Troubled Periphery

Troubled Periphery

Crisis of India's North East

SUBIR BHAUMIK

SAGE STUDIES ON INDIA'S NORTH EAST

SAGE www.sagepublications.com
Los Angeles • London • New Delhi • Singapore • Washington DC

First published in 2009 by

SAGE Publications India Pvt Ltd
B 1/I-1 Mohan Cooperative Industrial Area
Mathura Road, New Delhi 110044, India
www.sagepub.in

SAGE Publications Inc
2455 Teller Road
Thousand Oaks, California 91320, USA

SAGE Publications Ltd
1 Oliver's Yard, 55 City Road
London EC1Y 1SP, United Kingdom

SAGE Publications Asia-Pacific Pte Ltd
33 Pekin Street
#02-01 Far East Square
Singapore 048763

Published by Vivek Mehra for SAGE Publications India Pvt Ltd, typeset in 10/12pt Sabon by Star Compugraphics Private Limited, Delhi and printed at Chaman Enterprises, New Delhi.

Library of Congress Cataloging-in-Publication Data

Bhaumik, Subir.
  Troubled Periphery: crisis of India's North East/Subir Bhaumik.
      p. cm.
  Includes bibliographical references and index.
1. India, Northeastern—Social conditions. 2. India, Northeastern—Ethnic relations. 3. India, Northeastern—Religion. 4. India, Northeastern—Politics and government. 5. Social conflict—India, Northeastern. 6. Ethnic conflict—India, Northeastern. 7. Social change—India, Northeastern. 8. Religion—Social aspects—India, Northeastern. 9. Land use—Social aspects—India, Northeastern. 10. Political leadership—India, Northeastern. I. Title.

HN690.N55B48   306.0954'1—dc22   2009   2009038702

ISBN: 978-81-321-0237-3 (HB)

The SAGE Team: Rekha Natarajan, Meena Chakravorty and
                    Trinankur Banerjee
Photo credit: Subhamoy Bhattacharjee

To my father
Amarendra Bhowmick
and my little daughter
Anwesha,
a daughter of the North East

Contents

List of Tables

List of Abbreviations

AAGSP	All Assam Gana Sangram Parishad
AASAA	All Adivasi Students Association of Assam
AAPSU	All Arunachal Pradesh Students Union
AASU	All Assam Students Union
ABSU	All Bodo Students Union
ACMA	Adivasi Cobra Militants of Assam
AFSPA	Armed Forces Special Powers Act
AGP	Asom Gana Parishad
AJYCP	Assam Jatiyotabadi Yuba Chatro Parishad
AMSU	All Manipur Students Union
AMUCO	All Manipur United Clubs Organization
APHLC	All Party Hill Leaders Conference
ASDC	Autonomous State Demands Committee
ATF	Assam Tiger Force
ATPLO	All Tripura Peoples Liberation Organization
ATTF	All-Tripura Tiger Force
AUDF	Assam United Democratic Front
BCP	Burmese Communist Party
BIDS	Bangladesh Institute of Development Studies
BJP	Bharatiya Janata Party
BLTF	Bodoland Liberation Tigers Force
BNLF	Bru National Liberation Front
BPAC	Bodo Peoples Action Committee
BPPF	Bodo Peoples Progressive Front

BSF	Border Security Force
BVF	Bodo Volunteer Force
CHT	Chittagong Hill Tracts
CIA	Central Intelligence 'Agency'
CII	Confederation of Indian Industry
CLAHRO	Civil Liberties and Human Rights Organization
CNF	Chin National Front
COFR	Committee on Fiscal Reform
CMIE	Centre for Monitoring of Indian Economy
CPI	Communist Party of India
DAB	Democratic Alliance of Burma
DAN	Democratic Alliance of Nagaland
DGFI	Directorate General of Forces Intelligence
DHD	Dima Halan Daogah
DONER	Department of Development of North Eastern Region
FCI	Food Corporation of India
GMP	Gana Mukti Parishad
HSPDP	Hill States Peoples Demands Party
HUJAI	Harkat-ul-Jihad-al Islami
IDPs	Internally Displaced Persons
IIFT	Indian Institute of Foreign Trade
ILAA	Islamic Liberation Army of Assam
IMDT	Illegal Migrants Act
INCB	International Narcotics Control Bureau
INPT	Indigenous Nationalist Party of Tripura
IPF	Idgah Protection Force
IPFT	Indigenous People's Front of Tripura
ISI	Inter-Services Intelligence
ISS	Islamic Sevak Sangh
IURPI	Islamic United Reformation Protest of India
KCP	Kangleipak Communist Party
KIA	Kachin Independence Army
KLO	Kamtapur Liberation Organisation
KSU	Khasi Students Union
KYKL	Kanglei Yawol Kanna Lup
LOC	Letters of Credit
MASS	Manab Adhikar Sangram Samity
MLA	Muslim Liberation Army

MNF	Mizo National Front
MNFF	Mizo National Famine Front
MPA	Meghalaya Progressive Alliance
MPLF	Manipur Peoples Liberation Front
MSCA	Muslim Security Council of Assam
MSF	Médecins Sans Frontières
MSF	Muslim Security Force
MTF	Muslim Tiger Force
MULFA	Muslim United Liberation Front of Assam
MULTA	Muslim United Liberation Tigers of Assam
MVF	Muslim Volunteer Force
MZP	Mizo Zirlai Pawl
NCAER	National Council of Applied Economic Research
NCB	Narcotics Control Bureau
NDF	National Democratic Front
NDFB	National Democratic Front of Bodoland
NEEPCO	North Eastern Electric Power Corporation
NEFA	North-East Frontier Agency
NESO	North East Students Organizations
NLFT	National Liberation Front of Tripura
NNC	Naga National Council
NNO	Naga Nationalist Organization
NPMHR	Naga Peoples Movement for Human Rights
NSCN	National Socialist Council of Nagaland
NSDP	Net State Domestic Product
NUPA	National Unity Party of Arakans
NVDA	National Volunteers Defense Army
PCG	Peoples Consultative Group
PCJSS	Parbattya Chattogram Jana Sanghati Samity
PLA	People's Liberation Army
PREPAK	Peoples Revolutionary Party of Kangleipak
PSP	Praja Socialist Party
PULF	People's United Liberation Front
R&AW	Research and Analysis Wing
RGM	Revolutionary Government of Manipur
RGN	Revolutionary Government of Nagaland
RMC	Revolutionary Muslim Commandos
RPF	The Revolutionary Peoples Front

RSS	Rastriya Swayamsevak Sangh
SATP	The South Asia Terrorism Portal
SJSS	Sanmilito Jonoghostiye Sangram Samity
SMG	Sub-machine Gun
SOO	Suspension of Operations
SRC	State Reorganization Commission
SSB	Special Services Bureau
SSG	Special Services Group
TBCU	Tripura Baptist Christian Union
TNV	Tribal National Volunteers
TSF	Tribal Students Federation
TUJS	Tripura Upajati Juba Samity
ULFA	United Liberation Front of Assam
ULMA	United Liberation Militia of Assam
UMF	United Minorities "Front"
UMLFA	United Muslim Liberation Front of Assam
UMNO	United Mizo National Organization
UNLF	United National Liberation Front
UPDS	United Peoples Democratic Solidarity
UPVA	United Peoples Volunteers Army
UWSA	United Wa State Army
VHP	Viswa Hindu Parishad
YMA	Young Mizo Association

Preface

The North East has been seen as the problem child since the very inception of the Indian republic. It has also been South Asia's most enduring theatre of separatist guerrilla war, a region where armed action has usually been the first, rather than the last, option of political protest. But none of these guerrilla campaigns have led to secession – like East Pakistan breaking off to become Bangladesh in 1971 or East Timor shedding off Indonesian yoke in 1999. Nor have these conflicts been as intensely violent as the separatist movements in Indian Kashmir and Punjab. Sixty years after the British departed from South Asia, none of the separatist movements in the North East appear anywhere near their proclaimed goal of liberation from the Indian rule. Nor does the separatist violence in the region threaten to spin out of control.

That raises a key question that historian David Ludden once tried to raise while summing up the deliberation of a three-day seminar at Delhi's elite Jawaharlal Nehru University – whether the North East challenges the separation of the colonial from the national. Or whether it raises the possibility of reorganization of space by opening up India's boundaries. Opinion is divided. Historian Aditya Mukherji, in his keynote address at a Guwahati seminar (29–30 March 2009), challenged Ludden and his likes by insisting that the Indian nation evolved out of a national movement against imperialism and did not seek to impose, like in the West, the master narrative of the majority on the smaller minorities in the process of nation building. Mukherji insisted that the Indian democracy is unique and not coercive and can accommodate the aspirations of almost any minority group. In the same seminar, Professor Javed Alam, chairman of the Indian Council of Social Science Research, carried the argument forward by saying that a new phase of democratic assertion involving smaller minorities and hitherto-marginalized groups in the new century is now opening up new vistas of Indian democracy.

But scholars from the North East contested these 'mainland' scholars by saying that their experience in the North East was different. They point to the endless festering conflicts, which have spread to new areas of the region, leading to sustained deployment of the Indian army and federal paramilitary forces on 'internal security duties', that, in turn, has militarized rather than democratized the social and political space in the North East. These troops are deployed often against well-armed and relatively well-trained insurgents adept at the use of the hill terrain and often willing to use modern urban terror tactics for the shock effect.

It must be said that the military deployment has aimed at neutralizing the strike power of the insurgents to force them to the table, rather than seeking their complete destruction. So the rebel groups have also not been forced to launch an all-out do-or-die secessionist campaign, as the Awami League was compelled to do in East Pakistan in 1971. The space for accommodation, resource transfer and power-sharing that the Indian state offered to recalcitrant groups has helped India control the insurgencies and often co-opt their leadership. Now some would call co-option a democratic exercise. That's where the debate goes to a point of no resolution. What many see as a bonafide and well-meant state effort to win over the rebel leadership to join the mainstream is seen by many others, specially in the North East, as a malafide and devious co-option process, a buying of loyalties by use of force, monetary inducements and promise of office rather than securing it by voluntary and fair means.

Interestingly, the insurgencies have only multiplied in Northeast India. Whenever a rebel group has signed an accord with the Indian government in a particular state, the void has been quickly filled by other groups, reviving the familiar allegations of betrayal, neglect and alienation. The South Asia Terrorism Portal (SATP) in 2006 counted 109 rebel groups in northeast India—only the state of Arunachal Pradesh was found to be without one, though Naga rebel groups were active in the state. Interestingly, only a few of these are officially banned. Of the 40 rebel groups in Manipur, only six were banned under India's Unlawful Activities Prevention Act. And of the 34 in the neighbouring state of Assam, only two were banned. A good number of these groups are described as 'inactive' but some such groups have been revived from time to time. Since post-colonial India has been ever willing to create new states or autonomous units to fulfil the aspirations of the battling ethnicities, the quest for an 'ethnic homeland' and insurgent radicalism as a means to achieve it has become the familiar political grammar of the region. So insurgencies never peter out in the North East, even though insurgents do.

Phizo faded away to make way for a Muivah in the Naga rebel space, but soon there was a Khaplang to challenge Muivah. If Dasarath Dev walked straight into the Indian parliament from the Communist tribal guerrilla bases in Tripura, elected in absentia, there was a Bijoy Hrangkhawl to take his place in the jungle, alleging Communist betrayal of the tribal cause. And when Hrangkhawl called it a day after ten years of blood-letting, there was a Ranjit Debbarma and a Biswamohan Debbarma, ready to take his place. Even in Mizoram, where no Mizo rebel leader took to the jungles after the 1986 accord, smaller ethnic groups like the Brus and the Hmars have taken to armed struggle in the last two decades, looking for their own acre of green grass.

Throughout the last six decades, the same drama has been repeated, state after state. As successive Indian governments tried to nationalize the political space in the North East by pushing ahead with mainstreaming efforts, the struggling ethnicities of the region continued to challenge the 'nation-building processes', stretching the limits of constitutional politics. But these ethnic groups also fought amongst themselves, often as viciously as they fought India, drawing daggers over scarce resources and conflicting visions of homelands. In such a situation, the crisis also provided opportunity to the Indian state to use the four principles of realpolitik statecraft propounded by the great Kautilya, the man who helped Chandragupta build India's first trans-regional empire just after Alexander's invasion. *Sham* (Reconciliation), *Dam* (Monetary Inducement), *Danda* (Force) and *Bhed* (Split)—the four principles of Kautilyan statecraft—have all been used in varying mix to control and contain the violent movements in the North East.

But unlike in many other post-colonial states like military-ruled Pakistan and Burma, the Indian government have not displayed an over-reliance on force. After the initial military operation in the North East had taken the sting out of a rebel movement, an 'Operation Bajrang' or an 'Operation Rhino' has been quickly followed up by offers of negotiations and liberal doses of federal largesse, all aimed at co-option. If nothing worked, intelligence agencies have quickly moved in to divide the rebel groups. But with draconian laws like the controversial Armed Forces Special Powers Act always available to security forces for handling a breakdown of public order, the architechure of militarization remained in place. Covert intelligence operations and extra judicial killings have only made the scenario more murky, bloody and devious, specially in Assam and Manipur.

So when the Naga National Council (NNC) split in 1968, the Indian security forces were quick to use the Revolutionary Government of Nagaland (RGN) against it. Then when the NNC leaders signed the 1975 Shillong Accord, they were used against the nascent National Socialist Council of Nagaland (NSCN). Now both factions of NSCN accuse each other of being used by 'Indian agencies'. In neighbouring Assam, the SULFA (Surrendered ULFA) was created, not as alternate political platform to the ULFA, but as a tactical counter-insurgency plank, as a force multiplier for the Indian security machine. Engineering desertion and using the surrendered militants against their former colleagues have remained a favourite tactic for authorities in the North East.

Between 2002–2005, the Tripura police and the military intelligence managed to win over some rebels who had not yet surrendered and used them for a series of attacks on rebel bases just inside Bangladesh across the border with Tripura. The 'Trojan Horse' model thus used proved to be a great success in the counter-insurgency operations than getting rebels to surrender first and then be used against their former colleagues.

But for an entire generation of post-colonial Indians, the little wars of the North East remained a distant thunder, a collection of conflicts not worth the bother. Until someone's brother was kidnapped by the rebels, while working in a tea estate or in an oil platform. Or until someone's relative got shot in an encounter with them, while leading a military patrol through the leech-infested jungles of the region. Despite the 'prairie fires' spreading in the North East, the sole encounter of most Indians with this frontier region remained the tribal dancers atop colourful tableaux on Republic Day parades in Delhi. The national media reinforced the 'girl-guitar-gun' stereotype of the region's rebellious youth, while politicians and bureaucrats pandered to preconceived notions and formulate adhocist policies that would never work.

The border war with China, however, changed that. As the Chinese army appeared on the outskirts of Tezpur, the distant oilfields and tea gardens of Assam, so crucial to India's economy, seemed all but lost. Then came the two wars with Pakistan, and Bangladesh was born. In a historic move, the North East itself was reorganized into several new states, mostly carved out of Assam. While these momentous developments drew more attention towards the North East, the powerful anti-foreigner agitation in Assam forced the rest of the country to sit up and take notice of the crisis of identity in the region. What began as Assam's cry in the wilderness quickly became the concern of the whole country. Illegal migration from over-populated neighbouring countries came to be seen as a threat to national security. And since then, the North East has never again been the same. It just became more complex.

The anti-foreigner agitation unleashed both anti-Centre and anti-migrant forces. The ULFA grew out of the anti-foreigner movement against the 'Bangladeshi infiltrators', people of East Bengali origin who have been settling in Assam since the late nineteenth century. Slowly, the ULFA's anti-migrant stance gave way to determined separatism and it started blaming 'economic exploitation by Delhi' as being responsible for Assam's woes. But in the face of a fierce counter-insurgency offensive by the Indian army, it started targetting migrants again—this time not people of East Bengali origin but Hindi-speaking settlers from India's heartland 'cow belt' states.

In the first quarter century after independence, while the rest of the country remained oblivious to the tumult in the North East, the region and its people saw only one face of India. The young Naga, Mizo or Manipuri knew little about Mahatma Gandhi or Subhas Chandra Bose and failed to see 'the separation of the colonial from the national'. Indian independence did not matter for him or her. What these young men and women saw, year after year, was the Indian soldier, the man in the uniform, gun in hand, out to punish the enemies of India. He saw the jackboots and grew suspicious when the occasional olive branch followed. When rats destroyed the crops in the Mizo hills, leaving the tribesmen to starve, the Mizo youth took the Naga's path of armed rebellion. Far-off Delhi seemed to have no interest in the region and, like in 1962 when Nehru left Assam to 'its fate', the North East could be abandoned in the time of a major crisis.

In my generation, the situation began to change slowly, though the conflicts did not end. More and more students from the North East started joining colleges and universities in 'mainland' India, many joining all-India services or corporate bodies after that. The media and the government started paying more attention to the North East, and even a separate federal ministry was created for developing the region. Now federal government employees get liberal leave travel allowances, including two-way airfare for visiting the North East, an effort to promote tourism in the picturesque region. As market economy struck deep roots across India, Tata salt and Maruti cars reached far-off Lunglei, Moreh and even Noklak. For a generation in the North East who grew up to hate India, the big nation-state was now proving its worth as a common market and a land of opportunity. Something that even excites the managers of the European Union.

Boys and girls from the North East won medals for India, many fought India's wars in places like Kargil, a very large number picked up Indian degrees and made a career in the heartland states or even abroad. The success of North Eastern girls in the country's hospitality industry provoked a *Times of India* columnist to warn spa-connoisuers to go for 'a professional doctor rather than a Linda from the North East'. But a Shahrukh Khan was quick to critique the 'mainland bias' against the North Eastern Lindas in his great film 'Chak de India.'

More significantly, the civil society of heartland India began to take much more interest in the North East, closely interacting with like-minded groups in the region, to promote peace and human rights. Suddenly, a Nandita Haksar was donning the lawyer's robe to drag the Indian army to court for excesses against Naga villagers around Oinam, mobilizing hundreds of villagers to testify against errant troops. A Gobinda Mukhoty was helping the nascent Naga Peoples Movement for Human Rights (NPMHR) file a habeas corpus petition seeking redressal for the military atrocities at Namthilok. Scores of human rights activists in Calcutta, Delhi or Chandigarh were fasting to protest the controversial death of a Thangjam Manorama or in support of the eternally fasting Irom Sharmila, the Meitei girl who says she will refuse food until the draconian Armed Forces Special Powers Act is revoked. Jaiprakash Narain and some other Gandhians had led the way by working for the Naga Peace Mission but now the concern for the North East was spreading to the grassroots in the mainland. The fledgling Indian human rights movement, a product of the Emergency, kept reminding the guardians of the Indian state of their obligations to a region they said was theirs.

How could the government deny the people of North East the democracy and the economic progress other Indians were enjoying? What moral right did Delhi have to impose draconian laws in the region and govern the North East through retired generals, police and intelligence officials? How could political problems be solved only by military means? Was India perpetrating internal colonization and promoting 'development of under-development'? These were questions that a whole new generation of Indian intellectuals, human rights activists, journalists and simple do-gooders continued to raise in courtroom battles, in the media space, even on the streets of Delhi, Calcutta or other Indian cities. Whereas their fathers had seen and judged India only by its soldiers, a Luithui Luingam or a Sebastian Hongray were soon to meet the footsoldiers of Indian democracy, men and women their own age with a vision of India quite different from the generation that had experienced Partition and had come to see all movements for self-determination as one great conspiracy to break up India.

In a matter of a few years, the Indian military commanders were furiously complaining that their troops were being forced to fight in the North East with one hand tied behind their back. Indeed, this was not a war against a foreign enemy. When fighting one's own 'misguided brothers and sisters', the rules of combat were expected to be different. Human rights violations continued to occur but resistance to them began to build up in the North East with support from elsewhere in the country, so much so that an Indian army chief, Shankar Roychoudhury, drafted human rights guidelines for his troops and declared that a 'brutalized army [is] no good as a fighting machine'.

Human rights and the media space became a new battle ground as both the troops and the rebels sought to win the hearts and minds of the population. It would, however, be wrong to over-emphasize the success of the human rights movement in the North East. Like the insurgents, the human rights movement has been torn by factional feuds at the national and the regional levels. But thanks to their efforts, more and more people in the Indian heartland came to hear of the brutalities at Namthilok and Oinam, Heirangothong and Mokukchung. Many young journalists of my generation also shook off the 'pro-establishment' bias of our predecessors and headed for remote locations to report without fear and favour. We crossed borders to meet rebel leaders, because if they were our misguided brothers, (as politicians and military leaders would often say) they had a right to be heard by our own people. One could argue that this only helped internalise the rebellions and paved the way for co-option. But it also created the ambience for a rights regime in a far frontier region where there was none for the first three decades after 1947. Facing pressure from below, the authorities began to relent and the truth about the North East began to emerge.

The yearning for peace and opportunity began to spread to the grassroots. Peace-making in the region still remains a largely bureaucratic exercise involving shady spymasters and political wheeler-dealers, marked by a total lack of transparency. Insurgent leaders, when they finally decide to make peace with India, are often as secretive as the spymasters because the final settlements invariably amount to such a huge climbdown from their initial positions that the rebel chieftains do not want to be seen as being party to sellouts and surrenders. Nevertheless, the consensus for peace is beginning to spread. Peace without honour may not hold, but both the nation-state and the rebels are beginning to feel the pressure from below to make peace. And increasingly the push for peace is led not by big political figures like a Jayprakash Narain or a Michael Scott but by commoners—intensely committed men and women like brave ladies of the Naga Mothers Association who trekked hundred of kilometres to reach the rebel bases in Burma for kickstarting the peace process in Nagaland.

In the last few years, the North East and the heartland have come to know each other better. Many myths and misconceptions continue to persist, but as India's democracy, regardless of its many aberrations, matures and the space for diversity and dissent increases, the unfortunate stereotypes associated with the North East are beginning to peter off slowly. The concept of one national mainstream is coming to be seen as an anathema in spite of the huge security hangover caused by terror strikes like the November 2008 assault on Bombay. Even Shahrukh Khan did not miss the pointlessness of mainstreaming in his banter sequence on the Manipur girls' 'failure' to learn Punjabi in 'Chak De India'. The existence of one big stream, presumably the 'Ganga Maiya' (Mother Ganges), is perhaps not good enough for India to grow around it. We need the Brahmaputras as much as we need the Godavaris and the Cauveris to evolve into a civilization state that is our destiny. The country cannot evolve on the misplaced notion of a national mainstream conceived around 'Hindu, Hindi and Hindustan'. The saffrons may win some elections because the seculars are a disorganized, squabbling, discredited and leaderless lot, but even the Hindutva forces must stretch both ways to accomodate a new vision of India or else they will fail to tackle the crisis of the North East and other trouble spots like Kashmir and will fell apart.

India remains a cauldron of many nationalities, races, religions, languages and sub-cultures. The multiplicity of identity was a fact of our pre-colonial existence and will determine our post-colonial lives. In the North East, language, ethnicity and religion will provide the roots of identity, sometimes conflicting, sometimes mutually supporting. So a larger national identity should have more to do with civilization and multi-culturalism, tolerance and diversity, than with the base and the primordial. For the North East, the real threat is the growing criminalization of the movements for self-determination and the conflicting perceptions of ethnicity-driven homelands that pit tribes and races against each other. 'Freedom fighters' are being replaced by 'warlords'. They in turn may become drug lords because of the region's uncomfortable proximity to Burma, where even former communists have turned to peddling drugs and weapons. Money from organized extortion may have given the insurgents in northeast India a secure financial base to pursue their separatist agenda, but it has also corrupted the movements. And groups who have violently pursued the agenda of ethnic homelands and attempted ethnic cleansing have threatened to turn the region into a Bosnia or a Lebanon, increasing the levels of militarization and adding to the democracy-deficit that North East has always suffered from.

Despite these gloomy forebodings, some, like the visionary B.G. Verghese, see great opportunities for the region in the changing geo-politics of Asia. India's 'Look East' thrust in foreign policy may help the North East by way of better transport linkages with the neighbourhood and greater market access for products made in the region. But the government's Vision 2020 document admits that the region needs huge improvement in infrastructure to become sufficiently attractive for big-time investors, domestic or foreign. Petroleum products made in the Numaligarh Refinery in Assam are now being exported to Bangladesh by less expensive river transport, but Assam's crude output has sharply dwindled in recent years and at least a part of Numaligarh's future requirement may have to be imported via Haldia port in West Bengal.

Environmentalists and indigenous leaders have also opposed the huge Indian investments in the region's hydel power resources, saying that it may prove to be dangerous in a sensitive geo-seismic region. As India tries to open out the North East to possible big-time investments, particularly in hydel power, a new kind of conflict, emanating from contradicting perceptions of resources-sharing may replace the old style insurgencies. It all depends on how the leaders of the locality, province and nation shape up to the challenges of the future and make the most of the opportunities.

This book is an attempt to understand the crisis of India's North East. I have drawn primarily on my own experience and primary documentation gained during nearly three decades of journalism in the region and in countries around it. I not only managed rare access to both the undergrounds and officialdom, but also had the benefit of covering the most important events at very close quarters. The book may benefit from the rare insights I gained. During these eventful decades, when many profound changes unfolded in the North East, I had the benefit of witnessing them first hand, which then helped me look beyond the immediate. I wish to thank countless friends and sources in the region for their help, including many who wish to remain anonymous. A special word of gratitude for my friend, Ashis Biswas, who went through the script to weed out errors. Jaideep Saikia, my younger brother, contested many of my observations from his own experience as a former security advisor with the Assam and the Indian government, until I could hold my own. That exercise proved rather useful.

My friend, the late B.B. Nandi, also shared many great secrets about the Indian intelligence operations in and around the region and gave me some rare insights developed over a long and superb career in domestic and foreign intelligence. Armchair academics may not always appreciate the value of the likes of Saikia and Nandi—or for that matter, E.N. Rammohan, former DG, Border Security Force who also shared many unknown facets of the complex world of domestic and border policing—but I know for sure that they are much closer to the reality, which is what I want to bring home to readers. But some academics, who also have great experience as activists, like Ranabir Sammadar of the Calcutta Research Group, have always been an inspiration. As have been some of my great teachers—I owe to Jayantanuja Bandopadhyay my grounding in international relations, to B.K. Roy Barman my sense of North East and to Anthony Smith my understanding of ethnicity which proved so useful in understanding the North East. I am indebted to my countless friends in the North East—both in the underground and in the government and civil society movements—whose knowledge and perspective helped enrich my understanding of a complex region. For want of space, they all cannot be named.

I must also thank Sugata Ghosh and Rekha Natarajan at SAGE for agreeing to do my book. It is neither the usual format of an academic work nor the pseudo-fiction that 'trade publishers' generally like on North East. And therefore this could well fall between two stools, but I am grateful to SAGE for taking the risk.

1   India's North East: Frontier to Region

India's North East is a region rooted more in the accident of geography than in the shared bonds of history, culture and tradition. It is a directional category right out of colonial geographical usage—like the Middle East or the Far East. A young Assamese scholar describes it as a 'politically convenient shorthand to gloss over complicated historical formations and dense loci of social unrest'.[1] The region has, over the centuries, seen an extraordinary mixing of different races, cultures, languages and religions, leading to a diversity rarely seen elsewhere in India. With an area of about 2.6 lakh square kilometre and a population of a little over 39 million, the seven states of North East and Sikkim (which is now part of the North East Council) is a conglomeration of around 475 ethnic groups and sub-groups, speaking over 400 languages/dialects.

The region accounts for just less than 8 per cent of the country's total geographical area and little less than 4 per cent of India's total population. It is hugely diverse within itself, an India in miniature. Of the 635 communities in India listed as tribal, more than 200 are found in the North East. Of the 325 languages listed by the 'People of India' project, 175 belonging to the Tibeto-Burman group are spoken in the North East. While bigger communities like the Assamese and the Bengalis number several million each, the tribes that render the North East so diverse rarely number more than one or two million and many, like the Mates of Manipur, are less than 10,000 people in all.

In recent decades, groups of tribes emerged into generic identities like the Nagas and the Mizos. As they challenged their incorporation into India and launched vigorous separatist campaigns, they began to evolve into nationalities. The presence of a common enemy—India—often generated a degree of cohesiveness and a sense of shared destiny within these generic identities. For instance, the Naga's self-perception of a national identity was manifested in the emergence of the Naga National Council (NNC) as the spearhead of the separatist movement and Nagas continue to describe their guerrillas as 'national workers'.

The fact that most of the prominent Naga tribes continue to use names given to them by outsiders also contributed to the formation of generic identities. For example, the traditional names of the Angamis are Tengima or Tenyimia, the Kalyo Kengnyu are actually Khiamniungams, and the Kacha Nagas were variously called Kabui and Rongmai until they merged with the Zemei and Lingmai tribes to form a new tribal identity—the Zeliangrong.[2] These constructed identities often provided a platform around which tribal identities could group and grow into generic ones.

But the absence of a common language and the long history of tribal warfare in the Naga Hills served to reinforce tribal identities that weakened the emerging 'national' identity of the Nagas. Thus, China-trained Naga rebel leader Thuingaleng Muivah labelled all Angamis as 'reactionary traitors' and described all Tangkhuls (his own tribe) as 'revolutionary patriots' when he lashed out at the 'betrayal' of the Angami-dominated NNC for signing the Shillong Accord with India in 1975.[3] Muivah later formed the National Socialist Council of Nagaland (NSCN) to continue the fight for Naga independence against India and there were hardly any Angami Naga in the NSCN.

Twenty-two years later, Muivah himself started negotiations with India in 1997. After more than a decade of painstakingly slow negotiations, there are clear indications now that the NSCN is prepared to accept a 'special federal relationship with India'. In effect, he has given up the cause of Naga independence. Muivah, however, insists that India should agree to create a larger Naga state to include all Naga-inhabited areas in the North East. As a Tangkhul Naga from Manipur, 'Greater Nagaland' is more important for his political future than 'sovereign Nagaland'. But the Burmese Nagas, who provided sanctuary to the Indian Naga rebels for 40 years, are clearly beyond the scope of these negotiations with India and are quietly forgotten. Which is why India, despite its ceasefire with the NSCN's Khaplang faction, has only started negotiations with the Muivah faction. Khaplang is a Hemi Naga from Burma—so how can India possibly negotiate with him! A ceasefire is the maximum India could offer to his faction.

The Naga rebel movement has unwittingly accepted 'Indian boundaries' to determine their territoriality—and Muivah's rivalry with Khaplang has also influenced the decision. But despite all these fissures that limit the evolution of a Naga nationality, the NSCN or any other rebel groups are unlikely to give up the label 'national' even if they were to settle for a special status within the Indian constitution. Former Indian Prime Minister Atal Behari, by accepting the 'unique history of the Nagas', has strengthened their case.

The Mizo National Front (MNF), which was to the Mizos what the NNC was for the Nagas, continues to retain the marker 'national' nearly two decades after it gave up armed struggle and signed an agreement to return to the Indian constitutional system as a legitimate political party recognized by the Election Commission. Indeed, the MNF's journey has been unique. Started as a relief front to support Mizo farmers devastated by the rat famine, it later became a political party and contested elections in undivided Assam. Then it went underground to fight against India for 20 years before it returned to constitutional politics in 1986.

Mizoram also illustrates the inherent weakness of 'constructed' generic identities. The assertiveness of a major tribe and sense of marginalization among smaller ones often weaken an evolving generic identity, a 'Naga' or a 'Mizo' construct. The Hmars, the Lais, the Maras and even the Reangs in the MNF fought the Indian army shoulder-to-shoulder with the Lushais, the major tribe of the Mizo Hills. After 1986, all these tribes demanded their own acre of green grass. The Hmars and the Reangs wanted autonomous councils and took up arms to achieve their objective. On the other hand, the Lai, Mara and Chakma autonomous tribal district councils now complain of neglect by a Lushai-dominated government that, they say, has 'hijacked' the Mizo identity. Retribalization has followed—Hmars,

Reangs (or Brus as they are called in Mizoram), Lais, Maras and Chakmas have all chosen to assert their distinct tribal identities and are demanding a separate Union Territory in southern Mizoram. The tensions within the generic identities have often led to mayhem and violence in North East. India's federal government has often played on the tribal-ethnic faultlines to control the turbulent region.

THE NORTH EAST: A BRITISH CONSTRUCT

India's North East is a British imperial construct subsequently accepted by the post-colonial nation-state. It emerged in British colonial discourse as a frontier region, initially connoting the long swathe of mountains, jungles and riverine, tropical marshy flatlands located between the eastern limits of British-ruled Bengal and the western borders of the Kingdom of Ava (Burma). As the British consolidated their position in Bengal, they came into contact with the principalities and tribes further east. For purposes of expansion, commercial gain and border management, the British decided to explore the area immediately after the historic Treaty of Yandabo in 1826, which ended the First Anglo-Burmese War. A senior official, R.B. Pemberton, was asked to write a report on the races and tribes of Bengal's eastern frontier.

In 1835, Pemberton wrote a general survey of the area, titled *The Eastern Frontier of Bengal*. In 1866, Alexander Mackenzie took charge of political correspondence in the government of British Bengal. On the request of the lieutenant-governor, Sir William Grey, Mackenzie wrote a comprehensive account of the relations between the British government and the hill tribes on the eastern frontier of Bengal. When he completed his report in 1871, Mackenzie called it *Memorandum on the North Eastern Frontier of Bengal*. A revised and updated version of this report was published in 1882 as the *History of the Relations of the Government with the Hill Tribes of the North Eastern Frontier of Bengal*. It had taken more than 30 years for the 'East' to become 'North East' in British administrative discourse. To Mackenzie, however, it must not have been entirely clear why the 'East' had become 'North East', though he tried to delineate its geographical extent:

The North East Frontier is a term used sometimes to denote a boundary line and sometimes more generally to describe a tract. In the latter sense, it embraces the whole of the hill ranges North East and south of Assam valley as well the western slopes of the great mountain system lying between Bengal and independent Burma, with its outlying spurs and ridges. It will be convenient to proceed in regular order, first traversing from west to east the sub-Himalayan ranges north of Brahmaputra, then turning westward along the course of the ranges that found the Assam valley in the south, and finally, exploring the highlands interposed between Cachar and Chittagong and the hills that separate the maritime district of Chittagong from the Empire of Ava.[4]

As the British became firmly entrenched in Assam and their commercial interests expanded, they began to feel the need for a stable frontier. The hill tribes, particularly the Nagas and the Lushais (now known as Mizos), mounted several attacks on the tea plantations during which some British officials were kidnapped and killed. Further expansion of commercial interests and opening of trade routes to lands beyond Bengal and Assam necessitated control over the frontier region. J.C. Arbuthnott, the British commissioner of the hill districts, strongly advocated extension of control over areas 'where prevalence of head-hunting and atrocious barbarities on the immediate frontier retard pacification and exercise a prejudicial effect on the progress of civilization amongst our own subjects'.[5] Mackenzie also made it clear that 'there can be no rest for the English in India till they stand forth as governors and advisers of each tribe or people in the land'. Historical evidence now suggests that the British overplayed the threat of tribal raids to justify their incursions into the hill country east of undivided Bengal,[6] a bit of a nineteenth-century Blair-type 'sexing up of dossiers'.

The British were also desperate to check Burmese expansion. The First Anglo-Burmese War led to the expulsion of the Burmese armies from Assam and Manipur. The British promptly annexed Lower Assam to the empire. The occupation of the Brahmaputra, the Surma and the Barak Valleys opened the way for further British expansion into the region. Upper Assam was briefly restored to Ahom rule but the arrangement failed and the whole province was made part of the British Empire in 1838. The Treaty of Yandabo in 1826 restored the kingdom of Manipur to its Maharaja, and the Burmese were eased out of that province. The Ahoms, who had ruled Assam for six centuries after subjugating the Dimasa and Koch kingdoms and had fought back the Bengal sultans and the Mughals, were finally conquered.

The British, however, did not stop after taking over Assam. The Muttock kingdom around Sadiya (now on the Assam–Arunachal Pradesh border) was taken over immediately after the conquest of Upper Assam. The kingdom of Cachar was taken over in stages until it was completely incorporated into Assam in 1850. The Khasi Hills were annexed in 1833 and two years later, the Jaintia Raja was dispossessed of his domains. The Garo Hills, nominally part of Assam's Goalpara district, were taken over in 1869 and made into a district with its headquarters at Tura. The Khasi, Jaintia and Garo Hills now make up the present state of Meghalaya after having been a part of Assam until 1972. In the second half of the nineteenth century, the British sent military expeditions into the Naga and Lushai hills and both areas were subjugated after fierce fighting. They became separate districts of Assam and remained such until Nagaland emerged as a state of the Indian Union in 1963 and Mizoram became first a Union Territory in 1972 and then a full state in 1987.

The Daflas, the Abors, the Akas, the Mishmis and other tribes occupying what is now Arunachal Pradesh all attracted British reprisals, some for obstructing trade, others for cultivating poppy and some for disturbing the Great Trigonometrical Survey in 1876–77. A series of expeditions were conducted into the Sadiya, Balipara and Lakhimpur frontier divisions to bring these turbulent tribal areas under control. Apart from exploring trade routes, these expeditions were also aimed at securing a clear and stable frontier with China. But while these hill regions west of Burma and south of Tibet were steadily being brought into the empire, the British realized the futility of administering them directly.

In 1873, the Inner Line Regulations were promulgated, marking the extent of the revenue administration beyond which the tribal people were left to manage their own affairs subject to good behaviour. No British subject or foreigner was permitted to cross the Inner Line without permission and rules were laid down for trade and acquisition of lands beyond.

The Inner Line was given the difficult task of providing a territorial frame to capital … it was also a temporal outside of the historical pace of development and progress … the communities staying beyond the Line were seen as belonging to a different time regime – where slavery, headhunting and nomadism could be allowed to exist. The Inner Line was expected to enact a sharp split between what were understood as the contending worlds of capital and pre-capital, of the modern and the primitive.[7]

Although the British started large commercial ventures in Assam in tea, oil and coal and invested heavily in the province's infrastructure, they remained satisfied with token acceptance of suzerainty from the tribes living beyond the Inner Line and did little to develop their economies. The kingdoms of Manipur and Tripura were also left alone, as long as they paid tributes. A British political resident was stationed in both the princely states to ensure suzerainty and monitor any political activity considered detrimental to British interests. British money and development targeted only areas that yielded large returns on investment. The Assam plains were seen as the only part of the North East where investment would bring forth adequate returns.

The foothills of the Brahmaputra and the Barak Valleys marked the limits of regular administration—the hills beyond and the tribespeople living there were largely left alone. 'The Inner Line became a frontier within a frontier adding to the seclusion of the hills and enhancing the cultural and political distance between them and the plains.'[8] Assam, however, continued to grow as a province, both in size and population, and its demographic diversity increased. Under the British, its boundaries were extended steadily to include most areas of what is now India's North East. Initially, Assam's administration was placed under the lieutenant-governor of Bengal and the Assamese were forced to accept Bengali as the official language of their province. In 1874, however, a year after the promulgation of the Inner Line Regulations for the hill areas, Assam was reconstituted as a province. The Bengali-dominated Sylhet and Cachar districts, the Garo and the Khasi-Jaintia Hills, the Naga Hills and the district of Goalpara were all brought within Assam. Between 1895 and 1898, the north and south Lushai Hills and a portion of the Chittagong Hill Tracts were detached from Bengal and added to Assam. With a population of nearly 5 million and a territory close to 60,000 square miles, Assam emerged as one of the largest provinces in British India.

Greater Assam, first under the British and then in the first 25 years after Indian independence, remained a heterogenous entity—and a troubled one. The Assamese and the Bengalis were involved in a fierce competition to control the province, both sidestepping the aspirations of the numerous tribespeople whose homelands were incorporated into Assam (and thus into the British Indian empire) for the first time in their history. The British found it administratively useful to group together the totally diverse areas on Bengal's North Eastern frontier into Assam. Later, this exercise was followed by an attempt to integrate the frontier marches on the North East of Bengal with the hill regions of upper Burma in what came to be known as the Crown Colony proposal. This was not because the vast multitude of tribespeople in this long border stretch had anything in common except their Mongoloid racial features, but because the British saw in their antipathy to the plains people of India and Burma an opportunity to forge together a political entity that would tolerate the limited presence of British power even after it was forced to retreat from India after the Second World War.

So, the British were only too keen to exacerbate the hills–plains divide. The Government of India Act of 1919 (Montagu-Chelmsford reforms) provided powers to the governor-general to declare any tract a 'Backward Area' and bar the application of normal provincial legislation there. Within a decade, the Garo Hills, the Khasi-Jaintia Hills, the Mikir Hills, the North Cachar Hills, the Naga and the Lushai hills districts and the three frontier tracts of Balipara, Lakhimpur and Sadiya were all designated as Backward Areas. The Simon Commission recommended designating these Backward Areas as Excluded Areas and the 1935 Government of India Act reorganized the Backward Areas of Assam into the Excluded Areas of the North East Frontier Tract (now Arunachal Pradesh), Naga Hills District (now Nagaland), Lushai Hills District (now Mizoram) and North Cachar Hills District, while the Garo Hills, the Mikir Hills and the Khasi-Jaintia Hills (later to become Meghalaya) were reconstituted as 'Partially Excluded Areas'. As princely states, Tripura and Manipur remained beyond the scope of this reorganization.

In 1929, the Simon Commission justified the creation of Excluded Areas in this way:

> The stage of development reached by the inhabitants of these areas prevents the possibility of applying to them methods of representation adopted elsewhere. They do not ask for self-determination, but for security of land tenure and freedom in the pursuit of their ancestral customs. Their contentment does not depend so much on rapid political advance as on experienced and sympathetic handling and on protection from economic subjugation by their neighbours.[9]

The Simon Commission was boycotted by the Congress and the major Indian parties but when it arrived in Shillong, capital of Greater Assam, as many as 27 representations were made to it by the Bodos and other plains tribals, the Naga Club of Kohima, the Khasi National Durbar and even the Assam government.

Dr J.H. Hutton's representation on behalf of the Assam government was indicative of British thinking on how to administer the North Eastern frontier region. It also gave enough indication of the conscious attempt the British were to make subsequently to split up the huge province of Assam between its rich plains and remote hills. Hutton opposed joining the 'backward hills' with the 'advanced plains' because the 'irreconcilable culture of the two could only produce an unnatural union'. His key recommendation was:

> [...] the gradual creation of self-governing communities, semi-independent in nature, secured by treaties on the lines of the Shan States in Burma, for whose external relations alone the Governor of the province would be ultimately responsible. Given self-determination to that extent, it would always be open to a functioning hill state to apply for amalgamation if so desired and satisfy the other party of the advantage of its incorporation.[10]

Hutton's influence (and that of N.E. Parry, the deputy commissioner of the Lushai Hills District) on the final report of the Simon Commission was evident in its recommendations for the North Eastern frontier. On 12 August 1930, the Simon Commission suggested that 'it might be desirable to combine the administration of the backward tracts of Assam with that of the Arakans, Chittagong and Pakkoko Hill Tracts, the Chin Hills and the area inhabited by the Rangpang

Nagas on both sides of the Patkai range'.[11] The British were clearly contemplating a new political-administrative entity that would club together the hill regions of India's North Eastern frontier and Burma's northern and western hill regions.

A definitive proposal along these lines was drawn up by Sir Robert Reid, governor of Assam, between 1939 and 1942. In his *Note on the Future of the Present Excluded, Partially Excluded and Tribal Areas of Assam*, Reid observed:

> The inhabitants of the Excluded Areas would not now be ready to join in any constitution in which they would be in danger of coming under the political domination of the Indians. The Excluded Areas are less politically minded and I have no doubt as to their dislike to be attached to India under a Parliamentary system. Throughout the hills, the Indian of the plains is despised for his effeminacy but feared for his cunning. The people of the hills of Assam are as eager to work out their own salvation free from Indian domination as are the people of Burma and for the same reason.

Colonial administrators like Reid, Hutton and Parry, who were keen on the separation of the plains and the hills of Greater Assam, were reviving the idea of a North Eastern province of British Indian Dominions—a province that would bring the vast region from the southern tip of the Lushai (or Lakher) Hills to the Balipara Tract on the border with Tibet under one administration, encompassing the Chin Hills, the Chittagong Hill Tracts, the Naga Hills and the Shan states of Burma. Reid was also prepared to sever Sylhet and Cachar from Assam as he considered the union 'unnatural'. Reginald Coupland, Beit Professor at Oxford, also fostered the idea of a greater union of tribes and smaller nationalities on the India–Burma frontier that could emerge into a 'Crown Colony' once the British were forced to leave India. In his book, *British Obligation: The Future of India*, Coupland argued the case for a Crown Colony that would ensure British strategic presence, as in Singapore or Aden or the Persian Gulf, in the post-colonial subcontinent.[12] The only difference was that while Singapore, Aden or the Persian Gulf lay on key sea routes, the proposed Crown Colony on the India–Burma frontier would be an inland entity with possible sea access only through the Arakans.

However, London abandoned the idea of a union of tribespeople on the India–Burma frontier in 1943 in view of what it described as 'immense difficulties' involved in the exercise. Reid's successor, Sir Andrew Clow, opposed the breaking up of Assam, which, without the hill areas, would become 'a long narrow finger stretching up the Brahmaputra Valley'. He saw the Assam valleys as a 'viable commercial proposition' and preferred a future in which the Tribal Areas and the Excluded Areas were retained in Assam to provide for a stable administration of a difficult frontier. As the Second World War was drawing to a close, a meeting was held on 10 March 1945 at the Department of External Affairs in London. It was attended, among others, by Olaf Caroe, secretary of external affairs, J.P. Mills, adviser to the governor of Assam, and Jack Mcguire of the Scheduled Areas Department. The Burmese government was opposed to the suggested amalgamation of its hill areas with northeast India and therefore proposed merely 'an agency on the Burmese side and one on the Indian side under separate forms of administration eventually being contemplated as federating with Burma or India'.[13] It was generally agreed that 'the boundaries would be drawn with regard to ethnography rather than geographically' so that individual tribes would not be split up between two administrations.

For similar reasons, the Crown Colony idea was given a silent burial in the humdrum of the transfer of power in the Indian subcontinent. By then, however, the tribespeople had seen a world war on their home turf. They saw in the imminent withdrawal of the imperial power an opportunity to regain the freedom they had enjoyed before the advent of the British. But if British manoeuvres had slowly turned this diverse hill area from a listless frontier into an administrative region held together to promote imperial interests, then the partition of the subcontinent and the break-up of British Bengal completed the process of turning it into a distinct geographical entity precariously detached from the Indian heartland. Cyril Radcliffe's pen left Assam, its sprawling hill regions and the princely kingdoms of Tripura and Manipur clinging to the Indian heartland by a 21-km-wide corridor below Bhutan and Tibet.

Despite being incorporated into Assam, every distinct area on Bengal's North Eastern frontier had historically relied on one or two border districts of eastern Bengal or Burma as their conduit to the world. Assam and its southern belly consist of the Khasi-Jaintia and Garo Hills and the Bengali region of Cachar, and the trans-border reference point was Sylhet and Mymensingh. For Tripura, it was Comilla and for the Mizo Hills it was Chittagong and the Chin Hills of Burma. For the Nagas and the tribespeople of what is now Arunachal Pradesh, Burma's Kachin Hills, the Naga-dominated western Sagaing division and the southern reaches of Tibet were natural reference points as immediate neighbours. The geographical links that were sustained by proximity and trade were suddenly severed, forcing the inhabitants to look for alternatives. With Comilla in a different country, Tripura needed the Assam–Agartala road to stay in touch with India. With Chittagong gone, Mizoram needs the Silchar–Aizawl highway. Moreover, everyone in the North East— and the Indian heartland—need the Siliguri Corridor to make sense of what Hutton and Parry described as an 'unnatural union'.

The Radcliffe Award forced all these frontier people to turn towards each other for the first time in history. The Bengal they knew was gone, having become a different country. Bengal's western half, always closer to the Indian heartland than its eastern half, was now the region's tenuous link to the rest of India. The North East slowly evolved as a territorial-administrative region, as Greater Assam petered out as the familiar unit of public imagination. As Delhi sought to consolidate its grip on 2,25,000 sq. km of hills and plains east of the Siliguri Corridor and manage the conflicting agendas of the great multitude of ethnic groups living in this area surrounded by China, Pakistan (now Bangladesh), Burma and Bhutan, a directional category was found to be more useful—much like 'South Asia' has been found to be more preferable to 'Indian subcontinent' after the Partition. Just as physical distance exacerbated the cultural divide between the two Pakistan and ultimately led to their violent divorce, the broad racial differences between India and its North East and the tenuous geographical link contributed to a certain alienation, a feeling of 'otherness' that subsequently gave rise to a political culture of violent separatism.

As the British left, the Constituent Assembly set up an advisory committee to make recommendations for the development of the tribal areas of northeast India. A sub-committee headed by Gopinath Bordoloi, later chief minister of Assam, was set up with four other tribal leaders: Rupnath Brahma (a Bodo), Reverend J.J.M. Nichols-Roy (a Khasi), Aliba Imti (a Naga) and A.V. Thakkar (a Gandhian social worker active in the North East). The committee found that the assimilation of the North Eastern tribals into the Indian mainstream was 'minimal', and that they were very sensitive to any interference with their lands and forests, their customary laws and way of life. The sub-committee recommended formation of autonomous regional and district councils that could provide adequate safeguards to the tribals in preserving their lands and customs, language and culture. Opinions in the Constituent Assembly were divided, but persuasion by communist leader Jaipal Singh and decisive intervention by the Dalit leader B.R. Ambedkar carried the day. Ambedkar argued that while tribals elsewhere in India had become Hindus and assimilated with the mainstream culture, in northeast India they had remained outside the Indian influence. Indeed, Ambedkar went so far as to compare their condition with the 'Red Indians' in the US.

Under Ambedkar's influence, it was decided that the district and regional councils would be provided with sufficient autonomy and their administration would be vested in the governor rather than in the state legislative assembly. The Sixth Schedule of the Indian constitution was created, vested with the provisions for the creation of the autonomous regional and the district councils. The autonomy provisions were fairly extensive, covering powers to draft laws for local administration, land, management of forests and customary laws, education and health administration at the grassroots. In 1952, five district councils were created in Assam, one each for the Garo Hills, the united Khasi-Jaintia Hills (now in Meghalaya), the Lushai Hills (now Mizoram), the United Mikir (Karbi) Hills and the North Cachar Hills (still in Assam). The Naga Hills, where the Naga National Council had already demanded separation from India, was not given the benefit of autonomy under the Sixth Schedule for reasons never properly explained. As a result, armed separatism gained ground in the Naga Hills. The intensity of the rebellion there and the rout of the Indian army in the brief border war with China in 1962 finally prompted India to concede a full separate state to the Nagas in 1963.

And that was the first nail in the coffin of Greater Assam. Up until then, with the exception of Tripura and Manipur, the two erstwhile princely states administered as Union Territories since their merger with the Indian Union, the rest of India east of the Siliguri Corridor was Assam. Only the tribal areas of the frontier tracts bordering Tibet were administered separately from Assam as the North-East Frontier Agency (NEFA). In fact, the North East frontier (as opposed to the region that it is today) began to emerge in 1875–76, when the Inner Line of the Lakhimpur and Darrang districts of Assam were brought under Regulation II of 1873. In 1880, the Assam Frontier Tract Regulation was passed by the British; it started the process by which the administration of the frontier tracts of Sadiya, Lakhimpur and Balipara was slowly handed over to the governor of Assam as distinct from the government of Assam. The Indian constitution put the president of India in charge of the administration of these frontier tracts (different from its hill districts) and representation for NEFA was provided by an Act in 1950. The administration of these tracts continued to be carried out by political officers and their assistants.

In 1969, the Panchayat Raj Regulations already in effect elsewhere in India were extended to NEFA, leading to the creation of Gaon Panchayats, Anchal Samitis and Zilla Parishads under the supervision of the Pradesh Council. The Pradesh Council was the precursor of the state legislative assembly and consisted of Zilla Parishad members and those nominated by the chief commissioner of NEFA. NEFA became a Union Territory in 1973 with its name changed to Arunachal Pradesh. It finally became a full state in 1987, along with Mizoram.

GREATER ASSAM OR 'NORTH EAST'

The Indian National Congress, which ruled the country until its first defeat in the national parliamentary elections in 1977, had favoured the creation of linguistic states even before independence. So, it supported the annulment of the Partition of Bengal in 1905. In its Nagpur session in 1920, the Congress made it clear that the 'time has come for the redistribution of the provinces on a linguistic basis'. This was reiterated by the Congress in its many subsequent annual sessions and was also reflected in its election manifesto of 1945–46.

In 1948, the Linguistic Provinces Commission of the Constituent Assembly argued that for purposes of state reorganization, 'apart from the homogeneity of language, stress should also be given to history, geography, economy and cultural mores'. The State Reorganization Commission (SRC) was set up in December 1953 to 'dispassionately and objectively' consider the question of reorganizing the states of the Union. Though it recommended formation of states giving 'greatest importance to language and culture', the SRC said in a note:

> In considering reorganization of States, however, there are other important factors which have also to be borne in mind. The first essential consideration is the preservation and strengthening of the unity and security of India. Financial, economic and administrative considerations are almost equally important not only from the point of view of each state but for the whole nation. (emphasis mine)

Clearly, the SRC was unwilling to recommend the use of the linguistic principle in the North East because it was uncertain about how the stability of a sensitive frontier region would be affected by such a move. The Assam government, in its representation to the SRC, advocated the preservation of the *status quo*. It would not be opposed, it said, to the merger of Cooch Behar, Manipur and Tripura. Needless to say, all political parties in these areas opposed moves for a possible merger with Assam. Proposals were put forward for a Kamtapur state that would encompass the Goalpara district of Assam, the Garo Hills, Cooch Behar, Darjeeling and Jalpaiguri districts of West Bengal. (These proposals were recently revived by some tribal groups in the northern districts of West Bengal like the Kamtapur Peoples Party and the underground Kamtapur Liberation Organisation.) A proposal for a Purbachal state with the Bengali-majority Cachar district at its core was also placed before the SRC. Leaders of the Khasi-Jaintia and the Garo Hills led by Captain Williamson Sangma also raised the demand for a hill state because they felt the autonomy provisions of the Sixth Schedule did not adequately protect tribal interests.

In its final recommendations, the SRC argued for a 'large and relatively resourceful state on the border rather than small and less resilient units'—in other words, for Tripura's merger with Assam so that the entire border with Pakistan could be brought under one administrative unit. Stiff resistance in Tripura to any merger with Assam ultimately foiled this initiative. The state had enjoyed several centuries of sovereign princely rule and all political parties and ethnic groups, tribals and Bengalis alike, were opposed to a merger with either Assam or West Bengal. Finally, Tripura and Manipur became Part C states of India, NEFA was retained as a Frontier Agency and the rest of what is India's North East today remained in Assam.

The growing intensity of the armed separatist movement in the Naga Hills, the peaceful but determined mass movement for a hill state below the Brahmaputra Valley and finally, the outbreak of armed rebellion in the Lushai Hills district (renametd Mizo Hills district) led to the ultimate break-up of Assam within 15 years of the linguistic reorganization of India, which had left Assam untouched. The core of Assam was the Brahmaputra Valley. With the Surma Valley lost to East Pakistan, Assam was more Assamese than ever before. But the Bengali-dominated Barak Valley remained in Assam and the ethnic rivalry between the Bengalis and the Assamese continued to disturb peace and stability in the state. The Assamese elite were also seen as insensitive to the aspirations of tribal and hill people.

The worsening of relations with China that led to the border war of 1962 forced leaders in Delhi to turn their attention to the security and stability of India's North Eastern frontier. The Chinese army had advanced to Tezpur before suddenly retreating to their version of the Line of Actual Control (LAC). In far-off Delhi, there were speculations about what would have happened if the Naga guerrillas had worked as the 'fifth column' for the Chinese (which they did not) and if the Chinese had pushed into the Naga Hills from Tirap after overrunning the Walong salient. The Naga rebels had been receiving assistance from Pakistan since 1957, but not from China. It was only in 1965 that the Chinese finally agreed to help the Naga rebels. Nevertheless, the prospect of a Chinese military drive through eastern Arunachal Pradesh and northern Burma into the Naga Hills for a Tibet-style 'liberation' weighed heavily on Nehru and his colleagues when they decided to break away from the 'Greater Assam' model of administration in India's North Eastern frontier and confer full statehood to Nagaland.

Within a few months of granting statehood to the Naga Hills district, Nehru also opened peace talks with the Naga rebels. A

Nagaland Peace Mission was set up with respected popular figures like Jayaprakash Narayan and Assam's chief minister, Bimala Prasad Chaliha. He did not live to see the failure of the Peace Mission and the Naga problem remains unresolved to this day. The worst-case scenario of a Chinese drive into Nagaland and adjoining states has also not materialized. In fact, after supporting several insurgent groups from northeast India for 15 years, Beijing stopped support to these groups in the early 1980s.

Within three years of the 1962 border war with China, India had faced a Pakistani offensive to 'liberate' Kashmir in 1965 through Operation Gibraltar and Operation Grand Slam. By 1966, Naga guerrillas had started reaching China in large numbers for training and Mizo rebels had unleashed Operation Jericho on the last day of February 1966. Manipur and Tripura also experienced the first stirrings of ethnic unrest and underground armed activity. In 1967, as the first batch of Naga rebels were returning from China after several weeks of intensive training in revolutionary guerrilla warfare, the tribal peasants of Naxalbari, on the Siliguri Corridor that the army calls the 'Chicken Neck', unfurled the banners of India's first Maoist rebellion. West Bengal was soon to be engulfed in a perilous escalation of violence that subsequently spread beyond its borders. With Pakistan as hostile as ever and now joined by China intent on teaching India a lesson for 'its collaboration with the American imperialists on Tibet', the worst-case scenario envisioned by Delhi looked like coming true.

Response to this situation called for a right mix of political acumen and military drive. The dull, thudding counter-insurgency campaign by the Indian army could go on in the Naga Hills and in the Mizo Hills but the generals in Delhi could ill afford several divisions locked up there. More troops were needed to man the long and difficult Himalayan frontier with China and the multi-climatic border with Pakistan. For those guarding the borders, there was always a need to look behind the back in the event of a war. The guerrillas might unsettle the supply lines and join up with Chinese or Pakistani special forces to wreak havoc in the rear. Counter-insurgency units also had to look out across the frontier from where the guerrillas were obtaining training, weapons, funds and encouragement.

The creation of Nagaland and the peace talks of the mid-1960s was intended to start a process of political reconciliation that would lead to the territorial reorganization in Assam. The spread of the prairie fires in India's North East forced Prime Minister Indira Gandhi to consider wide-ranging concessions to the battling ethnicities. Assam had been India's delegated overlord in the North East—its upper-caste ruling elite had run the hill regions of the North Eastern frontier for close to a quarter century. Anyone who went to the hills was likely to meet a *Bora* or a *Buragohain*, a *Borthakur* or a *Barpujari* running the local administration as its deputy commissioner or police superintendent, as its chief engineer or chief medical officer. Now, however, there was too much pressure on them to make way for a missionary-educated neo-literate tribal political and professional class. If the Nagas could have a state of their own, the Mizos, the Khasis and the Garos, the Bodos and the Karbis all wanted one for themselves. The ethnic homeland was catching the imagination of the struggling tribal communities in North East. At the forefront of these movements for separate tribal homelands, one could not miss the lead taken by the neo-literate Christian converts. Be it a Phizo or a Muivah, a Laldenga or a Zoramthanga, a Nichols-Roy or a Williamson Sangma, or much later, even a Bijoy Hrangkhawl or a Ranjan Daimary, the cross on their chests could not be missed.

The Naxalite movement in West Bengal and the evolving crisis in East Pakistan occupied much of Prime Minister Indira Gandhi's attention as India entered its 'difficult years'. But she made the most of the opportunity. As she prepared for military intervention in East Pakistan after much initial reluctance, Mrs Gandhi used the military build-up on the border to crush the Naxalite movement in Bengal. Deployment of troops against the Maoist guerrillas concealed India's offensive intentions across the border until it was too late in the day for Pakistan. The same troops who combed the jungles of Birbhum during the monsoon of 1971 were, a few months later, marching to Jessore and Dhaka.

By decisively intervening in East Pakistan, Indira Gandhi cut off one of the main trans-border regrouping zones for the ethnic rebels of northeast India. A friendly government in Dhaka, though short-lived, ensured for Delhi that the jungles of the Chittagong Hill Tracts, Sylhet and Mymensingh were not available to the guerrillas from the Alee Command (Foreign Command) of the 'Naga Army' or the Zampuimanga battalion of the Mizo National Front. Despite other irritants in Indo-Burmese relations, Delhi followed up the success in Bangladesh by developing closer military cooperation with the Burmese. Indira Gandhi, however, was far too sagacious to rely exclusively on diplomatic and military options. She soon played the 'statehood' card in the North East to satisfy the aspirations of the battling ethnicities to consolidate the gains of the 1971 Bangladesh military campaign.

Even before the liberation of Bangladesh, Mrs Gandhi's government had taken the initiative for the territorial reorganization of the North East. The North-Eastern Areas (Reorganization) Act of 1971, which sought to 'provide for the establishment of the states of Manipur and Tripura and for the formation of the state of Meghalaya and of the Union Territories of Mizoram and Arunachal Pradesh by reorganizing the existing state of Assam', was finally passed in the parliament at almost the same time as the new secular and socialist Republic in Bangladesh was born. The vivisection of Assam and the creation of three new states and two Union Territories (finally upgraded to full states by Mrs Gandhi's son Rajiv in 1987) were intended to satisfy the aspirations of the neo-literate tribal political class so that they could draw away their fellow tribesmen from the path of armed opposition to the Indian state. The North-Eastern Areas (Reorganization) Act finally achieved what the likes of Hutton and Parry, Reid and Mackenzie had failed to carry out—the separation of the plains of Assam from its enchanting hills. Delhi did realize the need for some regional coordination when it set up the North Eastern Council to facilitate coordinated development and security planning. This was described by B.P. Singh, an Assam cadre IAS officer and later India's home secretary, as 'the new twin vision for the region'.[14]

In Indian—and South Asian—political-administrative discourse, Assam was finally replaced by 'the North East'. After the reorganization, Assam became just another state in the region east of the Siliguri Corridor, controlling a much smaller piece of territory made up of the Brahmaputra and Barak Valleys and the Karbi Anglong and North Cachar Hills. The other hill regions that had been added to Assam by the British were all gone. It is debatable whether India gained anything by creating so many small—and some say, economically non-viable—states in the North East. The region's leading historian, H.K. Barpujari, argued that breaking up Assam was a disaster. In his last book, he lamented: 'The policy-makers in Delhi utterly failed to realize that in a multi-racial and multi-lingual country, erection of linguistic states would unlock the Pandora's Box and open up the floodgates of racism, linguism and parochialism. This has happened elsewhere in India and is now happening in the North East'.[15] As time has shown, there is much truth in the last written words of Assam's greatest historian.

Although the North East has emerged as a distinct region in India, with clearly demarcated geographical contours, states within the region rarely betray any awareness of this. All the states carved out of Assam have border disputes with the mother state. Police forces of these states, particularly those of Nagaland and Assam, have fought pitched battles—the worst such clash occurring in 1985 at Merapani—to settle border disputes, the fighting sometimes resembling a border clash between separate countries. Furthermore, the region's many insurgent armies, as well as the state governments who try to combat them, have failed to work out any meaningful degree of cooperation among themselves.

Joint revolutionary fronts have been non-starters, unlike in neighbouring Burma, because even the Delhi-baiting rebels often find they are as different from their regional cousins as from the rest of India. Differences of ethnicity, religion and ideology have often blurred the tactical wisdom of joining hands against the common enemy. Some agitators, such as those leading the anti-foreigner agitation in Assam in the early 1980s, discovered, after initial hostility, that the Indian federal government was their only real safeguard against rampant illegal migration from Bangladesh that threatened to undermine the demographic character of Assam. The agenda of the Assam agitation is now considered a policy priority for the whole nation and Delhi, especially when ruled by a Hindu revivalist government appeared to be more enthusiastic than the Prafulla Mahantas and Bhrigu Phukans to identify and throw out illegal infiltrators from states bordering Bangladesh.

Despite its heterogenity, the 'North East' as a constituent region of India has come to stay as a distinct entity. If India's south, made up of the four states of Andhra Pradesh, Tamil Nadu, Kerala and Karnataka, is seen as India's 'Dravidian under-belly', very different from the country's northern cow-belt, the North East is considered racially distinct from the heartland. That clubbing together of hugely diverse identities into a post-colonial region may be the cause of many a policy failure but there's no denying that Delhi is now beginning to see the North East as a possible bridge with the tiger economies of South East Asia. That's why, in 2001, a cabinet-level Department for Development of the North Eastern Region (DONER) was launched to fast track the region's economic and infrastructure development. That makes the North East the only region whose development is the specific mandate of a stand-alone department of the federal government. There is an industrial policy for the region to attract private capital that's been sparse to come to the North East since the British left.

In fact, the government of India's Vision 2020 document for North East envisages the region as 'a prosperous part of India contributing, in some measure, to the growth of the national economy with the geo-economical disadvantages converted into productive opportunities'. The document says it wants to create 'a contented rural North East with developed primary sector impacting growth in the secondary sector, with minimum connectivity established and health and education for all ensured'. It further says that it aims at converting the North East into

> an important hub of trade and commerce in relation to South East Asia with border trade developed and firmly rooted, an empowered and informed people through skill development and technology intervention, a community participating and involving in socio-economic planning, projectizing, implementing and monitoring and a peaceful society with level of unemployment drastically brought down.[16]

In fact, India's Look East foreign policy—a special effort to develop close ties with largely Mongoloid South East Asia, China, Japan and Korea—sees the North East not as a periphery anymore, but as the centre of a thriving and integrated economic space linking two dynamic regions (South East and South Asia) with a network of highways, railways, pipelines, transmission lines criss-crossing the region.

The mainland Indian perception of the North East has also changed, albeit rather slowly. Assam's former governor, Lieutenant-General S.K. Sinha, proposed installing the statute of the great Ahom hero Lachit Barphukan in the National Defense Academy at Khadakvasla. The logic is not difficult to see: if Shivaji can be a national hero for fighting the Mughals, why cannot Lachit be one for his great victory against the Mughal army at the Battle of Saraighat. The historical legitimacy of regional 'Indian' heroes for their resistance to foreign invaders like the Mughals has been growing in a climate of Hindu revivalism. And in this changing Indian milieu, the exploits of the soldiers of the Naga and the Assam regiments of the Indian army in the far-off battlefields of Kargil has found a place in the nation's television-engineered collective memory. The country's soccer team has, at any time now, a 50 to 60 per cent representation from North East, especially Manipur—something that prompted young Calcutta-based sports historian Kaushik Bandyopadhyay to explore soccer's potential to draw away potential insurgent recruits in Manipur.

Times have changed in the North East as well. Thousands of Nagas lined up to pay homage at the funeral of Lieutenant Kengruse, the Naga officer of the Indian army martyred in Kargil, as they did during the cremation of the great 'Naga Army' General Mowu Angami, who led the several groups of Naga rebels to East Pakistan and China in a saga of bravery and grit recollected in Nirmal Nibedon's *Night of the Guerrillas*. Scores of Nagas and Mizos, Khasis and Garos join the central services, the Indian army and the paramilitary forces and other national organizations every year. The national parliament has had a president and a speaker from the North East. There has been even a Congress president from the region.

Since the missionary-educated tribals of northeast India have a lead in English education over most other tribals from the Indian heartland, they are beginning to secure more and more positions in the central services by taking advantage of the Scheduled Tribes quota. Those who join these services and other federal organizations end up as part of the 'mobile Indian middle class', the strongest cement of India's post-colonial nationhood. Their influence on local society is not inconsiderable and they provide a direction for new aspirants in the region. At last, the university campuses in Delhi, Bombay and Pune are beginning to be as attractive for the educated youth in the North East as the guerrilla camps in the troubled region.

The creation of the new states and autonomous councils in the North East have indeed opened a Pandora's Box. The Bodos, the Karbis, the Dimasas, the Hmars and even the Garos, who have produced more chief ministers in Meghalaya than the Khasis, have militant groups fighting for new states, autonomous regions and even independent homelands. If the Nagas and the Mizos can have states of their own, the argument goes, why cannot the Bodos or the Garos have likewise? But, none of the new states of northeast India can be called ethnically compact. They were formed by joining up the homelands of three, four or more important tribes. Meghalaya has three leading tribes, namely, the Khasis, the Jaintias and the Garos. Mizoram has the dominant Lushais but has to reckon with the aspirations of the Hmars, the Lais, the Maras, the Chakmas and the Reangs. Pure ethnic homelands have proved to be a costly mirage and North East's battling ethnicities, in their relentless pursuit of the same, could reduce the region to a Bosnia or a Kosovo.

Since the North East has emerged as a distinct geo-political region, its inhabitants have a good reason to make a common ground on a host of issues to achieve the best possible deal with India. It is time for all separatist groups in North East to explore the limits of the 'special federal relationship' that Delhi is prepared to offer to the NSCN. As India's relations with China and the countries of South East Asia begin to improve, the importance of the country's 'Mongoloid' fringe has not been lost on Delhi or her neighbours. In years to come, if regional cooperation in the eastern part of South Asia increases, as it did in the ASEAN region, India's North East can emerge as the country's bridge to several growth quadrants across its borders, a land of opportunity for outsiders and natives alike. At last, a disadvantageous geographic location could give way to great eco-strategic advantage for India. But before Delhi could exploit that, it will have to overcome two of North East's perpetual deficits: the deficit of democracy and development. Festering—and multiplying—low-intensity conflicts in the North East are clearly inconsistent with India's image as a rising power and Delhi would do well to resolve these conflicts even as it pushes ahead with the Look East policy to turn the 'arc of instability' (the rebellious Indo-Burma frontier region) into a shared economic space with great promise for growth and prosperity.

Notes

1. Sanjay Barbora, May–June 2008.
2. S.K. Pillai, November 1999.
3. 'Polarisation', an NSCN document written by its General Secretary Thuingaleng Muivah, 1985. Available with author.
4. Alexander Mackenzie, 1884.
5. J.C. Arbuthnott, 26 September 1907.
6. V.S. Jafa, August 1999.
7. Bodhisattva Kar, 2009.
8. B.G. Verghese, 1996.
9. The Simon Commission Report, 1930.
10. Ibid.
11. Ibid.
12. Reginald Coupland, 1944.
13. Robert Reid, 1983. He talks of 'immense difficulties' in implementing the Coupland Plan.
14. B.P. Singh, 1987.
15. H.K. Barpujari, 1998.
16. Northeast Region Vision 2020 document, finalised by the Department of Northeast Region (DONER) and Northeast Council on 12–13 May 2008 at the Council's meeting in Agartala.

2 Ethnicity, Ideology and Religion

The North East is seen as India's 'Mongoloid fringe', where the country begins to look less and less like India and more like the highland societies of South East Asia. Many argue that this racial element makes the North East very different from the rest of the country.[1] One of the last areas of the subcontinent to be conquered by the British, the 'North East' was never part of any trans-Indian empire in ancient or medieval times. Migration from the Indian mainland was limited to preachers and teachers, traders and soldiers of fortune. The mainland's 'Sanskritic' cultural influence touched only Assam, Manipur and Tripura, where the kings adopted variants of Hinduism as the state religion. But these kings also fought back attempts by the Bengal sultans and the Mughals to conquer their territories.

Before the advent of the British, successive waves of Tibeto-Mongoloid tribes and nationalities from north western China, northern Burma and even Thailand and Laos came and occupied various parts of the 'North East'. They fought each other, traded with each other, built small empires, but never allowed the area to be run over and controlled by anyone from the Indian mainland. That uninterrupted freedom for a great length of historical time and the region's racial distinctiveness gave its people a sense of being different from the rest of India.

All of India's major religions are practised here. Christianity dominates the hills; Hinduism and Islam are the major religions in the plains. Animistic faiths and Lamaist sects also thrive both in the hills and the plains. Assamese and Bengali speakers are the most numerous, but scores of other languages and dialects are spoken. Although ethnicity has dominated the social and political processes in the North East, the region has also been subjected to the complex interplay of ideology and religion before and after 1947. The tangled web of ethnic alignments has continuously influenced the evolution—and ruptures—of generic identities, with both political ideology and religion playing a part.

Tribes, Nationalities, Changing Identities

In parts of the North East, including Assam, Manipur and Tripura, language has sometimes served as the basis for ethnic identity, but often it has not. In the hill regions, the absence of a common language has actually forced evolving generic identities to develop pidgin lingua francas like Nagamese. Political expediency and the constant realignment of ethnic groups have also helped create new identities. The Paites were seen as part of the great Kuki-Chin family of tribes not so long ago. But in their quest for self-assertion, the Paites started projecting themselves as Zomis since the late 1980s, insisting they were not Kukis. When the militias of the Kuki and Naga tribes started fighting each other in the 1990s, the Paite militants sided with the Naga rebels against the Kukis. The Kukis and the Paites, however, speak variants of the same language and have more in common amongst themselves than with the Nagas.

In India's North East, where emphasis on ethnicity has often produced splintered identities, the Paites are a classic case of a breakaway identity, of a smaller tribe challenging the larger tribe within a generic formation, fragmenting the process of nationality formation. The withdrawal of the Lais and Maras from a 'Mizo' identity to avoid Lushai domination is a similar case. The reverse process has happened as well. Smaller tribes have identified with a bigger tribal or generic identity for self-preservation during conflict between battling ethnicities. In Manipur, smaller tribes like the Anals have identified with the broader Naga identity, reporting themselves as Nagas in successive censuses. And several tribes in Tripura have grouped themselves into an *Upajati* (literal meaning: tribal) identity just to prevent being subsumed by the dominant Bengali culture.

So while the autonomous councils for the Lais and Maras in Mizoram are coterminus with the boundaries of their ethnic homelands, the autonomous council for the tribals in Tripura covers the entire hill region barring the state's western plains and is called 'Tripura Tribal Areas Autonomous District Council'. In such an arrangement, the tribes have not moved towards a generic identity like the 'Naga' or the 'Mizo'—they have retained the distinct identity of the tribe but sought to project a broad tribal unity stressing their ethno-cultural differences from the Bengali settlers. The ruling Manikya dynasty of the state, despite their tribal roots, had accepted Bengali language and culture instead of promoting a generic identity of the tribes. But that's what the tribes of Tripura are now trying to undo—because unless they stress their ethnic difference from the Bengalis, they are likely to be absorbed by the Bengali nationality like the tribes in north Bengal. Even the Koch-Rajbongshis of northern Bengal are in a phase of retribalization, stressing their distinct ethnicity. This upsets the Bengalis who see their assimilation as final. Even senior Marxist politicians from north Bengal like the state's Urban Affairs Minister Asok Bhattacharya are no exception. In a television chatshow anchored by me in February 2006, Bhattacharya referred to the Koch-Rajbongshis as *Amaderi Moto Bangali* (Bengalis like us).

The royal houses of Tripura and Cooch Behar (in North Bengal) consciously adopted Bengali language and culture as the language and the culture of the court—and they expected their tribal subjects to follow. But later generations of tribals, feeling marginalized in their own homeland, began to consciously distance themselves from the dominant Bengali language and culture to preserve their distinctive ethnicity. The over-arching *Upajati* identity served the purpose in Tripura—it did not dilute the distinct tribal identities but it did provide a basis for 'we' and 'other' vis-à-vis the Bengalis. In North Bengal, the *Kamtapuri* identity has been whipped up by tribal movements—both by armed groups and those who follow the path of mass agitation—to fight for a separate state and break away from West Bengal. The *Upajati* identity in Tripura also has a close parallel with the evolution of the *Jumma* identity in the neighbouring Chittagong Hill Tracts (CHT) of Bangladesh. The circumstances were quite similar and the tribes of CHT needed an 'identity shield' against the country's majoritarian assimilationist drive, best exemplified by Sheikh Mujib-ur-Rehman's advice to Chakma leader Manabendra Narayan Larma in 1972 to *go home and become Bengalis*. Larma and his followers later took the path of armed movement against Bangladesh's successive military-driven governments.

In recent years, all across North East, generic identities that emerged during the last days of colonial rule and consolidated in the early years of the Indian republic have tended to splinterize. The material advantages that follow recognition as a Scheduled Tribe (ST) in India have encouraged retribalization. Reservations—like those for Scheduled Castes—in education and employment, legislatures and parliaments, have often prompted smaller ethnic groups in northeast India to seek recognition as STs. The Deshi Tripuras or the Lashkars in Tripura were happy to be recognized as 'local Bengalis' during princely rule but have subsequently sought recognition as a ST. The Meiteis in Tripura have done the same and their ethnic cousins in Manipur rue at not being able to get the same material benefits that Kukis, Nagas or Zomis tend to enjoy in Manipur.

The Bodos have long been denied the benefit of autonomy because as 'plains tribals' they were not covered by the Sixth Schedule of the Indian constitution, which provides autonomy to tribal areas. Now that the Indian government has finally signed an agreement with the Bodoland Liberation Tigers Force (BLTF), the Sixth Schedule has been amended to include the Bodoland Territorial Council in western Assam, and the Bodos have begun to enjoy the benefits that the Scheduled Tribes status brings. That has prompted the millions of *Adivasi*s in Assam to demand recognition as Scheduled Tribes. Their ancestors were brought to work on the tea gardens of Assam by the British from what is now the state of Bihar, Jharkhand and Madhya Pradesh. In those states, their ethnic cousins enjoy ST status—so the *Adivasi*s of Assam say they must get it.

Even linguistic preferences in India's North East have often shifted due to political considerations, concealing ethnic and religious divisions. In Assam, the migrant Muslim peasantry of Bengali origin chose to register themselves as Assamese speakers in every census since independence, so that they could assimilate into the local milieu. Unlike the tribal communities or the Bengali Hindus, these Muslims, mostly poor landless peasants, chose assimilation to secure their economic and political future in an adopted homeland, even when their co-religionists back in East Pakistan were fighting for the Bengali language and culture. And when Hindus of East Bengali origin fought for their linguistic rights in the Barak Valley of southern Assam, these Muslim migrants looked the other way, registering Assamese as their mother tongue in successive censuses.

The Assamese caste-Hindus co-opted these East Bengali Muslims into their fold as *Na-Asamiya*s or neo-Assamese only to ensure that Assamese speakers remained the largest linguistic group in the state. Constantly haunted by the perceived Bengali domination, the Assamese-caste elite were keen to retain the numerical preponderance of Assamese speakers in the state, since linguistic predominance ensures ethnic hegemony. With the support of the *Na-Asamiya*s, Assamese remained the major language in Assam and the caste elite sought to impose it on the Bengali-dominated Barak Valley, leading to the language agitations between 1960 and 1975.

Every year in the Barak Valley, Bengalis observe 19 May as their Language Martyrs Day in the memory of the eleven killed in police firing on that date in 1960. Nineteenth May has become somewhat like 21 February of Bangladesh—a Language Martyrs Day. In recent years, 19 May celebrations in Silchar have been graced by the visits of leading poets, writers and singers from both West Bengal and Bangladesh. The Muslims of Bengali origin in the Brahmaputra Valley, however, have largely stayed away from these celebrations to emphasize their linguistic preferences and have rather used their religious identity as the defining point of 'we' and 'others'.

Physical security and fear of eviction from the land they own are the obvious priorities for the Muslim peasant migrants from the erstwhile eastern Bengal who settled in the Brahmaputra Valley. Unlike their brethren in Bangladesh, West Bengal, Tripura and the Barak Valley, their passion for the Bengali language has been limited to the occasional folk song choirs in the *char* areas (river islands) during the harvest season. But the most popular singer of the *char*s, Aklima Akhtar, emphasizes the *Na-Asamiya* identity when she sings *Ami Charua, Kintu Na hau Bangladeshi, ami Axomiya*. (We are poor *char* dwellers but we are not Bangladeshis, we are Assamese.) *Na-Asamiya*s are richly contributing to contemporary Assamese writing and literature, though most of them continue to speak East Bengali dialects at homes, or within their villages or towns.

Only after these 'East Bengali' Muslims were specifically targeted by the Assamese militant student and youth groups during the bloody riots of 1982–83, did some of them register as Bengali speakers during the 1991 census in what was seen as a return to roots. This led to a fall in the number of Assamese speakers in the last two censuses of 1991 and 2001, but the *Na-Asamiya* identity, bestowed on the Muslim migrants and gratefully accepted by most of them, has not withered away even after the 1982–83 riots and the subsequent violence they have often faced from Assamese vigilante groups. Though the migrants, or at least many of them, now back aggressive minority parties like the Assam United Democratic Front led by Maulana Badruddin Ajmal to protect themselves and seek their piece of the political cake, moderate minority groups such as the Assam Mia Parishad seek minority protection through reconciliation with the Assamese sub-nationalist groups such as the All Assam Students Union (AASU) or the Assam Jatiyotabadi Yuba Chatro Parishad (AJYCP).

The six-year long Assamese movement against 'foreigners' and 'infiltrators' ruptured the ongoing assimilation process of the Muslims of East Bengali origin. The same Assamese who had called them *Na-Asamiyas* were now derisively calling them *Miyas* or 'Bangladeshis' and asking for their expulsion from Assam. The 1982–83 riot during the Assam agitation, of which the high point was the massacre at Nellie (police death-count: 219, press reports: 3300, unofficial sources: 5000), kickstarted a process of minority consolidation for self-preservation that has been reflected in the formation of minority political parties like the United Minorities Forum and now the Assam United Democratic Front. But as the East Bengali Muslims asserted themselves more as Muslims in recent years, the Muslims of Assamese origin (descendants of the Mughals who came to conquer Assam and then settled down in the state) have challenged the *Na-Asamiyas* in the state's minority space by aggressively promoting their *Khilongjia* (indigenous) credentials. The indigenous Assamese Muslims emphasize their roots in Assam not just to prove they are not 'infiltrators' or 'foreigners' but also to challenge the preponderance of the East Bengali Muslims in the state's minority political space.

In recent years, the question of illegal migration from Bangladesh has overshadowed other political issues in Assam. This, along with the rise of the Bharatiya Janata Party (BJP), has ensured that the linguistic mobilization of the 1960s has been replaced by the politics of religious fundamentalism. Bengali Hindus in large numbers throughout Assam have started supporting the BJP and Assamese Hindus have joined them because they feel regional parties like the Asom Gana Parishad (AGP) cannot deliver on their promise of deporting illegal migrants (read: Muslim migrants). The AGP–BJP political alliance in the 2001 state assembly elections, engineered by the state's governor, Lieutenant-General S.K. Sinha (retired), marked the high point of this new trend, but it prompted Muslims to group together and vote Congress to victory. The alliance has been renewed again in Assam before the 2009 Lok Sabha elections.

With north Indian migrant communities like the Biharis and the Marwaris supporting the BJP in ever-increasing numbers, the process of religious consolidation has begun to affect the politics of Assam more significantly than ever before. After all, Assam has the second highest percentage of Muslim population among Indian states after Kashmir and the impact of global and national realities on Assam's politics cannot be wished away. This has weakened the support base of Assamese separatism because the United Liberation Front of Assam (ULFA) has been operating from its bases in Bangladesh and its soft stand on the migration issue has not gone down well with Assamese upper-caste Hindus. The ULFA is opposed to the politics of religious fundamentalism, but when it went to the extent of supporting the 'Kashmiri freedom struggle' during the Kargil War, the Assamese saw in it a not-so-subtle attempt to please the ULFA's main external sponsors.

In the pre-British era, the population flow into what is now northeast India originated almost entirely from the east. Closer to the highlands of Burma and south western China than to the power centres of the Indian heartland, this region was exposed to a constant flow of tribes and nationalities belonging to the Tibeto-Burman and the Mon-Khmer stock, one settling down only to be overrun by the subsequent wave. The direction of population flow changed with the advent of the British. The colonial masters brought peasants and agricultural labourers, teachers and clerks from neighbouring Bengal and Bihar to open up Assam's economy. Traders from north India followed. The trickle became a tide, spreading to Tripura, where the Manikya kings offered Bengali farmers *jungle-avadi* or forest clearance leases. The move was intended to popularize settled agriculture in a largely hill state and improve the state's revenues.[2]

The hill regions were protected by the Inner Line Regulations, whereas the plains and the princely domains were not. The steady population flow from mainland India, particularly from Bengal, into the plains of Assam and Tripura, accentuated the ethnic and religious diversity and introduced a nativist–outsider dichotomy to the simmering conflict.[3]

Partition led to a rise in the flow of refugees and migrants from East Pakistan (now Bangladesh). Tripura's demography changed within two decades as Bengalis became a powerful majority. The pace of demographic change was slightly slower in Assam than in Tripura but it was enough to upset the 'sons of the soil', provoking both armed conflict and mass protest movements and sometimes a mix of both. The fear that other North Eastern states would go the Tripura way has weighed heavily on indigenous people and early settlers throughout the North East and provoked the more militant among them to take up arms.[4]

A tradition of armed resistance to invaders had developed in the region even before the arrival of the British. The Ahoms, who ruled Assam for several centuries, fought back the invading Mughals. The Manikya kings of Tripura not only fought the Bengal sultans back from their hill region but also managed to conquer parts of eastern Bengal at various times in history. The Burmese were the only ones who overran Assam and Manipur, only to be ousted by the British within a few years. When the British ventured into the North East, they encountered fierce resistance in the Naga and the Mizo (then Lushai) Hills regions, in Manipur and in what is now Meghalaya. The Naga and the Mizo tribesmen resorted to guerrilla war, holding up much stronger British forces by grit and ingenuous use of the terrain. As a result of the fighting, there were parts of the Mizo Hills where entire villages were reduced to being 'populated only by widows'.[5]

After the departure of the British, the Indian nation-state faced uprisings in Tripura almost immediately after independence and in the Naga hills since the mid-1950s. The communists, who led the tribal uprising in Tripura, called off armed struggle in the early 1950s and joined Indian-style electoral politics. Since the 1980 ethnic riots, Tripura has witnessed periodic bouts of tribal militancy, with the Bengali refugee population its main target. The Naga uprising, the strongest ethnic insurrection in northeast India, has been weakened by repeated splits along tribal lines. Talks between the Indian government and the stronger faction of the National Socialist Council of Nagaland (NSCN), which were started in 1997, are continuing, but a possible resumption of Naga insurgency cannot be ruled out completely.

Armed uprisings erupted in the Mizo hills following a famine in 1966. A year later, guerrilla bands became active in Manipur and Tripura. Almost all the separatist groups in the North East—Nagas, Mizos, Meiteis, Tripuris and now those from Meghalaya—have subsequently received shelter and support in East Pakistan and later in Bangladesh. By the early 1980s, the entire region was gripped by large-scale violence. There were fierce riots in Tripura and Assam. Separatist movements intensified in Mizoram, Nagaland and Manipur, later spreading to both Assam and Tripura. India's young Prime Minister Rajiv Gandhi took the initiative to arrive at settlements with the militant students of Assam, the separatist Mizo National Front and the Tribal National Volunteers of Tripura. Other insurgencies continued, however, and new ones emerged. Whereas earlier separatist movements, such as that of the Nagas and the Mizos, had challenged federal authority, the recent insurgencies of the Bodos, the Hmars, the Karbis and the Dimasas directly confront the regional power centres—the new states of North East.

Although the Nagas and the Mizos fought for a separate country and finally settled for a separate state within India, the smaller ethnicities like the Bodos and the Hmars have fought for autonomous homelands that they wish to carve out of states like Assam and Mizoram. The failure to achieve separate states radicalized the movements and made them turn to secessionist rhetoric. Territorial demands based on ethnicity in northeast India are very often sustained by historical memories of separate tribal kingdoms. The Bodos or the Dimasas fondly recall their pre-Ahom kingdoms, when they controlled large territories. The Tripuris and the Meiteis of Manipur look back at the long rule of their princely families to justify secession. A democratic dispensation like India's provides even the smallest of these groups scope to raise their demands. That Delhi has conceded many of them—and specially after some agitation or armed movement—have actually given these ethnic groups a feeling that they can obtain their imagined homelands with a little more effort, a push here, a shove there.

Very often in the North East, a negotiated settlement with a separatist movement has opened the ethnic fissures within it and created new homeland demands. The Hmars, the Maras and the Lais fought shoulder-to-shoulder with the Lushais against the Indian security forces during the 20 years of insurgency led by the Mizo National Front (MNF). But 20 years of bonding through the shared experience of guerrilla warfare failed to consolidate the greater 'Mizo' identity. After the 1986 accord with the MNF, India came to be seen as a source of protection and justice by the smaller tribes and ethnicities. Now, the Hmars and the Reangs want an autonomous district council for themselves, like the Lais, the Maras and the Chakmas already enjoy. Both tribes have militant groups (the Hmar Peoples Convention and the Bru National Liberation Front) who have resorted to violence and then came to some settlements with the state government in Aizawl.

The Bodos, the Karbis, the Dimasas and the Rabhas all joined the Assam movement to expel 'foreigners' and 'infiltrators'. But after the 1985 accord was signed by the Assam agitation groups with the Indian government, these groups felt the Assamese 'had taken the cake and left us the crumbs'.[6] The result: fresh agitations, often sliding into violent insurgencies, spearheaded by smaller ethnicities demanding separate homelands. Within two years of the 1985 accord, the Bodos were on the warpath with a new slogan: 'divide Assam fifty-fifty'. Militant Bodo groups took the road of armed rebellion and terrorism, blowing up bridges, trains and buses, attacking troops and policemen, politicians and non-Bodo ethnic groups.

In 2003, a settlement was reached with the Bodoland Liberation Tigers Force (BLTF) and that led to the creation of the Bodoland Territorial Autonomous Council. Sometime later, the National Democratic Front of Bodoland (NDFB) also emerged from the jungles and is now involved in negotiations with Delhi. In the meantime, clashes between the NDFB and the former BLTF has sharply increased across the Bodoland Council area—a conflict that is further sharpened by the religious divide amongst the Bodos, with adherents of the Bathou faith (ancient animists) and Hindus largely behind the BLTF and the neo-convert Bodo Christians largely behind the NDFB. Here's a classic case of religion fracturing a strong ethno-national bonding—like the one suffered by the Bengalis in what is now Bangladesh.

The ethnic imbalance in power-sharing has often caused retribalization, which in turn has limited the growth of local nationalisms that could challenge the Indian state.[7] After fighting India for fifty years, Naga nationalism remains an incomplete process due to at least three major splits within the separatist movement. Each of these splits—and the clashes that followed—followed tribal divides, leaving behind so much bad blood that all unity efforts to bring the factions closer have failed miserably. Even a China-trained leader like Muivah, a Tangkhul Naga from Manipur, has no hesitation branding Angamis as 'reactionary traitors' and his own tribe, the Tangkhuls (who form the bulk of the NSCN), as 'revolutionary patriots'.[8] On the other hand, the Tangkhuls are seen in Nagaland as *Kaccha Nagas* (impure Nagas).[9] Only when an emotive issue like 'Greater Nagaland' surfaces, pitting the Nagas against the Meiteis or the Assamese, do the conflicts within the Naga identity evaporate for a while, only to surface at a later stage. It has been argued that if the Naga separatist movement had not suffered so many splits on tribal lines, it might have secured a much better deal from India in the 1960s than what the NSCN is now capable of.[10]

The trend has been no different in Mizoram or Manipur. The Kuki's demand for a separate homeland that has pitted them against the Nagas has driven some smaller clans away and led to the emergence of a separate Zomi identity. The Hmars, Lais and the Maras have joined the Chakmas and the Reangs to challenge the Mizos. In Manipur, the Meitei identity has been reinforced through the rich Manipuri language and culture, but the Meitei refuse to recognize the Bishnupriyas as Manipuris. When the leftist government in Tripura recognized the Bishnupriya's right to primary education in their own mother tongue, the Meiteis in Tripura and Manipur came out in the streets to protest against it. In Tripura, the Mizos in the northern Jampui Hills demand a regional council within the Tribal Areas Autonomous Council of Tripura to preserve their 'distinct identity', whereas their ethnic kinsmen in Mizoram are wary of similar demands by smaller ethnicities. The Reangs in Tripura resent attempts by the Tripuris to impose the Kokborok language on them. And they look back at the brutal suppression of Reang rebellions by the Tripuri kings as 'evidence of ethnic domination that cannot be accepted anymore'.[11]

The tensions within the tribes, as much caused by the oral and written traditions of conflict between them as by contemporary tussles for power and influence, have weakened efforts to promote a compact 'Borok' or tribal identity against perceived Bengali domination. At times, several tribes sharing the same religion have tried to promote a common identity on its basis, albeit with little success. The separatist National Liberation Front of Tripura (NLFT) has tried aggressively to promote the Borok identity reinforced by Christianity, taking a cue from the Mizo and Naga rebel groups. The animist Reangs and the Vaishnavite Jamatias, however, resent imposition of the Christian-centric Borok identity and many of them have broken away from the NLFT.

Once India carved out the state of Nagaland in 1963, Assam's role as a sub-regional hegemon was threatened and its position as India's political sub-contractor in the North East was destined to end. Within a decade of the creation of Nagaland, Delhi effected a political reorganization of the whole region, through which three new administrative units were formed. All these three became full-fledged states in the 1980s, as India desperately sought to control violent ethnic insurgencies in the area. On the other hand, the break-up of Assam not only produced fresh demands for ethnic homelands within what has remained of it now, but it also drove a section of the ethnic Assamese to insurgency. With the hills gone, the Assamese turned to their valleys to find they were fast becoming a minority there. The anti-foreigner movement that rocked Assam between 1979 and 1985 led to large-scale, free-for-all ethnic riots. The ULFA, now the leading separatist organization in the state, was born out of that movement. Its initial credo was ethnic cleansing—it sought to drive the 'foreigners' (mostly migrants from what's now Bangladesh) out of Assam by force of arms.

Over a period of time, however, the ULFA's politics has changed. Sheltered in Bangladesh, Burma and Bhutan, and having to face the military might of the Indian state, the ULFA has denounced the Assam movement as 'one that was led by juveniles, who failed to understand that migration per se was not bad and had helped many countries like the USA to become what they are today'. The ULFA claims that Bengalis—Hindus and Muslims alike—have 'immensely contributed to Assam' and that 'those of them who feel themselves as part of Assam should be treated as its legitimate dwellers'.[12] It is difficult to ascertain how much of this policy shift on the part of the ULFA—

projecting itself as the representative of the *Asombashis* (dwellers of Assam) rather than the *Asomiyas* or ethnic Assamese—stems from tactical considerations, such as finding shelter in Bangladesh and gaining the support of Assam's large Bengali population, and how much of it is a genuine attempt to rise above the ethnic considerations to forge a secular, multi-ethnic identity.

The ULFA is only being pragmatic in trying to project territory and a multi-ethnic credo as the basis for a future independent Assam. It is merely acknowledging the polyglot nature of the state of Assam and of the rest of the region. Despite its racial difference from the Indian heartland, the North East is an ethnic mosaic, which is ironically reminiscent of India's own multi-lingual, multi-religious and multi-ethnic polity. The ULFA seeks to restore the multi-ethnic and assimilative nature of the Assamese nationality formation process that was disrupted by racial-linguistic chauvinism on the part of the upper-caste Assamese elite in the 1960s, as a result of which tribe after tribe chose to abandon Assam, fuelling demands for an ever-increasing number of ethnicity-based states in the North East. Significantly, though the ULFA has targeted Hindi-speaking populations for large-scale attacks after 1999, it has avoided any attack on Bengalis, Nepalis or tribal groups that it regards as potential allies in the struggle against 'Indian colonialism'. Hindi-speakers have been seen by ULFA leaders as 'Indian populations supportive of the colonial rule'.[13] Though it could well be that the ULFA intensified their attacks on the Hindi-speakers to pressurize Delhi to start negotiations with them on their own terms or under instigation from their external sponsors in Bangladesh and Pakistan. It backfired and led to intensified military operations against them because Delhi came under heavy pressure from political parties in Hindi-speaking states to act decisively against the separatists in Assam.

The ULFA's lack of faith in ethnicity as the basis for its political militancy stems from a realization that there could be no 'pure ethnic homeland' in Assam or anywhere else in northeast India. A broad-based Assamese nationalism, unless it caters to the distinct ethnic aspirations of the tribes and other communities in Assam, is a non-starter. The ULFA therefore, shrewdly enough, projects a future independent Assam as a federal Assam, where Bodo, Karbi, Dimasa, Rabha, Lalung or Mishing, or even Bengali homelands can coexist, so long as the 'basic values of Assamese society and culture are accepted'.[14] The ULFA says ethnicity has 'promoted more divisions within the revolutionary struggles and provided India's ruling classes with more and more opportunity to crush them'.[15] According to a former security adviser to the Assam government, this is 'a clever ploy to broaden the support base of the ULFA insurgency against India'.[16] But Assam's political leadership now speak the same language, of the need to satisfy the aspirations of the ethnic, linguistic and religious minorities to stave off another break-up of the state.[17]

Though ethnicity has been the mainstay of the region's separatist movements and often has formed the basis for creation of political-administrative units there, its self-corrosive properties have restricted the growth of local nationalisms strong enough to confront Delhi. It can create a Lebanon or a Bosnia out of northeast India but never a Bangladesh or an East Timor capable of breaking away from the post-colonial nation-state. All the states in the North East, most of which were created on the basis of ethnic distinctiveness, have failed to resolve their ethnic issues, thus exposing the illusion of a 'pure ethnic homeland'.

Meghalaya came into being as a tribal state because the leaders of the three major tribes (Khasis, Jaintias and Garos) felt that their aspirations were poorly served in Assam. Now they fight along ethnic lines for the spoils of political office and since Meghalaya, like most other North Eastern states, has a small legislature of 60 members, the state has to live with the instability of shaky coalitions. The latest power-sharing arrangement within Meghalaya's ruling regional coalition gives a politician of the Garo tribe (Purno Sangma) and one of the Khasi tribe (Donkuper Roy) two-and-half years each as chief minister. That Sangma, a former Speaker of the Indian parliament, comes back to his home state and becomes part of such a power-sharing arrangement to secure his dwindling political fortunes testifies to the power of ethnicity in Meghalaya—and perhaps in the rest of the region.

Mizoram also has problems with its ethnic minorities. The Reang and Chakma tribes complain of ethnic and religious persecution and allege that the dominant Mizos, who are mostly Christian, want to convert them to Christianity and to the Mizo way of life. The Lais and Maras want to join the Reangs and the Chakmas to form a separate unit, a Union Territory to be administered from the Centre.[18] The Naga–Kuki clashes throughout northeast India that left hundreds dead in the 1980s and 1990s raised the spectre of conflicting home-land demands that could lead to ethnic cleansing in pursuit of the impossible, namely, the creation of 'pure ethnic states'.

In Arunachal Pradesh, the largest state in northeast India, ethnicity has served to fragment the society and polity and has hindered political modernization. Its just over quarter of a million people are split up into 110 tribes and several plains communities. Twenty-six of these tribes are large and politically significant. The largest among them, including the Adis, the Nishis, the Singphos, the Khamptis and the Apa Tanis, are in perpetual competition for political power. They unite only when faced with a common scare and also when they find an acceptable scapegoat: the Chakmas and the Hajongs. Local politicians in the state whip up anti-Chakma passions to win elections or mobilize support during key political occasions.

The Chakmas and Hajongs fled from East Pakistan in the 1960s to escape economic pauperization and political persecution. One-fifth of the Chakmas were rendered landless in their Chittagong Hill Tracts homeland by the Kaptai Dam and had no choice but to flee into northeast India. The Indian government settled them in North-East Frontier Agency (NEFA), now Arunachal Pradesh. Since it was reckoned that both these communities would be loyal to India for the shelter and rehabilitation they received here, officials in the Indian Home Ministry felt that their presence in a state on the frontier with China would help India develop 'behind-the-lines partisan resistance' if the Chinese army were to overrun the province, as they partly did in 1962.

Local tribesmen, however, complain that the Chakmas and the Hajongs are infiltrators who were settled without their consent. Groups like the All Arunachal Pradesh Students Union (AAPSU) periodically voice their determination to push the Chakmas and Hajongs out of the state. They are seen as a threat by all the state's leading tribes because they now number between 60,000 and 70,000, which makes them more numerous than most of the larger local tribes. If they gain Indian citizenship in keeping with a Supreme Court order, they will unsettle current political equations in the state because they can join up with smaller tribes and chal-lenge the preponderance of larger tribes. For this reason, the larger local tribes of Arunachal Pradesh have resisted fiercely moves by Delhi to grant Indian citizenship to the Chakmas and the Hajongs.

And successive state governments have refused to implement the Supreme Court order that recommended Indian citizenship for the Hajongs and Chakmas.

While ethnicity remains the driving force in the separatist and autonomist movements of northeast India, it has also come to play a prominent role in the legislative politics of the region. The Congress party, which continues to dominate the region, running governments in most states, exploits ethnic and religious sentiments as much as the BJP or the communists. In Assam, the Congress, whose grip on local politics grew out of its leadership of the nationalist movement against the British, has been increasingly challenged by the Asom Gana Parishad (AGP). The AGP, a party barely two decades old, grew out of the anti-foreigner agitation in Assam that redefined Assamese identity on the basis of ethnicity, thus weakening its traditional multi-racial base. The exigencies of legislative politics forced it to appeal to non-Assamese segments of the population as well, if only in a limited way and to address only electoral issues.

So strong is the pull of ethnicity that even leftist parties, that had opposed the Assam agitation for its alleged chauvinistic character, supported the AGP in coalition politics. The BJP has also wooed the AGP to push its own religious agenda amongst the *Asomiya* caste-Hindus. In fact, the BJP has tried to complement the AGP's grip on Assamese caste-Hindus by attempting to add to it its own vote bank amongst Bengali and Hindi-speaking Hindus. More and more groups have used ethnicity in Assam to build parties and organizations. All tribes now have student organizations modelled on the AASU and they use ethnicity as the basis for political articulation. Across the spectrum, political organizations like the Bodo Peoples Action Committee and the Autonomous States Demands Committee of Karbi Anglong and North Cachar Hills are using an ethnic demand, like autonomy or statehood for an ethnic group, to gain political mileage.

The scene is no different elsewhere in the North East. The Naga regional parties—like the Naga Nationalist Democratic Party or coalitions like the Democratic Alliance of Nagaland that now rules the state—have a one-point programme: to push the Naga cause, be it by facilitating talks with the separatist groups or by demanding demographic security for the Nagas (by seeking the ouster of migrants) or by pressing for integration of Naga-inhabited areas of states neighbouring Nagaland. The Indigenous Nationalist Party of Tripura and the Tripura Upajati Yuba Samity, before it, have developed their entire politics around the ethnic concerns of the indigenous tribespeople of Tripura and the undercurrent of marginalization amongst them in view of a continuous influx of Bengali settlers from across the border.

Organizations like the Manipur People's Party and Mizoram's People's Conference draw their strength from ethnicity as do the regional parties in Meghalaya, like the Hill States Peoples Demands Party (HSPDP). And a party like the Mizo National Front, a former rebel group but now Mizoram's leading opposition party, is so narrowly focussed on Mizo ethnicity as the basis for its politics that it has managed to alienate ethnic minorities like the Chakmas, the Brus, the Lais and the Maras. In some states, regional parties were born out of the Congress, after desertions by legislators and senior politicians from the Delhi-oriented Congress. Some returned to the Congress, some did not. These parties, such as the Manipur Congress of W. Nipamacha Singh and the Arunachal Congress of Gegong Apang, have chosen to articulate ethnic concerns after the breakaway from the Congress in a rather brazen way.

Thus, the North East has witnessed the rise of three types of ethnicity-based parties and organizations: (a) those, like the AGP, that grew out of local protest movements with clear ethnic overtones, like the anti-migrant agenda in Assam; (b) those with separatist roots but then returned to constitutional politics, like the Mizo National Front and (c) those which broke away from the Congress or another national party and articulated ethnic issues. The preponderant influence of ethnicity is apparent in the politics and the protest movements of northeast India, in its social processes, at times even in economic decision-making. But its manifestation is never uni-directional. Ethnicity has fragmented and also consolidated generic identities in the region in a dynamic process of socio-political change.

'NATIONAL LIBERATION' OR 'INDIAN REVOLUTION'

In some parts of what became India's North East, communist parties subtly articulated ethnic issues to create a support base among the indigenous tribespeople. In Tripura, the communists played on the tribal's sense of loss and marginalization brought on by the end of princely rule and the kingdom's merger with India. Their leaders first gained popularity in the tribal areas through the 'Jana Shiksha' or the Mass Literacy movement. At the peak of its nation-wide armed movement in 1948, the Communist Party of India (CPI) absorbed into its fold the state's leading tribal organization, the Gana Mukti Parishad (GMP) or People's Liberation Council. The CPI adopted the GMP's political programme on tribal rights, loss of tribal lands and the threat to the distinctive social organization of the tribespeople. Unlike the Naga National Council, however, the GMP never demanded secession. The GMP guerrillas fought for an 'Indian revolution' rather than for an independent homeland like the Nagas.[19]

When the CPI gave up the armed struggle and denounced it as 'irresponsible adventurism', the tribal guerrillas in the communist Shanti Sena (Peace Army) gave up their weapons and returned to normal life. Taking advantage of the situation, the Congress-dominated state administration started resettling large numbers of newly arrived Bengali migrants in the tribal areas of Tripura. Since the tribespeople were largely supportive of the communists, the Congress wanted to alter the demographic profile of the constituencies by promoting the organized rehabilitation of the Bengali migrants. This did help the Congress in 1967, when it won both the state's parliament seats for the first time after having lost them to the communists in three successive elections. Having suffered in the numbers game, the tribals lost faith in the CPI and began to turn to militant ethnic politics.

After manipulating ethnic concerns to build up a party nucleus and a political base, the communists succumbed to electoral concerns in Tripura. With other tribal parties and insurgent organizations surfacing to articulate ethnic issues, the communists had to fall back on their growing support base among the Bengalis. Since 1978, they have won all but one of the state assembly elections, but their grip on the state's tribal areas has weakened. Twice in a decade, Tripura's ruling communists lost the state's Tribal Areas Autonomous District Council to a militant tribal party, first the Tripura Upajati Juba Samity (TUJS), then Indigenous People's Front of Tripura (IPFT), both strangely aligned to the Congress for purely electoral considerations.

The IPFT, now renamed the Indigenous Nationalist Party of Tripura (INPT), enjoys the backing of the separatist National Liberation Front of Tripura (NLFT). The NLFT's rhetoric is secessionist but its leaders have said they are open to negotiations on an 'appropriate power sharing arrangement for maximum possible tribal control in state assembly, the autonomous district council and on the state's resources'.[20] Two more tribal parties have merged with the INPT—the TUJS, the first exclusive tribal party in the state, and the Tribal National Volunteers (TNV), which led a bloody ten-year insurgency during 1978–88. The ruling communists staved off the INPT challenge in two successive state assembly elections in 2003 and 2008. The tribal party's alliance with the Congress did not work and the majority Bengali voters were alarmed by the INPT's close links with the NLFT.

The communists in Tripura used a tribal organization and its leadership to promote their complex ideology in backward agrarian society where slash-and-burn agriculture (locally called *jhum*) was still prevalent and industry was virtually absent. The GMP had retained its distinct character even after its merger with the Communist Party organization, including its anomalous family-based membership. During the two decades that followed the end of the communist armed struggle, however, the GMP's influence on the communist political agenda dwindled sharply. Having widened their political base to win elections, the communists tried to sidestep the ethnic issues until they were forced to support the tribal autonomy movement in the 1980s. The tribal parties moved into the vacuum, aggressively ethnicizing the state's political discourse and questioning the relevance of communist ideology for the tribespeople. Unlike the TUJS, which accepted the role of a junior partner in the coalition with the Congress that ruled Tripura between 1988 and 1993, the INPT is more assertive, especially when it comes to articulating tribal issues and interests.

In Manipur and Assam, the communists continue to win a few seats in the state assembly. The CPI has strong pockets of support that were built up during the struggle for peasant rights, but it shares power only as minor partners in regional coalitions. In Manipur, the CPI has joined the Congress-led ruling coalition formed in February 2002 to keep the BJP out of power in the state. In Assam, on the other hand, it opposed the Congress in the 1996 state elections and came to power by forming a coalition with the AGP. The AGP grew out of the anti-foreigner agitation of the 1980s, which the communists had opposed as 'parochial' and 'chauvinist'.[21] Just before the 2001 Assam state assembly elections, however, the AGP abandoned the communists and forged an alliance with the BJP. In view of emerging national equations, the communists in Assam may be compelled to support the Congress, particularly on the aliens issue. The Congress and the communists want to protect the migrant minorities, whereas the AGP, the BJP and other Assamese regional groups want 'detection and deportation of all illegal infiltrators'.

The communists failed to develop a support base in any of the North East's tribal-dominated states, where ethnicity and religion, rather than ideology, dominated politics and protest movements. The communist ideology, in its Maoist manifestations, did, however, find takers among some secessionist groups in the North East. Throughout the 1980s, the People's Liberation Army (PLA) of Manipur claimed it was 'part of the Indian revolution' and that its mission was to 'bring down the bandit government of Delhi'. Only much later did it limit itself to fighting at the 'vanguard of the struggle for Manipur's independence'.[22] Its assessment of the Indian polity as 'semi-colonial and semi-feudal' bears striking resemblance with the class character analysis of the Indian state done by India's Communist Party (Maoist).

But the Maoists have failed to make any significant inroad into the North East, though the CPI (Marxit-Leninist) had some influence in pockets like Assam's North Cachar Hills and Karbi Anglong, where they provided leadership to the local autonomy movements. The Maoists enjoy tactical relations with ULFA, using the latter to procure weapons from Burma. But ULFA fighters have at least once closed down by force one secret Maoists hideout, asking them to stay away from Assam. The Maoists resent the ULFA's attacks on the Hindi-speakers and say they cannot have fraternal relations with the ULFA until such time the Assamese separatist group stops attacking the Hindi-speaking settlers and accept them as 'Indian proletariat'.

The Revolutionary Peoples Front (RPF)–PLA of Manipur have, however, maintained close fraternal relations with the Maoists. In October 2008, the Maoists signed an accord with the RPF–PLA to fight for the 'overthrow of the semi-feudal, semi-colonial Indian regime'. The accord was signed by S. Gunen, secretary-general of the RPF, and 'Comrade' Alok (pseudonym) of the CPI(Maoist). The RPF–PLA agreed to support the 'great Indian class struggle led by Maoists' while the CPI(Maoist) agreed to support the 'cause of Manipur's liberation from Indian colonialists'.[23]

The Maoists have also tried to interact with the NSCN leadership, particularly with the China-returned Muivah, only to be dismayed by Muivah's persisting negotiations with India inspite of a failure to achieve a breakthrough. But it is not clear whether the Maoists support for the 'nationality struggles' of northeast India stems from definite ideological convictions or is a mere tactical ploy to spread their influence in a region, where there is only limited receptivity to radical Marxism-Leninism.

The PLA's core leadership was trained in China. Though the ethnic rebel armies of the Naga and the Mizo hills had received military training in China before them, the Chinese tried to politicize only a few Naga leaders like Thuingaleng Muivah, the present general secretary of the NSCN. Muivah says he had some exposure to Marxist-Leninist ideology before he led the first group of Naga rebels to China in 1966 at the beginning of the Cultural Revolution.[24] But the Chinese made no effort to politicize the Mizo and most of the Naga rebels who were devout Christians. China merely wanted to use them against India. The PLA's core leadership (the first batch of eighteen *Ojha*s, or pioneers) was the first group of North East Indian rebels who were given 'extensive political training' by the Chinese. They had hoped that the PLA and ULFA would be able to coordin-ate their struggles with the Indian Maoist groups and strengthen the cause of the Indian revolution in the eastern part of India.[25] There are again some unconfirmed Indian intelligence reports of a fresh batch of PLA and ULFA guerrillas receiving training in guerrilla warfare in China since mid-2009.

Later, the ULFA, a separatist organization committed to Assam's liberation from India, voiced the Marxist-Leninist 'colonial thesis' that Assam was an 'internal colony' of India. Individual ULFA leaders, some of whom came from leftist political backgrounds, have expressed admiration for CPI(M-L) leader Charu Majumdar, hailing him as the 'first real hope of the Indian revolution'.[26] The Autonomous State Demands Committee (ASDC), which advocates an autonomous state for the Karbi tribesmen in central Assam, has close connections with the CPI(M-L)—at least two of their senior leaders have been in the CPI(M-L)'s central committee. The ASDC, however, has lost out on influence to a new insurgent group, the United Peoples Democratic Solidarity (UPDS). This replicates the Tripura scenario, in which pro-Left organizations sought to use ethnic issues to build up influence, but finally lost out to groups that directly articulate ethnic concerns.

The Maoist groups in India's heartland, despite their lack of presence in the North East, have supported the 'struggle of the oppressed nationalities' in the region.[27] In private, Maoist leaders differentiate between those struggles led by a 'conscious leadership' (meaning those who place their faith in Marxism-Leninism) and the rest.[28] The Maoists are aware of the need for a tactical understanding with the ethnic separatist groups in the battle against the Indian state, but they have their preferences. The ULFA in Assam (if it stops attacking Hindi-speaking settlers), the PLA in Manipur or even the NSCN led by Thuingaleng Muivah would be more acceptable to them than a National Liberation Front of Tripura, which not only pursues violent ethnic cleansing against Bengalis and smaller tribes like the Reangs and the Chakmas, but also declares 'evangelization' of the tribes of Tripura as a key objective.

In the North East, even the political use of ideology has been largely determined by ethnic considerations. With the subcontinent on the throes of a fervent religious mobilization, however, Marxism-Leninism could become less attractive than the forces of Hindutva, militant Islam or born-again Christianity. In addition, new ethnic equations could emerge, shaped by these religious forces. The communists continue to rule Tripura and are part of a ruling coalition in Manipur and were in a ruling coalition in Assam until recently. Their appeal to the new generation in northeast India, however, is decidedly on the wane.

CROSS, CRESCENT AND THE SAFFRONS

Though ethnicity and ideology, the former more than the latter, remain major influences on separatist and autonomist groups in northeast India, religion is increasingly beginning to influence the political agenda of some of these groups. Religious distinctiveness, when coterminous with ethnicity, exacerbated the sense of otherness in the Naga and Mizo hills. The tribespeople in both these former head-hunting hill regions had been largely converted to Christianity during the last quarter of the nineteenth century and felt emotionally alienated from the Indian cultural ethos, which was often equated with the 'Hindu entity'.[29] Christianity reinforced and complemented, rather than supplanted, the sense of distinct ethnicity and otherness amongst the Nagas and the Mizos. Separatist groups like the Naga National Council (NNC) and the Mizo National Front (MNF) laced their separatist rhetoric with free use of Biblical imagery. The MNF even named their military operations after Biblical events. For example, they described their first uprising (on 28 February 1966) as 'Operation Jericho'. Rebel regiments, on the other hand, were named after Mizo heroes of yore, like Zampuimanga, and not after Biblical heroes.[30]

When the NNC decided to send the first group of Naga rebels to China, the powerful Baptist church was upset with the rebel leaders. The NNC and the NSCN, led by Thuingaleng Muivah, who was trained in China, have subsequently made conscious efforts to appease the church. Muivah, much less a practising Christian than NSCN Chairman Issac Chisi Swu, coined the phrase 'Nagaland for Christ' that found its way into the NSCN's lexicon. This slogan would boldly hang over the churches in the NSCN camps, where the Sunday services were regularly performed by the NSCN's 'chaplain kilonser' (religious affairs minister) Vedai Chakesang and his team.[31] Although in private, Muivah revered Mao Zedong and Zhou-en-Lai as 'some of the greatest leaders of the twentieth century',[32] he was quick to see that most of his leaders and fighters were devout Christians, and that religion and ethnicity could complement each other to promote an identity that would hold up against Indian assimilationist attempts. Even S.C. Jamir, former Congress chief minister of Nagaland, would often observe that 'there is no village in Nagaland without at least one church'.

The MNF was much more serious about its Christian identity, about fostering religiosity in the rank and file. Senior leaders like Zoramthanga, then MNF vice-president (and now chief minister of Mizoram), personally conducted church services in the rebel camps and many MNF leaders, like Malswamma Colney, became preachers after their return to normal life. Consumption of alcohol and drugs, so easily available in the North East because of its proximity to Burma's infamous Golden Triangle, were strictly prohibited among the guerrillas and they were encouraged to propagate their 'evil influences'.[33] MNF chief Laldenga, however, after becoming chief minister snubbed the church leaders when they started pressurizing his government for total prohibition. Laldenga was loath to lose one of the most important sources of revenue for his government. The Congress was quick to take advantage. To secure the support of the church, it proclaimed in its election manifesto that it was committed to the promotion of 'Christian socialism' in Mizoram.[34]

The MNF was defeated in the ensuing elections in 1989 because the church went against it and backed the Congress. I was a witness to how senior Congress leaders from other parts of India switched to jeans and T-shirts from their *dhoti-kurta*s when they arrived in Mizoram for election campaign in 1989 to play down Indian looks and use dresses that the young Westernized Mizos would identify with. After Laldenga's death, Zoramthanga took over as party president and repaired the MNF's relations with the church. He assured the church leaders of his commitment to continue with the prohibition imposed by the Congress government. The MNF has regained the support of the church leaders and that has helped it win two successive elections.

In neighbouring Tripura, first-generation Christian converts constituted a large percentage of the leadership and the fighters of the Tribal National Volunteers (TNV). Its chairman, Bijoy Hrangkhawl, remains a devout Christian. Non-Christian tribesmen who joined the TNV were encouraged, though not forced, to convert. The state's strongest rebel group now, the NLFT insists on conversion of non-Christian recruits. Some of those who have broken away from the NLFT, like a former commander Nayanbashi Jamatia, are Hindus or animists who say they resent 'the leadership's interference with personal faiths and religions'.[35]

The NLFT, in keeping with their stated objective of turning Tripura into 'the land of Christ', has also issued fiats to tribal communities to convert to Christianity as a whole.[36] That has provoked the predominantly animist Reangs and the Hindu Jamatia tribesmen to resist them. Even after the NLFT 'banned' the worship of Durga (Goddess of Power), Saraswati (Goddess of Learning) and Laxmi (Goddess of Wealth) in the hills, the spiritual head of the Jamatia tribe, 'Hada Okrah' Bikram Bahadur Jamatia performed the *puja*s (worship).[37] But his followers had to face attacks and Jamatia escaped two assassination attempts. Some leading tribal priests like Shanti Kali were killed by the NLFT and their womenfolk were raped by the rebels. On 7 August 1999, the NLFT kidnapped four senior leaders of the Hindu nationalist Rastriya Swayamsevak Sangh (RSS). All four are feared dead. The NLFT allegedly enjoys the support of the Tripura Baptist Christian Union (TBCU). According to sources in the TBCU, both voluntary and forced conversions to Christianity have increased among the tribespeople in Tripura since the TNV and the NLFT intensified their activity.[38] For many tribesmen, Christianity is a source of a new extra-territorial identity that reinforces the ethnic group's confidence to challenge the dominant cultures of the Bengali migrants rather than being absorbed by it.

In Manipur, the Meitei separatists, mostly born Hindus, advocated a revival of the state's leading pre-Hindu faith, Sanamahi. They also tried to stop the use of the Bengali script for the Meitei language and promoted the Sanamahi script to encourage ethno-religious revivalism and thus strengthen the appeal of the separatist movement. Meitei revivalism in different forms has periodically surfaced in Manipur to dominate popular consciousness since the days of Naoriya Phullo, the founder of the first such organization, the Apokpa Marup. As political separatism gained momentum in the Imphal Valley, the rebel groups demonstratively abandoned their Hindu identity in a hostile gesture towards the Indian state. Some of them promoted the Sanamahi cult to emphasize the distinct history and the identity of the Meiteis. Some local political parties have cultivated these revivalist organizations for electoral considerations.

In Assam, the ULFA remained silent on the question of religion and its guerrillas played a visible role in containing religious riots in the Hojai region of Nagaon district.[39] It has been accused of recruiting Muslims of Bengali origin in greater numbers in the last few years, apparently to appease sentiments in Bangladesh, where they continue to find refuge. This writer, however, has been to several ULFA camps and has interacted with a wide cross-section of ULFA leaders and guerrillas, some still fighting and others surrendered, and has not seen any religious activity in the camps. Hindu, Muslim and Christian cadres of the ULFA participate in Assamese festivals such as Bihu, which celebrates primarily the harvest in what is still essentially a peasant society.[40] The Meitei guerrilla groups, like the ULFA, have also refrained from demonstrative religiosity.

In the tribal areas of Assam, however, Christian priests are trying to use ethnicity to promote evangelization among tribes and ethnic rebel groups pander to religious concerns. The church has played for long a peace-making role in Nagaland and Mizoram, but in some states of northeast India, where the church is expanding and gaining new converts, it has also covertly pandered to the militant groups. The National Democratic Front of Bodoland (NDFB), like the NLFT, is said to be supportive of the church but does not demonstrate it as openly. In recent months, as ethnic clashes between the Hmars and the Dimasas multiplied, a Manipur-born US-based priest, Dr Rochunga Pudaite, who set up a US-based missionary institution called 'Bible for the World', sought to interpret the conflict as one between the Hindu Dimasas and the Christian Hmars. Pudaite's propaganda against the Dimasas gained worldwide attention when a US-based website, www.worthynews.com, carried his rather inflammatory article.

In his article, Pudaite urged all the Christians throughout the world to collect funds for the cause of the Hmars. The website, which solicited online donations, is a non-denominational Christian news service headquartered in Baltimore in the United States. The website reports news from a Christian perspective and carries mainly news stories on persecution against Christians throughout the world, a topic which, according to the website, 'is not covered by the national media'. One of the website's subsequent editions carried a story on the atrocities perpetrated by Hindus on Christians in Tripura. It accused the recent Indian census of discrimination because the census has not accepted the Dalit Christians as a separate category. In another article, the website stressed the need to increase missionary activities in the North East and described India as the 29th most dangerous place in the world for Christians after the Middle east countries.

Like in Tripura, religion has also played a divisive role in the Bodo separatist movement in Assam. The NDFB is predominantly Christian. It supports the church's demand for the use of the Roman script for the Bodo language (similar to the NLFT's support for a similar church demand to use Roman script for the Tripuri Kokborok language) and its guerrillas have killed many Bodo intellectuals, cultural icons and writers who oppose the demand. Their victims include a former president of the Bodo Sahitya Sabha (Bodo Literary Society). The All Bodo Students Union (ABSU), the Bodo Peoples

Action Committee (BPAC) and the (BLTF), which has now surfaced after signing an autonomy deal with the Indian government, remain committed to the 'traditional Bodo way of life' and oppose the use of Roman script for the Bodo language.

The overt Christian religiosity of some separatist groups has led Hindu nationalist groups like the Rashtriya Swayamsevak Sangh to suspect a 'foreign hand' behind the ethnic rebellions of northeast India. RSS leaders, upset by the spread of Christianity in ever-new areas of the North East and by rebel attacks on their leaders and institutions, point to the church's use of 'liberation theology' slogans like 'to Christ through People's Movements' (used by some Baptist denominations in the North East) as evidence of its connivance with ethnic separatism.[41] To counter this alleged nexus, the RSS is trying to infiltrate a number of ethnic movements, mostly spearheaded by smaller tribes who oppose the imposition of Christianity by bigger ethnic groups and rebel armies. On the Tripura–Mizoram border, the RSS has a strong presence in the camps where Brus Reangs displaced by violent evangelical Mizo groups have taken shelter. There have been reports that the Bru National Liberation Front (BNLF) has received backing from the RSS, as have the Jamatia Hoda Okrah, for opposing the NLFT. The RSS has even asked the federal home ministry to provide arms and funds to the Reang and the Jamatia armed groups when the BJP was in power in Delhi.

In recent years, the RSS and the Viswa Hindu Parishad (VHP) have also strongly backed efforts to codify and promote traditional animistic faiths and beliefs in Arunachal Pradesh. Former Chief Minister Gegong Apang received RSS backing in his efforts to promote the 'Donyi Polo' faith and a number of organizations were set up to support it. Apang fell out with Christian leaders in the Congress party in the North East and finally formed the Arunachal Pradesh Congress to oust the Congress from power. Later his government was brought down by dissidents within his party and Apang alleges that the NSCN and the Baptist church played a major role in bringing about his downfall. He claims that the church saw him as a bulwark against Christian missionary activities in Arunachal Pradesh and wanted to replace him.[42] Apang's ties with the Sangh Parivar continued to grow after his ouster from power and the activities of the 'Donyi Polo' mission, which seeks to institutionalize the animistic faiths of the Arunachali tribes, have not suffered. Belatedly, as he made a successful bid to return to power by splitting from the Congress party, Apang is said to have repaired his relations with the church and the NSCN. He made no secret, however, of his political and religious preferences when, after toppling the Congress-led government of Mukut Mithi, he promptly joined the BJP with all the legislators of the breakaway coalition that had assumed power in the state.

Nowhere has the RSS–VHP–BJP combine been more active than in Assam. It is trying to hijack the anti-foreigner plank from regional groups like the AASU by supporting controversial legislations that seeks to oppose illegal migrants. The VHP leader Praveen Togadia has even called for an 'economic boycott of the Bangladeshis in Assam'. This raised the spectre of a religious showdown that prompted Assam Chief Minister Tarun Gogoi to consider his arrest. The process of religious consolidation that the BJP started through its alliance with the AGP in the 2001 assembly elections is what the RSS–VHP combine would like to carry forward when it describes Assam as the 'next big battleground after Kashmir'.[43]

Despite its secular protestations, the Congress has also used the religious factor in the North East. It promoted a Zeliang Naga leader, Rani Gaidiliu, to counter the Naga separatist movement. Rani's followers practised the animistic Haraka faith and were opposed to Christianity. Unlike the RSS, which sees religion as the major cause of the ethnic divide in the North East, the Congress used religion to oppose the separatist movements and weaken them by playing on the religious (Haraka versus Christian) and the ethnic (Zeliangs as different from Nagas) divides simultaneously.[44] Its stand on the religious question in the North East has been dictated by power—political and electoral concerns—from the use of the sects of Anukul Thakur and Anandmoyi Ma (both Hindu cult figures) to win the Bengali Hindu votes in Tripura, to the use of Pir of Badarpur or Jamait-e-Ulema-e-Hind leader Assad Madani to win the Muslim vote in Assam to the championing of 'Christian Socialism' in Mizoram; its use of religious issues in the North East has often smacked of rank opportunism.

Although the RSS has been stridently vocal about the church–separatist nexus, its preoccupation with the emerging threat of Islamic radicalism in the North East and in the rest of the country has occasionally prompted its leaders to try and promote 'Hindu–

Christian understanding' in the region. Former RSS chief V. Sudarshan has said that 'the resurgence of militant Islam based in neighbouring Bangladesh and continuous infiltration from that country was the biggest threat to the region that Hindus and Christians must fight together'.[45] However, efforts to bridge the Hindu–Christian divide in the North East by playing up the issue of illegal infiltration from Bangladesh have not been very successful because Hindu radicals elsewhere in India attacked Christian preachers. Furthermore, the brutal murder in Orissa of Australian priest Graham Staines evoked extensive protest amongst the Christians in the North East.

By the time India was partitioned, the Muslim population in the North East was concentrated mostly in Assam with a small sprinkling in Tripura. Assam, like undivided Bengal, was ruled by a Muslim League government during the Second World War. During that phase, large numbers of peasants from East Bengal were encouraged to settle down on the *char*s of the Brahmaputra and its tributaries. Just before the Partition, however, Sylhet was given over to Pakistan. Some Hindu leaders felt that 'amputation of the diseased arm' was good for Assam.[46] But the inflow of Muslim migrants to Assam continued even after the break-up of Pakistan. Some religious parties in Bangladesh still feel that Assam should have gone to East Pakistan during the Partition because of its large Muslim population.[47] In fact, Islamic parties tried to merge both Assam and princely Tripura with Pakistan around the time of Partition. Parties such as the Jamait-e-Islami in Bangladesh continue to maintain that these areas of northeast India would be a 'normal appendage' of Bangladesh.

Until the rise of the BJP in India and its growth in parts of Assam by skilful exploitation of the Babri Masjid issue, Islamic radicalism was practically absent in Assam and the rest of the North East. The riots during the Assam agitation, though apparently aimed at 'outsiders' and 'infiltrators', did target Muslims of Bengali origin. More than 2,000 Muslim Bengalis were killed in the riots at Nellie and Chaulkhowa Chapori in February–March 1983. The ferocity of the violence split the groups leading the Assam agitation along religious lines and a number of Assamese Muslim leaders broke away from the AASU and the All Assam Gana Sangram Parishad (AAGSP) immediately after the 1983 riots, alleging that the agitating groups had been 'infiltrated by the RSS'.[48]

There was no violent Muslim backlash, however. Only some defence groups were organized in the predominantly Muslim areas. Although political parties and the police in Assam made exaggerated projections of their strength and intentions and the local Assamese press floated stories about their links to Islamic fundamentalist groups in Bangladesh, these groups were essentially defensive in nature until the mid-1990s. Immediately after the riots and the Assam accord of 1985 that brought an end to the agitation, Muslims of Bengali origin joined their linguistic Hindu brethren to form the United Minorities Forum (UMF). Traditionally they had voted for Congress but they had felt let down by the Congress government in 1983. One of the founders of the UMF said:

> For the first time in post-Partition Assam, the Bengali Hindus and Muslims felt the need to come together to protect their interests. We found we were in the same boat. Since we were more than forty percent of the state's population, we were sure we could defend our interests against rising Assamese chauvinism.[49]

But after the rise of the BJP, Bengali Hindus in Assam, unlike their brethren in West Bengal and Tripura, largely turned towards the politics of Hindutva. Muslims were left with little choice. In elections, they began to vote Congress and most UMF leaders returned to the Congress. The younger and more religious elements did form a few militant groups, defensive to begin with but becoming increasingly pro-active. The Idgah Protection Force (IPF) was formed just before the demolition of the Babri Masjid at Ayodhya and some of its supporters were responsible for the massacre of nearly 100 Hindus at Hojai in 1992. Incidentally, the victims were mostly Bengali Hindus who had started supporting the BJP and its campaign to construct a Hindu temple at Ayodhya in place of the disputed Babri mosque.

After the Hojai riots, a number of Muslim radical groups have surfaced in Assam, essentially feeding on the community's growing insecurity in a state where the power-holding elites see them as 'agents of Pakistan or Bangladesh'. The Assamese fear of being reduced to a minority in their own land, fuelled by the changing demography of the state during the last 40 years, has given rise to strong anti-Muslim feelings. Assamese political groups were pushing for the scrapping of the Illegal Migrants (Determination by Tribunals) Act, 1983. These groups say the Act, by placing the burden of proof of someone's foreign identity on the state, is actually protecting 'illegal foreign migrants' in Assam.[50] These Assamese groups have received strong support from the BJP, which now has a strong base both amongst Bengali and Assamese Hindus. The Illegal Migrants Act was finally scrapped by the Indian Supreme Court in July 2005, increasing insecurity amongst the Muslims.

In successive Assam assembly elections, the AGP and the BJP have fought the elections together. For the first time, Assam witnessed the politics of 'religious consolidation', though the AGP says it is not reconciled to the BJP's political stand of treating Bengali Hindus as refugees and Bengali Muslims as infiltrators. The Congress came back to power on the strength of its influence amongst Muslims and the 'tea tribes' (descendants of those who came from central India to work on the British tea estates in the nineteenth century), who, between themselves, accounted for more than 40 per cent of the electorate. Subsequently, the BJP tried to penetrate the tea tribes, exploiting the religious divide within the community (Assam's tea labourers are largely first- or second-generation Christian converts, but many remain Hindus).

Assam's Muslim and Christian minorities, faced with 'religious consolidation' of the Bengali and Assamese Hindus who would account for more than 40 per cent of the population, have decided to stick it out with the Congress. Their combined strength gives them a chance to share power and ensure security. But in the 2006 elections, a new Muslim party, the Assam United Democratic Front (AUDF) surfaced under the leadership of Maulana Badruddin Ajmal and it cashed on the Muslim's anxiety after the Illegal Migrants (Determination by Tribunals) Act, 1983, was scrapped by the Supreme Court. The AUDF won 10 seats from Muslim areas in the March–April 2006 elections, slicing into traditional Congress vote banks.

Some Muslim hardliners in Assam have also formed armed militant groups. The Muslim United Liberation Tigers of Assam (MULTA) is the strongest of these groups.[51] Formed in 1997, the MULTA has close connections with the Sunni radical Sipai-e-Saheba of Pakistan. The MULTA leaders signed an agreement with the Sipai-e-Saheba leaders at a meeting at Jamait Ul Uloom Ali Madrassah in Chittagong in February 2001. The Sipai-e-Saheba decided to back the MULTA in its militant activities in Assam. At the political level, the MULTA demands a 30 per cent reservation in education and employment for Muslims in Assam and also a similar reservation for seats in the state assembly, in keeping with their numbers. But at the religious level, they want the establishment of a chain of Islamic courts in Assam to dispense with justice in keeping with the tenets of Shariat.[52]

The Assam police have arrested some MULTA activists while others have surrendered. During interrogation, some of them confessed to have received training at Al-Qaida and Taliban camps in Afghanistan, with logistic support provided by Pakistan's Inter-Services Intelligence (ISI).[53] The MULTA also participated in a convention of Islamic radical groups in Bangladesh held at Ukhia near the coastal town of Cox's Bazaar on 10–11 May 2002. Six Bangladesh-based Islamic militant groups, like Harkat-ul-Jihad-al Islami (HUJAI) and Islamic Shashantantra Andolan, were joined by two Burmese Rohingya Muslim rebel groups and the MULTA at the convention, which was attended by more than 60 delegates. The convention decided to form an umbrella organization to coordinate the jihad for turning Bangladesh from a *Dar-ul-Harb* (Land of Infidels) into a *Dar-ul-Islam* (Land of Islam), but it also decided to intensify efforts for creation of a 'Brihat Bangladesh' (Greater Bangladesh) by incorporating areas of Assam and Burma's Arakan province that are now largely settled by Muslims of Bengali origin. Indian intelligence agencies see the Bangladesh Islamic Manch as a replica of the United Jihad Council in Pakistan. While the United Jihad Council coordinates the struggle for Kashmir's merger with Pakistan, the Bangladesh Islamic Manch, in its inaugural declaration, pledged that it would work for the 'wilful merger' of areas of Assam and Arakan into Bangladesh.[54]

The alarming scenario that generations of Assamese have been fed on is finally coming true. Groups that would prefer to merge Assam's Muslim-majority areas with contiguous Bangladesh have finally arrived. Security analysts in Assam envisage the 'eastward surge of the Jihadis', that is, a projected growth of Islamic militant activity in the arca that begins at India's Siliguri Corridor, goes through Bangladesh and stretches into India's North East and Burma's Arakan province with wider links to Pakistan, the Middle East, Malaysia, Indonesia and the Philippines.[55] The presence of Islamist parties like the Jamait-e-Islami and the Islamic Aikyo Jote in ruling coalitions of Bangladesh has fuelled fears that the country founded on the ideals of Bengali nationalism might become the fulcrum of *jihad* in the eastern part of South Asia.[56] The attacks on Hindu, Christian and Buddhist minorities in Bangladesh during and after the 2001 parliamentary elections, widely reported in Bangladesh's vibrant and largely secular press, have provided substance to such apprehensions.[57]

If globalization is the mantra of the new millennium, conflicts as much as economies are likely to be globalized. Moreover, if the religious divide fuels a 'clash of civilizations', South Asia and even its more remote regions, including the North East, could be sucked into it. Religion, which led to the Partition of the Indian subcontinent but did not much influence the 'little nationalisms' of northeast India, may begin to play a more important role in the politics of the region. The October 2008 riots in Assam's Darrang and Udalguri districts, where Assamese, Bodos, Bengali Hindus and *Adivasi*s ganged up against immigrant Muslims, may be a pointer. But with Bangladesh swinging back to its secular Bengali nationalist base following the Awami League's massive election victory in the December 2008 Jatiyo Sangsad (national parliament) polls, the forces of radical religiosity may take a beating in the eastern slice of South Asia. Influenced by local dynamics and those in its immediate neighbourhood, the swing-game between ethnicity, ideology and religion will continue in the politics and identity-formation in India's North East.

NOTES

1. Nandita Haksar, India's leading human rights lawyer active in northeast India, says 'the North East is very distinct from the rest of India essentially because of race'. See Haksar, 1996.
2. J.B. Ganguly, 1987.
3. See Myron Weiner, 1978 and Sajal Nag, 1990.
4. Subodh Debbarma, vice-president of the Tribal Students Federation (TSF) of Tripura, told a news conference in Guwahati, Assam, that 'Assam would soon become another Tripura, where the sons of the soil have become aliens within half a century'. Reported in *The Sentinel*, Guwahati, 3 June 2002.
5. Suhas Chatterjee, 1985.
6. The late Upendranath Brahma, former president of ABSU in an interview with the writer at Agartala, 16 April 1988. Subir Bhaumik analyzed the phenomenon of minor tribes and clans challenging the preponderance of the bigger ones in a 'northeast India: The Second Ethnic Explosion', presented at the Queen Elizabeth House, Oxford University, 22 January 1990.

7. Subir Bhaumik, 1998.

8. 'Polarisation', NSCN document, published in 1985 at Oking (headquarters), written by Thuingaleng Muivah, NSCN's general secretary.

9. Subir Bhaumik, 1994.

10. Subir Bhaumik, 2001b.

11. Dhananjoy Reang, founder of the National Liberation Front of Tripura (NLFT), interview with author at his residence in Kumaritilla, Agartala, 16 October 1999. Reang was earlier vice-president of the Tribal National Volunteers (TNV) and a pioneer in the tribal guerrilla movements of Tripura. Now he complains bitterly that Reangs have been intimidated, their women raped and men killed by the NLFT.

12. In the ULFA's document 'Purba Bongiyo Jonoghoshti Loi ULFA-r Ahvan' (ULFA's appeal to East Bengali groups) published in *Budhbar* Assamese weekly on 24 June 1992, the ULFA attacked the Assam agitation groups as 'juvenile' and defended Bengali migrants—Hindus for their contribution to education and services, Muslims for their contribution to Assam's agriculture. The document claimed that 82 per cent of Assam's current food output comes from the *char*s tilled by the Bengali Muslim migrants. The document also made it clear, however, that there is 'no further space left in Assam to accommodate current migrants'.

13. The Assam Tiger Force (ATF) claimed responsibility for attacks on the Hindi-speakers in Assam, but Assam police say it is certain that ATF was an ULFA front.

14. *Freedom*, ULFA's weekly e-newsletter, 25 May 2001.

15. *Freedom*, 28 May 2003.

16. Jaideep Saikia, security advisor to the government of Assam, speaking on *Mukhomukhi* (Face-to-Face), a chat show hosted on Doordarshan's Seventh Channel by Rainbow Productions, Calcutta, 17 February 2002.

17. Assam's Minister of State for Home Pradyut Bordoloi, in an interview with the writer, aired on the BBC World Service on 29 March 2002. Bordoloi described Assam as a 'multi-racial, multi-ethnic, multi-lingual and multi-religious entity'.

18. Memorandum jointly submitted by the Lai, Mara and Chakma district councils to the Indian government on 17 August 2000.

19. For details on the communist uprising in Tripura, see Bhaumik, 1996 and Harihar Bhattacharya, 1999.

20. NLFT leader Nayanbashi Jamatia, telephone interview with the writer, reported in BBC Bengali service on 3 March 2002. Jamatia said the NLFT leadership had communicated their desire to negotiate with Delhi through the Assam Rifles officials.

21. *Peoples Democracy*, mouthpiece of the CPI(M), 27 March 1981.

22. *Dawn*, mouthpiece of the PLA of Manipur, 3 June 1980.

23. 'India Maoists Forge New Alliance', *BBC Newsonline*, 24 October 2008. Available online at http://news.bbc.co.uk/2/hi/south_asia/7688358.stm. Accessed on 3 August 2009.

24. Thuingaleng Muivah, 'Never Say Die', interview at Mannerplaw in Thailand with Subir Bhaumik, published in *Sunday* magazine, Calcutta, 16–22 June 1996.

25. Former PLA chief Nameirakpam Bisheswar Singh, interview with author at his Babupara residence in Imphal, 16 May 1986. Bisheswar was elected to the Manipur assembly after his release from jail but he was later killed in a mysterious attack.

26. On 6 May 2000, in a personal e-mail to the writer, Arun Mahanta, an important ULFA functionary, made this comment about Charu Majumdar.

27. *Biplobi Yug* (Revolutionary Age), monthly journal of the Bengal unit of Peoples War, 18 August 2001.

28. Comrade Sagar, central publicity secretary of Peoples War, in interview with the writer, aired on BBC Radio World Today programme, 19 May 2001.

29. The NSCN manifesto says:

   though as a doctrine, Hinduism is not a recruiting force, it is backed by a Hindu government. The forces of Hinduism, viz, the numberless Indian troops, the retail and wholesale dealers, the teachers and instructors, the intelligentsia, the prophets of non-violence, the gamblers and the snake-charmers, the Hindi songs and Hindi films, the rasgulla makers and the Gita, are all arrayed for the mission to supplant the Christian God, the eternal God of the Universe. The challenge is serious.

   The manifesto was issued from Oking, the NSCN headquarters inside Burma, on 31 January 1980, by its Chairman Issac Chisi Swu.

30. Nirmal Nibedon, 1983.

31. Muivah, interview in *Sunday*, ibid.

32. Subir Bhaumik, 'Brothers in Arms', *Sunday*, 14–20 June 1987.

33. MNF 'order' no. 3 of 1986, entitled 'Eradication of Drugs and Liquor in Mizo society' issued to all units of the organization.

34. Congress (I) manifesto for the 1989 Mizoram state assembly elections, issued at Aizawl, Mizoram.

35. NLFT leader Nayanbashi Jamatia.

36. The constitution of the NLFT, 'Sacrifice for Liberation', issued on 22 December 1991, describes its armed wing as the 'National Holy Army'.

37. Statement of the 'Hada Okrah' Bikram Bahadur Jamatia, reported in the *Dainik Sambad*, Bengali daily published at Agartala, Tripura, on 16 September 2000.

38. TBCU sources say that the number of Christian converts has gone up sharply since first the TNV and then the NLFT started operating in the hilly interiors of Tripura. In 1981, Tripura's Christian population stood at 24,872. By 1991, it had risen to 46,472. TBCU sources say there are nearly 90,000 Christians in the state now, almost entirely made up of converts. The TBCU's mouthpiece, *Baptist Herald* details the major acts of conversions.

39. 'ULFA Jangira Bandhuk Uchiye Danga Thamalen' (ULFA stops riots at gunpoint), a report in *Ananda Bazar Patrika*, Bengali daily published at Calcutta, 21 December 1992.

40. This writer has visited extensively a number of ULFA camps in Bhutan and Burma, as well as those of other northeast Indian rebel groups. The absence of religious activity is conspicuous in ULFA camps and those of the Meitei rebel groups.

41. V. Sudarshan, RSS chief, interview with the writer in Calcutta, 20 January 2002.

42. Gegong Apang, interview with author, 21 May 2002.

43. *Assam Tribune*, 9 June 2003.

44. S.C. Dev, 1988.

45. Sudarshan's news conference reported in the *Shillong Times*, Meghalaya, 16 May 1997.

46. Sardar Patel, quoted in R.N. Aditya, 1970, p. 63.
47. Jamait-e-Islami monograph *Bharat Baghe Mussalmanra ki Hariyeche* (Dhaka, 1969).
48. Seema Guha, 'Assam Movement: Shadow of the RSS', *Sunday* magazine, 28 Feb–6 March 1983.
49. Gholam Osmani, former UMF president now back in Congress, interview with the writer, 28 May 1995.
50. Sarbananda Sonowal, AASU president, interview with the writer, aired in South Asia Report, BBC World Service Radio, 22 August 1994.
51. The Assam Police lists a total of 17 Muslim fundamentalist groups reportedly active in Assam, including the MULTA. The other groups are the Muslim United Liberation Front of Assam (MULFA), Adam Sena, the People's United Liberation Front (PULF), the Muslim Security Council of Assam (MSCA), the United Liberation Militia of Assam (ULMA), the Islamic Liberation Army of Assam (ILAA), the Muslim Volunteer Force (MVF), the Islamic Sevak Sangh (ISS), the Islamic United Reformation Protest of India (IURPI), the United Muslim Liberation Front of Assam (UMLFA), the Revolutionary Muslim Commandos (RMC), the Muslim Liberation Army (MLA), the Muslim Tiger Force (MTF), the Muslim Security Force (MSF), the Harkat-ul-Jihad al Islami of Bangladesh and the Harkat-ul-Mujahideen of Pakistan. Except the MULTA, whose cadre strength is more than 1,000, the rest of the groups have between 100 and 300 activists. Organizational details of these groups are listed in Jaideep Saikia, 'Terror Sans Frontiers: Islamic Militancy in northeast India', ACDIS Occasional Paper, University of Illinois, July 2003.
52. Jaideep Saikia, 2001.
53. Ibid.
54. Report entitled 'Bangladesh Islamic Manch—Formation and Alignments' prepared by the Special Bureau's Bangladesh Desk, June 2002.
55. Saikia, 'Terror Sans Frontiers'.
56. Bertil Lintner, 2002a.
57. Bangladesh press reports detailing atrocities on minorities quoted in the Annual Autumn Souvenir of the Bangladesh Hindu-Buddhist-Christian Council, 2002.

3   Land, Language and Leadership

Before the British conquered the 'North East', the region was sparsely populated. So when the British started tea plantations and began to exploit Assam's oilfields, they felt a labour shortage—of toilers and white-collars alike. To overcome this, they started importing labourers from Bihar and Orissa, and clerks and teachers from Bengal. Later they started bringing in East Bengali peasants to reclaim Assam's wastelands for increasing food output for the growing population of outside labourers. As migration from the Indian heartland to Assam increased, the state's demography began to undergo an unprecedented change. This, in turn, affected the pattern of land ownership, the linguistic balance and the nature of social and political leadership in the area. Land in pre-industrial societies like the 'North East' is not merely an economic resource but is often seen as a symbol of the collective—and loss of land is generally seen as the beginning of loss of social and political power.

Despite Nagaland's special constitutional position guaranteeing protection of tribal lands, Dimapur and its adjacent areas have recently witnessed extensive settlement by Muslims of Bengali origin to the extent that major political parties in Nagaland have started considering fielding Muslim candidates for some legislative assembly seats in the region.[1] This has upset local Naga groups who feel that a major demographic change will inevitably affect political equations and marginalize indigenous tribespeople. In recent months, Naga organizations have targeted Bengali Muslims and hitherto unknown groups like the Khel Association have asked Muslim shopkeepers to leave Nagaland or face 'dire consequences'. The National Socialist Council of Nagaland (NSCN) (Khaplang faction) has asked all Muslims to register and secure 'work permits' from the so-called 'Government of the People's Republic of Nagaland' or face eviction.[2]

Demographic change is usually followed by settler community's demands for land rights, recognition of their language and claims to leadership. In Tripura, the migrant Bengali Hindus have completely taken over the state's political and cultural leadership. In Assam, the migrants, especially the Muslims of East Bengali origin, play a very decisive role in the state's politics, essentially on the strength of the growing number of legislators from the community. In Indian-style ballot box democracy, numbers count and demographic change surely affects leadership patterns and the division of scarce resources among the competing communities.

LAND: ROOT OF CONFLICT

Land alienation in India's North East has led to serious ethnic tensions. In the past 30 years, land alienation has been at the root of the most horrible, headline-grabbing ethnic carnages that have shaken the region. In June 1980, at least 300 Bengali Hindu settlers were butchered by indigenous tribespeople in Mandai. In just one day in February 1983, more than 2,000 Muslims of Bengali origin were massacred by Lalung tribesmen in Nellie in central Assam. Naga militiamen beheaded eighty-seven Kuki villagers in one night at Zopui in February 1993. Since the carnage in Mandai, there have been nearly 200 massacres with body counts of 30 or more.[3] Massacres with body counts of between 10 and 30 people are several times more.

Investigations revealed that armed militiamen representing an ethnic group formed the core group that perpetrated the violence. There were also signs of systematic incitement in an atmosphere already vitiated by agitations or insurgencies. However, the high number of casualties during the massacres were caused by the extensive participation of the local peasantry, who resent loss of land to settlers. The nature of injury in most cases also indicated the high level of local involvement: most victims were killed by cuts and stabs rather than by firearms. The size of the armed mobs, often running into hundreds and sometimes into thousands, confirms the trend.

In almost all these cases, the tribesmen listed land loss to settlers as their main grievance, nursed for years before a spark exploded into a furious outburst of ethnic violence. Armed Bodos, Assamese, Lalungs, Mishings, Tripuris, Karbis, Dimasas, Nagas and Kukis have all attacked communities that they considered encroachers or outsiders—the hated enemy who, having deprived them of their lands, could then upset their vision of a compact ethnic homeland. Land alienation sowed the seeds of ethnic hatred, first at the level of the individual and then at the level of the collective. The fierce urge to recover lost lands has led to repeated bouts of anomic violence in the North East, at times degenerating into systematic ethnic cleansing with radical groups utilizing the groundswell of hatred to promote an aggressive ethnic agenda.

Although some of the largest communities in the North East—the Assamese, the Bengalis and the Meiteis—are not tribals, every state in the region has a high content of tribal population. According to the 2001 census data, tribals constitute more than 80 per cent of the state's population in Meghalaya, Mizoram, Nagaland and Arunachal Pradesh. In two other states—Tripura and Manipur—the tribals made up 25–30 per cent of the population. Only in Assam did tribals account for less than 10 per cent of the population. One of the region's senior bureaucrat-scholars, who rose to become India's home secretary, says: 'The proverbial attachment of a tribal to his land is a complex web of relationships, the primary force being no doubt economic. But it is also related to tradition, family ties and religion.'[4]

Another legendary police official, who served in the North East, observes:

> Land, whether it be homestead land which is the habitat of the family or land for cultivation, constitutes the life blood of the tribal community, as much in the Christian as in the non-Christian villages. Particular locations are considered the dwelling place of the spirits, good and evil, that have to be periodically placated. Other locations are associated with the shades of devoted ancestors and are held in special respect and reverence ... for a tribal, every corner of his home has its associations.[5]

When the land is lost, therefore, either to a manipulating non-tribal or to a large government project like a dam or to real-estate sharks, the tribal is severed from his home and his roots and his sense of loss and anger is profound. When individual experience finds resonance in that of the collective, ethnic hatred becomes a powerful social force, which, if harnessed by radical political elements, can lead to high degrees of violence and dislocation. In northeast India, indigenous people have lost land to settlers, government projects and urbanization on a large scale. And they have hit back against communities they saw as encroachers and outsiders. In Assam and Tripura, both in the hills and the plains, tribals lost lands to the migrant settlers in keeping with the steady demographic change in the state. This forced one of the region's senior bureaucrats to remark: 'Future attempts at social cohesiveness and the maintenance of peace greatly depend upon the way the land problem of the tribals is tackled in coming years.'[6]

There are different provisions for administration of land in the region's hills and plains districts. In the hills, land is owned communally and not by the individual, so there is no individual right of transfer. Under the Sixth Schedule, the authority for land administration is vested in the autonomous district councils, which are guided by traditional customs. In Assam's plains districts, 37 tribal belts and blocks were constituted immediately after independence under executive orders that were added to the Assam Land and Revenue Regulation of 1886. A separate chapter was formulated in 1947 to stop further alienation of tribal lands and to prevent plains tribals like the Bodos from being driven further into the interior.

Three studies on the land situation in Assam[7] suggest that in the two hill districts of Assam (Karbi Anglong and the North Cachar Hills), the formal transfer of lands from tribals to non-tribals is only nominal but the actual transfer is very extensive. The report, authored by the Tribal Research Institute, indicates that through the systems of Pakis, Sukti Bandhak, Koi Bandhak and Mena, large swathes of tribal lands had temporarily passed into the hands of non-tribals. Tribals continue to practise *jhum* or shifting cultivation in these two districts, taking advantage of which the non-tribals have grown crops in their lands and earned a much better surplus income that is subsequently used to corner more landed assests. The report concluded: 'Within the next few years, this temporary alienation of land might lead to complete distortion of the tribal economy if it is not nipped in the bud.'[8]

Neither the Karbi Anglong (Transfer of Land) Act of 1959 nor the tribal-dominated District Council could prevent the alienation of tribal lands because non-tribals determined to take over tribal lands have always found ever-new ways to hoodwink local authorities. The new generation of Karbi rebels—the United Peoples Democratic Solidarity (UPDS)—point to the autonomous council's failure to protect tribal lands as one major raison d'etre of their armed movement. In the plains districts, the alienation of tribal lands has been even more serious. The integrity of tribal belts and blocks were never preserved and non-tribals of different population groups were allowed to secure lands in those areas. The 1976 report on Assam's tribal belts and blocks noted that

> the first and foremost duty of the revenue administration should be to eject all those ineligible encroachments both from *sarkari* as well as *patta* land (in individual possession with proper deed) within all the tribal belts or blocks in a time bound programme and all such lands made free from encroachments should be simultaneously handed over for possession to eligible landless persons in the blocks and belts.[9]

The per capita agricultural holdings in Assam has declined by 26 per cent against the national average of 16.3 per cent during 1961–71 alone. The average size of ownership holdings, now around 1.25 hectares, has also declined and the number of landless peasants has gone up sharply with the number of households not owning lands going up to 27.77 per cent of the total population. Prior to the Partition, landlessness was practically non-existent in Assam, despite continuous migration in the first half of the twentieth century. After 1947, the situation changed sharply.

According to an estimate by Dr K. Alam of Gauhati University, the growth rate of population in lands under food crops shot up to 74 per cent in Assam against the national average of 32 per cent. The pressure on forest lands also mounted in Assam due to heavy migration. Assam's forest lands were reduced from 38.32 per cent to 28.07 per cent of the total surface area between 1950 and 1973. According to one of the North East's leading analysts: 'The land question in Assam is extremely complicated and even more than the ethnic dimension and the threat to identity it was the land question that invested the Assam agitation with a measure of legitimacy.'[10]

During the 1983 legislative assembly election held at the peak of the anti-foreigner agitation in Assam, violence erupted on a massive scale at Gohpur, Nellie and a host of other places. At Gohpur, which is located in a tribal belt, angry Bodos upset with large-scale land alienation attacked Assamese caste-Hindus to whom they had lost much of their lands. At Nellie, Lalung tribesmen attacked Muslims of Bengali origin to whom they had lost lands. The free-for-all violence of February–March 1983 was marked by the absence of a single target community. The only uniform trend was that the attackers were tribals whereas the target communities were non-tribals, including Assamese caste-Hindus, Bengali Hindus, Muslims of Bengali origin, Nepalis and migrants from Bihar.

The violence perpetrated by Bodo underground groups against non-Bodo settler communities since 1987, when they started their agitation for a separate state, has been at its most intense in areas where the Bodos have lost lands on a large scale. In fact, when they demanded the division of Assam on a fifty-fifty basis to pave the way for a separate state, Bodo leaders did not realize that their ethnic kinsmen would not form a majority in most parts of the proposed state, and certainly not in its urban locations. When the first Bodo accord was signed in 1993, the Assam government refused to give up some 3,000 villages falling in the proposed Territorial Council area on the grounds that the Bodos were less than 50 per cent of the population in those villages.[11] Bodo leaders argued that this was a tribal-compact area and that they could not be denied autonomy over it merely because of its changing demography.[12]

In fact, some Bodo militant leaders decided that they would 'create a majority even if we do not have one because this is our land and [it] cannot go to anyone else'.[13] Bodo militants then started attacking non-Bodo settlers (the Assamese, Bengali Hindus and Muslims, Nepalis and finally the Santhals, Mundas and Oraons, who had migrated from central India) in early 1994, killing hundreds of them. Their purpose: ethnic cleansing in order to create majorities needed to back claims for a separate Bodo state. The Karbi and the Dimasa rebel groups have also unleashed similar violence against 'outsiders'. In fact, the United Peoples Democratic Solidarity (UPDS), fighting for a Karbi homeland, and the Dima Halan Daogah (DHD), which is fighting for a Dimasa homeland, both have attacked non-tribals and massacred them in large numbers in an attempt to drive them out of their area.

In Tripura, the royal administration passed a land law in 1886 that dealt with rights on different types of land, transfer of *raiyati* rights, rates of rent that a landlord could charge from his tenants and rights of the reclaimer. Those who reclaimed waste and fallow land or forest obtained *jote* or *raiyati* rights and had to pay very nominal rent rates for 20 years. Invariably, the peasants who qualified for these *jungle-avadi* lease were peasants from the eastern districts of undivided Bengal bordering on Hill Tipperah. These provisions 'clearly paved the way for the growth of individual proprietorial cultivation in Tripura'.[14]

Since the beneficiaries of this arrangement were almost exclusively Bengali peasants, it was bound to cause much heartburn. Moreover, due to their relatively more advanced methods of cultivation, Bengali peasants started producing a surplus that, when sold for cash, gave them more funds to either buy more tribal lands on distress sale or loan out money to tribals against the mortgage of land with a set time-frame for land transfer if the tribal failed to repay the debt in time. Since the tribals lacked adequate title on lands they owned, they also lacked the legal basis to protect their lands in a changing tenurial system where communal ownership was being overtaken by principles of individual proprietorship.

As long as the tribals had enough land and the pressure of the Bengali population was limited to certain pockets, land alienation of tribals did not become a major problem. This began to change with independence and the merger of princely Tripura into the Indian Union. Between 1947 and 1971, 6,09,998 Bengalis displaced from East Pakistan came to Tripura for rehabilitation and resettlement. Since the total population of the state in 1951 was 6,45,707, it is not difficult to gauge the enormous population pressure created on tiny Tripura. During this period, the state government primarily resettled the refugees on land under different schemes, some by enabling them to settle down with financial assistance and some by just helping them buy land. The operation of these schemes accelerated the process of large-scale loss of tribal lands.

The marginalization of the tribals can also be discerned from the growing number of tribal agricultural labourers in three decades since Partition. In 1951, cultivators constituted 62.94 per cent of the total tribal workforce in the state, while only 8.93 per cent were in the category of agricultural labourers. In 1981, however, only 43.57 per cent of the tribal workforce were cultivators and the number of agricultural labourers had risen to 23.91 per cent.[15] The land loss at the level of the individual was further compounded by loss of tribal lands to huge government projects like the Dumbur hydro-electric project, where an estimated 5,000 to 8,000 tribal families lost their lands. Only a small fraction of them owned title deeds as evidence of ownership that could ensure their rehabilitation.

The pauperization of Dumbur's once prosperous tribal peasantry and the huge benefits reaped by Bengali urban dwellers (through electricity) and by Bengali fishermen (through fishing in the large reservoir) were not lost on a generation of angry tribal youths who took up arms and left for the jungles to fight an administration they felt was only working in the interests of the Bengali refugees. Insurgent leader Bijoy Kumar Hrangkhawl, now back in mainstream politics after his Tribal National Volunteers (TNV) signed accord in 1988, used to always refer to Chief Minister Nripen Chakrabarty as the 'refugee chief minister' of Tripura.[16]

Under the Congress administration, some Bengali refugee leaders even set up 'land cooperatives' like the Swasti Samity in northern Tripura. These cooperatives violated the Tribal Reserves regulations and began to take over large swathes of tribal lands, a process that was legitimized by conniving bureaucrats. The Communist Party mobilized the tribesmen and even took the matter to court to secure a favourable verdict that was not honoured by the bureaucracy. Anger at such rampant loss of traditional lands motivated the first significant underground group in post-merger Tripura, the Sengkrak or 'Clenched Fist' to started armed action.[17]

This writer conducted a correlation analysis between land alienation and tribal insurgency in August 1984 by choosing to interview the family members of eighty-four guerrillas of the TNV. These people had been gathered at a government building as part of Nripen Chakrabarty's 'Motivation Drive' to work on the guerillas through their families. It was found that 64 per cent of the families had suffered loss of land to Bengalis while 32 per cent of them were from families of *jhumia*s or shifting cultivators who were under increasing pressure to find fresh land for cultivation due to the growing occupation of hill stretches by Bengali refugees. Only 4 per cent came from families with enough land not yet lost to the settlers.[18]

The loss of land by an individual tribal should be seen in the over-all context of land alienation. In Tripura's pre-industrial society, it was linked by the indigenous tribesmen to the loss of political power caused by the transfer of authority from a princely administration run by their own king to an electoral democracy where the growing numbers of Bengali settlers would always marginalize them. The fact that post-merger Tripura has had only one tribal amongst the state's eight chief ministers is used to back such an argument that the tribal has become a foreigner in his own land and will never be in control of his own destiny unless he manages to throw out the Bengali settlers in large numbers and create enough pressure on the government to reserve enough seats for tribals in the state assembly and other elected bodies.

Tripura and Assam are glaring examples of land loss, changing demography and shift in political power running along a single continuum, one following the other as a logical outcome. But the problem does not end there. In Meghalaya, the tension between indigenous tribesmen and outsiders (*Dhkars* in Khasi language) has been largely restricted to the state's capital Shillong, once the capital of the larger state of Assam. When Assam was ruled from Shillong, the administration leased out land liberally to expanding government offices, security organizations and also for private residential colonies, for markets, business establishments, hospitals, churches and educational institutions.

The process continued well into the early 1980s when violence against the settlers started. Since loss of tribal lands in Meghalaya has been restricted mostly to Shillong and its surroundings, violence against settlers has been most intense in and around Shillong. In 1973, after the creation of Meghalaya, the state government set up a Land Reforms Commission to codify the customary land laws and streamline land holdings in the state. But the Khasi tribesmen were apprehensive about the implications of the commission's report and feared it could lead to more taxation and tighter land ceilings. They even opposed the government's efforts to undertake a cadastral survey of land—streamlining of holdings could lead to more commercial purchases by buyers from outside the community.

Nagaland and Mizoram have been protected by the Inner Line legacy and formal loss of land at the level of the individual tribesmen has not been a problem as yet. But thousands of Nagas and Mizos have been uprooted from their ancestral lands by security forces during the counter-insurgency operations and never allowed to go back. This disrupted their control over the land, which slowly went waste. Almost half of those affected permanently lost their lands either through disuse or by ownership transfer. Agricultural output in both the states suffered and the indigenous tribesmen became ever more dependent on the Indian public distribution system. One study estimates that at least 80 per cent of the population of the Mizo Hills, later Mizoram, was uprooted by the Village Regrouping programme of the Indian army.[19] Estimates from the Naga Hills (now Nagaland) suggest that around 35 per cent of the population was relocated under the army's counter-insurgency programme, though not as sweepingly as in Mizoram.

In fact, Village Regrouping, a counter-insurgency tactic used by the British army in Malaya and by US troops in Vietnam, was adopted by the Indian army in the North East to cut off the rebels from the village people so that they could be denied food, shelter, clothing and other essential supplies as well as the population cover necessary for concealment. But since thousands of Naga and Mizo peasants were uprooted from their ancestral lands with no other assets or skills to fall back on, many of them were left with no other option but to become wage labourers in road-building programmes of the Border Roads Organization or to migrate to the towns and semi-urban locations in search of unskilled jobs. This uprooted population has been prone to drug trafficking, violent crime and prostitution. In retrospect, the socio-economic stability of a self-sustaining tribal peasantry in both the Naga and the Mizo hills has been seriously affected with rather far-reaching consequences.

In Manipur's hill regions, land alienation was growing until the Manipur Land Revenue and Reforms Act was passed in 1960. This act prohibited the sale of tribal land to non-tribals and also provided for the restoration of alienated tribal lands. As in Tripura, the restoration of alienated tribal lands has not been possible because tribals rarely retain records of transfer and restoration attempts themselves could spark off ethnic unrest. Due to growing pressure in the Imphal

Valley, however, Meiteis have also been losing land, not necessarily to outsiders but to their own wealthier kinsmen. This again has forced many landless peasants to migrate to the towns. They swelled the ranks of rootless men and women, from whom the insurgents draw their recruits.

In Arunachal Pradesh, tribespeople are apprehensive that the loss of land by their ethnic kinsmen in Assam could happen to them. They resent the settlement of the Chakmas and the Hajongs, who came from what is now Bangladesh, because many of these Chakma and Hajong hamlets have expanded into land once held by the state's indigenous tribes. Land is still abundant in Arunachal Pradesh—the largest state in the North East has the lowest population density in the country. Added to this is the 'Inner Line' legacy, so land alienation has not been a major problem in Arunachal Pradesh. Small wonder that this has remained the most peaceful state in the North East, at least so far.

LANGUAGE AND SCRIPT: PASSION BEHIND CONFLICT

In pre-industrial agrarian societies like India's North East, sharp demographic changes and the pattern of land ownership are linked to the issue of ethnic identity. A century of continuous migration from eastern Bengal (now Bangladesh) and the consequent rise in the Bengali population have raised the question of whether Assam will be a state of and for ethnic Assamese or will it be a polyglot entity with many languages used as medium of instruction. The state's official language has been one of the contentious issues that have unsettled Assam ever since 1947. The ethnic Assamese have insisted that only Assamese can be the official language of the state and that all business and education should be conducted in Assamese. Bengalis have demanded parallel status for their language, justifying it with their growing numbers. So have tribal groups such as the Bodos.

British administrators, like the deputy commissioner of Sibsagar, George Campbell, pushed to bring immigrant cultivators from eastern Bengal to improve Assam's food production after the state's population started rising in the wake of the expanding plantation and oil economy. Initially, the Assamese, particularly their landed gentry, looked upon the hardy East Bengali peasants as a source of cheap labour for their huge estates or for cultivating the *char*s or river islands. In March 1897, the secretary of the Assam Association, Babu Gunjanan Barua, submitted to the government that 'as there is 70.15 per cent of land lying waste [in Assam], the government should give encouragement to their settlement by offering them [the migrants] land on favourable terms as a speedy and effective means of bringing waste lands under settlement to produce all sorts of cash crops'.[20] Leading Assamese intellectuals like Anandaram Dhekial-Phukan argued that 'the people of some badly provided parts of Bengal could be invited to immigrate'.[21]

By the end of the First World War, however, the demographic change was becoming evident in Assam. Districts like Barpeta, Dhubri and Goalpara already had a Bengali majority; so did the whole of the Barak Valley area. This made the Assamese, who had once supported immigration, very restive. Under pressure from Assamese organizations, the government tried to implement the Line System by creating a line to delineate the segregated areas of a frontier district where migrants could settle down. But the Line System failed to control immigration and the number of Bengalis continued to rise. By 1931, the Bengali-speaking population had crossed the 1 million mark, with the ethnic Assamese numbering just below 2 million.[22]

In 1836, Bengali was introduced as the official language of Assam, provoking stormy protest among the Assamese and the foreign missionaries who were committed to promoting local languages in northeast India. The British were convinced that Assamese was a mere variant of Bengali and not an independent language. Chief Commissioner Henry Hopkinson said: 'I can come to no other conclusion that they [Assamese and Bengali] are one and all … with an admixture of local archaic or otherwise corrupted and debased words.'[23]

But the incipient Assamese middle class were determined not to accept the imposition of Bengali. Intellectuals, like Anandaram Dhekial-Phukan, who had supported Bengali immigration, now turned to fight the imposition of the Bengali language in Assam. Dhekial-Phukan wrote an anonymous pamphlet titled *A Few Remarks on the Assamese Language*, which was published by the Baptist Mission Press in Sibsagar and distributed free to British officials. In it, Dhekial-Phukan argued for the antiquity of the

Assamese language and referred extensively to its ancient literature: 62 religious works and 40 dramas based on the Hindu epics were cited. Finally, the British gave in. In July 1873, the lieutenant-governor of Bengal ordered that 'Assamese be used in judicial and revenue proceedings' and recognized it as 'the ordinary language of the five valley districts of Assam—Kamrup, Darrang, Nowgong, Sibsagar and Lakhimpur'.[24]

The reintroduction of Assamese language did not allay the fears of the Assamese. In 1874, when Assam became a chief commissioner's province, Bengal's Sylhet district and the Bengali areas of Cachar and Goalpara were added to Assam. Bengalis started pressing for Bengali-medium schools as their numbers increased. Assam Congress leaders like Gopinath Bordoloi tried in vain to persuade the Bengali leaders to accept privately run mixed schools. As separate Bengali and Assamese-medium schools flourished, the linguistic divide widened and set the stage for the confrontation.

The Assamese were further shaken up when Muslim migrants from eastern Bengal, relatively less educated than Bengali Hindus, supported the cause of Bengali. Bengali Hindus, mostly urban dwellers employed in administrations, the professions and business, thus found support from the mainly rural Muslim Bengali migrants. Matiur Rehman Miah, an immigrant peasant leader from west Goalpara, told the Assam assembly on 16 February 1938: 'We are Bengalees. Our mother tongue is Bengali ... under the circumstances, if this Assamese language be on our shoulders, on our children's shoulders and if we are deprived of our mother tongue then that will amount to depriving our children from opportunities of education.'[25]

The linguistic factor began to shape the contours of ethnic competition and conflict between the Assamese and the Bengalis more sharply as the British withdrawal from the subcontinent became imminent. The Assamese became more and more protectionist and resentful of Bengali immigration and they wanted Sylhet and other Bengali-majority areas to be removed from Assam. In 1927, during his presidential address at the annual session of the Asom Sahitya Sabha (Assam Literature Society), Tarun Ram Phukan said:

We *Asomiyas* [Assamese] are a distinct nationality amongst Indians. Though our language is Sanskrit based, it is a distinct language. A rising nationality shows signs of life by way of extending domination over others. Alas, it is otherwise; we are not only dependent, our neighbour [Bengal] is trying to swallow us taking advantage of our helplessness. Brother *Asomiyas*, reflect on your past glory to have an understanding of the situation.[26]

The Assamese soon realized the futility of confronting Bengalis as an ethnic group and decided to play on the religious and class divide. Realizing that they faced a more immediate challenge from the relatively more educated Bengali Hindu middle class for positions in bureaucracy and the professions, they tried to cultivate the less-educated Bengali Muslim peasants and win their support on the language question. In the 1931 annual session of the Asom Sahitya Sabha, Nagendra Nath Choudhury said in his presidential address:

> To the immigrants from Mymensingh, I want to say they are not Bengalees anymore but Assamese. They are equal partners in the happiness, pains and the prosperity and deterioration in this province... They should learn the local language and they are learning. At present the similarities they have with the Bengali language is almost nil. Moreover, they are quite a distance from the main Bengali language. We hereby welcome them today. Let them join and contribute to the development of Assamese culture and nationality.[27]

At the 1944 annual session of the Asom Sahitya Sabha, Nilmoni Phukan, a pioneer of the protectionist movement, made it clear that 'Assam is for the Assamese', though he was quick to add: 'Anybody who lives in Assam has the right to become Assamese by adopting Assamese language and culture.'[28]

Partition resulted in Sylhet going over to East Pakistan, thus reducing the numerical preponderance of the Bengalis. With the immediate threat of Bengali domination gone, the Assamese turned to consolidate their linguistic grip on post-Partition Assam. Their repeated attempts to impose Assamese on the Bengali-dominated Barak Valley region sparked off fierce protest movements culminating in the police firing in Silchar on 19 May 1960. The 11 who died on that day have since been treated as martyrs in the cause of defending the Bengali language, much like the martyrs of the movement against the imposition of Urdu in East Pakistan in 1952 have been treated as national heroes in Bangladesh. Now political parties and social groups in the Barak Valley are demanding that the railway station of Silchar, the biggest town in the valley, should be renamed 'Bhasha Shahid' (language matyrs) station in memory of the 19 May martyrs.

But it was not only the Bengalis who resented Assamese linguistic chauvinism. When the Assam government tried to impose Assamese as the official language of the state in 1960, the tribal groups joined the Bengalis in protest. Assam's large population of tribespeople—the Nagas, the Mizos, the Bodos, the Khasis and the Jaintias—who had accepted Assamese as the link language resented its imposition as the official language of the state, which would foreclose the use of their own languages as media of instruction or communication in the hill regions.

Most of these tribes had been exposed to Christian evangelization for a century and had converted in large numbers. The church in the North East promoted smaller tribal languages and worked for their development through the Roman script with some success. Most of these languages had developed their grammar and vocabulary and had emerged as effective vernaculars capable of being used as the official language of the autonomous district councils set up under the Sixth Schedule. So the policy of imposing Assamese did not go down well with these tribes. Long after Assam had broken up, a tribal politician of Meghalaya who rose to become the speaker of the Lok Sabha said: 'We all spoke Assamese, we still can. But we are not Assamese, so we could not accept the imposition of Assamese. That's why Assam broke up.'[29]

In fact, the tribal groups joined the Bengalis to organize the 'All Assam Non-Assamese Language Conference' in Silchar on 2 July 1960, two months after the police firing in the same town at the peak of the Bengali language movement. The resolution adopted at the conference went as follows:

> The conference of the Non-Assamese speaking people of Assam strongly opposes the move to impose Assamese as the official language for the state of Assam and that the *status quo* based on the intrinsically multilingual character of the state must be maintained for the peace and security of the eastern region of India.[30]

As the protest against the imposition of Assamese grew stronger, the hill leaders demanded that English be made the official language of Assam. Some Bodos demanded that Hindi be the official language, while the Bengalis requested that their mother tongue be awarded the status of an official language in the Barak Valley. In some ways, the attempt to impose the Assamese language on non-Assamese nationalities in Assam proved to be a catalytic event that led ultimately to the fragmentation of this large imperial province.

Tribal groups like the Bodos saw in the move an attempt to deny them autonomy and undermine their distinct ethnic identity. Bodos had formed their own Sahitya Sabha in 1952 and an influential group within the community was trying to introduce Roman script for the Bodo language. Assam's chief minister, Bimala Prasad Chaliha, one of the few Assamese leaders who was willing to accommodate the aspirations of the non-Assamese, agreed to the use of the Bodo language as a medium of instruction in Bodo-dominated areas in 1963. In February 1969, the Script Sub-committee of the Bodo Sahitya Sabha submitted its final report on the script issue. Almost immediately, the Bodo Sahitya Sabha adopted the report that recommended the abolition of the Assamese script and its replacement with the Roman script.

When the Bodo primer *Bithorai* (Balab-se), in Roman script, was introduced in Bodo medium schools in 1974, the Assam government stopped financial grants for Bodo primary schools in an attempt to force them back to the Assamese script. This led to a massive movement in the Bodo areas that was marked by the boycott of educational institutions and the *gherao* (encirclement) of government offices. Thousands of Bodo tribesmen stormed government offices, forcing the police to fire in at least six places. Hundreds of Bodos were arrested and some killed in the police firing. The Assam government called for negotiations with the Bodo Sahitya Sabha but the state's education minister insisted that the Bodos should continue to use the Assamese script.

When Bodo leaders approached the Union government, Prime Minister Indira Gandhi advised them to adopt the Devnagari (Hindi) script for the Bodo language. These leaders, as a former member of parliament Dharanidhar Basumatary later put it, were caught 'between a lion and a crocodile'.[31] In April 1975, as the impasse dragged on, the two Bodo Sahitya Sabha representatives camping in Delhi (Thaneswar Boro, later minister in the Asom Gana Parishad (AGP) government, and Ramdas Basumatary) submitted a proposal to the Union government, in which they agreed to adopt the Devnagari script for the Bodo language. The Sahitya Sabha later endorsed this decision at its 16th annual conference held at Dhing on 25–27 April 1975.

This decision, however, divided the Bodo community along an increasingly religious divide and threatened their cohesion as a nationality. If language is the bedrock on which a nationality rests, the vicious divide over the script for the Bodo language has been a major setback for the Bodos and it continues to cast a shadow over the autonomy and the separatist movements launched by Bodo militant groups. Christian Bodos, the church and most of the Bodo students educated in Shillong strongly advocate the use of Roman script and they now enjoy the backing of the separatist National Democratic Front of Bodoland (NDFB), which killed a former Bodo Sahitya Sabha president and other Bodo politicians for opposing the introduction of the Roman script. Groups opposed to the NDFB and the church, including the All Bodo Students Union (ABSU) and the Bodo Peoples Action Committee, stridently oppose the Roman script. They practice the indigenous Bathou faith or adhere to Hinduism.

The tussle now has less to do with the suitability of one script over another and more to do with the politics of identity—whether the Bodos should present themselves as an evangelized tribe like the Nagas, the Khasis or the Mizos, or whether they should emphasize their links to the 'Indian mainstream' and be seen as a tribe with its own distinct traditions and religious practices free of Christian influences.

The advent of Hindutva groups in northeast India and the patronage they provide to animist and Hindu tribal groups to hold their own against the church has further complicated the language issue, not only among the Bodos but among other tribes who stand divided between the pull of Christianity and their traditional faiths. Converts to Christianity in northeast India have always advocated the use of Roman script for their languages and dialects. They see in the Roman script a way of identifying closely with the West, with Christianity, with modern education. They believe that use of traditional scripts like Assamese and Bengali will keep them tied to dominant ethnic groups and hinder the creation of an independent identity, with its attendant political and economic consequences.

Like the Hindutva groups, the communists have also backed the use of Bengali and Assamese scripts for most tribal languages and dialects. In Tripura, they strongly supported the use of Bengali script for the Kokborok language, which is spoken by the Tripuri tribes. The state's legendary communist leader (later chief minister) Dasarath Debbarma, Sudhanya Debbarma, leftist writer Mahendra Debbarma and Radhamohan Thakur have all advocated the use of the Bengali script for the Kokborok language. The undivided Communist Party deployed linguists like Kumud Kundu Choudhury to conduct research for the development of the Kokborok.

When Kokborok was given the status of the second official language of Tripura after the communists came to power in 1978, it was steadily introduced in village schools in tribal-dominated areas. Kokborok textbooks were prepared in Bengali script and circulated widely. The communist state government continues to promote the use of the Bengali script, but in the Tripura tribal areas autonomous district council, where the Indigenous Nationalist Party of Tripura (INPT) had come to power earlier in this decade, the Roman script has been steadily introduced with the full backing of the ruling party, the Baptist church and the Tribal Students Federation (TSF). Some linguists argue that the Roman script will create a gap between the language and those who use it because the Tripuris are long used to Bengali script.[32]

The new generation of tribal youths and the organizations that claim to represent their aspirations, like the TSF and the INPT, support all-round introduction of the Roman script. In the politics of tribalism and ethnic identity that has strongly challenged the multi-ethnic model of communist politics in Tripura, the issue of a suitable script for Kokborok is no longer seen as an issue of linguistic convenience. The use of the Bengali script is seen as a manifestation of an undesirable dependence on Bengali culture and Bengali-style leftist politics and a historical link with the Bengali people that the new generation of tribals is not willing to retain.

For these tribal youths, Shillong rather than Calcutta is the model for education, culture and politics. The Mizo, the Khasi and the Garo have adopted Roman script for their languages and the new generation of Bodo or Tripuri youth wants the same to happen. The politics of armed separatism may not work; total ethnic cleansing of the Bengali population may not be attainable either. The use of the Roman script, however, may serve to put an end to the love affair between Bengal and Tripura that began with the Manikya kings several centuries ago, as a result of which Bengali remained the official language of princely Tripura and Rabindranath Tagore remained the favourite royal guest at the Tripura court, even when British-ruled Bengal used English as its official language.

When the politics of ethnic identity swept through northeast India in the early 1980s, some Manipuri revivalist organizations, like the Apokpa Marup and later the Meitei National Front, demanded the abolition of the Bengali script, which had been used for the Meitei language since the eighteenth century. These revivalists saw the adoption of Bengal's Vaishnavite faith and the Bengali script for the Meitei language by the kings of Manipur as part of a process of cultural surrender that undermined the Meitei identity. As organizations across the state stepped up their agitation for the inclusion of Manipuri in the Eighth Schedule of the Indian constitution, these revivalist groups pushed for use of the Meitei script. It did not work because (a) the Meitei script is too archaic for contemporary use; (b) the threat of Bengali domination does not work as a convenient trigger in Manipur, as it does in Tripura, because Bengalis are a very small population group in Manipur and (c) the Bengali script has been used for two centuries in Manipur and the people have got used to it. Manipuri is not a new language like Kokborok and has a rich literary tradition and a change of script will not be easy to adjust to.

In Mizoram, the promotion of the Roman script for the Mizo language has never been challenged because smaller tribes who resent Mizo domination nevertheless find it easy to use the language as a lingua franca or language of communication among themselves. The Hmars, the Lais, the Maras and the Brus rarely hesitate to use Mizo as an official language, but the Chakmas resent the imposition of the Mizo language because their own language is rich in folk traditions. In Meghalaya, the politics of linguistic primacy has not yet started because the three major tribes live in physically distinct zones in which they use their own languages for administrative and educational purposes, whereas the elite has access to English education.

The absence of a Naga language is regarded as a major weakness of the Naga nationality-formation process. The use of Nagamese, a pidgin mixture of Assamese and other tribal dialects and Indian languages, as a working lingua franca has been limited and the development of separate dialects as languages has further reinforced the element of tribalism in Naga society. In Arunachal Pradesh, the prevalence of tribalism and the absence of a lingua franca have made possible the entry of Hindi as the language of the marketplace. Tribals from the state have even carved out chequered careers in Hindi television. This could have happened in Nagaland as well but for the long separatist movement there, which projected Hindi as the language of the occupation force. Since the church has promoted separate tribal dialects amongst the Nagas and English as the common language of communication, all newspapers in Nagaland are published in English.

The scene is no different in Arunachal Pradesh, but the heavy Indian military presence and the amicable civil–military relations there have favoured the acceptance of Hindi even at the village level. Rebels have much to do with the acceptance of a language that's not local. Separatist rebels in Manipur and Assam have banned Hindi movies but have allowed halls to run Korean and Thai movies or those from other South East Asian countries. That's restricted the popularity of Hindi in these states, despite the presence of a community of Hindi-speakers in them.

Leadership: The Platform for Conflict

The advent of the British was followed by the growth of the railways, the tea and oil-based industries in Assam and the spread of English education through the efforts of Christian missionaries in the hill areas of the North East. It also led to the growing import of labour and professionals from outside the region. The traditional feudal elite of Assam—priests and teachers, government officials and *satradhikars*—and the tribal chiefs in the hill regions were slowly but surely challenged in their leadership role by an emergent middle class that consisted of the newly-educated locals as well as educated professionals from neighbouring Bengal and traders from Rajasthan who enjoyed patronage of the colonial overlord.

After a brief period of cooperation with the British, the local middle class in Assam assumed the leadership of the nationalist movement in the state. Their agitation against the British rule was reinforced by the antipathy towards the migrant middle class that was seen as an appendage of colonial rule and a competitor for a share of jobs and professions. The British partly appeased the Assamese middle class by replacing Bengali with Assamese as the official language of the province but immediately thereafter upset them by adding Sylhet and Cachar (then covering the whole of Barak Valley) to Assam. The 'Sylhetis' could boast of a vibrant and enterprising middle class that was more than a match for the nascent Assamese middle class in the competition for political office, administrative positions and the professions.

Thus, the conflict of interests between the Bengali and the Assamese middle classes became one of the recurring features of middle-class competition in Assam and it influenced the nature of social and political leadership that emerged in the province. After independence, with Sylhet gone to East Pakistan, the Bengali middle class lost the territory and the resources that supported it and, weakened by the religious divide, its influence slowly became limited to the Barak Valley districts of southern Assam. In Tripura, however, the Bengali middle class became more dominant after the princely state merged with the Indian Union. The end of the princely order led to the withering away of the tribal feudal elite, the palace-based Kartas and the tribal chiefs heading the dafas. Their preponderant position in political and administrative decision-making was taken over by the incoming Bengali middle class from East Pakistan until a neo-literate tribal middle class emerged in the late 1960s to challenge the Bengali domination.

In Manipur, a class of officials owing allegiance to the kings had provided social and political leadership until the state became part of India. Like the Ahom elite, they gave free service to the *maharaja* for 10 in every 40 days under the Lalup system. After independence, a middle class emerged in both the hills and the plains through the avenues of modern education and new political and administrative opportunities. The Meitei middle class in the plains, like the Bengali middle class in the nineteenth century, emerged as the most creative in the North East, leaving its imprint on the arts, literature, music, theatre and sports. But it remained disgruntled with India because of the lack of opportunities. It failed to gain the benefits of reservation that were available to the tribal middle classes in Nagaland, Mizoram, Meghalaya and Arunachal Pradesh or the resources and the locational advantage available to the Assamese middle class.

The new middle class in northeast India has come to consist of (a) indigenous tea planters, merchants, agent-proprietors, contractors, food-grain dealers and retail shop-owners; (b) salaried employees of government and private companies; (c) self-employed professionals like doctors, accountants and lawyers; (d) civil servants serving all-India services and state services; (e) teachers and creative intellectuals and (f) professional politicians. Over the last few years, a new element has been added to the middle class in the region—the agitator and the rebel. Radical students, youths, insurgent leaders and activists have been co-opted into the system through the process of reconciliation initiated by the state and the federal government. Their class origins are mostly rooted in the urban or rural lower middle class or peasantry and the subsequent prominence secured by them is indicative of the fluidity and socio-economic mobility in the process of middle-class formation in the region.

> One of the significant achievements of the political leadership (in Northeast India) in the initial years of their management of the polity was in the establishment of new centres of education to train local youths for jobs in administration as well as in such professions as medicine, engineering and architecture. Actuated by a strong desire to subserve the interests of the expanding indigenous middle class, the political leadership was expected to give preference to local talent as far as employment was concerned. As a result, the various middle class elements of the region concentrated on wresting the control of district and state administrative organs from their earlier dominant groups, mostly outsiders. The migrant middle class however continued to retain as well as expand its control over agencies and also had a major say in the utilization of development funds.[33]

Over the last two decades, the migrant middle class has lost out in the competition for all-India services. Newly educated tribals, with the benefit of missionary education, have taken advantage of reservations and found ever more places in the all-India services. No longer are Assamese or Bengali officers from Assam the only ones to be mentioned in the headlines. More often than not, it is a

J.M. Lyngdoh (former India's chief election commissioner, who hails from Meghalaya) or a Sangliana (Karnataka police official responsible for hunting down notorious sandalwood smuggler Veerappan, who hails from Mizoram) or a Donald Ingti (one of the finest customs officers from the North East) who are in the limelight. The tribal middle class has also wrested total control over state services and other jobs and professions in the states of Nagaland, Mizoram, Meghalaya and Arunachal Pradesh. They have limited control over trade and business, but they are beginning to compete with traditional Indian business communities, such as the Marwaris, whose presence in the 'North East' is considerable. In Manipur and Tripura, the tribal middle class has also emerged and they have found themselves in acute conflict with the Meitei or the Bengali middle class because their aspirations, political style and cultural mores differ sharply.

It would be wrong, however, to assume that the new middle class completely replaced the traditional elite in the North East. In every state of the region, when the traditional elite lost political power, they turned to modern education. Their progeny returned to positions of social and political leadership within a few years, sharing power with the new elites. The Sailos in Mizoram, the Ahom aristocracy in Assam and the Syiems in Meghalaya all had lost power and found a fresh share of it within a generation by exploiting the opportunities of modern education and reservations in higher education and jobs. There has been 'a convergence between the interests of the middle class and the traditional ruling elites or bourgeoisie in the North East. By and large, this combined group has felt confident enough to control the levers of power through the instrumentality of universal suffrage'.[34]

The conflict of interests between the indigenous and the migrant middle class has been a recurrent theme in the evolution of the leadership in northeast India. The indigenous middle class has also suffered fragmentation along ethnic lines, preventing the growth of regional consciousness and leadership. Since the growth of the new indigenous middle class has been largely shaped by the politics of ethnic identity, the leadership it provides has rarely transcended the boundaries of tribal or sub-national identity. The resourceful *Asomiya* middle class failed to provide leadership to the rest of the region because it could not rise above linguistic sectarianism. The Naga insurgent leadership, though made up of the neo-literates brought up in Christian missionary schools, failed to rise above the compelling identity of the tribe. Despite the exposure of some of their leaders to Marxism-Leninism in China, they failed to create a multi-tribal base for Naga nationalism. Most other regional parties or insurgent groups have been limited by the politics of tribalism or linguistic parochialism.

In northeast India, the national political parties largely dominated by the traditional power-holding elites were first challenged throughout the region by the neo-middle class leadership of the insurgent organizations in the 1960s. In the 1970s, their grip on the region's politics was further eroded by radical student and youth groups. Student activism sprang up throughout northeast India as the region's neo-literates made a determined bid to redefine the parameters and idioms of politics. The Congress—which had led the national movement in Assam and took credit for being able to retain the province in India by thwarting the attempts of the Muslim League to merge it with East Pakistan—wilted under pressure from the student leadership during the anti-foreigner agitation.

In the hills, the character of Congress leadership underwent a change as the traditional loyalists yielded to the neo-middle class. A number of regional parties emerged from the student and youth movements or from the ranks of the insurgent groups that had called it a day. The regional parties failed to consolidate their position, however, because of (a) the immaturity of the leadership; (b) corruption and failure to provide an alternative vision; (c) lack of a broad base and the limitations of tribal identity and (d) failure to evolve a multi-ethnic, trans-ethnic political ethos.

The character of leadership in northeast India has been shaped by (a) the absence of a traditional capitalist class capable of enterprise and the consequent lack of indigenous capital formation; (b) the continuous conflict between the indigenous and the migrant middle class and the failure of both to find common meeting grounds of aspirations and interests; (c) growing control by the indigenous middle class over the state apparatus but its failure to wrest control over business and trade, manufacturing and industries from the migrant trading communities and (d) polarization of the indigenous middle class with one section accepting co-option into the national political system to access greater opportunities and another section remaining tied to regional roots and the insurgent movements that grew out of it.

The Marxist political leadership in Tripura did make a difference. Unlike the Congress, which provided a multi-ethnic model of political mobilization and leadership from the top, the Marxists promoted a multi-ethnic ethos of politics from the grassroots, one that made a serious attempt to reconcile the quest for security and livelihood of the Bengali settlers with the aspirations of autonomy and self-rule of the indigenous tribesmen. While the Congress tried to promote a coalition of indigenous and migrant middle class leadership through power-sharing and resorted to vote bank politics in Assam and elsewhere in the region, the Marxists in Tripura promoted the autonomist aspirations of the tribal leadership even at the cost of risking their Bengali vote bank.[35]

The courage displayed by the Marxists in pushing forward the creation of the state's tribal areas autonomous district council within a year of the 1980 ethnic riots and in attempting a political rather than a military solution to the problem of armed tribal separatism in Tripura attest to the quality of statesmanship provided by the Marxist triumvirate: Chief Minister Nripen Chakrabarty, Deputy Chief Minister (later chief minister) Dasarath Deb and Biren Dutta, the founder of the Communist Party in Tripura. Under Chief Minister Manik Sarkar, the Marxists remain committed to ethnic reconciliation and class politics, but as the older generation of party-builders fades away, the new generation of appratchiks seems to be losing touch with the grassroots from their comfortable porticoes of power. Corruption and complacency, the bane of most indigenous middle classes in northeast India, is catching up with the Marxist ruling elite in Tripura that has been largely free of it for several decades.

In the years to come, the immigrant middle class in the North Eastern states will also be locked in greater conflict with emergent tribal middle-class elements who are demanding new autonomous administrative units. The conflict between the Assamese neo-middle-class leadership (those who led the anti-foreigner agitation) and the Bodo middle-class leadership represented in similar youth organizations has already set a pattern for the future. The conflict of interest within smaller tribal middle classes, reinforced by the religious divide or political manipulation by the national parties, may also increase. But since the emergent leadership is more driven by ethnicity than by ideology, it is prone to promote conflict rather than ethnic reconciliation. But they remain prone to co-option by Delhi, often joining India's corrupt national elite by choice.

Notes

1. Interview with former Congress Minister Imtisungit Jamir, who lost his seat in Dimapur during the February 2003 elections. Jamir predicted that there would be 'at least two Muslim candidates' for the Congress in the following Nagaland state assembly elections.
2. Press handout of the Khel Association, Kohima, reported in the *Nagaland Post* on 27 April 2003. NSCN (Khaplang faction) press handout, reported in the *Nagaland Post* on 2 February 2003.
3. Clippings from the Guwahati-based Eastern Press Service indicate that between 1980 and 2008, there were 197 mass killings in India's North East, in which more than 30 people were killed in a single incident. The death toll was highest in Nellie, with about 1,800 killed on the first day of violence.
4. Balmiki Prasad Singh (Governor of Assam) 1987.
5. Nari Rustomji, 1983.
6. Balmiki Prasad Singh (Governor of Sikkim) 1987.
7. *The Problem of Transfer and Alienation of Tribal Land in Assam* issued by the Assam Tribal Research Institute in 1974 was somewhat supplemented by the Advisory Council's Sub-Committee for Welfare of Schedule Tribes (Plains) Report on Settlement of Land in Tribal Belts and Blocks and of Forest Land, 1976. The report of the committee on the Welfare of Scheduled Castes and Scheduled Tribes, presented to the Assam Legislative Assembly in April 1979, also contributes to the understanding of the problem.
8. Tribal Research Institute, 1974, Guwahati.
9. Report of the Sub-Committee of the Advisory Council for Welfare of Schedule Tribes (Plains) on Settlement of Land in Tribal Belts and Blocks and of Forest Land.
10. M.S. Prabhakara, 1987.
11. Assam Chief Minister Hiteswar Saikia in interview with the writer at Guwahati, 12 November 1993. Saikia argued that the 'interests of the non-Bodos' in the proposed Bodoland Council had to be protected.
12. Sangsuma Khungur Bwismutiary, chairman of ABSU, in an interview with the writer at Kokrajhar (western Assam), 11 December 1993.
13. D. Zabrang, military wing chief of the National Democratic Front of Bodoland, in an interview with the writer at the Manas Reserve Forest, 7 May 1995.
14. J.B. Ganguly, 1987.
15. Census of India, series 21, Tripura.

16. B.K. Hrangkhawl's several letters written to Chief Minister Nripen Chakrabarti during 1984–87, quoted in Subir Bhaumik, 1996.
17. For details on the Sengkrak movement and the large-scale land alienation leading to it, see Bhaumik, *Insurgent Crossfire*.
18. Press Trust of India, 5 August 1984.
19. Amrita Rangaswami, 'Mizoram: Tragedy of our Making', paper read at Queen Elizabeth House, Oxford University, 12 October 1989.
20. Gunjanan Barua on behalf of the Assam Association in memorandum to chief commissioner of Assam.
21. Anandaram Dhekial-Phukan, quoted in A.T.M. Mills, *Report on the Province of Assam* (Calcutta: 1854).
22. As per the 1931 census, Assamese speakers numbered 19,81,369 or 42 per cent of the population while Bengali speakers numbered 10,87,776 or 23 per cent of the population.
23. Quoted in Sajal Nag, *Roots of Ethnic Conflict: Nationality Question in North East India* (Delhi: Manohar Publishers, 1990).
24. Bengal Government Proceedings, General Department, Order of the Lieutenant Governor, 25 July 1873.
25. Speech in Bengali, Assam Legislative Assembly Proceedings, 1938 (pp. 67–71).
26. Atul Hazarika (ed.), 1957.
27. Ibid.
28. Ibid.
29. Purno Agitok Sangma, during a press conference at Guwahati Circuit House, 4 May 1996.
30. Text of the resolution reproduced in the *Hindustan Standard* (Calcutta), 11 July 1960.
31. Dharanidhar Basumatary, interview with the author, 17 August 1993.
32. Anadi Bhattacharya, 1987.
33. Balmik.Prasad Singh (Governor of Assam), 1987.
34. Ibid.
35. Mohan Choudhury, chief of the party's armed wing Shanti Sena in the 1950s, in an interview with the author on 12 March 1992.

4   Insurgency, Ethnic Cleansing and Forced Migration

Ever since decolonization, India's North East has been scarred by violent agitations, sustained separatist insurgencies, ethnic riots and heavy-handed state response, all leading to considerable bloodletting. The region has witnessed large-scale insurgent violence, frequent fighting between militia factions representing different ethnicities or competing for the loyalty of the same ethnic group and the huge deployment of security forces on a sustained basis. The consequent militarization has impeded the growth of civil society and restricted the space in which it can thrive. Rampant violations of human rights and use of terror by both state and non-state actors, ethnic cleansing and extra-judicial killings have weakened the political system and the social fabric and have led to substantial displacement of populations.

It is unfair, however, to signpost this remote periphery as a region of 'durable disorder', to see its angry youth through the prism of the 'gun, guitar, girl' syndrome. There are provinces in India's Hindi-speaking heartland—Bihar, Jharkhand or Chattisgarh—where the level of social and political conflict and the activity of armed radicals, especially the Maoists, are comparable to the North East. The legislative instability in contemporary Uttar Pradesh is also comparable to that of smaller North Eastern states like Meghalaya, and even parts of the 'cyber state' of Andhra Pradesh are as backward or poor as in the North East.

But the North East is surely the one area of post-colonial India where the outbreak of insurgency has been more frequent than elsewhere in the country and where recourse to armed struggle has often been the first, rather than the last, option of a recalcitrant tribe or a larger ethnic group. The prairie fires that began in the Naga Hills and Tripura have continued to spread. Successive generations of youth in the Naga and the Mizo hills, in Manipur and Tripura and then in Assam, have lived under the shadow of the gun. Even the once peaceful states of Meghalaya and Arunachal Pradesh have been affected by recent violence perpetrated by homegrown insurgents and/or by stronger rebel outfits from neighbouring states.

The insurgencies that have afflicted the North East during the last 50 years do not represent a stereotype and their similarities often end with the factor of choice: the use of violence to attain stated objectives. Very often, their goals are as much in conflict with each other as with those of the Indian state. Although any typology of the insurgencies of northeast India is unlikely to be adequate, they can be broadly classified into six broad categories:

1. Insurgencies pronouncedly secessionist in aspirations—the Naga insurgency would fall in this category, though its leaders are now seeking a negotiated settlement after being weakened by several splits and military setbacks.
2. Insurgencies that are separatist in rhetoric but autonomist in aspiration, thus can be co-opted—most insurgencies in the North East fit this category.
3. Insurgencies with separatist overtones but ultimately co-opted by the Indian state through sustained negotiations—the Mizo insurgency is perhaps the only one in this category.
4. Insurgencies with trans-regional dimensions that sought or found allies in mainland India—the early Manipur PLA or communist insurgents of Tripura in 1948–50 would fall into this type.
5. Insurgencies with pronounced autonomist aspirations that seek separate states or autonomous units for a particular tribe or an ethnic group—like the Bodo, the Dimasa, the Karbi, the Bru or the Hmar rebel groups.
6. Insurgencies that work as satellites of more powerful groups—like the Dragon Force or the United Peoples Volunteers Army

(UPVA) of Arunachal Pradesh which are small organizations sustained by larger Assamese or Naga rebel groups and rarely display any independence of action or articulation.

India has been able to control, though not end, these insurgencies by a complex mix of force, political reconciliation, economic incentives and by splitting the insurgents. I have argued that the post-colonial Indian state did not follow Western colonial or post-colonial, not even British models of counter-insurgency in the North East—except picking up some military concepts like the village regrouping of Malaya. Rather it went by the precepts of the traditional Hindu realpolitik statecraft, by the teachings of the great Kautilya (also known as Chanakya) who advised India's first trans-regional empire builder Chandragupta Maurya after Alexander's departure from India.

Kautilya's four principles of *Sham* (political reconciliation), *Dam* (monetary inducement), *Danda* (force) and *Bhed* (split) has been amply applied in dealing with the insurgents of North East—more than anywhere else in post-colonial India.[1]

After the initial use of force has helped contain the insurgent movements, the Indian state has been quick to offer political negotiations (*Sham*) to talk the insurgents into settlements that offered substantial autonomy (including separate states) and liberal doses of federal development funds (*Dam*). But if that did not work, India has freely used its covert agencies to split the insurgents on ethnic, religious or ideological lines to take the sting out of the separatist movements (*Bhed*). Splits worked well as short-term strategy of military containment but became an impediment when the Indian state looked for a durable settlement with the insurgent movements. Multiplicity of insurgent groups fighting over the same political space have often created conditions of 'competitive radicalism'—groups making impossible demands on the state just to outgun rivals within the movement and thus delaying an ultimate settlement. The 1986 Mizo accord worked because the whole of the Mizo National Front accepted the deal. But fratricidal feuds within insurgent movements in North East—be it in Nagaland or Assam—have complicated the reconciliation process and delayed settlements, though it offered the Indian security forces and covert agencies opportunity to weaken the movements by playing one group against another. The constant splits in the insurgent movements partly explain the proliferation of such groups in the North East.

India's counter-insurgency doctrine in the North East always used military action (Danda) not as a stand-alone element but placed it within the broader holistic political approach of the Indian state, which treated the recalcitrant ethnicities of a troubled frontier region not as enemies but as 'our misguided boys and girls'—so the army operations had to be immediately supplemented by a 'hearts and minds' campaign followed by consistent efforts to develop local governments through democratic processes and economic development.[2] The proliferation and intensity of the insurgencies, however, compelled India to enforce draconian laws like the Armed Forces Special Powers Act and that has added to the region's deficit of both democracy and development. India's conflict-management strategy in the North East has also been seen as a cause for the proliferation of insurgency. If less than one million Nagas could get a separate state primarily through an armed movement, bigger population groups like the Bodos had good reasons to feel they could get one by walking the same path.

THE NAGA PATH

The Naga insurrection posed the first major challenge to India's post-colonial nation-building project. It has also been South Asia's longest-running guerilla campaign. For four decades (1956–96), Naga separatists with support from a cross-section of Naga society fought India's military machine to a stalemate, compelling Delhi to look for a negotiated settlement. Negotiations continue but progress is slow and a host of contentious issues threatens to delay, if not derail the peace process. A settlement is now only possible if the Indian government agrees to create a greater Naga state, that is, one that integrates Naga-inhabited territories in the North East with the state of Nagaland. Because the strongest Naga rebel main faction has indicated that they may give up their long-standing demand for sovereignty only if 'Greater Nagaland' is established. Or else the rebels will have to climb down from their 'Greater Nagaland' demand and accept 'special federal relationship' with India.

Political parties and insurgent groups in Assam, Manipur and Arunachal Pradesh have fiercely opposed a 'Greater Nagaland' as they stand to lose a lot of territory. That's put Delhi in a bind. It desperately wants to end the long-festering Naga problem because it cannot afford two powerful insurgencies in the east and the west, where the Pakistan-backed *jihad* in Kashmir continues unabated. But, at the same time, Delhi cannot afford fresh trouble spots in the North East, which is what 'Greater Nagaland' may end up creating, because rebel groups in Manipur and Assam, once close to the Naga rebels, have threatened to intensify their violent campaigns if parts of their state's territory are parceled off to Nagaland to create a larger Naga state.

The Nagas were never a homogenous ethnic entity. The varied tribal character of their polity prior to their conquest by the British has been acknowledged by Western, Indian and Naga scholars. The British contained clan warfare and head-hunting amongst the Naga tribes, largely monetized their economy, encouraged the spread of Christianity and introduced Western-style education to pave the way for the emergence of an incipient middle class of teachers, traders and officials.

> This class would, in years to come, played a pivotal role in the politics of the Naga Hills. Christianity and Western education went hand in hand in the Naga Hills … somewhat cut at the traditional power structure of the villages and helped to weaken exclusive clan allegiance, thereby paving the way for the growth of a pan-Naga consciousness.[3]

The first definite expression of the Naga desire for self-determination goes back to the visit of the Simon Commission in 1929. The Naga Club, the first political group among the Nagas, told the commission in a memorandum that the British should 'leave us (Nagas) alone once you leave so that we determine for ourselves as in ancient times'.[4] The Naga Club and its successor organization, the Naga Tribal Hill District Council faded away despite British patronage, but their efforts evoked much suspicion among the Indian nationalist leadership. In their post-colonial nation-building vision, the freedom-loving Nagas were seen as a problem, not as a possible partner. As India moved towards freedom, the Nagas wanted theirs. Only visionaries like Mahatma Gandhi could have reconciled the Indian's desire for independence with the similar aspiration amongst the Nagas. Gandhi died within a year of India's independence and Subhas Bose, the other nationalist leader sympathetic to the Nagas, mysteriously disappeared during the last days of the Second World War.

By then, much was changing in the Naga Hills. In February 1946, the Naga National Council (NNC) was formed with 29 members and two central councils, one based in Kohima and the other in Mokukchung. The pan-Naga character of the NNC was evident from its composition—although the two leading tribes, the Angamis (with seven members) and the Aos (with five members), dominated the NNC, all major Naga tribes with the exception of the Konyaks were represented in it. Its birth represents a landmark in the history of Naga political mobilization. For the first time in history, there was an attempt to bring the disparate Naga tribes on a common political platform. To the 'Naga' identity, which encompassed two dozen odd tribes, was now added the label 'national'. The nationality-formation process, stimulated by the emergence of a common adversary in India, picked up momentum, though the NNC's organization, modelled on the traditional power structure, promoted tribalism and clan loyalties and weakened the very process it was meant to carry forward.

In June 1946, when the Cabinet Mission plan was announced, the NNC adopted a resolution supporting the demand for autonomy within Assam. It opposed the proposal for a Crown Colony as well as the Grouping Scheme. That should have dispelled any doubt about the intention of the Naga leadership—they were not interested in playing the white-man's game. In August 1946, Jawaharlal Nehru as Congress president wrote to NNC leader Theyieu Sakhrie, advocating the integration of Naga Hills with India. Nehru wrote:

> It is obvious that the Naga territory in Eastern Assam is much too small to stand by itself politically or economically. It lies between two huge countries, India and China. Inevitably therefore the Nagas must form a part of India and of Assam with which it has developed such close associations.[5]

Nehru made two mistakes: he tried to dictate what was 'inevitable' for the Nagas and he gave them no real choice by asking them to be a part of Assam. Given the unique historical position of the Nagas, it would have been wise for Nehru to offer them an autonomous unit within India, perhaps a Union Territory. Erstwhile princely states of Manipur and Tripura opposed being joined to Assam because they were proud of their distinct past. So if they could get Union Territory status, why not the Naga Hills because the Nagas were never part of Assam. Even the creation of a Naga Autonomous Region within Assam, with India as the guardian power, might have worked. An effective structure of grassroots autonomy and a power-sharing arrangement might have satisfied both the Naga chiefs and the middle class that formed the core of the NNC leadership.

But Nehru's insistence that the Nagas should form a part of India—and Assam—cost India one real opportunity to befriend the NNC and the Naga chiefs at the same time.

The NNC was divided on many issues pertaining to future of the Naga Hills—some in it wanted complete independence, some preferred British guardianship and some were inclined to accept autonomy within Assam. On one point there was no division of opinion—that Nagas were never part of India and therefore should be allowed to decide democratically on their future without any Indian pressure. In May 1947, when the Indian Advisory Committee on the Aboriginal Tribes visited Kohima, the NNC put forward a proposal that provided for (a) a 10-year interim government for the Naga people, having full powers in respect to legislation, executive and judiciary; (b) full power for collection of revenue and expenditure; (c) an annual subvention by the guardian power to cover the revenue gap and (d) a force maintained by the guardian power for defence and to aid the civil power.

Negotiations between the Advisory Committee and the NNC broke down over the question of autonomy and the relationship the Nagas would have with the guardian power. The committee refused to make any recommendation to the Constituent Assembly on the 10-year guardianship proposal. The NNC refused to accept the Indian constitution because it already had its own. The Assam Governor Akbar Hydari's subsequent agreement with the NNC brought back the Nagas to the path of reconciliation. The NNC was recognized as the sole representative of the Nagas, even though its popularity had never been tested through a democratic process.

Later, ambiguity in parts of the agreement led both India and the NNC to interpret it in ways that suited their own standpoints. Though the NNC had accepted the Hydari agreement by a majority vote, the dispute over Article Nine of the agreement completely marginalized its moderate elements. The hardliners led by Angami Zapu

Phizo took over the organization, declared independence a day before India became free and set the Nagas on a path of conflict with India. Nehru, during his meeting with NNC General Secretary Aliba Imti, made one last attempt to save the situation by promising autonomy to the Naga Hills under the Sixth Schedule, but it was too late. Imti had been marginalized within the NNC by Phizo and was in no position to accept the offer. The Indian leadership had underestimated the NNC's popularity and the Naga's desire for self-determination. And though Nehru remained conscious of the need to extend fuller autonomy to the Nagas, events overtook him.

The 1952 parliamentary elections produced a negligible turnout in the Naga Hills, while the plebiscite organized by the NNC produced a near-total response in support of self-determination. During his visit to the Naga Hills in 1953 with Burmese Prime Minister U Nu, Nehru felt slighted by the poor turnout at the rally he addressed in Kohima. As the NNC opted for armed struggle, Nehru authorized security operations that started the long road to conflict. The NNC created an armed wing, the Naga Army, and a parallel Federal Government of Nagaland. The first recruits to the Naga Army fought the Indian troops with locally-made weapons or those left over by the Japanese and the Allies during the 1944–45 Kohima campaign. While they engaged in guerrilla operations, the Naga Army also fought from well-defended positions in an attempt to hold on to their base areas.

The Indian army initially assisted the para-military Assam Rifles in breaking up rebel concentrations but later it took charge of the operations as the rebellion spread. The 181 brigade was the first army unit to fight the Naga rebels but eventually three other infantry brigades—201, 301, 192—joined them, all ultimately reorganized into the 23rd Infantry division under a Major General. Later, this division was re-raised as the 8th Mountain Division and at the peak of its strength in the Nagaland–Manipur theatre, had 36 battalions under it. Slowly, the Indian army succeeded in storming the big Naga rebel concentrations one after another—first at Khekiye, then at Kyutsukilong and the biggest one at Khulvi on the Kohima–Mokukchung highway defended by the legendary Naga Army commander Kaito Sema. But even as they were being driven on the defensive, the Nagas managed to get the support from Pakistan. Phizo reached East Pakistan in 1956 and soon after left for London to internationalize the Naga issue with Pakistani help. Batches of Naga guerrillas, numbering 200–300 each, started leaving for East Pakistan to seek weapons and training. Within five years, the Naga Army had grown into a force of nearly 5,000 trained guerrillas, backed by a less equipped support force of close to 15,000 militiamen.

But even under such circumstances, Nehru did not allow the army a free run. The commanders were asked not to use force indiscriminately because Nehru saw the Nagas as his own countrymen, not as foreign enemies, who had to be won over, not destroyed. Nehru repeatedly turned down the army's requests for offensive air support and only allowed the air force for transport, supply and reconnaissance, essentially to scare and not to strike. In retrospect, Nehru's insistence on avoiding an overkill—the bane of US counter-insurgency action from Vietnam to Iraq—was politically sound. By treating the Nagas as citizens and not as enemies, Nehru managed to check the levels of alienation amongst the Nagas, always keeping open the doors for a possible settlement. Ruthless use of force—as by the Pakistani army in its eastern wing in 1971—often creates successful conditions for secession and the Indian state has always been aware of that, in Nagaland and elsewhere.

The Naga insurgency has been through five distinct phases: (a) the 1957–64 phase, when the Pakistan-trained rebels intensified the guerrilla war in the Naga Hills; (b) the 1964–71 phase when the movement peaked in military intensity but also split along tribal lines at least twice and lost East Pakistan as a base area after the creation of Bangladesh in 1971; (c) the 1971–75 phase, when the movement weakened and was compelled to sign the Shillong Accord in 1975 that could justifiably be called as abject surrender; (d) the 1975–87 phase, during which the NNC split and the breakaway National Socialist Council of Nagaland (NSCN) emerged to give the Naga rebel movement a fresh lease on life and (e) the post-1987 phase, when the NSCN also split along tribal lines and both factions ultimately started negotiations with India.

Throughout the 1960s, the conflict in the Naga Hills went through its ups and downs. As the movement intensified, Delhi backed up its military effort with a political move that began with the signing of the Sixteen-Point Agreement with the moderate Naga leadership in 1960 and culminated with the creation of the separate state of Nagaland three years later. After handing the Indian army a humiliating defeat in 1962, the Chinese started helping the Naga rebels. The first group of Naga guerrillas went to China in 1966 and several others followed. Though bolstered by help from China and Pakistan, the Naga movement was considerably weakened from within. In 1968, the Sema leaders broke away to form the Revolutionary Government of Nagaland (RGN), which started cooperating with Indian security forces.

The Indian counter-insurgency strategy attempted to (a) block the exit–entry routes for the Pakistan and China-bound guerrilla columns; (b) deny base areas for those guerrilla squads active within the Naga Hills; (c) negotiate with tribal elders and chiefs to secure the surrender of guerillas belonging to particular tribes; (d) encourage fragmentation by exploiting tribal divisions within the NNC and (e) strengthen the electoral system and provide huge development funds to Nagaland. The defeat of the Pakistani forces and the creation of Bangladesh dealt a severe blow to the Naga rebel movement. An immediate base area for training, regrouping and arming was gone in one stroke. Though groups of Naga rebels kept going to China until 1976, the sheer length of the trek, the increased vigil on the route by the Indian and Burmese armies and the help given to the security forces by the RGN rebels made it more and more difficult for the Naga Army to use foreign bases for training and weapons.

The Naga guerrillas who returned from China, however, gave the Indian army a torrid time. The army lost nearly 30 soldiers in a ten-day operation trying to track down a large group of these guerrillas around the Jotsoma knoll not far from state capital Kohima. The rebels also started attacking railways by setting off explosions in stations on the Assam–Nagaland border. As the guerrilla campaign intensified with the return of the first batch of China-trained Nagas, the Indian army started using the RGN and the civil administration and concentrated on winning over the tribal chiefs, who could then be used to bring about the surrender of guerrilla captains by a systematic exploitation of clan loyalties. In his memoirs, a former Nagaland administrator, S.C. Dev, gives a detailed account of this strategy and the manner in which it unfolded.[6]

In retrospect, it seems that if the Indians had made a mistake by failing to offer a settlement to the Nagas in the early 1950s, the NNC leadership made an equally serious mistake by failing to reach an agreement with Prime Minister Indira Gandhi. The NNC had forced

Delhi into a tight corner through a fierce guerrilla war, it had obtained the backing of two of India's major enemies (China and Pakistan), it had blazed a path of rebellion, which other ethnic militias were beginning to follow in northeast India. It enjoyed an exceptionally favourable bargaining clout that no insurgent organization had ever enjoyed or perhaps will ever enjoy in India. A climbdown from the demand of sovereignty and a commitment to remain within the Indian Union would have assured Nagaland something of a Bhutan-style protectorate status.[7] But the moment Indira Gandhi sensed the growing schism within the Naga movement, she went ahead with an effective divide-and-rule initiative that split the NNC down the middle. She then followed it up with a massive counter-insurgency operation sustained up until the Bangladesh operations in 1971. That forced the NNC to a corner and set the stage for the Shillong Accord of 1975.

The Shillong Accord signed by the NNC leaders (it is not clear whether Phizo had consented to it) with the government was an apology of a settlement. It merely reiterated the will of the two sides to achieve a final solution to the Naga problem. The NNC got no political dividend from the Accord. Instead, it split again and was eventually overshadowed by the breakaway NSCN that was formed by the China-returned Muivah and Issac Swu. The NSCN revived the armed movement with its initial support base limited to Manipur's hill regions and fringe areas of Nagaland, like Tuensang and Mon. The Konyaks of the Mon–Tuensang area, the Tangkhuls of Manipur and the Hemi Nagas of Burma largely made up the NSCN ranks.

Within a decade, the NSCN had achieved a position of primacy among the rebel groups in the North East. Officials in Delhi started describing the NSCN as the 'mother of all insurgencies' in the region. At its peak, the NSCN commanded a force of 1,500–2,000 guerrillas with a backup force of thousands of Naga Lim Guards, mostly concentrated in the Naga areas of Manipur to fight the Kuki militias. Most of the NSCN's top leaders, including Muivah, were from Manipur's Naga areas and it is not difficult to see why the proposed integration of Naga territories rather than sovereignty for the Nagas finds such an important place in the NSCN's agenda.

Muivah's success in propping up the NSCN to a position of primacy in the insurgency theatre of northeast India owes much to his strategy of creating 'satellites'—smaller insurgent groups of other tribes and ethnicities in neighbouring states who were trained, armed and equipped by the NSCN in return for safe bases, routes to reach key foreign destinations and support in operations against Indian security forces. By developing such 'satellites' in Tripura, Assam, Mizoram, Manipur and Arunachal Pradesh, the NSCN managed to broaden the scope of its operations and the support base for its activities, extending its reach well beyond the areas inhabited by the Nagas. The notion that the NSCN is the 'mother of all insurgents' in the North East goes a long way to prove that Muivah succeeded in what he set out to do: marginalize the NNC completely and emerge as the role model for other 'revolutionary groups' in the region, thus giving the NSCN a bargaining clout much greater than its actual capabilities. Che Guevara's strategy of igniting more prairie fires than the enemy can extinguish has paid dividends to Muivah.

But the 1988 split within the NSCN, again along tribal lines, pitted Muivah and Swu against their one-time comrade, the Burmese Hemi Naga leader S.S. Khaplang. The NSCN (Issac-Muivah) was denied the base area in Burma's Sagaing Division and with direct Chinese and Pakistani support not forthcoming anymore, Muivah's options were becoming limited. The fratricidal feud with Khaplang cost both factions dearly. After a series of setbacks in 1994–95 (the arrest of several of its senior leaders in and around the town of Dimapur, a mysterious explosion that sank one of the NSCN's weapons-carrying ship near the Gulf of Martaban and the interception by the Indian army of a huge rebel column bringing in weapons from the coast of Bangladesh), the NSCN decided to open negotiations with India.

At the moment, both the NSCN factions observe a ceasefire with Indian forces but fought freely amongst themselves. Negotiations have been conducted in foreign capitals like Bangkok and Amsterdam; the NSCN has pushed India to appoint a senior politician—Oscar Fernandes—to deal with them, replacing the retired Union Home Secretary K. Padmanabiah. The NSCN leaders have made it clear that there can be 'no compromise on the question of integration of Naga-inhabited areas'.[8] For Muivah, who is himself part of an ethnic group (the Tangkhul Nagas) who are often treated as Nagas in Manipur and as Manipuris in Nagaland, it is impossible to rise above the 'Corsican syndrome'. Without a Greater Naga state that includes his native Ukhrul district, Muivah is left without an effective locus standi in Naga politics. But for this contentious territorial element that the

NSCN insists on for a durable settlement to happen, there has been much progress in the negotiations and both sides have worked on developing the concept of a 'special federal relationship' as a bedrock of a final settlement. That means the NSCN is prepared to drop the sovereignty demand in the interest of durable peace while India is prepared to work on a novel constitutional arrangement that could later be used to placate and pacify other similar movements.

Naga politicians like former Chief Minister S.C. Jamir have been calling for a comprehensive dialogue involving all Naga rebel factions. The emerging Naga civil society—the Naga Mothers Association, the Naga Peoples Movement for Human Rights, the Naga Hoho, the Naga Students Federation—also call for a comprehensive dialogue that would involve all Naga rebel factions. They argue with much justification that a settlement with one rebel faction may not be acceptable to other factions and would defeat the cause of peace, which is what the civil society is keen to achieve. They also want a collective bargaining position for the Nagas to get the best possible deal from Delhi and that can only be achieved by 'a unity of positions' amongst the Nagas. So the March 2009 reconciliation meetings in Nagaland not only aimed at achieving a ceasefire between the two warring NSCN factions to stop the fratricidal bloodletting, but it took the first steps to work out a 'collective bargaining position' for the 'Indo-Naga political talks'.

It remains problematic for India to negotiate with Khaplang. Indian forces can observe a ceasefire with the Khaplang group but to open formal negotiations with the Burmese Naga leader will not be easy to explain. The trappings of the nation-state and the way it defines its citizens sit heavy even on insurgents who challenge it. After the NSCN split and the hostilities between the Muivah and Khaplang factions escalated, the NSCN's main faction led by the Indian Naga leaders have quietly stopped talking about 'Eastern Nagaland' (that is, Burmese Naga areas) as part of the Greater Naga state they are fighting for.

As their negotiations with India enters a new decade, Muivah and Swu's priorities are clearly changing. Now in their seventies, the two great veterans of the long marches to China are aware that the generation that fought so fiercely for Naga independence is fading away. The next generation is more inclined to accept the reality of India and profit from it. Thousands of Nagas turned out in Dimapur for the funeral ceremony of a Naga officer of the Indian army who had died fighting the Pakistani intruders in Kargil—an honour previously reserved only for the fallen heroes of the Naga Army. The Nagas value their freedom but they are clearly suffering from the 'conflict fatigue' and are desperate for peace. Since the negotiations with the NSCN started, the influence of the civil society has grown in Nagaland. Groups representing human rights, gender concerns and the aspirations of youths and students are beginning to play a bigger role in the shaping of the Nagas' future. They have ensured that the talks stay on course, despite the huge delays and large-scale frustration in the rebel ranks.

The idyllic vision of a Greater Nagaland is also fading. Eastern Nagaland is no longer a priority for Indian Nagas because the need for a foreign base area in Burma, in view of the ceasefire with Indian forces, is no longer a priority. Working with the civil society and keeping the channels of communication open with all major Indian parties, human rights groups and the media have become more important in Muivah's new battle strategy. Indeed, the Naga guerrilla veterans sense a great opportunity in Delhi's need for a new 'subcontractor' in the North East. Muivah and his lieutenants have actually displayed some skill at Indian-style manipulative politics that characterize the country's ballot-box democracy. In two state assembly elections (2003 and 2008), they supported the opposition Democratic Alliance of Nagaland (DAN)—a coalition of Naga regional parties and the Bharatiya Janata Party (BJP)—and worked to ensure their victory. NSCN guerillas visited villages, asking Nagas to vote for the DAN coalition or face the consequence. Other militant groups in the North East have done this before (the ULFA in Assam and the TNV and the NLFT in Tripura) but the combined use of terror and persuasion by the NSCN first brought down the Congress government in 2003 and foiled its bid to regain power five years later. The NSCN later faced accusations of engineering the defections that brought down the Congress government in Arunachal Pradesh as well, again much to the glee of the BJP.

After more than a decade of negotiations, the NSCN has got used to working within the Indian system, though they may not admit it. So long as the Indian state looks the other way to NSCN's tax collections, recruitments and 'area domination' tactics and does not make much of its ceasefire violations, Muivah and Swu will keep the talks going. India's longest running ethnic insurrection has no problem in pursuing what is also the country's longest running state-insurgent political dialogue because of a convergence of interests. Changing regional realities in South Asia and the 'conflict fatigue' of the Nagas, the weakening of the insurgent movement due to fratricidal strife, the growing global outcry against terrorism and armed action by non-state actors—all this makes it difficult for Muivah and Swu to revive the guerrilla war against India, settlement or no settlement. And for India, it is a priority to ensure the Naga guerrillas, the toughest in the region, do not renew their armed campaign against India. Durable peace is desirable but not if it means fresh trouble in the neighbourhood. So long as a settlement is not reached with the NSCN, India will be happy to keep them confined to their barracks—or fighting each other.

THE PRAIRIE FIRES SPREAD

After the Naga insurrection in the 1950s, the North East witnessed three distinct phases of insurgency: (a) the late 1960s, when insurgency erupted in the Mizo Hills and spread to Manipur and Tripura; (b) the late 1970s, when it intensified in Manipur, Assam and Tripura along with Mizoram and Nagaland and (c) the late 1980s, when a number of insurgent groups surfaced among the smaller ethnic groups like the Bodos, the Hmars, the Dimasas, the Karbis, the Khasis and the Garos. At the moment, the territorial spread of the insurgent movement had peaked because every state in the region was affected by some insurgent activity or the other. Since the NSCN is at the negotiating table and the United Liberation Front of Assam (ULFA) is no longer near its peak strength, the intensity of the insurgencies is much less than it was the case a decade ago. The existence of a greater number of insurgent groups, however, means greater complexity for peace-makers because settlement with one could well provoke another to more violence.[9]

Unlike the Naga insurgent movement, which was built up slowly over several years in the 1950s, the uprising in the Mizo Hills has a definite birth date. A devastating rat famine—*Mautam*—ignited passions in the Mizo Hills in the mid 1960s. The people's anger was directed at both the Assam government and the leadership of the

Mizo District Council. The Mizo National Famine Front (MNFF), formed by some former Mizo soldiers of the Indian and the Burmese armies, became active, but after the immediate need for relief was addressed, the MNFF dropped the 'Famine' and became a political party: the Mizo National Front (MNF). While it contested elections for the Assam assembly, its leadership quietly prepared for rebellion. At midnight on 28 February 1966, the MNF unleashed 'Operation Jericho'—a blitzkrieg operation that led to the capture of as many as 11 towns in the Mizo Hills by the rebels. Only one Assam Rifles unit held on to its defence perimeter in the capital Aizawl, supplied sporadically from the air.

The Indian army had to organize one of the most comprehensive counter-insurgency operations it has ever undertaken to take back the towns and semi-urban townships in the Mizo Hills—an operation that took more than a month and saw some bitter fighting. As the army regained control of the towns, the MNF guerrillas moved into the hills and the countryside, keeping up a barrage of attacks against the mobile army columns. To deny the guerrillas popular support and a secure line of supply, the army initiated a village regrouping programme that hit at the heart of the Mizo village economy. The MNF pulled back most of its better-armed guerrilla units into the hills, the leadership escaped into pre-selected locations in East Pakistan and only small strike squads composed of highly motivated fighters were left behind in the towns to take out selected targets, such as moderate Mizo politicians, senior police or military officials or those serving the federal government. In one such strike in 1975, the MNF killed three senior police officials inside the police headquarters in Aizawl: an inspector-general, his deputy and a superintendent of the special branch.

Between 1967 and 1969, the army undertook a very comprehensive groupings of villages in the Mizo Hills. The relocation of the population out of their traditional villages into sites (euphemistically called 'Progressive and Protected Villages') along the national highway that the army could control was seen as essential to isolate the MNF from the Mizo people. One of North East's leading bureaucrat-scholars writes that at least 80 per cent of the population of the Mizo Hills was affected by the regrouping programme: 'The general humiliation, loss of freedom and property and, very often, the injury and death involved in the so-called grouping of villages ... was tantamount to annihilation of reason and sensibility and certainly not the best policy to follow against our own ethnic minorities.'[10]

As in the Naga Hills, military repression only added to resentment and the swelling of the guerilla ranks in the Mizo Hills. Burnt-out villages, roughed-up families and angry chiefs sent more and more able-bodied males to join the MNF in their bases in the Chittagong Hill Tracts of East Pakistan. By the end of the decade, Mizo guerrillas also started reaching China for training and weapons. Like in Nagaland, so in the Mizo Hills, the Indian army deployed a full division to fight the insurgents. The 57th Mountain Division was responsible for the Mizo Hills, as the 8th Mountain Division was for the Naga Hills. Later, when the situation had improved in both Mizoram and Nagaland, units of both these divisions were used for counter-insurgency purposes in neighbouring states or in Kashmir, where the prairie fires were spreading.

The creation of Bangladesh affected the MNF more than the NNC. Its immediate trans-border bases used for regular exit and entry by strike groups were neutralized by the Indian army during its push into East Pakistan. By the time these bases could be revived in the late 1970s, after a military coup in independent Bangladesh, the MNF had a rival in the Chittagong Hill Tracts. The Chakma insurgents of the Shanti Bahini, backed by India, were all too keen to hound the MNF to avenge the ill-treatment the Mizos meted out to the Chakmas in Mizoram.

The Mizo insurgency has traversed three distinct phases: (a) outbreak and peak intensity in 1966–71; (b) decline in intensity, splits in the MNF and the Calcutta accord in 1976 and (c) sporadic action and occasional negotiations after 1977 leading to the final settlement in 1986. By the late 1970s, the MNF's resolve to fight India had weakened, with scores of surrenders to Mizoram's chief minister, Thengpunga Sailo, a former Indian army officer. I have argued elsewhere that the Mizo insurgency would have ended in the late 1970s if (a) the new military regime of Bangladesh had not allowed the MNF to reactivate their lost bases in the Chittagong Hill Tracts; (b) if the Janata government headed by Prime Minister Morarji Desai had not treated MNF supreme Laldenga shabbily and (c) if Chief Minister Sailo had not opposed a settlement involving an interim administration that would accommodate the MNF in a power-sharing deal even before it had won an election.[11]

Negotiations with the MNF broke off in January 1982 but were resumed once Sailo's Peoples Conference lost the elections in Mizoram. The new chief minister, Lalthanhawla, was elected on a promise that he will step down from office in the interest of peace. And Lalthanhawla did not let his people down. Indira Gandhi's assassination delayed the process but her son Rajiv Gandhi carried the negotiations to a successful conclusion by giving Mizoram full statehood and by accommodating the MNF in an interim power-sharing arrangement with his own party. Of the many accords that Rajiv Gandhi signed, the Mizo accord signed in June 1986 has been the most durable. Peace in Mizoram has been held, the MNF has ruled the state for two full and one part tenure and no breakaway group has emerged to return to the jungles again. The present disturbances in Mizoram are caused by insurgent groups that represent smaller tribes, like the Hmars and the Brus demanding autonomy. Even these smaller tribal militias have now reached agreements with the state government.

The Mizo accord has worked because Delhi came to a settlement with the entire Mizo insurgent leadership, not with a splinter group. The MNF did split later, but those who left the party were mostly former student and youth leaders who had joined it only after it came overground. Even after Laldenga's death, the veterans of the two-decade-long guerrilla war have held together under the leadership of the triumvirate formed by Zoramthanga, Tawnluia and Rualchhina. There is a morale in Mizoram's story for Delhi to ponder: whereas divisions within an insurgent organization are desirable when the aim is to fight and annihilate it, for the purposes of a durable settlement the same divisions can become a problem. Parallel power centres in the underground not only complicate the process of negotiation—which group should be given how much weightage, what issues should be discussed with whom and when—but also interfere with the very modalities of the dialogue. To demonstrate their own clout, insurgent leaders may become involved in competitive radicalism—if one Naga rebel leader settles for more autonomy, another will demand a Greater Nagaland as the condition for a settlement and yet another may decide to remain in the jungles to fight for independence. Delhi was spared such a scenario in Mizoram because the entire movement stood behind Laldenga in accepting the final settlement.

The insurgencies in Manipur, Tripura and Assam, which represent communities thought to have been absorbed within the Sanskritic cultural ambit, pose a different kind of challenge for Delhi. Unlike the insurgencies in Nagaland or Mizoram, where tribesmen had little exposure to Indian politics or culture before or during the British rule, unrest in Manipur, Tripura and Assam was not born out of inherent separatist tendencies. Rather, it was engendered by acute frustration among the region's youth caused by a stifling lack of the opportunities that were made available to the hill states like Nagaland, Mizoram or Arunachal Pradesh, and by an abysmal failure of governance. Economic backwardness in these three states, which had been exposed to leftist ideology, soon came to be seen as an outcome of 'semi-feudal, semi-colonial exploitation' by the Indian state.

THE PRINCELY STATES

In Tripura, the undivided Communist Party provided leadership to the armed struggle of the tribespeople, who were upset with the uncertainties brought about by the end of princely rule. But the Communist Party gave up the 'Ranadive line' of armed struggle in 1950 and joined India's electoral democracy. The change in Tripura's demographic character provoked a group of young tribesmen to form a succession of insurgent groups that promised to throw out the Bengali settlers and liberate Tripura from an administration dominated by them. The Sengkrak (literally meaning 'clenched fist') grew in the late 1960s to protest against the rampant and systematic alienation of tribal lands encouraged by Tripura's Bengali-dominated Congress government and its lesser functionaries. It was annihilated by the mid 1970s after it lost its trans-border bases in East Pakistan following the liberation of Bangladesh.

The Tribal National Volunteers (TNV) emerged in 1978, sustained by the politics of tribalism promoted by the Tripura Upajati Juba Samity (TUJS). It relied on the extreme fringe of the TUJS to recruit its guerrilla cadres, again sustained by a hatred for the Bengali settler. It returned to normal life in 1988, following an accord with the federal government. Within four years, however, the state had seen the birth of two guerrilla organizations: the All-Tripura Tiger Force (ATTF) and the National Liberation Force of Tripura (NLFT).

Both are sustained by their zeal to drive out Bengali settlers, who are seen as responsible for the physical, cultural, political and economic marginalization of the indigenous tribesmen. With the exception of the ATTF, which has drawn many of its guerillas from the communist mass fronts and which uses leftist polemics in its articulation, the other insurgent groups were fiercely anti-communist. They blamed the Communist Party and its successor, the CPI(M), for failing to stop the continuous influx of Bengalis and ensuring a better deal for the tribals.

The TNV and now the NLFT have strong evangelist overtones. They regard the acceptance of Christianity by the tribesmen as the one and only way to break away from the dominant Hindu-Bengali culture, which they blame for the sorry plight of the tribespeople. Their leaders urge their followers to look elsewhere in the North East and they point to the dominance of tribesmen in all walks of life in the Christian-dominated states. Christianity, for these rebel groups, is the source of a secure and self-confident identity to the tribespeople, unencumbered by a culture that is identified with the majority Bengali-Hindu residents of Tripura.

While the ATTF has wisely stayed away from the religious debate and identified itself with the 'colonial thesis' of the ULFA and the Manipur Peoples Liberation Front (MPLF), the NLFT has faced a major split by over-emphasizing its agenda of evangelization. A faction led by Nayanbashi Jamatia broke away from the NLFT after the rebel leadership ordered the execution of the Jamatia spiritual guru, Hada Okrah Bikram Bahadur Jamatia. Bikram Bahadur escaped two assassination attempts but another tribal guru, Shanti Kali, was killed. This provoked the tribes that value traditional religious practices.

While the Sengkrak and later the TNV attacked Bengali settlers and security forces in a bid to protect tribal settlements or push out the settlers from tribal-compact areas, the ATTF and the NLFT have adopted a different strategy. They resorted to large-scale kidnappings, mostly targeting Bengali settlers. Between 1995 and 2005, nearly 3,500 abductions were reported to the police. Many went unreported because the families paid up silently in order to secure the release of the victim. Many of those kidnapped failed to return even after their families paid a ransom. So widespread was the problem that the state government had to initiate a move to change the succession laws because many families were not in a position to run their businesses after the head of the family had been abducted. Since the head would normally be the superintending authority of the business and since he could not be declared dead until the body was recovered, banks and financial institutions would not accept the legal authority of the successors. With the change in the laws, a person gone missing for a long period of time is treated as dead in the eyes of law and succession takes effect.

The campaign of kidnappings had a double effect: it spread the message of terror among the Bengali settlers, forcing hundreds to vacate locations in remote areas and head for safer locations, and it earned huge amounts of liquid cash for the coffers of the rebel groups, enabling them to buy weapons and communication equipment and even pay their fighters a monthly allowance. Abduction as an insurgent strategy is not unique to Tripura. Insurgents in Assam, Manipur and Nagaland, now even in Meghalaya, have adopted this tactic to extort funds from the business community and the upper middle class. Insurgent groups in other North Eastern states have resorted to abductions only when repeated 'tax notices' failed to force the targets to pay. For the insurgents in Tripura, on the other hand, kidnappings for ransom were undertaken without notice. In some cases, the insurgents have gone to the inhuman extent of demanding payment for the dead bodies of victims who died in their captivity.

The ATTF is militarily weaker than the NLFT but is the more cohesive and focused of the two. It also enjoys close links with the ULFA and the Manipuri rebels, while the NLFT has close links with the NSCN and the National Democratic Front of Bodoland (NDFB), which is fighting for an independent Bodo homeland. This represents a growing ethno-ideological divide in the separatist politics of northeast India. Groups with leftist tendencies or origins like the ULFA, the Manipur groups or the ATTF have come together, while organizations more narrowly focused on ethnic concerns and united by their faith in Christianity (like the NSCN [slogan: 'Nagaland for Christ'], the NLFT [slogan: 'a Christian Tripura'] and the NDFB) find themselves on the same side of the fence.

Tripura's Left government managed to contain the tribal insurgency after 2003 through a combination of determined police action, covert trans-border raids and relentless political offensive to effect splits and bring about surrenders from the rebel ranks. In one year after G.M. Srivastava had taken over as the state's police chief and pushed the Tripura States Rifles into a comprehensive 'area domination' by making them live off the land in the hilly interiors, the militancy-related incidents fell dramatically—from 380 in 2003 (average more than one a day) to 210 in 2004. Only 30 civilian fatalities were reported in 2005 and just 14 in 2006. Nearly 600 rebels surrendered in the 2003–04 phase, weakening the ATTF and the NLFT, the latter more than the former, considerably. A dramatic decline in kidnappings—from 445 in 2000 to 311 in 2003 to 115 in 2005 to a further 73 in 2006—also testifies to the much weakened tribal guerrilla movement. Both the state police and the military intelligence used 'Trojan horse' techniques to attack rebel bases and leaders across the border in Bangladesh—they encouraged recalcitrant guerrillas to surrender only after they have carried out these attacks. The growing criminality of the rebel groups added to their unpopularity in tribal areas—especially the NLFT's widespread abuse of women in tribal areas including those recruited by the rebel group.

The decline in the rebel activity helped the ruling Left Front regain the Tripura Tribal Areas Autonomous District Council in 2005, after having lost it five years ago to the NLFT-backed Indigenous Nationalist Party of Tripura (INPT). The Left Front has also won all state elections since 1993—after 2003, their performance in the tribal areas has also improved considerably. At the moment, the Left Front's political position in Tripura is considered best among the three states it rules—West Bengal and Kerala being the other two.

In Tripura, the communist movement, despite beginning with armed struggle, focused on tribal concerns but never became separatist in form or content. In Manipur, the icon of the communist movement, Hijam Irabot Singh, displayed clear separatist tendencies in his ideological orientation. He opposed Manipur's merger with India and proposed a Purbanchal state that was to include Manipur, Tripura, Cachar and the Mizo Hills. He abandoned the Indian communist movement for its failure to address the 'national question' in peripheral areas like Manipur, advocating instead that 'Manipur should be a republic with a responsible form of government with headquarters at Nongda'.[12] He demanded the restoration of the

Kabaw Valley to Manipur and even sought the help of the Burmese Communist Party for 'the revolution in Manipur'. Irabot's dreams remained unfulfilled due to his long years in prison but his leftist ideology favouring Manipuri separatism continued to inspire a whole generation of freedom-loving Meiteis.

In 1964, the state's first overtly separatist group, the United National Liberation Front (UNLF), was formed, but it soon split on the question of revolution. The UNLF advocated a programme of social reform, but a faction within it advocated outright revolution. It called itself the Revolutionary Government of Manipur (RGM) and sent its members to East Pakistan for training. Though Pakistan had welcomed Naga and Mizo rebels and provided them with sanctuary, training and weapons, it refused to help the Manipuri rebels. They were all arrested and released near the Indian border, only to be arrested by the police in Tripura. The RGM was again split. Its leader, Sudhir Kumar, believed in Meitei revivalism but he was challenged by a leftist group, led by Nameirakpam Bisheswar Singh, that believed in a Marxist-Leninist revolution. Sudhir was shot dead by his rivals and endemic factionalism put on hold the formation of a strong Manipuri separatist group until Bisheswar and his comrades established the Peoples Liberation Army (PLA) on 25 July 1978.

The PLA expressed unreserved faith in Marxism-Leninism and in Mao Zedong's Thought. It supported 'class war', abolition of private property after the revolution, and cooperation with the Indian proletariat. It opposed sectarian politics based on ethnic or religious appeal and stated that it wanted to 'bring down the bandit government of Delhi'. The PLA leadership identified China as the 'fountainhead of international proletarian revolution' and even credited Beijing with preserving Nepal's sovereignty from Indian expansionist designs. It further accused Nehru for 'attempting to take over Tibet to create an all-India empire'.[13] Another similar insurgent group that surfaced around the same time was the Peoples Revolutionary Party of Kangleipak (the ancient name of Manipur) which was better known by its acronym, PREPAK. It was more pronounced in its separatist designs when it declared to fight for Manipur's independence and it warned it would suppress 'all counter-revolutionaries, Mayangs [outsiders], neo-colonialist stooges [read Indian security forces] and class enemies' and establish a classless society in Manipur.[14]

The PLA leaders—the *Ojha*s (pioneers or torch-bearers)—were trained entirely in China in three batches. Upon their return they set up cells, built up an arsenal of stolen weapons (unlike the liberal supply secured by the Nagas and Mizos) and went about recruiting. By then, the PREPAK had also readied itself and the UNLF had reorganized itself under Raj Kumar Meghen (party name: Sanaiyama). By mid 1979, the three groups unleashed a fierce spell of urban and semi-urban guerrilla warfare in the Imphal Valley. Special laws were soon extended to Manipur and the army was deployed in some strength to combat the Meitei insurgents. Smaller groups, like the Kangleipak Communist Party (KCP), also added to the tumult in the Imphal Valley.

Indian intelligence managed to infiltrate the Meitei groups by the end of 1981. Almost the entire China-trained leadership of the PLA was captured or killed in just two encounters. In the first confrontation at Thekcham in August 1981, the PLA's chairman, Nameirakpam Bisheswar Singh, was arrested. In the second one at Kadamkopki in April 1982, Bisheswar's successor, Kunjabehari Singh alias Raghu, was killed. After the arrest of the PREPAK's charismatic supremo, R.K. Tulachandra, that organization split up into two factions, one led by Leima Chamu and the other by Maipak Sharma. Despite these setbacks, the PLA regrouped and hit back at the security apparatus with regularity. The UNLF also stepped up its operations, despite a split that led to the breakaway Oken faction siding with the NSCN.

Unlike most other insurgent groups in northeast India, the Meitei rebels have a well-defined social programme. While some elements of the once-disciplined NSCN have been found trafficking in heroin, both the PLA and the UNLF have played the social watchdog with unfailing zeal, shooting drug traffickers, imposing a ban on liquor, 'culturally obscene' Hindi films and even tobacco. A new rebel group, the Kanglei Yawol Kanna Lup (KYKL), has even attacked students who cheat in exams and teachers who help them. They cannot give up their assumed responsibility of 'cleaning up the society in which the revolution has to take place'—a leftist moral hangover not found in most other ethnicity-oriented rebel groups in the North East.

Meitei insurgency has experienced four distinct phases: (a) the early beginnings, with the formation of the UNLF, the Meitei State Committee and the RGM, which petered out by the end of 1970;

(b) the birth of the PLA in 1978, with Chinese help in the beginning, heavy violence throughout the Imphal Valley before the severe setbacks in the major Meitei insurgent groups; (c) the regrouping of these groups, redefinition of their political objectives and revival of insurgency in the valley between 1988 and 1998 and (d) fresh impetus to insurgency after the creation of the Manipur Peoples Liberation Front.

After major setbacks, the PLA and the UNLF both regained their bearings by the end of the 1980s. In the last decade, both have emerged stronger, with more and better-trained fighters, more weapons and a more focused political programme devoid of the ideological baggage relating to an 'Indian revolution'. Fraternal ties with Indian Maoists still exist, but are limited to expressions of support. The two groups suffered another major setback in November 2001, when the Burmese army raided their camps around the border town of Tamu and recovered some 1,600 weapons. 192 guerrillas, including several top leaders, like UNLF Chairman R.K. Meghen and PLA Commander Jibon Singh, were arrested. They were later released amidst allegations that the Burmese military authorities had received nearly $7,50,000 from the rebels. The size of the cache surprised Indian intelligence and gave definite indications that the two top Meitei separatist groups had extensive financial resources, access to weapons, enough recruits (a combined strength of around 8,000 now) and safe bases in Bangladesh, Burma and within Manipur.

Since 2003, the Manipuri rebel groups, specially the UNLF, have grown stronger and have done what even the Naga Army could not do at its peak—held on to base areas in the face of determined military offensive. In early 2003, the UNLF forces effectively thwarted repeated efforts by the Border Security Force (BSF) to overrun their main area at Sajit Tampak in Chandel district bordering Burma. Since 2006, the UNLF has managed to stymie repeated military offensives by the Indian army to overrun their base areas in Sajit Tampak and Churachandpur. The Indian army, in a clever move, signed a Suspension of Operations (SOO) with eight Kuki groups in an effort to use them against the UNLF, particularly in the Kuki-dominated Churachandpur district. The Kukis have subsequently blamed the UNLF for 'terrorizing them', even accused them of raping Kuki women. The UNLF has hit back, killing a top Kuki leader Hansing in far-off Delhi by using a former BSF soldier as a contract killer.

The Indian army's 'Operation Khengjoi', a huge counter-insurgency offensive to regain control over the UNLF base areas, has only led to limited success. The UNLF has heavily mined approaches to their key bases and the army has failed to wrest control over many of them, despite heavy casualties.

The UNLF's intelligent use of landmines, mixing of urban terror tactics with those of traditional hill guerrilla warfare, successful propaganda by clever use of media, has all paid rich dividends. The UNLF chief Sanayaima has clearly refused any negotiations with the Indian government and instead dared it to hold a referendum in Manipur on the issue of secession.[15] Heavily armed UNLF platoons, fighting between carefully mined areas, have engaged Indian troops with even mortars and machine-guns and efforts by Indian troops to rush the UNLF positions have only led to heavy casualties in the concealed minefields. Desperate Indian soldiers have forced local villagers to walk ahead of them in the mined areas, only adding to the greater resentment. The PLA's actions have been more modest—limited to ambushes of military convoys and a few bomb explosions to create terror. But the combined effect of their actions has provoked military atrocities on civilian populations, particularly during cordon-and-search operations, leading to strident demands for abolition of the Armed Forces Special Powers Act.

A Manipuri woman, Irom Sharmila, has been on fast since the beginning of the decade, saying she will only eat when the controversial Act will be revoked. She has been force-fed in prison. A huge agitation to abolish the Act erupted when a Manipuri woman Thangjam Manorama was allegedly raped and killed by the paramilitary Assam Rifles in July 2004. Elderly Manipuri women undressed in front of the Assam Rifles headquarters at Fort Kangla in state capital Imphal, with placards that said 'Indian army, come and rape us'. That shocked the whole nation and Delhi set up a committee by a former Supreme Court judge Jeevan Reddy to review the Act.

The orchestrated nature of mob violence during the agitation against the extension of the Naga ceasefire to all parts of the North East in 2001 also gave rise to suspicions that Meitei underground groups were behind it. Not one Naga was killed during the violence, but the office of every major political party in Manipur, the assembly building and the residences of several top politicians were burnt down. It was a powerful but a controlled mass agitation that was threatening to grow into a replica of Assam's anti-foreigner agitation until the Centre decided to reverse its decision to pacify the Meiteis. The atmosphere of uncertainty in Manipur and the fear that the state's Naga-inhabited areas might be given over to a greater Naga state to assuage Muivah and the NSCN stirred up Meitei passions. That has actually helped groups like the UNLF to step up recruitment in a big way.

Unless the Centre gives an unqualified assurance that Manipur's territorial boundaries are non-negotiable and keeps its word, the state is heading for considerable unrest—a situation sure to benefit the UNLF and other Meitei insurgents. 'Bringing down the bandit government at Delhi' had limited appeal for the Meiteis, whereas preventing the break-up of the state is a greater immediate concern. Delhi now faces a serious dilemma: in order to arrive at a settlement with the NSCN, it will have to concede their demand for integration of Naga areas of Manipur and other North Eastern states, but if that happens, Manipur will likely go up in flames. Groups like the UNLF would receive huge popular support and their campaign would intensify throughout the state.

In the last five years, as the situation in Tripura has considerably improved, that in Manipur has gone from bad to worse. A 2006 year-end assessment by the South Asia Intelligence Review described Manipur as the most violent state in India's North East. That year, there were 280 fatalities in Manipur—45 per cent of the total fatalities that year in the North East, whereas Manipur only accounts for just under 6 per cent of the region's population. The problem is further compounded by the inter-ethnic strife. It started with the large-scale clashes and massacres between the Naga and the Kuki rebel militias in the early 1990s. Now Meitei groups like the UNLF have been at dagger's drawn with the Kuki militias, who they allege, are working as support groups of the Indian army. The Indian army's signing of the SOO with eight of the Kuki-Zomi groups is seen as evidence of such claims. The rise in militant and state-sponsored violence is palpable in Manipur, as is the all-pervasive law-lessness that is exemplified by large-scale extortions and the frequent blockade on its major highways by rebel groups. But the Indian army says it has made steady tactical gains in the state since 2006—the year when it signed the SOO deals with the Kuki-Zomi groups and started using them as part of their counter-insurgency drive to deprive the Meitei rebels of their secure base areas. Unless the scenario changes dramatically, Manipur is heading to be India's Bosnia, an inter-ethnic killing field, as my friend and fellow journalist from Manipur, Yambem Laba, had feared.

BURNING ASSAM

Assam's experience in India has been the opposite of that of the Nagas. When India became free, Assam was the prima donna of the North East. The entire region, except the erstwhile princely states of Manipur and Tripura, was tied to the state in some form or other. I have argued before that the Assamese elite and middle class, through their involvement with the Indian nationalist movement, emerged as Delhi's most acceptable 'political sub-contractor' in the North East. As India faced one hill insurgency after another and demands for separate tribal states spread, however, Delhi alienated the Assamese by politically reorganizing the North East in 1972.[16]

It would be wrong, however, to think that this alienation was sudden and merely linked to Delhi's decision to dissect Assam. In fact, it began immediately after the Partition, when Assam was forced to accept a huge flow of refugees from East Pakistan. Assam's Congress Chief Minister Gopinath Bordoloi opposed federal government moves to settle the Bengali Hindu refugees from East Pakistan and later expressed his determination to stop illegal Bengali Muslim migration from there. Despite Bordoloi's strident opposition to settle Bengali refugees from East Pakistan, he was pressured by the Centre to accept more than 600,000 refugees by 1961. Bordoloi had pointed out that there were 1,86,000 landless Assamese peasants waiting to be settled on reclaimable lands. Patel wanted the reclaimable land to be evenly distributed between landless Assamese peasants and Bengali Hindu refugees. Nehru threatened Bordoloi with denial of federal development funds unless Assam agreed to share 'India's refugee burden'.[17] That did not go down well with the Assamese.

Though the Assamese elite had a stake in India's nation-building project in the North East, its middle class and rural masses were immensely resentful of the state's changing demography, land loss to Bengali migrants and 'colonial exploitation' by the Indian state. When India decided to build a refinery at Barauni in Bihar to process Assamese crude oil transported through a long pipeline, the state erupted in agitation. That failed to stop the pipeline but secured for Assam a small refinery later built at Guwahati (derisively described in Assam as a 'toy refinery'). An all-party Sangram Parishad coordinated the agitation and even the state Congress leadership expressed its opposition to the Barauni refinery. Chief Minister Bishnuram Medhi, when told that a large refinery in Assam would be a security risk because of the proximity of borders with China and Pakistan, argued, with much justification, that by the same yardstick, Assam's oilfields and long railway network would be at risk as well.

If one were to construct a typology of the protest movements in northeast India, Assam would stand out at the end of a continuum, with Nagaland occupying the other extreme. The Nagas resorted to insurgency as the first option of protest after negotiations with the Indian leadership had failed in the early 1950s. The Assamese middle class and the peasantry exhausted their options of non-violent protest and not-so-peaceful mass agitations before they resorted to a violent separatist insurgency. The Mizo insurgency and the ones in Tripura and Manipur would fall between Assam and Nagaland, because the insurgent movement gained momentum in those areas through years of neglect and deprivation.

The oil refinery agitation raised the issue of Assam's 'exploitation' by the Indian state. From the initial 0.1 million tonnes in 1947, Assam's annual crude output touched a peak of 5 million tonnes in the 1970s. Before the anti-foreigner agitation, Assam received only Rs 42 per tonne of crude oil as royalty. The Centre collected six times that amount in cess. Assam would get only Rs 54 as sales tax on a tonne of crude oil while the Centre collected Rs 991 on the same quantity. For plywood extracted from Assam, the state received only Rs 35–40 lakhs a year while the Centre got Rs 80 crore. Assam's sales tax collections from tea hovered around Rs 20–30 crore per year until the outbreak of the anti-foreigner agitation in 1979, whereas West Bengal made 60–70 per cent more because the head offices of the tea companies were located there.

To this feeling of economic exploitation, which some Assamese would compare to the exploitation of Pakistan's eastern half by the

more dominant western half, were added powerful linguistic sentiments and a lurking fear that the Assamese would one day be out-
numbered by migrants and become foreigners in their own land.
Assam Chief Minister Bimala Prasad Chaliha, introduced the Official
Language Bill in 1960. While the move was strongly supported by
the Asom Sahitya Sabha and other student-youth organizations, it
provoked fierce protests among the tribals and the Bengalis. Sporadic
clashes and agitations continued to rock Assam until the outbreak
of war with China. Nehru's farewell speech, leaving Assam 'to its
fate' in the face of the Chinese advance, made the Assamese feel they
were expendable during crisis.

In the late 1960s, as insurgencies spread to new areas of the North
East, Assam's Brahmaputra Valley was engulfed by a spate of agitations. The statewide food agitation in 1966 was followed by the
agitation against the proposed break-up of Assam in 1967–68. The
call for boycott of Republic Day Celebrations and observance of 'Unity
Day' in 1968, the attack on non-Assamese business communities
that year because they were regarded as the immediate exploiters of
Assam, gave the first indications that a constituency for secession was
starting to build up. In the following year, the Left and regional parties
organized an agitation in favour of a second oil refinery in Assam to
process the state's growing crude oil output. The new refinery was
set up in Bongaigaon, but the resentment refused to die down. The
fragmentation of Assam in 1972 was pushed through despite large-
scale protests throughout the Brahmaputra Valley. It was followed
by a statewide agitation led by the All Assam Students Union
(AASU) in 1974 to demand the state's rapid economic development.

In some ways, these mass agitations were a dress rehearsal for the
'mother of all agitations' that was to follow. The bye-elections to
the Mangaldoi assembly constituency in mid 1979 provided the fuse
for India's most powerful and sustained mass agitation after
independence. During a routine update of the electoral rolls, 45,000
illegal migrants were found in the voter list by a tribunal set up by
the state government. On 8 June 1979, the AASU observed the first
statewide strike to protest the infiltration issue. It was quickly followed two months later by the formation of the All Assam Gana
Sangram Parishad, which was composed of several regional parties,
youth organizations, the AASU and the Asom Sahitya Sabha. The
leaders of the agitation had one specific demand: the use of the 1951

National Register of Citizens as the baseline to determine Indian citizenship of all those living in Assam. All those identified as non-citizens would have to leave, they said.

For six years, the Assam agitation was sustained by a high level of cross-ethnic participation. Assamese and tribals throughout the state, cutting across political affiliations and age groups, took to the streets to demand the ouster of illegal migrants. 'Janata curfews', civil disobedience programmes and oil blockades paralyzed the administration across the state as slogans like 'Mare Asom, jiye kon, jiye Asom, Mara Kon, jai aai Asom' (if Assam dies, who will live, if Asom lives, none will die, long live mother Assam) and 'Jadi na hua *Asomiya*, Asom eri gusi joa' (if not an Assamese, please leave Assam and go) set the tenor of the agitation. Assamese student and youth groups coerced linguistic and religious minorities during the agitation and violent attacks on them were reported from all across Assam.

There is no denying that the agitation received unprecedented popular support that led one analyst, Mahesh Joshi, to comment: 'Assam is fighting India's battle'. Within two decades, the need to control illegal migration from Bangladesh had come to dominate India's national agenda, but in the early 1980s, Delhi was still not sensitive to the threat posed to the states on India's eastern borders by the demographic changes caused by illegal migration. Thus, the government chose to combat the popular agitation by unusually severe measures, which peaked during the 1983 assembly elections in Assam. As the agitation leaders called for a boycott of the elections until the electoral rolls were rid of foreigners, the government had to resort to heavy-handed use of police. More than 130 people died in police firings during the election month. The elections were a farce in the Brahmaputra Valley, where one Congress candidate won his seat after polling a mere 300 votes out of a total electorate of 69,000. But they were also marked by unprecedented violence against minorities. The worst massacre occurred at Nellie, a village on the highway that connects Guwahati with Nagaon, where more than 2,000 Muslims were butchered by Lalung tribesmen.

The assumption of power by the Congress in an election deprived of any legitimacy marked a break with the past. State repression and the farcical elections convinced many Assamese students and youths that they would not get justice within the Indian system and that their concerns would be rudely overlooked. As they started going underground to join the ULFA, which had been formed in April 1979, a new era in Assam's relation with India was about to begin. It would be wrong to think of the ULFA as growing out of the Assam movement, as is commonly suggested. Its formation precedes the first statewide strike called by the AASU in June 1979 on the issue of foreigners. The ULFA lay low after its formation—its leaders did not consider the time to be ripe for armed revolution because the Assamese middle class and the rural masses still retained faith in mass agitation, which had characterized their participation in the Indian national movement.

The ULFA drew many of its recruits from the AASU and the Gana Sangram Parishad, but many of its leaders and ideologues came from Left-nationalist groups like the Assam Jatiyotabadi Yuba Chatro Parishad (AJYCP). The AJYCP propagates a curious mixture of Assamese nationalist and radical Marxist views ('build communism on a nationalist base'), it shuns parliamentary politics and advocates the Assamese's right to dual citizenship and self-determination. The ULFA's emphasis on 'scientific socialism' and 'two-phase revolution' has often been taken far too seriously by Indian leftist radical groups as indicative of the group's Marxist-Leninist tilt. The ULFA advocated 'denationalization of ethnic communities' to ensure they accept the broad parameters of Assamese nationalism and it promised to implement 'scientific socialism to build Assamese society after the liberation from Indian colonial rule'. In 1992, as the ULFA sought to widen its popular base among non-Assamese ethnic groups, it articulated its concerns for the *Asombashi* (dwellers of Assam) rather than the *Asomiya*s (ethnic Assamese).

During the years of the Assam agitation, the ULFA remained a largely dormant force. During the Congress regime, it undertook bank robberies and made select assassination attempts. It came into its own in 1985, after the Assam Accord, when the newly formed Asom Gana Parishad (AGP), riding the crest of a popularity wave, swept to power. Unlike the Naga or Mizo rebels, the ULFA avoided any major confrontation with the Indian security forces. Given the flatland terrain from which it was operating, such a tactic was also not possible. The ULFA therefore used a combination of selective terror, assassination and parallel taxation to build up an organizational base. It capitalized on its close connections with the AGP leadership and ministers to undermine the administration by hounding out officials identified with the state repression of the Congress regime. The ULFA's military wing chief, Paresh Barua, later admitted that he had received Rs 30 lakh from the Chief Minister's Fund in 1986, which was used to fund the training of the second group of ULFA guerrillas in the Kachin hills of Burma.[18]

In the five years of AGP rule, the ULFA killed nearly 100 people who had been branded 'enemies of the people of Assam'. The victims were mostly Assamese, though the killings of some high-profile non-Assamese businessmen like Surrendra Paul and Haralalka, politicians like United Minorities Front leader Kalipada Sen and police officials like Dibrugarh police superintendent Daulat Sing Negi, received much more publicity. The ULFA also built up a huge war chest by systematic extortion, raising a few hundred crore rupees from tea companies and other businesses in Assam. It entrenched itself in rural Assam through the Jatiya Unnayan Parishad, a front that undertook public works in order to endear itself to the masses. Having had several batches of its guerrillas trained by the Kachin Independence Army (KIA) and later by the NSCN, the ULFA developed a force of some 1,500 fighters, all armed with weapons bought in Burma. Slowly but steadily, it built up a parallel administration like the NNC or the MNF had done.

Successive military operations in 1990–91 (Operation Bajrang and Operation Rhino) upset the ULFA and led to the first surrenders from the group in 1992. The Indian army smashed its major base areas within Assam and in neighbouring states. Many senior ULFA leaders—district commanders, those heading special units or cells like the group's highly effective publicity wing—were killed or captured. Indian intelligence managed to establish contact with the ULFA leadership once in 1992 and three of its top leaders (Chairman Arabinda Rajkhowa, Vice-Chairman Pradip Gogoi and General Secretary Anup Chetia) were flown to Delhi where they promised to begin talks for a peaceful settlement by giving up their demand for Assam's sovereignty.

The ULFA's organization, however, like the KIA of Burma that trained its fighters, has always been dominated by the military wing and its chief Paresh Barua was unwilling to give up the fight for secession from India. When Rajkhowa, Gogoi and Chetia returned to

Bangladesh to bring Barua round, they were humiliated and punished for 'dealing with the enemy without organizational sanction'. Since Barua controlled the guerrillas and the weapons and much of the war chest, there was nothing that the political leadership could do but fall in line. So the armed rebellion of the ULFA continued. Once it became clear that it would not negotiate with the Indian state, the ULFA has faced perhaps the most ruthless counter-insurgency action ever faced by any rebel group in the North East.

Indian intelligence used mercenaries and surrendered militants to attack ULFA leaders, specially Paresh Barua and his close associates, in Bangladesh. Many ULFA leaders, like Swadhinata Phukan, were liquidated in fake encounters. Even their close relatives were not spared and whole families of rebel leaders like Mithinga Daimary (real name: Dipak Das) were liquidated by surrendered militants backed by the Assam police and the Indian army. The 'secret killings' (*Gupto Hatya* in Assamese, a term widely used by the Assamese vernacular press to describe the massacre of ULFA families) have never been properly investigated by human rights groups. The government enquiry about the 'secret killings', initiated by Chief Minister Tarun Gogoi to placate Assamese sentiments, did not go very far in nailing those police and military officials widely believed to be responsible for initiating them because they enjoyed Delhi's unstinted patronage. And when the top ULFA commanders—Robin Neog, Asantha Bagh Phukan, Bening Rabha and Robin Handique—were nabbed by the Bhutanese army during their 'Operation All Clear', they all mysteriously disappeared. They were perhaps killed by the Bhutanese but it is hard to believe the Bhutanese would do that without Indian prodding.

The Naga, the Mizo or the Manipuri separatists have been much more vicious in their military challenge to the Indian state than the ULFA. The Bodo rebels have attacked more 'soft targets' by exploding bombs in crowded markets or public transport. But none of their leaders were ever attacked in a foreign country, neither were whole families of rebel leaders targeted with similar ruthlessness as during the 'secret killings' in Assam. Muivah was arrested by the Thai police in Bangkok, mistaken as a North Korean saboteur, after he had started negotiating with India. Delhi enjoyed his discomfiture and did not try to bail him out, but never did Indian intelligence try to influence the Thais to liquidate him. Though he was suspected for continuing his links with Pakistani intelligence, Muivah at that point had started talking to India.

Delhi sees negotiations by rebels as one sure indication of the acceptance of its overlordship—from which point, outright secession is no longer possible. Also, Delhi is very uncomfortable when groups representing a major nationality revolt—be it the Sikh Khalistanis of Punjab or the Bengali Naxalites or their Maoist successors in the Indian heartland states or the Assamese ULFA. The possibility of a settlement with such groups is remote—so they face ruthless repressive action. Smaller tribes and ethnic groups provide better chances for co-option and are therefore handled less ruthlessly.

The ULFA also resorted to unabashed terror and in the process lost much of its popular support. It started attacking oil installations, railways and other industrial locations that it initially had refrained from targeting and its guerillas killed a number of off-duty military and police officials. The tenure of the first AGP government (1985–90) was the high point for the ULFA. That was when they literally ran a parallel government. The imposition of president's rule in 1990 and the subsequent military operations were followed by the return to power of Congress in 1991. The ULFA struck immediately, kidnapping 16 senior officials on the same day. Soviet coal engineer Sergei Gritchenko was killed while trying to flee from the ULFA's custody while an Oil and Natural Gas Corporation (ONGC) engineer, T. Raju, was killed in crossfire between the police and the ULFA. Chief Minister Hiteswar Saikia refused to budge, after the ULFA refused 'reasonable terms' offered for releasing the abducted officials. The officials were finally released and a confident Saikia, determined to avenge the slight, authorized heavy military action and started splitting the ULFA. Allegations that the Assam police was using the surrendered militants to hunt down their colleagues in the underground started mounting.

When the AGP came back to power in 1996, it promised to take up 'the issue of Assam's self-determination'. But once firmly in control, Chief Minister Prafulla Mahanta not only accepted the formation of the Unified Command to provide security forces the necessary structure and leadership to fight the rebels, but also asked his police to go after the ULFA. Mahanta was under pressure from Governor S.K. Sinha to intensify anti-ULFA operations and when he obliged, a grateful governor refused to authorize prosecution sanction against the chief minister in the multi-million rupee Letters of Credit (LOC) scam. Mahanta was also determined not to have his government pulled down by Delhi yet again by allowing the ULFA a free run.

The rebels struck back and nearly assassinated Mahanta in the heart of Guwahati. The explosions hit his security detail as his vehicle sped past. Then the ULFA went for his colleagues. Zoinath Sarma, like Mahanta a hero of the anti-foreigner agitation and a minister in his government, was attacked by two rebel boats while crossing a river in his legislative constituency. Later, an important minister in Mahanta's cabinet, Nagen Sarma, was blown up with explosives planted on the road over which his convoy was passing. Scores of AGP leaders at the zonal and district level were killed. The ULFA made sure that the AGP lost every election, including the 2001 assembly elections, through a campaign of systematic terror.

After the Congress victory in 2001 assembly election, the new chief minister, Tarun Gogoi, promised to bring the ULFA to the ne-gotiating table. There was a perceptible fall in ULFA violence but it was only towards the end of Gogoi's first tenure that the ULFA finally started parleys. A committee of Assamese notables from civil society, local media and pro-ULFA political groups called the Peoples Consultative Group (PCG) was established in 2005 and it held a few rounds to talks with federal negotiators. But the peace process floundered because the ULFA refused to declare a ceasefire and the army continued to attack the rebels because there was no formal cessation of hostilities. The talks broke down in 2006 and could not be revived, despite the best efforts of Assamese writer Indira Raisom Goswami. The ULFA continues to insist that Assam's sovereignty will have to be included in the agenda for talks—something that Delhi is clearly unwilling to accept.

The ULFA still depends on Paresh Barua to decide on crucial issues and unless Barua agrees to talk, no one else seems capable of upstag-ing him. Surrenders from ULFA have weakened the organization but no senior leader who surrendered (like Luit Deuri, Kalpajyoti Neog, Tapan Dutta, Avinash Bordoloi, Sunil Nath, Jiten Dutta or Mrinal Hazarika) have the stature to initiate a peace process. Barua, in frequent contact with the author from his undisclosed hideouts in Bangladesh, made it clear that he would negotiate only if the Indian government agreed to a discussion of Assam's sovereignty. In spite of suffering huge military setbacks and large-scale desertion from the ULFA ranks, Barua is 'only willing to retreat, but not surrender'. He told the author that he does not have much faith in negotiations with India because Delhi 'only uses talks to buy time, as they have done with the NSCN'. Of the four options that he thinks the ULFA now has—fight-to-death, surrender, negotiate or retreat—Barua clearly favours a tactical retreat. And he is quick to note that even revolutionary greats like the legendary Mao used retreat as an offensive tactic, as during the great Long March.[19]

But Barua's options, specially after the return to power of the Awami League in Bangladesh following the December 2008 parliament elections, are far more limited than Mao's ever was. Even far more limited than the men who liberated Bangladesh and East Timor. The Bangladesh government has now issued a look-out notice for Paresh Barua, implicating him in the April 2004 Chittagong arms haul case, and blaming him in the redrafted charge sheet as the intended recipient of the huge cache of weapons that were seized by Bangladesh police at Chittagong port. Demoralized by the change of guard in Bangladesh, more and more ULFA guerillas are surrendering. With the Burmese army launching periodic attacks against the NSCN(Khaplang) bases in upper Burma, which the ULFA has been sharing, Barua will find it difficult to organize a safe neighbourhood sanctuary. With Bhutan gone, the Burmese bases under attack and the new regime in Bangladesh determined to punish the ULFA for their alleged bias towards the political rivals of the Awami League, Paresh Barua has only one hope—Chinese support. He has told this author that the Chinese are upset with India's growing 'strategic relationship' with the United States and he sounds optimistic of securing Chinese backing. But that does not seem to be happening immediately and Barua's only real option lies in opening a dialogue with India, even if it is for limited purposes to seek a breather.

Going by available indications, the Indian intelligence agencies will continue to make efforts to lure Paresh Barua out of his lair in Dhaka for talks—and on their terms. If they fail, they will try to attack him and try open negotiations with Chairman Arabinda Rajkhowa and other moderates, even as the security forces deployed in Assam attack locally deployed rebel units, encouraging them to surrender or face liquidation. Paresh Barua, for his part, is known to be watching closely the negotiations between Delhi and the NSCN. A breakthrough in Nagaland may encourage him to come forward for negotiations, but for any change of line, he would have to look sideways to ensure the absence of dissent within his own group.

Unlike the ULFA, the National Democratic Front of Bodoland (NDFB) has already started negotiations with Delhi after suffering huge reverses in Bhutan during 'Operation All Clear'. Much younger than the ULFA, the NDFB (originally Bodo Security Force) grew out of the Bodo movement for a separate state. In 1987, the All Bodo Students Union (ABSU) and the Bodo Peoples Action Committee (BPAC) began their agitation for a separate Bodo state carved out of Assam. From the very beginning, the Bodo movement was marked by extensive violence. For the first time, armed Bodos used terror tactics, such as blowing up of buses and trains. The Bodo Volunteer Force (BVF), which maintained close links with the ABSU–BPAC combine but operated on its own, was behind the violence. The AGP government, pushed on the back foot by the Bodo agitation demanding that Assam be divided 'fifty-fifty', resorted to heavy-handed police operations to quell its pitch. State repression provoked the Bodos to more violence. They controlled the gateway to the North East and terror attacks on the region's road and rail networks gave the Bodos a clout much in excess to their numerical strength and resources.

After Assam came under president's rule, intense behind-the-scenes negotiations with the ABSU–BPAC leaders started. With the Congress back in power, Indian minister Rajesh Pilot piloted an agreement in 1993 with the ABSU–BPAC combine that promised a territorial council for the Bodos in western and central Assam. Chief Minister Saikia felt slighted because the deal was struck behind his back. He made sure it did not work. The Assam government refused to hand over thousands of villages that would fall into the agreed boundary of the Bodoland Territorial Council. The impasse on the council's boundary torpedoed its future. Saikia got one of his favourites in the Bodo movement to head the Territorial Council on an interim basis, but the body never went through elections and failed to find an institutional footing.

As the ABSU–BPAC combine stood discredited 'with a kingdom which had no boundaries', the NDFB emerged from the shadows to intensify its armed insurgent movement. Besides taking a leaf out of the ULFA's book—by using systematic extortion of the tea industry and other businesses in the Bodo area, shifting major bases to Bhutan and resorting to select assassination of rivals within the community—the NDFB also went about its programme of ethnic cleansing. The Assam government was refusing to give the proposed Bodoland Territorial Council possession of 2,570 villages because it claimed there Bodos were less than 50 per cent of their population. In order to create a Bodo majority in areas lacking one, the NDFB unleashed a violent campaign, targeting one non-Bodo community after another. The worst of these campaigns led to the death of hundreds of *Adivasis* (descendants of the Santhal, Munda and Oraon tribesmen brought to Assam from central India by the British) during the 1996 elections.

The *Adivasis* soon set up their own militant group, Cobra Force, to fight back the NDFB and it also found a challenger within the Bodo community itself. The remnants of the old BVF had organized themselves into the Bodoland Liberation Tigers Force (BLTF) on the demand of a separate Bodo state. The BLTF, which was backed by the ABSU–BPAC combine, endorsed an autonomist agenda because it found the NDFB's secessionist agenda 'far too unrealistic and unattainable'. The BLTF also teamed up with groups like the Bengal Tigers, formed to defend the Bengalis attacked by the Bodos, to fight the NDFB. So while the ULFA, though much weakened, has never had a rival in the ethnic Assamese community to challenge its primacy in the underground, the NDFB is locked in a fierce fratricidal feud with the BLTF elements who have surrendered after the 2003 accord but then organized themselves into a political party, Bodoland People's Progressive Front (BPPF).

The BPPF led by the former BLTF veterans not only control the Bodoland Territorial Council that was set up under terms of the 2003 BLTF–Centre accord but its support is crucial for the survival of Tarun Gogoi's Congress-led coalition government in Dispur. Rarely has a Bodo political group controlled its own 'homeland' area so strongly and has simultaneously had so much influence in a state government in Assam. That gives the BPPF leader Hangrama Mohilary an unusually dominant position amongst the Bodos and he appears to be in no mood to share his preserve with a NDFB that's much weakened after the reverses suffered in Bhutan. That the BLTF was used by Indian security forces against the NDFB is now an open secret and that its former guerrillas, now with the BPPF, retain much of their pre-accord arsenal is clear from the gun battles it is fighting with the NDFB. But the BPPF is now split and Mohilary and his colleagues are smeared by allegation of large-scale corruption. The one-time feared bomber, known within his underground group by the pseudonym of Thebla, is reported to have spent millions of rupees on his marriage in 2008 and when Assam's leading newspaper *Asomiya Protidin* reported it in some detail, Mohilary's supporters banned the entry of the daily in areas under the Bodoland Council and burnt down copies of it to enforce their diktat.

On the other hand, the NDFB hardliners were implicated by the Assam police in the serial bomb explosions that rocked Assam on 30 October 2008. The explosions were funded by the ULFA, says the Assam police special investigation report, but it was carried out by a section of the NDFB loyal to the Chairman Ranjan Daimary. The rebels connected with the explosions were identified and some were arrested as well. In a surprise move, most of the top NDFB leaders engaged in negotiations with the federal government, ganged up and expelled Ranjan Daimary from the organization. They reiterated their faith in negotiations with the Indian state and have agreed to refrain from any violent action by maintaining the ceasefire.

Like the Bodos, other ethnic groups in Assam have demanded their own homelands and fought with arms to achieve them. The Dima Halan Daogah (DHD) says it is fighting for a homeland for the Dimasas. Initially it received support from the NSCN but now the NSCN is uncomfortable with the DHD's vision of a separate Dimasa homeland that includes parts of Nagaland. The DHD argues that even Nagaland's main commercial hub of Dimapur had a Dimasa majority not so long ago. The United Peoples Democratic Solidarity (UPDS) is similarly fighting for a separate Karbi homeland. Both the DHD and the UPDS have fed on the failure of the earlier generation of Karbi and Dimasa leadership, who used agitprop methods to secure autonomy but failed to reach a settlement. The local tribesmen also resent land loss to outsiders and attack settlers who have encroached on tribal lands or reserves. But both the Dimasa and Karbi rebels attack security forces to snatch weapons as well and they target Assam's rail network that runs through their areas.

The North Cachar Hills and Karbi Anglong districts form the link zone between the Brahmaputra and the Barak Valleys. Naga and Manipuri rebels have used these hills to reach their hideouts in East Pakistan, now Bangladesh. northeast India's north-to-south railroad networks passes through these hills. The Dimasa and the Karbi insurgent groups are territorially limited because of their smaller population base, but with the right kind of alliances, they can still pose a problem. The mayhem caused by the DHD's breakaway 'Black Widow' faction (the main faction is now negotiating with Delhi) led by Jewel Garlossa (arrested in June 2009) and the panic his fighters managed to cause amongst railway employees in mid-2008 has forced the Assam government to resort to a huge deployment of security forces in these two hill districts. The ULFA has tried to create bases in these hills after suffering reverses in Bhutan. It maintains close links with Manipuri rebel groups and the corridor to Manipur lies through the Barail ranges on the eastern edges of Karbi Anglong. The NSCN has tried to run 'satellite insurgent groups' in these hill districts and continues to operate there. Given the strategic importance of the two hill districts, the Assam government is planning to intensify its counter-insurgency operations in the area. Because ever new groups like the Karbi Longri National Liberation Front have surfaced to unleash fresh violence even when earlier militant groups have weakened.

PATTERNS OF DISPLACEMENT

The ethnic conflicts in northeast India have led to considerable internal displacement of victim populations. Both migrant settlers and indigenous populations have faced eviction and displacement owing to conflicts. Military operations like the controversial village regrouping drive in Mizoram (1966–69) and development projects like dams have displaced large number of people belonging to indigenous tribes and economically weaker groups. The Dumbur hydroelectric project in Tripura's south uprooted thousands of ethnic tribespeople, but it benefited both migrant Bengali fishermen (who obtained fishing opportunities in the reservoir lake) and urban dwellers (who received electricity from it). Many tribal insurgents in Tripura come from families displaced by the Dumbur project. In neighbouring Meghalaya, Khasi and Jaintia tribespeople have stridently opposed uranium mining by Indian federal agencies in the state's Domiosiat region because they anticipate serious health hazards, like those faced by tribespeople living in and around India's other uranium mining zone in Jadugoda in Jharkhand state.

In the North East, internal displacement has been caused by (a) development projects; (b) violent conflicts; (c) counter-insurgency operations by security forces; (d) natural disasters, such as floods and (e) takeover of land by migrating communities. Reliable data on displacement caused by floods and takeover of land by migrating communities are not available either from the government or from NGOs. Data on displacement caused by counter-insurgency operations is also not very reliable. Only in Mizoram, where the army enforced village regrouping, can a reasonably accurate assessment about the extent of displacement be made. Displacement caused by development projects is available in certain specific cases, but not in all cases. But relatively reliable data is available only for displacement caused by violent conflicts in the North East.

The concept of 'internal displacement' is new to northeast India—media reports and official correspondence continue to refer to those internally displaced as 'refugees'. Tripura newspapers, for example, talk of 'Reang refugees' (those Brus displaced from Mizoram and were forced to live in Tripura) in the same manner as they talk of 'Chakma refugees' (those Chakmas who fled into Tripura from Bangladesh after large-scale fighting broke out between Bangladesh security forces and Shanti Bahini guerrillas in the Chittagong Hill Tracts during the 1980s and 1990s). Government reports also make no distinction between those 'internally displaced' and those who have come for refuge from other countries. Camps sheltering internally displaced persons (IDPs) are also called 'refugee camps' in government reports and official correspondence. Only some non-governmental groups with exposure to the global discourse on refugees and internal displacement tend to make this distinction.

At a time during the late 1990s, the North East accounted for almost half of India's conflict-induced IDPs, if not more. The Global IDP survey, first published in 1998, estimated the number of conflict-induced IDPs in India at 3,90,000. This survey, however, gave incorrect data about the IDPs in Assam, where 1000s of Santhals, Mundas and Oraons have been displaced due to violence by Bodo guerrillas. It said: 'While the majority of *Adivasi*s (Santhals, Mundas and Oraons) numbering about 80,000 have returned home, about 70,000 of them remain in relief camps.'[20] The Assam government claims that the process of return started only in August 2002 and it remains very slow. Until August 2002, however, a total of 37,677 families (2,37,768 people) were staying in makeshift camps in three districts of western Assam, namely, Kokrakjhar, Bongaigaon and Dhubri.[21] It is only after the creation of the Bodoland Territorial Council after the 2003 accord that most of the internally displaced have returned home. The Bodos, having secured autonomy and political power, no longer have to prove a majority to achieve it. And they are too busy fighting amongst themselves for the spoils of office (so the BPPF has already split into two warring factions) and for primacy (the BPPF–NDFB feud) to bother about the non-Bodos who are no longer politically vocal in the Bodoland area.

Thus, the Global IDP survey's statistics about IDPs in Assam at the time it was published were incorrect. The statistics about IDPs elsewhere in the region provided in the survey were also inaccurate. In March 2001, during the budget session of the Tripura legislative assembly, the state budget stated that there were 'about 37,000 Reangs displaced from Mizoram, staying in North Tripura'.[22] Therefore, it is not correct to put the number of Reang IDPs in Tripura at 15,000, as the Global IDP survey had done. In 1998, the total number of conflict-induced IDPs in North East was close to 3,00,000—that was clearly more than half the national figure.

The North East has witnessed eight major cases of conflict-induced internal displacement in recent years: (a) the displacement of Hindus and Muslims of Bengali descent from and within Assam; (b) the displacement of *Adivasis* (also called Tea Tribes) and Bodos within and from western Assam; (c) the displacement of the Bengalis from Meghalaya, particularly Shillong; (d) the displacement of Bengalis from and within Tripura; (e) the displacement of the Nagas, Kukis and Paites in Manipur; (f) the displacement of the Reangs from Mizoram; (g) the displacement of the Chakmas from Arunachal Pradesh and Mizoram and (h) the displacement of Karbis and Dimasas during the DHD–UPDS feud in October 2005.

The first major displacement in post-colonial northeast India was reported in Assam, where religious riots displaced around 1,00,000 Muslims in post-Partition riots: 60,000 from Goalpara district, 20,000 from Kamrup district, 14,000 from Cachar district and 6,000 from Darrang district. Almost the entire displaced population that migrated to East Pakistan returned to Assam after the Nehru–Liaquat Pact of 1950.[23] It would be suitable to categorize this displacement as a refugee situation, because it was not strictly internal to Indian territory, as the displaced Muslims had left for Pakistan and then returned to India after an agreement between the two nations. Since the displacement started because of violence that preceded the Partition, however, there is an element of internality to the displacement.

The first major ethnic conflagration in Assam after the Partition riots occurred during the language movement in 1960. When the Assam government decided to make Assamese the official language of the province, Bengalis protested because they feared loss of opportunities. The Bengali-dominated Barak Valley erupted in agitation and there was a spate of police firings. Elsewhere in the state, particularly in the Brahmaputra Valley, Assamese mobs started attacking Bengali settlements in large numbers. During the worst phase of the violence between July and September 1960, nearly 50,000 Bengalis, almost entirely Hindus, crossed over to West Bengal, seeking shelter. The chief minister of West Bengal, Dr B.C. Roy, wrote to Prime Minister Jawaharlal Nehru:

> The exodus has taken place in three distinct waves. The first lot of 4,000 came between 5 and 11 July. These were the real fugitives fleeing from the fury of the Assamese. Between the 12 and 20 July, there was a small trickle of 447 people who may not have all been victims of violence. From the 31st of July, however, the floodgates have really opened.[24]

Dr Roy, in a subsequent letter, said that 45,000 displaced Bengalis had taken shelter in West Bengal: 'We have no more space for them. In spite of all the Assam government has done recently, more than a thousand people are coming away to West Bengal every day, most of whom are not direct victims of violence but are migrating for fear of disturbances.'[25] The violence was most intense in 25 villages in Goreswar in Kamrup district and a one-man enquiry commission under Justice Gopalji Mehrotra was set up in November 1960 to investigate them. The commission's report observed that 4,019 huts and 58 houses of Bengalis had been vandalized and destroyed in the 25 villages, nine Bengalis had been killed and more than 100 injured; there had been at least one instance of attack on women.

This was certainly not the first time that Bengalis had been attacked in Assam. The Bangal Kheda (drive away Bengalis) movement originated in 1948 with the looting of Bengali shops in Guwahati. Wide-spread disturbances took place in the district of Goalpara during the visit of the State Reorganization Commission. The 1960 disturbances sparked off an exodus of Bengalis to West Bengal and to other Bengali-dominated areas of northeast India, like Tripura and Assam's Barak Valley. While 45,000 Bengalis fled to West Bengal, almost twice as many relocated to other Bengali-dominated areas of Assam and Tripura. Fresh language riots erupted in 1972 and large-scale violence was again reported throughout the Brahmaputra Valley.

Again Bengali Hindus were the main target because they were at the forefront of opposing the imposition of Assamese language. More than 14,000 Bengalis were displaced during the 1972–73 language disturbances and fled to West Bengal and elsewhere in the North East. The real extent of Bengali displacement from Assam, however, is far greater than these figures suggest. While only those who took refuge in camps in West Bengal were accounted for in government records, thousands who took shelter with relatives or just relocated themselves by buying property in West Bengal after selling off their possessions in Assam escaped government or media notice. Moreover, those who continued to leave Assam for fear of future attacks after the riots had ended were also not taken into account.

Bengali Muslims largely escaped attacks by the Assamese during the language riots because they had mostly accepted the Assamese language, but they also faced substantial displacement during the war with Pakistan in 1965. 'Instead of sealing off the border with Pakistan and preventing possible infiltration from there, the government in Assam launched a massive manhunt for the "Pakistani nationals" in Assam. The operation of the Prevention of Infiltration from Pakistan (PIP) scheme terrorized the defenceless and virtually unorganized rural Muslim peasantry.'[26] Assam's late Chief Minister Hiteswar Saikia later admitted that between 1961 and 1969, 1,92,079 Muslims of Bengali descent were deported to East Pakistan.[27] While this cannot be categorized as 'internal displacement' and would rank as outright pushback, it is not clear how many Muslims moved to other parts of India or the North East. There is some indication that many did, but since none of them went to government camps for fear of detection and possible pushback, there are no statistics available on their displacement.

During the six-year anti-foreigner agitation in Assam (1979–85), there was substantial internal displacement of both Hindus and Muslims of Bengali descent. The displacement occurred in two phases: the initial phase of the movement in 1979–80 and during the second phase of massive violence in and around the assembly polls in February–March 1983. During the initial phase of the movement, attacks were reported on Bengali Hindu and Muslim settlements throughout the Brahmaputra Valley. Incidents such as the killing of a Bengali technical officer, Rabi Mitra, at the Oil India headquarters in Duliajan in Upper Assam led to panic among Bengalis. While at least 7,000 Bengali Hindus crossed into West Bengal in 1979–80, the Muslim peasantry of Bengali descent stayed put. They became targets of attacks by the supporters of the agitation in February–March 1983, when at least 1,800 were butchered in Nellie in one day. This was easily one of the worst pogroms faced by a minority community in post-Partition India. Nevertheless, the Muslim peasantry of Nellie, as indeed in many other places in the Brahmaputra Valley, where they had become targets of the agitation supporters, returned to their lands within a few days of the massacre. As marginal peasants whose ancestors had left East Bengal in search of land and survival, they had nowhere to go and very little to lose, except their lives.

Even those who braved the attacks, however, were eventually displaced under sustained pressure from the Assamese-dominated administration. In 1985, the new AGP came to power. It was composed almost entirely of student and youth leaders who had led the Assam agitation. AGP supporters backed by the administration went about hunting for 'foreigners'. Thousands of Bengali Hindus and Muslims fled to the Barak Valley and to West Bengal and many Muslim and lower-caste Bengali Hindu peasants vacated their cultivable lands and went into hiding deep into forest areas. Nearly 1,50,000 were allowed to settle down in the disputed border region of Assam and Nagaland in order to prevent encroachment and forced settlements by Naga tribespeople who were continuously pushing westwards. Indeed, the same administration that was pushing these Bengalis—both Hindu and Muslim—out of Assam was willing to use them as a protective buffer against Naga expansion so that Assam's territorial boundaries, constantly under challenge from aggressive neighbouring tribal groups, could be preserved.

After the Assam agitation, Muslims and some lower-caste Hindus of Bengali extraction started entering Nagaland in substantial numbers. Recently a Naga rebel group, the National Socialist Council of Nagaland (NSCN—Khaplang faction) has asked 'all Muslims in Nagaland to take work permits' from its offices or face 'dire consequences'.[28] Nagaland government sources estimate that the *Semiya*s (so called because Muslims are referred to as *Miya*s in the region and have mostly inter-married with the Semas in Nagaland) now number at least 80,000–1,00,000, though some intelligence agencies sometimes place their number at 2,50,000 to 3,00,000.[29] Nagaland's former governor, Shyamal Dutta, and his one-time colleagues in the Intelligence Bureau (of which he was the chief) see the *Semiya*s as a major threat to Nagaland's demography and a possible source of future tension.

It is difficult to say whether all of them have migrated from Assam or have used Assam as a corridor to reach Nagaland, but intelligence reports indicate that most of the Muslims in Nagaland are of East Bengali extraction and could be second or third-generation settlers in India and have moved out of Assam to settle down in Nagaland.[30] Even if we accept the intelligence version that many of these Muslims of Bengali extraction are 'illegal infiltrators', it would be reasonable to accept that tens of thousands of them moved to Nagaland after displacement from Assam during the violence of the early 1980s. The Bengali Hindus and Muslims from Assam quickly settled down wherever they relocated themselves. Even those (about 25,000) who were displaced in attacks by guerrillas of the Bodo tribe in western Assam during the 1993–94 violence either returned to their lands or quickly settled down in the place of their relocation.

The *Adivasi*s or Tea Tribes who were displaced in attacks by the Bodos in western Assam, on the other hand, remained in makeshift camps in large numbers and for a much longer period—nearly 15 years. Many Bodos, also displaced during clashes with the *Adivasi*s, also remained in the camps for around nine to 10 years. Since 1987, Bodo groups intensified their movement for a separate state, setting off explosions in trains, buses and rail tracks. At this stage of their movement, however, the Bodos did not attack non-Bodo population, though many were killed in explosions set off by them. The Assam government, then run by the AGP alleged that federal intelligence agencies were backing the Bodo militants to bring down their government.[31]

In 1993, the Indian government and the Assam government, then run by the Congress party, finally agreed to set up an autonomous region for the Bodo tribe and an agreement was signed with the agitating Bodo groups. The agreement proved to be a non-starter because the Assam government refused to hand over to the Bodoland Autonomous Territorial Council those areas where Bodos were not a majority. Bodo hardliners argued that 'those areas historically belong to the Bodos and will be part of our independent homeland'.[32] Even moderate Bodo groups, discredited by their failure to work the autonomy arrangement, said that the area demanded by the council was their 'historic homeland' and if the Bodos had become a minority in some areas, it was because governments in Assam had failed to stop 'illegal infiltration' into those areas.[33] The separatist National Democratic Front of Bodoland (NDFB), which had opposed the agreement, was vindicated and many Bodo militants who had decided to return to normal life returned to the jungles.

The stage was set for a fierce ethnic conflagration. In October 1993, within a few months of the Bodoland Accord, Bodo militants began large-scale attacks on Muslims of Bengali descent. These migrants, mostly of peasant stock, had taken over land throughout Assam, initially causing displacement of ethnic Assamese and the tribal peasantry. In the 1980s, they were targeted by Assamese agitators. A decade later, they became targets for the Bodo militants. During the attacks in October 1993, more than 20,000 Muslims were displaced in Kokrajhar and Bongaigaon districts. The attacks continued in 1994, covering four western Assam districts of Barpeta, Bongaigaon, Dhubri and Kokrajhar. More than 60 villages were completely devastated. Casualty figures varied, government sources placing them at 300–400 dead, while Monirul Hussain, one of Assam's noted academics, says 1,000 Muslims, mostly women and children, were killed.[34] Intelligence reports from the area suggest that this estimate is on the higher side—Assam police estimated around 400 Muslims dead.[35] The Bodo militants did not even spare camps set up for the displaced Muslims. One large camp at Banhbari was subjected to a night attack and nearly 90 camp inmates were massacred, even as the police guards stood by, too frightened to take on the heavily armed Bodos.

What started with specific attacks on Muslims of Bengali descent slowly engulfed other non-Bodo communities, like the Bengali Hindus and the *Adivasi*s. Unlike some of the previous ethnic pogroms in Assam, in this instance the pattern of violence appeared to be very calculated. Bodo militants first targeted Muslims of Bengali descent in 1993–94. Then in 1995–96, they started attacking Bengali Hindus. Finally in May–June 1996, they launched massive attacks against the *Adivasi*s throughout western Assam. But unlike the Muslims, *Adivasi*s and Bengali Hindus formed their own militant groups and started attacking Bodo villages.

The Adivasi Cobra Militants of Assam (ACMA) and the Bengal Liberation Tigers, a group formed by Bengali Hindus, joined hands and attacked several Bodo villages after the massive Bodo-sponsored violence of May–June 1996. Besides extensive displacement, the mushrooming of ethnic militias has created a Bosnia type situation, in which federal and provincial authorities become helpless spectators, capable merely of setting up camps for displaced persons but totally unable to stop the proliferation of militias and their depredations. The Assam government claims that more than 2,50,000 people were displaced, of which at least 2,37,668 people—1,81,932 *Adivasi*s and the rest Bodos—had taken shelter in camps.[36]

After the first outbreak of Bodo–*Adivasi* violence in May–June 1996, clashes between the two ethnic groups became a regular feature in western Assam. They began with the recovery of the dead bodies of three Bodo girls at Satyapur in the jurisdiction of the Gosaigaon police station. While Bodos say they were raped and killed by *Adivasi* militants, the ACMA alleges that they were prostitutes from the Bhutanese border town of Phuentsoling who were killed and left in a jungle to spark off the riots.[37] These murders sparked off fierce attacks by the Bodos but the *Adivasi*s also retaliated, killing the kin of a Bodo legislator.

In 1998, the violence intensified just when some of the displaced people were returning home. Thousands fled their villages again, exacerbating the displacement. The Assam government admitted that 1,213 people had died in the violent incidents of 1996 and 1998, but since militias continue to attack rival communities, the casualty toll mounted. The Assam government decided to keep the displaced in 47 relief camps, improving their security but not providing them with enough rations and medicine.[38] At the same time, both the

Indian federal and the Assamese provincial government steadfastly opposed the entry of international organizations like Médecins Sans Frontières (MSF) to work in the camps. Since it was not immediately possible to send the displaced people back to their villages as long as the militants were at large, the Assam government decided to initiate extensive counter-insurgency operations in the area. With the split in the Bodo underground movement, and the Bodoland Liberation Tigers Force (BLTF) coming out openly against the NDFB, the government found it convenient to quell the pitch of the Bodo insurgency. While it started negotiations with the BLTF and got it to scale down its demands of a separate Bodo state within India, the NDFB remained the target of the counter-insurgency operations until it also started negotiations with India.

In August 2002, the Assam government finally started sending the *Adivasis* and the Bodos from the makeshift camps back to their villages. The government drew up a detailed plan to rehabilitate these displaced people in four phases, beginning with the resettlement of 16,783 families in the first phase. Kokrajhar deputy commissioner A.K. Bhutani said that the process of rehabilitation would be slow because the situation in the area was still far from normal.[39] The situation remained tense even after the 2003 accord between the BLTF and the Indian government, despite the best efforts of the BLTF to assuage the non-Bodos' fear.[40] Some non-Bodo groups in the area formed an organization called the Sanmilito Jonoghostiye Sangram Samity (SJSS) or United Nationalities Struggle Committee.

The BLTF and other groups, such as the ABSU and the BPAC, were upset with the SJSS and the activities of the All Adivasi Students Association of Assam (AASAA), which threatened an economic blockade of the Bodo areas if the council was created.[41] The BLTF spokesman Maino Daimary (real name: Kampa Borgiary, now executive member of Bodoland Territorial Autonomous Council) said in an interview: 'If the Bodos fail to get meaningful autonomy soon enough, relations between them and the other communities in the area will further worsen.'[42] But finally when the 2003 accord was implemented and the Bodoland Territorial Council was formed, the situation began to ease. The non-Bodos started returning to their villages, much less to fear. After the NDFB guerrillas came out of the jungles and were placed in the designated camps, the non-Bodos were no longer facing the threat of organized militant attacks against their villages. The sending back of the non-Bodo displaced from the camps is now almost complete.

Bongal Kheda (Drive Away Bengalis) as an organized campaign of ethnic cleansing originated in Assam but was not restricted to the state. In the early 1980s, it spread to Tripura and Meghalaya. In both states, ethnic tribespeople attacked Bengalis, resenting their growing numbers or dominance in jobs and business or both. In Meghalaya, the mayhem was largely restricted to Shillong, the former capital of undivided Assam, where Bengalis dominated the bureaucracy and the professions. In 1980, a Bengali legislator was killed and many Bengali localities came under systematic attack. The pattern was repeated at regular intervals, mostly before or during the main Bengali Hindu festival of Durga Puja.

In the 1990s, Bengalis remained the prime target of tribal violence but other non-tribal communities like the Biharis and the Marwaris also came under attack. More than 50 people have died in these attacks during the last two decades—a small number compared to neighbouring Tripura or Assam—but they were disturbing enough to trigger a Bengali exodus. Since the early 1980s, an estimated 35,000–40,000 Bengalis have left Shillong and some other parts of Meghalaya and settled down in West Bengal and other states of India. In 1981, there were 1,19,571 Bengalis in Meghalaya, equivalent to 8.13 per cent of the state's population. Ten years later, it stood at 1,44,261, now only 5.97 per cent of the population.[43]

Attacks on Bengalis in neighbouring Tripura have been much more widespread than in Meghalaya, where it was restricted to urban localities like Shillong. Since Bengalis had taken over land on a large scale from the indigenous tribespeople and reduced them to an ethnic minority in Tripura, ethnic hatred was much more intense and widespread. Land alienation and loss of political power after the end of princely rule explain the continued intensity of the violence. It started with the fierce ethnic riots of June–July 1980, in which 1,076 Bengalis and 278 tribals were killed. Three hundred twenty seven Bengalis were butchered in one village, Mandai. During the riots in June 1980, 1,89,919 people, 80 per cent of them Bengalis and the remaining 20 per cent tribals, were displaced and took shelter in 186 camps that was set up for them. Bengalis were sheltered in 141 camps, while the tribals took refuge in the other 45 camps.[44]

Most of the displaced went back to their villages but after a while, the Bengalis started relocating their villages closer to police outposts, semi-urban centres and roadside positions. Mandai is a classic example: the old Bengali part of the settlement has now been largely taken over by tribals and the Bengalis have moved away to New Mandai, a fledgling semi-urban location guarded by a paramilitary camp. In fact, most new Bengali settlements came up near the camps where they had taken shelter. The villages in which they had lived earlier were abandoned and in most cases taken over by tribals. Many Bengali farmers tried to cultivate their land holdings from their new locations and often became victims of sneak attacks by rebel tribesmen. On the other hand, the tribals who were displaced returned to their ancestral villages though many of their young men, implicated in rioting cases and hunted by the police, left for the hills and joined the TNV and the All Tripura Peoples Liberation Organization (ATPLO), the two rebel groups that had emerged in post-1980 Tripura. The ATPLO surrendered in 1983 and was disbanded but the TNV continued its depredations until they gave up insurgency in 1988.

More than 600 Bengalis died in the TNV raids between 1982 and 1988, over 100 of them in two months preceding the 1988 state elections. Although the TNV gave up the path of insurgency, two rebel groups, the ATTF and the NLFT emerged with the same kind of agenda of ethnic cleansing: to drive the Bengali migrants away from Tripura. These two rebel groups adopted a new tactic. Instead of merely launching TNV-style night attacks on Bengali villages and killing scores of Bengalis, which they sometimes resort to, they also started kidnapping Bengalis en masse—officials, businessmen, anyone with the capacity to pay up. Between March 1992 and March 2002, 823 Bengalis were killed by the rebels and 3,312 were kidnapped. About one-seventh of those kidnapped did not return.[45] Since many abductions are not reported to the police and the families pay up quietly, the actual number of abductions of Bengalis could be much more, almost one abduction per day on the average. Most of the families who had someone abducted have been rendered penniless by the rebels, who extort every bit of family property before releasing the victim. The NLFT and the ATTF have periodically issued 'quit Tripura notices' to the Bengalis who entered Tripura after the state merged with the Indian Union in 1949. Bengali settlements have been regularly attacked and subjected to systematic massacres.

Since the June 1980 riots, more than 1,00,000 Bengalis have been displaced. During particularly violent phases of the rebel campaigns, camps were opened in violence-affected areas like Khowai but were quickly closed down, unlike in Assam. In Khowai alone, 2,600 families, almost entirely Bengalis, were displaced by NLFT and ATTF attacks between 1998 and 2001. Some of these displaced Bengalis even went back to Bangladesh, from where they had come to Tripura few years back. In other parts of West Tripura district (in areas under Sadar and Bishalgarh subdivisions) another 2,400 families were displaced between 1998 and 2001 alone. Government officials said the total displacement of Bengalis in Khowai, Sadar and Bishalgarh subdivisions between 1995 and 2002 could be more than 7,000 families, or between 40,000–50,000 people in all. This is corroborated by collation of data between the two most recent censuses (1991 and 2001), which indicates changes of residence by nearly 50,000 people in these three subdivisions of Tripura.

Throughout the hills of Tripura, a silent exodus has taken place. Bengali peasants and small traders from the hills have fled to roadside locations or crowded into the outskirts of the towns that dot Tripura's western border with Bangladesh. In March 2002, a large number of Bengalis displaced from Takarjala, Jampuijhala and Gabardi on the outskirts of Agartala crowded into the city and took over the town's main cultural hall, Rabindra Bhavan. The ruling Marxists said the opposition Congress was provoking them to embarrass the government, but the displaced Bengalis said they were protesting to highlight their problems before an 'insensitive government'.[46] The major trend of Bengali migration from Assam has been repeated in Tripura: those fleeing to West Bengal in anticipation of attacks were greater in number than those who fled after suffering attacks.

In both Assam and Tripura, which has accounted for the bulk of the internally displaced population in northeast India, the situation remains fluid. Fresh conflicts cannot be ruled out and the threat of large-scale displacement remains a distinct possibility in both these states. Heavy migration that alters the demographic balance of these states and threatens to reduce the indigenous groups to a minority has provoked nativist violence, often degenerating into insurgencies. Competition for jobs, business opportunities, land and political power has pitted the Assamese, the Bodos and the Tripuris against the migrant Bengalis and other communities from the Indian heartland. Since the beginning of 2000, guerrillas of the ULFA have been frequently attacking Hindi-speaking settlers throughout Assam. More than 200 of them have been killed so far. The ULFA has asked these Hindi-speaking settlers to quit Assam. If the military confrontation between the ULFA and the Indian security forces ease, these settlers may get a respite, but otherwise the ULFA will regularly attack them as 'soft targets'. Following these attacks, there has been an exodus of Marwari and Bihari settlers from upper and central Assam, but a definitive estimate was not possible because the Marwaris moved over to other Indian states that provided the best business opportunities. The Biharis are believed to have moved to safer areas within Assam or back to some of the Hindi-speaking states or to northern Bengal. The Hindi-speaking settlers are also being displaced in the Karbi Anglong and North Cachar Hills districts, where rebel tribal groups attack them at regular intervals. Similar attacks have started in Manipur in recent weeks and an exodus of Hindi-speakers from that state has started.

Tribal Warfare and Ethnic Cleansing

The situation may not be as critical in other North Eastern states as in Assam and Tripura, but tense relations between battling ethnicities and counter-insurgency operations have led to substantial internal displacement in Manipur, Mizoram and Arunachal Pradesh. These states that border Burma have been spared the kind of rampant migration from across the border that has upset the demographic balance of Assam and Tripura, but various tribes who entered these states in medieval times entertain conflicting homeland demands that have often led to conflicts and created substantial internal displacement.

After the Partition, the Indian government kept the North East outside the purview of the linguistic reorganization process. In the rest of the country, states were created around population groups largely speaking one language. Since the North East was diverse, this principle was not extended to this region. An exception was made in 1963, when Nagaland was created. This was done to defuse the powerful

Naga insurrection and provide moderates with some political space to manoeuvre. Once the Nagas had a separate state, however, other ethnic groups began to demand theirs. In 1972, the North East was politically reorganized and new tribal states like Meghalaya were created. Mizoram and Arunachal Pradesh obtained full statehood in 1987. This spurred many ethnic groups to demand homelands and adopt armed militancy to achieve them. These armed groups often attack settler communities or rival tribes as part of a strategy of ethnic cleansing to achieve ethnically compact homelands, but often they strike soft targets to pressure the government to grant their demands.

Manipur has witnessed substantial internal displacement and ethnic relocation in the wake of the Naga–Kuki and the Kuki–Paite feuds in the 1990s. These feuds led to nearly 1,700 deaths and destruction of property worth millions of rupees. There were also riots between the Hindu Meiteis and the ethnic Manipuri Pangal Muslims in 1993. The vision of an independent homeland called Nagalim propounded by the NSCN includes all but one of the five hill districts of Manipur. Churachandpur, where Kukis hold more than 95 per cent of the land, has never been part of the Nagalim demand. The United Naga Council of Manipur, which has close relations with the NSCN's Issac–Muivah faction, which is active in Manipur and is the stronger of the two NSCN factions, issued a 'quit notice' to all Kukis who lived in areas of the state that the Nagas wanted to include in an independent Nagalim.

A new militia, the Naga Lim Guards, formed by Manipuri Nagas as a backup force of the NSCN, came into existence and started attacks against the Kukis. The worst carnage occurred at Zopui, a remote hill village north of the state's capital Imphal, where 87 Kuki males were beheaded in one night. The NSCN alleged that the Kuki National Front and some other Kuki militant groups enjoyed support of the Indian army and were, in fact, helping them against the NSCN.[47] Kuki militias retaliated but only in a few areas that they controlled. Soon, Manipur was gripped by a fierce spiral of tribal feuds that threatened to spin out of control.

The Indian government and the state government of Manipur increased the presence of security forces but did little else to control the violence. Delhi appeared keener to use the issue to discredit the NSCN at international fora. Naga human rights groups had been active at international fora since the early 1980s, offering regular documentation of human rights violations by Indian security forces. Now the Indian agencies were using the same stick to beat the NSCN. The Kuki Inpi, the tribe's most representative body, submitted a series of memoranda to the Indian and the Manipur governments, demanding more security and restoration of lands to their Kuki owners. Only in 1998, six years after the outbreak of violence, did the Indian government formally react: the Home Ministry asked the government of Manipur to furnish details and comments on the charges made by the Kuki Inpi.[48] By then, Delhi had initiated negotiations with the NSCN (Issac–Muivah faction). The Kukis remain apprehensive over the demand for a Greater Nagaland, which the NSCN has not given up. Though they are more numerous than the Nagas in Manipur, the latter have a longer tradition of guerrilla warfare against the Indian state and are better prepared for armed conflict.

The violence was finally controlled after the Baptist church intervened and got leaders of both the Naga and Kuki communities to accept a ceasefire that would be binding on their militant elements. The Paites, who are ethnic cousins of the Kukis but had developed close ties with the Nagas, were also involved in a bitter feud that led to hundreds of deaths. A similar agreement between the leaders of the Zomi Council and the Kuki Inpi brought to an end the Kuki–Paite feud. Peace has thereafter reigned in the violence-ravaged hills of Manipur but it is too early to say whether these bitter tribal feuds are truly over. The displacement of population was limited because neither the Nagas, the Kukis nor the Paites remained in camps for very long. They returned to their ancestral villages at the first opportunity. In some cases they relocated entire villages to safer areas but did not give up control over their lands.

The Manipur government says that only 15,000 Nagas and Kukis have been permanently displaced. In mixed Naga–Kuki districts like Senapati, Tamenglong and Chandel, where the violence was fierce and sustained, the Nagas and the Kukis stuck to their lands and homesteads in most cases. Only in districts where one ethnic group was in total dominance did the other find their position untenable and was forced to move. For instance, the town of Moreh (population: 15,000) on the border with Burma, on a lucrative drug route, no longer has a single Naga living there. Recently, when I visited Moreh, the vehicle in which I was travelling was halted by Kuki vigilantes who were looking for Nagas. Three Buddhist women from Arunachal

Pradesh who perhaps resembled Nagas were dragged out of the vehicle. Only when the women produced their Indian voter identity cards that gave their place of residence as Arunachal Pradesh did the Kukis relent and release them.

At least 600 villages were burnt down during the Naga–Kuki feud, in which nearly 10,000 houses were destroyed. Eight hundred ninety eight Kukis were killed by Nagas during the eight-year feud and 312 Nagas were killed by the Kukis. Two hundred ten Kukis were killed in clashes with the Paites, who lost 298 of their own tribesmen. Three thousand houses in 47 villages were destroyed and 22,000 Kukis and Paites were displaced. During riots between Meiteis and Pangals, more than 100 were killed while 196 houses in nine villages were destroyed.[49]

In June 2001, the Indian government extended the ceasefire with the NSCN to Manipur and the rest of the country. This provoked fierce protests in the Imphal Valley; angry Meiteis burnt down the state assembly building, offices of political parties and houses of senior politicians. Twenty Meiteis were killed in a police firing. The agitation created panic amongst the Nagas. The fact that not a single Naga was attacked anywhere in the Imphal Valley testifies to the political maturity of the organizations leading the agitation. But more than 10,000 Nagas left the plains and moved to Manipur's hill districts or to neighbouring Nagaland. Most of them have not returned. Some Nagas I interviewed said they feared a massive backlash against them if any part of Manipur was included in a settlement between the Indian government and the NSCN. Therefore, they did not think it safe to remain in the Imphal Valley.[50]

In 1998, Mizo tribesmen unleashed a wave of terror against the minority Brus (called Reangs in Tripura) who live in Mizoram's western border with Tripura. From October 1998, hundreds of Reangs started fleeing into neighbouring Tripura, complaining of persecution. The refugees spoke of villages burnt down, Bru women raped and men beaten up and killed.[51] The Bru National Liberation Front, or BNLF, started attacking Mizoram police. This further provoked the Mizos to commit atrocities against the Brus. The Tripura government claims that 30,690 Brus belonging to 6,859 families have fled into Tripura until 2001, when the exodus stopped. The Mizoram government refused to accept them, claiming that the

Tripura government has not provided details of residence for 10,435 people belonging to 2,075 families.

Mizoram Chief Minister Zoramthanga told me in an interview that 'the Brus are from Tripura and if they are not happy in Mizoram, they are welcome to go back to Tripura'.[52] The chief minister also alleged that the Brus would try to come back with more of their ethnic kinsmen—a situation that must be stopped. In an attitude reminiscent of the Bhutanese authorities' unwillingness to take back refugees of Nepalese origin, the Mizoram government tried to stall the return of the Bru refugees until Delhi piled huge pressure after 2004. Tripura's Left government managed to convince Delhi that Zoramthanga was playing foul and while the Left had greater influence in Delhi after the Congress came to power, Zoramthanga lost the influence he had on the BJP government for playing the mediator between them and the NSCN.

The Indian home ministry's efforts to prevent ethnic persecution of smaller tribes in Mizoram are not new. The Chakmas have always faced discrimination and pressure from the Mizos, particularly after the rebels of the Shanti Bahini, which fought the Bangladesh security forces in the neighbouring Chittagong Hill Tracts, attacked the MNF's bases in that area at the behest of the Indian government during 1978–85. When the MNF returned to normal life in 1986, it became a legitimate political party. Zoramthanga, who was chief minister, had run the MNF bases in the Chittagong Hill Tracts and faced the Shanti Bahini attacks. Immediately after the 1986 accord, the MNF put pressure on the Indian government to abrogate the Chakma autonomous district council, but the Indian government did not agree. Rajiv Gandhi told a rally in Aizawl that if the Mizos expect justice from India as a small minority, they must safeguard the interests of still smaller groups like the Chakmas.

Mizo officials, however, have deleted names of Chakma electors from the voter's list at random, so much so that even a former Chakma legislator, S.P. Dewan, had his name struck off the rolls. Besides the Chakmas, there are two other autonomous district councils in Mizoram meant for the smaller Mara and Lai tribes. They want to join hands with the Chakmas and turn the territory of the three district councils into a centrally administered area, that is, a Union Territory.[53] If that movement gains momentum, Mizoram police and administration will attempt to curb it with a heavy hand and thus create fresh displacement.

The Mizos themselves were victims of large-scale displacement in the late 1960s, when the Indian army started Vietnam-style village regrouping to contain the MNF rebels. Nearly 45,000 Mizos from 109 villages were herded into 18 group centres, each guarded by a military company (120 soldiers) in the first phase of the regrouping. In the second phase, another 87,000 Mizos were grouped in 84 regrouping centres. The regrouping forced the Mizo farmer away from his lands; he was forced to settle in roadside locations guarded by the army. This was meant to denude population cover and food support for the rebels. According to Amrita Rangaswami, it ended up destroying Mizoram's rural economy. Almost half of the population of the Mizo Hills was affected by this displacement engineered by the army. The final phase of the regrouping could not be carried out due to a stay order issued by the Guwahati High Court, the only High Court in northeast India.[54]

Unlike in Mizoram and Manipur, the conflict between the indigenous tribes of Arunachal Pradesh and the Chakma and Hajong refugees has been simmering but has not exploded into a bloody feud. The Chakmas and the Hajongs fled from what was then East Pakistan to escape persecution and displacement in the mid 1960s. Nearly 15,000 of them belonging to 2,748 families were settled in 10,799 acres of land in Lohit, Subansiri and Tirap districts of Arunachal Pradesh (which was then centrally administered by the North Eastern Frontier Agency). Indigenous tribes like the Adis and the Nishis resent the settlement of the Chakmas and the Hajongs, who now number around 65,000.

In the last few years, groups such as the All Arunachal Pradesh Students Union (AAPSU) have periodically enforced economic blockades in areas inhabited by the Chakmas. Many villages have been attacked and some houses set on fire. The indigenous tribes were angered by a 1996 Supreme Court order that directed the state government to forward to the federal government applications for citizenship by the refugees. The AAPSU and other local groups argue they have no objection if the Chakmas and the Hajongs are granted citizenship as long as they are shifted to another part of India. They fear that, in a sparsely populated state like Arunachal Pradesh with a population of less than half a million, the grant of citizenship to so many settlers would upset the power-political equations and make the Chakmas and Hajongs a decisive factor in the legislative politics of the state.

The World Chakma Organization (WCO) alleges that more than 5,000 Chakmas have already left Arunachal Pradesh, unable to bear the persecution. They continue to be stateless and have great difficulty in securing education, jobs and businesses. Many have come to Assam, though in 1994, the Assam government issued shoot-at-sight orders along the border with Arunachal Pradesh. Some have gone to Tripura, where the Chakmas do not face the wrath of the local tribesmen like in Mizoram and Arunachal Pradesh. The WCO and other Chakma human rights groups say that unless the Chakmas and the Hajongs are granted citizenship and provided protection, they will be forced to look for some other place to settle. A human rights activist describes the condition of the Chakmas and the Hajongs as 'stifling, because they live in the constant dread of pogroms, economic blockade and large-scale displacement'.[55] On the other hand, some bureaucrats in the region have argued that giving the Chakmas and the Hajongs citizenship and allowing them to stay in Arunachal Pradesh may lead to violence like in other North East Indian states. Clearly, there is a crisis in the making in Arunachal Pradesh and only a dubiously maintained *status quo*—in which even the Supreme Court order has not been implemented—has prevented an explosion.

DEVELOPMENT AND DISPLACEMENT

Development-induced displacement has been a widespread phenomenon in northeast India, like elsewhere in the country. Development projects like dams, oil and gas fields, mines and indust-rial projects have displaced thousands of people in the North Eastern states. Among development projects, dams have so far been the single largest source of displacement in northeast India. The Dumbur dam of the Gumti hydroelectric project in South Tripura district, intended to generate a meagre 8.6 MW of power, completely displaced a total of 5,845 tribal families—between 35,000 and 40,000 people in all. This displacement aggravated the degenerating ethnic relations between Bengali migrants and ethnic tribespeople. It is incumbent on the state government, dominated primarily by Bengalis, to undo this historical injustice by decommissioning the Dumbur dam, since Tripura has now discovered vast natural gas reserves and several large gas-based thermal projects are planned, more than capable of taking care of the state's power needs.

The Loktak hydroelectric project in Manipur displaced around 20,000 people as their villages went under water. The Pagladia dam in Assam, predominantly an irrigation and flood control project, is likely to displace nearly 1,50,000 people when completed in 2007 and a people's committee to protest work on the dam has already emerged. The Tipaimukh dam, which will generate 1,500 MW, is also likely to face stiff resistance because it has the potential to displace close to 40,000 people, though the North 'Eastern' Electric Power Corporation (NEEPCO) that was to execute the project claims the potential for displacement has been much exaggerated by NGOs.

Besides displacing so many people, the Tipaimukh Dam, like the Dumbur Dam, also has the potential to exacerbate the hills–plains conflict because it will submerge lands of the hill people in Manipur and benefit the Barak Valley districts of Assam, which are inhabited by a Bengali majority. Several thousand tribespeople are likely to be displaced in Arunachal Pradesh in the next 20 years, as many large and medium-sized dams are constructed there. Worse would be the damage to the local environment, including many bio-diversity hotspots. And since the North East is prone to earthquakes (two major ones in 1897 and 1950 in Assam), India would do well to reconsider its latest drive for building huge dams in Arunachal Pradesh with the lower riparian communities in mind.

Various oil and gas fields when drilled and commissioned have displaced up to 15,000 farmers in Assam and Tripura. The tribals have resisted displacement in Domiosiat and Wakkhaji in Meghalaya's West Khasi Hills district, where a huge uranium deposit has been struck. They fear radiation hazards. If the government pursues the mining of uranium, the level of panic prevalent in the area will force nearly 7,000–8,000 Khasi tribesmen to flee the area. Paper mills in Assam and Nagaland and other industrial projects, including the yet-to-be-implemented Reliance gas cracker project at Lepetkata, have displaced nearly 10,000 people. Even the setting up of the Indian Institute of Technology on the outskirts of Guwahati has displaced up to 600 families (around 3,500 people). These numbers may not appear large by the standards of displacement that projects like

Narmada dam may bring about, but in ethnically sensitive North East India, even small levels of displacement can produce bitterness and conflict if one community benefits from the projects and another suffers. Such conflicts may produce more displacement than those caused by development projects. Displacement caused by takeover of tribal lands by migrants has invariably led to continuous ethnic conflict and could lead to more.

If large-scale displacement in conflict-prone regions like North East India has to be avoided, the government must adopt certain measures at the policy level:

1. Migration from other Indian states into the region should be discouraged. There must be a strict national labour policy to protect the interests of indigenous populations. Only if higher skills are not locally available should people from other states be allowed to work in the North East. This surely contradicts provisions of the Indian constitution and any executive order designed to protect the interests of local labour is likely to be challenged in the courts, but keeping social unrest at a minimum is a sure way of avoiding conflict.
2. Protection of indigenous land is imperative because land alienation is one of the major sources of ethnic conflict in northeast India. If tribals lose land in large measure, insurgency is likely, followed by large-scale displacement.
3. Illegal migration into the region from Bangladesh, Nepal and Burma must be stopped. Since resources are scarce and the region's agrarian economy cannot support more populace, any major inflow of population is bound to create ethnic or religious backlash or both. For example, the Mizos, who once considered themselves ethnic cousins of the Chins from Burma, now resent fresh Chin migration into Mizoram. The reasons are primarily economic. The MNF, which led a 20-year separatist campaign, advocated 'Greater Mizoram' as its ultimate goal. Even Brigadier Thengpunga Sailo's Peoples Conference supported the integration of Mizo-inhabited territories in India, Burma and Bangladesh. Now all major Mizo political parties, including the MNF, which is at the helm of government, oppose Chin migration. Mizos see the Chins as unwelcome intruders for economic reasons.

4. Extensive autonomy for tribal regions must be established before they start resorting to violence, not after they have already taken the road to militancy.

5. Having recommended autonomy for indigenous peoples and protection for their land and share of scarce resources, it is important to work out a multi-ethnic ethos of governance. No province can be totally homogenous in ethnic or religious terms and minorities are bound to persist. Even if the minorities happen to be illegal migrants who had entered the region at some stage, their present generation cannot be faulted for the decision of their ancestors.

6. Empowerment of indigenous populations should not prevent a tough policy towards insurgents who resort to ethnic cleansing and violent militancy. There is no reason why such groups should be legitimized or unnecessarily placated because the assumption that violence can be politically and financially rewarding only encourages the formation of other rebel groups.

7. Once displacement has taken place, it is important to provide security to the affected population and organize their return to ancestral villages as soon as possible. Delay in rehabilitation creates problems. The ordeal of the *Adivasis* is a case in point: they have stayed in makeshift camps in large numbers and rued the experience, while their younger elements have formed a new militia because they had no faith left in the ability of the state to defend them.

Ethnic feuds in the North East thrive as much on the region's enormous diversity, as due to conflicting aspirations of ethnic groups and also because the Indian state have often backed one against the other as part of its counter-insurgency strategy. Conflict over scarce resources like water may further complicate the process.

NOTES

1. Subir Bhaumik, 'Insurgencies in India's North East: Conflict, Co-option and Change', Working Paper No. 10, East-West Center, Washington, July 2007.
2. Rajesh Rajagopalan, 2008.
3. Udayon Misra, 2000.

4. Naga Club's memorandum to the Simon Commission, 1929.
5. Quoted in M. Alemchiba, 1970.
6. S.C. Dev, 1987.
7. Details provided in Subir Bhaumik, 2000.
8. Thuingaleng Muivah, quoted in the BBC report, 2003.
9. 'The New Ethnic Explosion: Lesser Tribes Want Their Say', paper presented at the Queen Elizabeth House, University of Oxford, 2 February 1990.
10. V.S. Jafa, 1999.
11. For a detailed analysis of the Mizo insurgency, see Subir Bhaumik, 'Operation Jericho and After', 1996.
12. V. Venkata Rao, 'Meitei Nationalism', paper presented at the northeast India History Association's annual conference at Imphal, 1983.
13. *Dawn*'s issues between September 1978 and July 1979 (translation by R.K. Kamaljit Singh, editor of *Marup-Agartala*).
14. See PREPAK's political manifesto, which also called for total nationalization of trade and commerce, revival of voluntary labour and the creation of a government based on communist and ancient Manipuri ideals.
15. R.K. Meghen alias Sanayaima, in interview to BBC World Service, aired on World Today programme, 16 June 2005.
16. Subir Bhaumik, 'The Evolution of a Post-Colonial Region', in Partha Chatterjee (ed.), 1997.
17. For details on the conflict between Assam and the Indian Congress leadership, see Udayon Misra, *The Periphery Strikes Back: Challenges to the Nation-State in Assam and Nagaland* (Shimla: Indian Institute of Advanced Study, 2000).
18. Paresh Barua's interview with Subir Bhaumik, broadcast on the BBC Bengali Service on 20 July 2008. In this long interview, he spoke of ULFA's future and Indian strategy and even expressed a glimmer of hope for the ULFA in the changing context of Sino-Indian relations in view of India's growing 'strategic relationship' with the United States. Barua said a great conflict between China and India is in the offing and emphasized that 'smaller forces like ours will either be sandwiched in this conflict or will emerge independent'. It is not however clear whether the Chinese have already offered help to the ULFA.
19. Ibid.
20. Omprakash Mishra et al., 2000.
21. A.K. Bhutani, deputy commissioner of Kokrajhar district, western Assam, quoted in *Times of India*, 22 August 2002.
22. Retired Lieutenant General A.K. Seth, budget speech in the Tripura legislative assembly, March 2001.
23. Monirul Hussain, 2000.
24. West Bengal Chief Minister Bidhan Chandra Roy's letter to Prime Minister Jawaharlal Nehru dated 23 August 1960, quoted in full in Saroj Chakrabarty, 1984.
25. Dr B.C. Roy's letter to Jawaharlal Nehru dated 30 August 1960, in Chakrabarty, *The Upheaval Years in northeast India* (Calcutta: Saraswati Press, 1984).
26. Monirul Hussain, ibid.
27. Hiteswar Saikia, quoted in Monirul Hussain, ibid.
28. NSCN–Khaplang faction's order dated 26 July 2002, reported in BBC World Service, 29 July 2002.

29. Subsidiary Intelligence Bureau, *Monthly Summary of Information from Kohima Branch Office*, March 2002.

30. Ibid.

31. Prafulla Kumar Mahanta, Assam chief minister, quoted in Reuters report, 12 April 1989.

32. Ranjan Daimary alias D.R. Nabla, chairman of the National Democratic Front of Bodoland (previously Bodo Security Force), interview with the writer, quoted in Reuters report, 21 January 1994.

33. Press statement of the Bodo Peoples Action Committee, 12 October 1993.

34. Monirul Hussain, ibid.

35. Assam Police Special Branch report dated 4 November 1993.

36. Figures quoted in Assam government's rehabilitation plan for displaced persons in western Assam, made available to the writer by A.K. Bhutani, deputy commissioner of Kokrajhar district and cross-checked by local journalist Shib Shankar Chatterji.

37. Adivasi Cobra Militants of Assam (ACMA) memorandum to Assam Chief Minister Tarun Gogoi, dated 5 February 2002.

38. Ibid.

39. A.K. Bhutani, deputy commissioner of Kokrajhar district, western Assam, quoted in *Times of India*, 22 August 2002.

40. Maino Daimary, central publicity secretary of the BLTF, in an interview with the writer broadcast on BBC World Service, 12 August 2002.

44. Justin Lakra, president of the All Adivasi Students of Assam, quoted in *Times of India*, 3 October 2002.

42. Interview with Maino Daimary.

43. Meghalaya Census Reports, 1981 and 1991.

44. Dinesh Singh Committee report into the disturbances of June 1980 in Tripura.

45. Compiled from Monthly Crime Summaries of Tripura Police, April 1996 to June 2002.

46. *Dainik Sambad*, 11 April 2002.

47. NSCN press note dated 23 November 1993.

48. T.T. Haokip, 2002.

49. Ibid.

50. In February 2002, 25 Nagas who had fled from Imphal were interviewed by the writer in Ukhrul and Senapati.

51. In October 1998, the writer interviewed the first group of 38 Reang families who crossed over from Phuldungsei in Mizoram to Kanchanpur subdivision in North Tripura district. The BBC broadcasted the story on 23 October 1998 in its *World Today* programme.

52. Zoramthanga, interviewed by the writer and broadcasted on BBC World Service on 14 May 2001.

53. Joint memorandum by the Chakma, Lai and Mara district councils to the Indian government submitted to Home Minister L.K. Advani on 13 December 2000 in Delhi.

54. Lianzela, 2002.

55. Interview with Mrinal Kanti Chakma of the Japan Committee on Chittagong Hill Tracts.

5   The Foreign Hand

India's North East borders on four countries. To its north are China and the Himalayan kingdom of Bhutan, to the east is Burma (Myanmar) and to the west is Bangladesh, which was East Pakistan until 1971. Its link with the Indian heartland is through the tenuous 21-km-wide Siliguri Corridor, which is flanked by Bhutan, Bangladesh and Nepal. The North East accounts for 7.6 per cent of India's land area and 3.6 per cent of the population, but it makes up 40 per cent of India's land borders. The country's seven North Eastern states share 5,200 kilometres of frontier with China, Bhutan, Burma and Bangladesh. During the last 50 years, these neighbours have either been hostile towards India or have failed to quell turmoil in their own frontier regions, thus aggravating the North East's troubled condition.

The most powerful rebel army on Burma's western borders, the Kachin Independence Army (KIA), developed close links with North East Indian separatist groups like the Naga National Council (NNC), the National Socialist Council of Nagaland (NSCN) and the United Liberation Front of Assam (ULFA). They first helped the Naga rebels to reach China in 1966—and then they trained and armed the NSCN, the ULFA and at least two Manipuri rebel groups. Pakistan and China, and then the Islamist regime in Bangladesh, have aided and abetted rebel groups from North East as part of a deliberate design to destabilize India's frontier regions. Chinese support for these rebels started in the mid 1960s and is said to have ended in the early 1980s, but there are some fresh indications that Chinese intelligence are in touch with at least two North East Indian rebel groups after India signed a nuclear deal with the United States and decided to enter into a 'strategic relationship' with them. Pakistan and Bangladesh continued to support rebel groups from the North East, providing them sanctuaries and safe houses, weapons and training facilities. The new Awami League government has, however, said it will not allow its soil to be used for anti-Indian activities and there are some indications that it has put the North Eastern rebels on notice to leave or face the inevitable pushout.

India, too, has used this strategic frontier region to support insurrections in neighbouring countries. During the Bangladesh liberation war, India trained thousands of Bengali guerrillas to fight Pakistani forces in the camps of Tripura, Meghalaya and Assam. When India's relations with Bangladesh worsened after the assassination of the country's founding father, Sheikh Mujibur Rehman, India's external intelligence agency, the Research and Analysis Wing (R&AW) armed and backed the Shanti Bahini guerrillas fighting for self-rule in Bangladesh's Chittagong Hill Tracts (CHT). Support for the Shanti Bahini, which operated from camps in Tripura and Mizoram, was discontinued in the mid 1990s and there are indications that Delhi pressurized them to sign a peace deal with Dhaka in 1997 after the Awami League had come to power for the first time since the forced ouster in 1975.

In the 1990s, India cultivated a host of Burmese ethnic armies not to use them against the military junta in Rangoon but rather to get them to stop aiding North East Indian rebel armies or preventing rising Chinese influence in Burma. Throughout the 1950s, Indian intelligence used the entire stretch of its Himalayan frontier zone to bolster the Tibetan armed struggle against Chinese occupation. Thus, this remote region, with its daunting topography and complex regional surroundings, has witnessed a near continuous spell of 'insurgent crossfire' between India and all her neighbours, with the sole exception of Bhutan, against whom India has steadfastly refused to back any dissidence. I have argued before—and so have many other studies on insurgency—that the element of foreign support has been crucial to the survival of the insurgencies in South Asia, especially in its eastern slice.[1]

By the early 1980s, China and India had stopped backing guerrilla armies against each other. Indian backing for the Burmese rebel groups has also stopped as Delhi appears keen to appease the Burmese military junta, which in turn undertakes occasional military campaigns against North East Indian militants based in its Sagaing Division. Indian support for the insurgency in the CHT has also been abandoned and the rebels of the Shanti Bahini have surrendered. All this, however, has not meant the end of Pakistani and Bangladeshi support for the ethnic rebel armies of northeast India. By all accounts, Pakistan's Inter-Services Intelligence (ISI) continues to maintain close rapport with the ULFA and other North East Indian rebel armies. Bangladesh's military intelligence, the Directorate General of Forces Intelligence (DGFI), has also provided weapons, training and sanctuary to North East Indian rebels on a regular basis. Dhaka alleges that Indian intelligence shelters some of its top criminals and political dissidents in northeast India. Although it is true that some Awami League leaders and secular intellectuals have found shelter in Tripura, and also in West Bengal, there is no evidence that they are receiving support for armed activity from Indian federal agencies.

Unlike Bangladesh, Bhutan has never denied the presence of North East Indian rebels in its territory. It first tried to persuade the ULFA and the National Democratic Front of Bodoland (NDFB)—and also the Kamtapur Liberation Organisation (KLO) of Northern Bengal—to leave the kingdom. But when that did not work, the Bhutanese army started 'Operation All Clear' in December 2003. The fierce military offensive led to the demolition of the bases of all the three rebel groups and forced them to leave Bhutan. But Bhutan is an exception to the regional trend. It is the only neighbour who, after the initial dithering, acted decisively against the anti-Indian rebel groups. Buoyed by its diplomatic success in pressurizing Bhutan to act against the rebels, India is now trying out similar 'push' tactics with Burma and Bangladesh—but with not much success so far. South Asia's 'insurgent crossfire' is far from over, especially in the east.

It all began with the Pakistani support to the Naga insurgency in 1956. NNC chief Angami Zapu Phizo crossed into East Pakistan's Sylhet region in late 1956 after a march through the Karbi Anglong Hills of Assam. The Pakistanis welcomed Phizo as soon as they realized what he was up to. Between 1956 and 1971, Pakistan's ISI backed the NNC, the Mizo National Front (MNF) and the Sengkrak of Tripura. It refused to help the Revolutionary Government of Manipur (RGM) from Manipur because it found the leftist ideological orientation of the Manipuri rebels unacceptable. China started aiding the NNC, the MNF and later the People's Liberation Army (PLA) of Manipur but discontinued all help after 1980. There have been reports of the ULFA and the Manipuri groups receiving substantial quantities of Chinese weapons through Bhutan and Burma, but my own investigations indicate that these weapons are coming through Yunnan-based mafia groups like the Ah Hua and the Blackhouse—and in the last four–five years through the United Wa State Army, in whose 'liberated areas', the Chinese have actually allowed weapons manufacturing franchise. These mafia groups also buy the heavier weapons like mortars from China's government ordnance factories like Norincho and it is hard to accept that Beijing and its vigilant intelligence agencies will not know of these surreptitious weapons sale to the enemies of India. But it is difficult to establish whether Beijing is supplying weapons to rebel groups in northeast India by fronting the mafia proxies.

Bangladesh backs almost all North Eastern Indian militant groups—the guerillas from Assam, Meghalaya, Manipur and Tripura have around 125 camps, smaller hideouts and safe houses in its territory. The NSCN had several bases in the CHT but ever since it started negotiations with India in 1997, these camps have not been functional. India backed the Bengali war of liberation in 1971 and trained thousands of guerillas in Tripura, Assam and Meghalaya. Later, many political opponents of the Bangladesh military junta escaped into northeast India and were sheltered there. The Bangladesh liberation war-hero Kader (Tiger) Siddiqui escaped into Meghalaya and was allowed to stay in the town of Burdwan in West Bengal for around 18 years. India also ran training and operational camps for the Shanti Bahini in Tripura and Mizoram for more than twenty years (1975–96). It ran camps for the Tibetan guerrillas in 1956–62. Indian intelligence maintained hideouts and arms caches in Arunachal Pradesh, Nagaland, Manipur and Mizoram for the KIA, the Arakan Army and the Chin National Front of Burma. The NNC and NSCN, the MNF and the Manipuri rebel groups maintained camps in Burmese territory and it is primarily to dislodge them from there that India started cultivating Burmese rebel groups.

THE SINO-PAKISTANI AXIS

After Phizo secured Pakistani support, the first batch of NNC guerrilla fighters reached East Pakistan for training and weapons in 1958. The speed of their march through the Barail ranges (on trijunction of Assam, Nagaland and Manipur), the Karbi Anglong and the Garo hills foxed Indian intelligence. The charismatic Naga rebel commander Kaito Sema is said to have led this group with great elan. The first Naga rebel camps came up in Sylhet region of East Pakistan and the first batch of Naga rebels returned after four months of training, equipped with automatic weapons that even the Indian army did not possess at that time. After Kaito's dash, it became difficult for the subsequent batches of Naga guerrillas to follow the same route. They took a more difficult and longer route, cutting through eastern Manipur, then turning west through the Chin Hills into the southern Mizo Hills and finally into the CHT of Bangladesh. So, most of the Naga rebel camps after 1958 came up in the CHT because the columns were reaching there.

Between 1958 and 1971, when Pakistan lost its eastern wing, 11 batches of Naga rebels reached East Pakistan for training and weapons. One of the two largest groups of Naga guerrillas, more than 500 fighters led by Dusoi Chakesang, took the long route to East Pakistan through the Chin Hills in October 1963 and returned in October 1964.[2] Taking advantage of the ceasefire in 1964, Zuheto Sema led the largest ever batch of Naga guerrillas (more than 1,000 guerrillas) to East Pakistan by the same route. Military officials estimate that more than 3,000 Naga guerrillas were trained in East Pakistan. Seven camps were set up for the Naga Army—five in the CHT and two in the Sylhet region. The five camps in the Chittagong Hills were located at Alikadam, Rumabazar, Rankhiang, Silopi and Thanchi, while the two camps in Sylhet were located in Srimangal and Khasiapunji.

The camps in Sylhet were used primarily to receive smaller groups who continued to sneak in through the Barail-Karbi Anglong-Garo hills route. The camps in the CHT were meant for the bigger columns who took the longer route through the Chin Hills. Naga guerrillas were trained by instructors from Pakistan's Special Services Group (SSG), an elite special forces unit specializing in behind-the-lines partisan warfare. The SSG had trained the *mujahid*s who entered Indian Kashmir as part of Operation Gibraltar in 1965. One veteran SSG officer, Colonel S.S. Medhi, who had trained both the Nagas and the Kashmir *mujahid*s, later told me:

> The Nagas were far better fighters than the Kashmir *mujahids*. They were disciplined and dedicated and quickly picked up tactics and weapons skills. They clearly had a cause. The *mujahids* from Azad Kashmir were unruly. It was clear they had more interest in women and loot waiting for them in the Srinagar Valley. And morale—the *mujahid* would flee at the first sight of an Indian counter-attack but the Nagas would fight until the bitter end unless he was asked to retreat by his commander for tactical reasons. We only hope we had the Nagas in the west.[3]

Naga rebel leaders and Indian military intelligence, however, do not agree on the number of weapons they received from the Pakistanis. The Indians say every Naga fighter brought back a weapon, but Naga rebel leaders claim that only half of the total number of guerrillas who went to East Pakistan returned with weapons. The rest had to carry back the huge quantity of ammunition without which the guerrillas would not be able to sustain long months of combat. Both sides admit that Pakistani support to the Naga Army was crucial in turning it into a well-knit guerrilla organization in its formative years. The Naga fighters did not lack natural battle instinct, knowledge of the terrain and motivation, but without a reasonably large nucleus of trained guerrillas and modern weapons, they could not have survived against India's professional army. If Pakistan helped build up the Naga Army as a fighting organization, Chinese training and weapons gave it the cutting edge after 1966.

After its short border war with India in 1962, China opened up to the NNC. The first batch of Naga Army left for China from the border village of Totok in June 1966. Led by Thinoselie, the military commander, and Muivah, the commissar, this batch of more than 300 fighters reached Yunnan after a march of 97 days through the Hukawng Valley and the Kachin Hills of Burma. Muivah was taken to the College of Diplomacy in Beijing, where he was indoctrinated in Marxism-Leninism and Mao Zedong's thought, coached in leadership techniques and taken on a brief tour of Vietnam to experience the 'People's War' at close quarters.

While the rank and file of the Naga Army were put through rigorous guerrilla training in three camps in Yunnan, some of their unit commanders were also taken to a camp of the Burmese Communist Party, which was also training thousands of its fighters later used in the big push into Burma's Mong Ko region in 1967. The second batch of Naga Army, about 250 strong, went to China in 1968 under the leadership of Mowu Angami, military commander, and Issac Chisi Swu, commissar. While the first batch came back unscathed, the second batch suffered casualties during encounters with the Burmese army and most of its fighters were betrayed by the Semas of the Revolutionary Government of Nagaland (RGN), who had broken away from the NNC and were being used by the Indian army.

The Chinese trained four subsequent batches of Naga guerrillas. The first two batches were large but the subsequent batches were much smaller. The Naga rebel leadership faced a dilemma in deciding the size of the batches they would send for training—if the batch was small, it could be annihilated by a major Indian or Burmese military operation and would not be able to fight its way out, but at the same time small batches would be harder to detect and might slip through. On the other hand, if the batch consisted of a few hundred guerrillas, it would be difficult to conceal, its supply problems would increase, but it would come back with a much larger body of trained guerrillas and more weapons. For tactical reasons, the Nagas chose to send large batches to Pakistan and China in the initial stages because they had the element of surprise. Subsequent batches were smaller so that they could slip through.

Indian military intelligence estimates that Pakistan and China trained nearly 5,000 Naga guerrillas in all. A special batch of 300 guerrillas, including some from batches previously trained and new recruits, underwent special training in advanced guerrilla warfare and special operations in 1969 in the CHT. Chinese and Pakistani instructors jointly imparted training to this batch. By then, India's two hostile neighbours had set up a joint 'China-Pakistan Coordination Bureau' to coordinate the guerrilla war in the North East. Two intelligence officers from the Foreign Liaison Committee of the Chinese Communist Party and four from the Chinese PLA's training division, including a full colonel, were based in Dhaka and Chittagong under diplomatic cover.

They teamed up with a Pakistani SSG complement supported by the ISI's East Pakistan regional headquarters. The 12-member Coordination Bureau consisted of six Chinese and six Pakistani officials, but there were no representatives from the North East Indian rebel groups. This is where it differed from the nine-member Co-ordination Committee set up to coordinate the guerrilla campaign in Tibet: it contained two US officials, the Central Intelligence Agency (CIA) station chief in Delhi and his deputy, four officials from India's Intelligence Bureau (at that time responsible for both domestic and external intelligence) and three commanders from the Tibetan National Volunteers Defense Army (NVDA).

After the Mizo insurrection, Pakistan opened many more camps for the MNF in the CHT. Between 1967 and 1971, 11 camps were housing 6,000–7,000 Mizo guerrillas in the CHT. Most of them underwent training imparted by SSG instructors and received weapons. When the Bangladesh Liberation War broke out, the MNF units fought with the Pakistani troops against the Bengali 'Mukti Fauj' (liberation army). Four batches of Mizo guerrillas went to Yunnan for training after 1971, when the MNF turned to China for training and weapons after losing its base area in East Pakistan. The first MNF batch led by Damkoshiak Gangte started for China in 1973 but it took them a march of 13 months to reach Tinsum County in Yunnan.

After training, the Chinese gave them some weapons and gold chains, some of which they had to hand over to the Kachins on their way back. An Intelligence Bureau (IB) official has revealed that Damkoshiak had been recruited as a junior operative by the IB's station chief in Manipur, B.R. Sanyal, and then infiltrated into the MNF. This official claims that Damkoshiak just walked back to the IB's outpost in Moreh with most of his China-returned guerrillas and surrendered on 30 June 1975 after being in touch with the IB from his temporary locations in Burma.[4] Subsequent batches of MNF were small and their experience with the Chinese was far from happy. Like the Nagas, the Mizos had to hand over half of the weapons they got from the Chinese to the KIA. The Kachins were always business-like: what they gave the Nagas and Mizos by way of temporary shelter, food and clothes, guides up to the Chinese border and medical help, they got it back in weapons—and gold chains.

A comparative analysis reveals two distinct patterns of sponsorship to guerilla campaigns in South Asia. The Indians and the Americans trained much larger batches of Tibetan guerrillas in a short time between 1956 and 1961 than the number of Naga insurgents trained by China and Pakistan. In five years of peak sponsorship, more than 20,000 Tibetan fighters underwent training in India and the United States, while the Chinese and the Pakistanis trained only one-fourth that number of Naga guerrillas over a much longer duration. More than 60,000 Bengali guerrillas were trained by India in eight months in 1971 that sharply contrasts the number of Mizo rebels—only around 7,000—that were trained by Pakistan and China. Second, the training spans of the Tibetans were shorter than the Nagas. While a Tibetan fighter spent two to three months in an Indian training camp and perhaps as much in a specialist American facility, the Nagas underwent four to five months of training on the average. The training span of the Bengali guerrilla was shorter than the Tibetan as well—30–45 days and 60 in the case of those given specialist sabotage training or special tasks. The Nagas suffered the absence of a common border with the sponsor countries and had to take long circuitous routes that added to the training time. Some would argue that while the Indian or American sponsorship to the Bengali or the Tibetan guerrilla campaigns were meant to provide decisive results within a definite time-frame, the Chinese and the Pakistanis were more keen to keep the pot boiling and bleed India by a policy of 'thousand cuts'.

The Sino-Pakistani sponsorship to the Naga and Mizo insurgencies reached a critical stage with the formation of the Coordination Bureau when it was cut short by the Bengali revolt of 1971 and the Indian military intervention in East Pakistan. In fact, a senior IB-R&AW official stated that Indian support for the Bengali revolt was crucial to counter-balance the Sino-Pakistani sponsorship of the guerrilla struggles in the North East in an almost 'who-gets-whom-first' situation.[5] The much smaller numbers of Naga and Mizo rebels trained by Pakistan and China, compared to the large contingent of Tibetans trained by India and the United States and the huge numbers of Bengali guerrilla fighters trained by India, could be attributed to the following:

1. Pakistan was primarily interested in snatching Kashmir from India. Support for the rebels in the North East was tactically limited to creating a second front of durable turmoil for India that would ensure dispersal of Indian forces on two flanks and help Pakistani-backed irregulars to liberate Kashmir.
2. Nagaland has no common border with either East Pakistan or China and only when the Mizo insurrection started could the two work on a strategy to unsettle the North East by using the border which the Mizo Hills shared with East Pakistan.
3. The border that the Mizo Hills shared with East Pakistan was narrow and could easily be blocked by Indian troops whereas India's border with Tibet was too long to be completely sealed off by the Chinese, atleast in the 1950s.
4. China was backing the rebels in northeast India only to deter India from actively backing the Tibetan guerrillas.
5. India was burdened with a huge flow of refugees from Tibet and Bangladesh, while Pakistan or China faced no refugee exodus from the North East. India therefore pitched its sponsorship of guerrilla armies in Tibet and Bangladesh at a much higher level because it was keen to resolve the crisis quickly.

Apart from the NNC and MNF, the Sengkrak of Tripura also set up bases in the CHT. There is no evidence, however, that they received weapons and training from the Pakistanis, though the latter allowed the rebels from Tripura to operate out of their territory. The Manipuri rebels, on the other hand, were pushed back into India by the Pakistanis. At a later stage, the Chinese supported the Manipuri PLA. Much after it had stopped helping the Naga or the Mizo rebels in the late 1970s, China was still aiding the Manipuri rebels, though the nature of assistance had changed. The Chinese had trained large batches of Naga and Mizo rebels; up to 300 guerrillas had been trained at one time. Instead of training such large batches of Manipuri rebels, however, they decided to train only small batches of leaders. The *ojha*s (pioneers or torchbearers) of the Manipuri PLA were trained and indoctrinated in Marxism-Leninism in small batches of 15 to 20. They were not given arms but were asked to return to Manipur and build up their own arsenal and organization by conducting a Maoist style 'People's War' campaign. Since the PLA leaders were adherents of Marxism-Leninism, the Chinese were inclined to put them through the process of revolutionary struggle without accepting too much liability.

The Nagas and Mizos had gone to China for training and weapons at the peak of the Cultural Revolution, when the Communist Party was keen to export the revolution and support national liberation movements. China supported the outbreak of the Naxalite struggle and hoped that at some stage the ethnic rebel armies of northeast India would forge some ties with the Marxist-Leninists of Bengal and mainland India. That did not happen. After the Shillong Accord, the Naga movement split up and weakened. The MNF also started to move towards a final settlement with India after the 1976 Calcutta agreement. China, under Deng Xiaoping, started to look for ways to normalize relations with India and export of revolution was seen as an unwanted revolutionary baggage of a Maoist past.

The Manipuri PLA was supported because of its ideological affiliations, but only just. When it started to lose its way in the face of strong counter-insurgency measures, China stopped aiding it. Repeated efforts by the ULFA and the NSCN in the late 1980s to secure Chinese help did not lead to any direct assistance from Beijing. Indian intelligence does have some evidence that Chinese intelligence put the NSCN, led by the China-trained Muivah, in touch with the Khmer Rouge (another China-backed group) in Cambodia. That connection helped the later generations of Naga, Assamese and Manipuri rebels secure large quantities of weapons from the Khmer Rouge or from black market operators in South East Asia.[6]

THE UNEASY HILL TRACTS

The end of Chinese support for the North East Indian rebel groups and of Indian support for the Tibetan guerrilla fighters and the dismemberment of Pakistan marked the end of a phase of insurgent crossfire in the subcontinent. India's worst worries, expressed by IB-R&AW eastern region chief P.N. Banerjee, had passed over. Bangladesh became a free nation, expected to be friendly to India, though such expectations were quickly belied. Within four years of liberation, Bangladesh experienced a brutal coup in which the country's founding father, Sheikh Mujibur Rehman, was killed along with many members of his family. In another four years, Bangladesh found itself firmly under military rule and the junta started to cultivate the militants from northeast India again. The immediate provocation for this turn was India's sponsorship of the Shanti Bahini guerrillas in the CHT.

During the Bengali uprising in 1971, India waited for the first two months before Prime Minister Indira Gandhi decided to aid the guerrillas. Indian intelligence had opened some channels of communication with the Awami League in 1968. A senior Awami League leader, Chittaranjan Sutar, had set up base in Calcutta around the time when the situation in East Pakistan was starting to spin out of control. The brutal Pakistani military crackdown in March 1971 against the Awami League and its fraternal groups sent tens of thousands of refugees fleeing to India, among them many of the League's leaders. After some indecision, Mrs Gandhi ordered support for the provisional Bangladesh government formed on Indian soil and the training and arming of the Mukti Fauj went ahead at great speed. Between 200 and 250 camps for the Mukti Fauj were set up in West Bengal and in the three North Eastern states of Tripura, Meghalaya and Assam and thousands of guerillas were trained in them.

Unlike the Pakistani support for the Naga and the Mizo rebels, the element of clandestinity in Indian support was absent from the very beginning. Journalists, foreign diplomats and dignitaries visited Bangladeshi refugee camps and also those where the Mukti Fauj were being trained. The Bengali guerrillas would use these camps for launching operations inside East Pakistan and then return to base. Every time they came back, they briefed Indian intelligence and military officials in detail, procuring information that would ultimately be useful for the Indian military offensive. Unlike the Naga and Mizo rebels, who were trained and told to return to fight in their hills against Indian forces with no regular control by the distant 'handlers', the Bengali guerrillas remained in close contact with Indian officials.

By mid 1971, the Indian military and intelligence establishment was preparing for a final push into East Pakistan because there seemed to be no scope for mediation of the conflict after the genocide. The level of support to the movement was transparent and concentrated; the Bengali guerrilla army operated in close coordination and conformity with the broad directions of Indian military planning. Most of the devastating sabotage operations, like the targeting of all major river and sea ports of East Pakistan in August 1971, were done at the behest of the Indian army. By November 1971, regular Indian Border Security Force units and even army units had started slipping into East Pakistan. A fortnight before war was finally declared, Indian tank regiments were already fighting 60–70 kilometres inside East Pakistan.[7]

The level of coordination between the Indian military machine and the Mukti Fauj began to grow firmly with the progress of the guerrilla campaign and was finally formalized with the setting up of the Joint Command just before the war. By mid 1971, Mrs Gandhi had decided on military intervention to break up Pakistan, which explains why the Indians were supporting the Mukti Fauj quite openly. The successful conclusion of the Bangladesh Liberation War owed as much to Indian support for the guerrilla movement and Mrs Gandhi's decision to decisively intervene militarily as to Pakistan's own failures in crisis management. By committing one of the worst genocides of post-war world, the Pakistani military itself created civil war conditions. The establishment of martial law forced the Awami League into revolutionary guerrilla warfare that it was just not prepared for. The huge refugee exodus forced India to act, or at least gave it a rationale to justify military action, for which global support was carefully drummed up by the Indian leadership.

Within four years of the liberation of Bangladesh, India unleashed another sponsored guerrilla campaign in that country. The immediate provocation for the Indian sponsorship of the Shanti Bahini guerrillas, made up of Chakma, Marma and Tripuri tribesmen, was the military coup that killed Sheikh Mujibur Rehman and many members of his family. To Indira Gandhi, the coup was a political act in defiance of India. Within a week of the coup, senior R&AW officials arrived in Tripura's capital, Agartala, with a clear brief for their subordinates: 'Get us those Chakma leaders who want to fight Bangladesh.'[8]

The Parbattya Chattogram Jana Sanghati Samity (PCJSS) was a political party that had contested elections and sent representatives to the Bangladesh parliament. It wanted extensive autonomy for the

CHT, a hill region dominated by tribes that were neither Muslim nor Bengali. Having failed to get autonomy from an unsympathetic Awami League government, the PCJSS was slowly taken over by hardliners determined to take the path of guerrilla warfare. But unlike the Awami League, the PCJSS had always nurtured a military wing. Armed with weapons left behind in large numbers by the defeated Pakistani army in 1971, the Shanti Bahini had taken on rival groups of militants, like those belonging to the Sarbahara (Proletariat) Party in their CHT homeland. Largely credited with bringing the brigandage and lawlessness in the CHT under control, the Shanti Bahini was ready for action when the opportunity came in 1975.

After the initial parleys in Delhi, PCJSS leaders returned with assurance of Indian support. By mid 1976, the first batch of Shanti Bahini leaders had finished training at a military facility near Dehradun. Larger batches of guerrilla fighters were also trained at Haflong in Assam, where a large training facility for the Special Services Bureau (SSB) existed. By the end of 1979, India had trained 700 guerrillas of the Shanti Bahini including their entire military leadership. A former sector commander of the Shanti Bahini, Suddattapriya Chakma alias Major Roxio, said:

> The Indian training was intensive and tough as the instructors had served with military units in Nagaland and Mizoram. The leadership element of the course was gruelling and involved war games and dummy attacks. The instructors would observe how we went about the attack and whether we had absorbed the theoretical lessons. They would severely admonish us if we were found lacking. They always reminded us of the military maxim that you train hard in peace to bleed less in war.[9]

Just before Mrs Gandhi was defeated in the 1977 parliamentary elections, R&AW officials asked the Shanti Bahini leaders to prepare for 'a big push forward'. They were told that India was prepared to support a strength of up to 15,000 guerrillas with an adequate complement of light automatics and heavier weapons like mortars. Shanti Bahini leaders remember how they were asked to get used to dry Indian-made rations for deep penetration strikes inside the CHT.[10] Indian intelligence was impressed by the success of the Shanti Bahini guerrillas, who were quick to exploit the weakness of the Bangladesh army in mountain warfare. In ambushes, the Shanti

Bahini could manage to kill between 20 to 50 soldiers quite often. Indeed, once the casualty figure of a patrol of the Bangladesh army crossed 50. Tattindralal Chakma alias Pele Talukdar emerged as the most successful Shanti Bahini commander.

It is not clear whether the Indians planned a repeat of 1971 in the CHT. The geo-strategic situation still favoured such an initiative: the United States was licking its wounds from the Vietnam War, the Soviets were still game for decisive intervention, the Chinese were dealing with huge changes in their power structures after Mao's death, Pakistan was in no position to challenge India and Bangladesh was still a country in flux, incapable of any resistance. If India wanted, it might have decisively intervened in the CHT. There is no denying that the strategic location of the CHT was an obvious temptation for any government in Delhi. Almost the entire tribal population of the CHT wanted to be part of India rather than an Islamic country whose military rulers were beginning to change the demography of the area by systematic re-settlement of Bengali Muslim plainsmen.

It is not clear how far Mrs Gandhi wanted to go and it is possible that, after the liberation of Bangladesh, she could see that a successful foreign campaign could boost her dropping popularity back home. But her defeat in the 1977 elections changed the course of events. The R&AW plans to intensify the guerrilla war in the CHT were put on hold when Morarji Desai took over as the prime minister. After Desai's meeting with Bangladesh's military dictator, Zia-ur-Rehman, the R&AW top brass was categorically told to lay off the CHT. The R&AW did not take kindly to this instruction, so it continued to shelter the Shanti Bahini and supply weapons and ammunition, though on a much reduced scale.

When Mrs Gandhi returned to power, the CHT operations were resumed. By then, however, the PCJSS–Shanti Bahini was torn apart by a fratricidal feud that considerably weakened the once powerful guerrilla organization. The feud led to the assassination of its leader M.N. Larma in a camp near the Indian village of Bhagabantilla in November 1983. The R&AW firmly intervened to settle the differences within the PCJSS. Under the memorandum of understanding signed by leaders of the two factions in 1985, the Priti Chakma faction was designated the 'Niskriyo' (inactive) group and the Santu Larma faction was designated the 'Sakriyo' (active) faction.

The settlement was drafted by the R&AW station chief in Agartala, Parimal Kumar Ghosh, who pushed it through despite reservations entertained by the Priti Chakma faction.[11]

The Santu Larma faction continued to receive some support from the R&AW. In the summer of 1986, it unleashed a fresh offensive in the CHT. But the rift within the organization had reduced it to a pale shadow of what it was in the 1970s. Its failure to stop the implementation of a new legislation that divided the CHT into three administrative districts showed its limitations as a guerrilla force capable of influencing events. Only a radical change of tactics, such as unleashing a decisive attack against the Kaptai Dam, might have forced Bangladesh to call off the elections. But neither was India willing to step up the ante in the CHT in view of changing regional realities nor was the Shanti Bahini capable of delivering such a massive blow. After the fall of General Ershad and the takeover of power by an elected government in 1991, the Shanti Bahini started negotiations with the Bangladesh government that culminated in 1997 settlement after the Awami League had come back to power in Dhaka.

BANGLADESH: FRIEND TO FOE

Bangladesh's military rulers started providing shelter to the rebels from northeast India in 1978, three years after India started training and arming the Shanti Bahini. The MNF was the first to set up camps in the CHT after the birth of Bangladesh. In 1971, they had fled from the area after Indian troops and the Mukti Fauj swept into the country. The MNF leadership, including Laldenga, travelled down the Karnaphuli River to Burma's Arakan province, where Pakistani intelligence officials operating under consular cover in Burma provided them with false travel documents and flew them out to Karachi. Laldenga and his wife travelled under the false name of Mr and Mrs Zolkeps.

The rest of the MNF fighters trekked back to Mizoram and hid in the remote mountains. In April 1978, the MNF first came back to the CHT and within four months set up six camps: central headquarters at Chhimtlang, supply headquarters at Rumabazar, general headquarters at Alikadam, tactical headquarters for the Dampa

Area Command (west Mizoram) at New Langkor, tactical head-quarters at Lama, and two smaller transit camps close to Parva and Tuipuibari villages in Mizoram. These camps were located in the present Bandarban district near the junction with Burma and in the remote northern Sajek ranges near the junction with Tripura. These areas were not populated at all or were sparsely populated with smaller tribes like the Bawm and the Pangko. The MNF avoided setting up any camp in Chakma areas for fear of attack by the India-backed Shanti Bahini.

But as the MNF increased its presence in the CHT and the number of its transit camps increased to 13 by 1982, it inadvertently stepped into Chakma-dominated areas. In that period, to oblige the R&AW, the Shanti Bahini attacked the MNF columns and camps at six different places. The MNF suffered up to 30 casualties and their operations were stifled. Its animosity towards the Chakmas increased. By 1984, the Tribal National Volunteers (TNV) of Tripura had also set up six camps in the Sajek ranges and four camps in other parts of what is now the Khagracherri district of the CHT. The TNV headquarters were located at Singlum, the military wing head-quarters were located at Thangnan. A ring of transit camps, like those set up by the MNF, were established by the TNV as well. This author has seen many of these camps, having visited them on foot.

In 1984, Bangladesh's Directorate General of Forces Intelligence (DGFI) set up a post at Marisha and another at Alikadam to coordinate with these MNF and TNV bases. Later that year, TNV leader B.K. Hrangkhawl visited Pakistan along with two MNF leaders. Subsequently, the NSCN also returned to the CHT and set up three bases, including the one at Silopi that was earlier used by the NNC. After 1990, the DGFI developed close links with the ULFA, the NDFB, the PLA and United National Liberation Front (UNLF) of Manipur. Now even Meghalaya rebel groups like the Achik National Volunteers Council and Tripura rebel groups like the All-Tripura Tiger Force (ATTF) and the National Liberation Front of Tripura (NLFT) are all based in Bangladesh. The Indian government has recently claimed that 108 bases belonging to as many as 11 rebel groups from northeast India exist in Bangladesh.

The two Tripura rebel groups, the NLFT and the ATTF, accounted for the maximum number of bases—48 in all. But some of these bases have closed down after the Awami League came to power in January 2009. The rebels were anticipating end of Bangladesh patronage and decided to move out before it was too late. The Achik National Volunteer Council (ANVC), ULFA and NDFB had 37 bases, the Manipur rebel groups had 17, and six are maintained by smaller Islamic militant groups like the Muslim United Liberation Tigers of Assam (MULTA) and the People's United Liberation Front (PULF), which represents the Pangal Muslims of Manipur. Again, some of these bases have also closed down for similar reasons. The NSCN is said to have closed down their bases in Bangladesh in 1999. My own extensive investigations into the North East Indian rebel presence in Bangladesh suggest that the Indian claims are far over the mark. The methodology used by Indian intelligence to collate the number of bases described by surrendered or arrested guerrillas during their interrogation is not sound. Since guerrillas refer to all small and big hideouts and even safe houses as 'bases' and several guerrillas use different location names to describe the same base, the estimate by Indian intelligence is far in excess to those that are actually operational.

For instance, a detailed verification of the number of bases used by Tripura rebels has revealed that the two NLFT factions (one headed by Biswamohan Debbarma and the other by Nayanbashi Jamatia) and the ATTF maintain not more than 30 bases in Bangladesh. Almost all these bases are located in the two districts of the Sylhet region (Habiganj and Maulavibazar) and three districts of the CHT (Khagracherri, Rangamati and Bandarban). The Sylhet bases provide the rebels access to north and west Tripura and those in the CHT give them easy entry and exit into south Tripura and Dhalai district. The state police special branch has listed 30 bases that are being used regularly by the ATTF and the two NLFT factions:[12]

1. ATTF:
   - Satcherri (Headquarters), Chunarughat Police Station, Habiganj district
   - Dalucherra, Chunarughat Police Station, Habiganj district
   - Srimangal, Chunarughat Police Station, Habiganj district
   - Moskinserghat, Chunarughat Police Station, Habiganj district
   - Balla Forest base, Chunarughat Police Station, Habiganj district

- Khasiapunji, Kamalganj Police Station, Maulavibazar district
- Machaicherra, Kamalganj Police Station, Maulavibazar district
- Matiranga (Wachu), Matiranga Police Station, Khagracherri district, CHT
- Taraban (shared with ULFA), Dighinala Police Station, Khagracherri district
- Biswa Road (Administrative Headquarters, Leaders Safehouse), Dhaka City (the ATTF is said to have opened another large safe house at Shyamoli)

2. NLFT (Biswamohan faction):
- Dudhpatilghat, Srimangal Police Station, Maulavibazar district, Sylhet Region
- Niralapunji, Kamalganj Police Station, Maulavibazar district, Sylhet Region
- Semai (Hongkong), Group-Headquarters, Sajek Hills, Rangamati district, CHT
- Lallu Kalu (Thunder Regiment headquarters), Sajek Hills, Rangamati district, CHT
- Tanglaikanta (Ranger Regiment headquarters), Sajek Hills, Rangamati district, CHT
- Thangnan (Panther Regiment headquarters), Sajek Hills, Rangamati district, CHT
- Khagrapur (Family Quarters), Dighinala Police Station, Khagracherri district, CHT
- Sajek (Family Quarters), Sajek Hills, Rangamati district, CHT
- Sajek (Rest and Medical Camp), Sajek Hills, Rangamati district, CHT
- 9-Mile Camp (Stores), Matiranga Police Station, Khagracherri district, CHT
- Ujancherri, Sajek Hills, Rangamati district, CHT
- Gilgal (taken from NSCN), Thanchi Police Station, Bandarban district, CHT
- Ramu, Ramu Police Station, Cox's Bazaar district
- Halishahar (administrative headquarters), Chittagong City

- Sugandha Colony (used as safe house by leaders), Pahartoli, Chittagong City

3. NLFT (Nayanbashi Jamatia faction):
   - Bhanumara (headquarters), Chunarughat Police Station, Habiganj district, Sylhet
   - Nalua forest camp, Chunarughat Police Station, Habiganj district, Sylhet
   - Kalanjipunji (tactical camp), Kamalganj Police Station, Habiganj district, Sylhet
   - Mangaljipunji (training camp), Kamalganj Police Station, Maulavibazar district, Sylhet Kudalia (Gajipur), Burichong Police Station, Comilla district

Sylhet and the CHT have large tribal populations of Tripuri stock, so the Tripura rebels find it more convenient to set up operational camps in those areas. The hilly jungle terrain also favours easy concealment. The ATTF's major bases are in Sylhet because they control the contiguous areas of Tripura's west district. From the rest of the state, they have been driven out by the NLFT. But the NLFT's main faction lost most of its Sylhet bases to the breakaway faction after the split in the party. The Biswamohan faction tried to set up a base in Burichong but they were beaten back by the Nayanbashi faction. Bangladesh was embarrassed by these factional feuds and later, in a BBC interview, Bangladesh's former Foreign Minister Morshed Khan had to accept that the NLFT factions had clashed in its territory.[13]

Though Bangladesh officially denies the North East Indian rebel presence and routinely commits not to allow its territory to be used by Indian rebels, its police has arrested more than 40 Tripura rebels, including those arrested after a truck with huge quantity of weapons belonging to the ATTF was seized at Kahalu *upa-zilla* in Bogra district of western Bangladesh. Joges Debbarma, *upa-zilla* chairman of Satcherri for more than 14 years and a well-known patron of the ATTF, was among those arrested. That pointed to the ATTF's involvement—and perhaps that of the ULFA—in a gun-running racket intended to supply weapons to mainland Maoist rebels through Bangladesh.

The DGFI has two units, one at Srimangal and the other at Rangamati to liaise with the Tripura rebels. The units operate under the DGFI's Operations Bureau. The same bureau also liaises with the ULFA leaders. After being pushed out of Bhutan, the ULFA has set up at least eight bases in the Mymensingh region bordering the Indian state of Meghalaya. Dristhi Rajkhowa, one of the ULFA's top hit men who killed Assam's minister Nagen Sarmah with a bomb planted on a road, has been promoted to area commander of the Mymensingh area. The ULFA had traditionally maintained only a transit camp at Sherpur but now its presence in the area has grown. The largest ULFA camp is said to be based in Halughat, not far from the border with Meghalaya. The ULFA's leadership, however, has stayed in Dhaka, maintaining at least 12 safe houses over the past 15 years.[14]

The locations have been changed from time to time to avoid attacks by Bangladeshi criminal syndicates funded by Indian intelligence. The ULFA military wing chief Paresh Barua has been attacked at least five times at separate locations: on a road that connects Khagracherri to Chittagong, then in an apartment at Dhaka's posh Gulshan locality and again in another apartment at Kakrail in Dhaka, then once near a Chinese restaurant in Gulshan and once finally when he was leaving the office of a transport company at Segun Bagicha in Dhaka's old town. The ULFA general secretary Anup Chetia was arrested from Dhaka's Mohammedpur locality and has served a long sentence in a city prison. After their pullout from Bhutan, Bangladesh is the major foreign area for the ULFA and for other rebel groups from Assam and Meghalaya.

The NDFB and the ANVC bases are also located in the Mymensingh region, not far from the ULFA bases. These two rebel groups have been 'taxing' the coal exports to Bangladesh. During the recent kidnappings of coal traders and customs officials from the Garo Hills, the families of the victims were asked to reach Bangladesh to make the payment in US dollars. The Manipur groups, especially the PLA, have more bases in Burma's Sagaing Division than in Bangladesh, but it runs not less than six bases in the Sylhet area. The largest PLA camps in Bangladesh are located at Chotodemai and Bhanugach. Both these camps house 50 to 70 guerrillas at any point of time.

When Awami League came to power in the 1996 elections, it promised to deal firmly with any anti-Indian rebel group that had bases in Bangladesh. Anup Chetia was arrested within a few months of the League's return to power. But the Awami League had limited control over the country's military establishment and the secret services. There is also evidence that some rebel groups who did not enjoy direct access to senior intelligence officials survived in Bangladesh by paying off local Bangladesh Rifles (BDR) camp commandants. The rates of payment varied between 15,000 and 25,000 Bangladeshi takas per camp per year.

The number of North East Indian rebel camps in Bangladesh may have been exaggerated by Indian intelligence, but there is no denying that at least 63 camps and large hideouts or safe houses of eleven rebel groups from northeast India remain operational. Without doubt, it is the largest foreign base area for the rebels of the North East. The wheel has come full circle. India backed the Bengali liberation war and intervened militarily in East Pakistan to achieve its strategic objective of dissecting Pakistan to create a friendly neighbour in the east. That was crucial to the security of the eastern and North Eastern states. After the 1975 coup, India-baiting became a useful political tool in Bangladesh. Its military and intelligence services reverted to the policy of the Pakistani era—of backing North East Indian militants.

Bangladesh also serves as the base for many Islamic *jihadi* groups, domestic, regional and foreign. Western media reports have indicated the arrival of many Al-Qaida and Taliban elements who have found shelter with the homegrown *jihadi*s like Harkat Ul Jehad al Islami.[15] From the hijackers of the Indian Airlines flight that was taken to Kandahar to the attackers of the American Cultural Centre in Calcutta to the serial bombings of Malegaon, Bangalore, Jaipur and Ahmedabad, all important *jihadi* attacks in India in recent years have been launched by elements with a base in Bangladesh. The ISI has expanded its networks in Bangladesh, closely backed by the DGFI and Islamic fundamentalist groups. Thus, India's strategic objective in the creation of Bangladesh has been largely defeated and undermined.

BURMA: CHANGING EQUATIONS

Ever since the British left Burma, the country has been in the throes of a civil war. Its western borders with India were relatively less volatile than its eastern borders with Thailand and northern borders with China, where powerful rebel groups took control of 'liberated areas' in the 1950s. When the Kachins revolted in 1961, however, Burmese control over parts of its western borders began to weaken. The Chin and Arakanese rebels were not strong enough to offset the Tatmadaw (Burmese army) but the KIA liberated large tracts of the Kachin Hills with a powerful ethnic rebel army that could boast of more than 8,000 guerrillas.

The Kachins—a martial people like the Gurkhas of Nepal—had played a key role in blocking the Japanese advance towards North Burma that could have cut off the Stillwell Road and the Allied supplies to China. The 'Kachin Levies' earned the sobriquet of 'Little Assassins'. By the mid 1960s, the KIA controlled most of the Kachin state, including the north western border with India. From 1966, the KIA started providing the corridor for Naga and Mizo rebel columns going to China. Later, when China stopped helping the guerrillas from northeast India, the KIA provided them with bases, training and weapons—all at a price.

By the end of the 1980s, Indian intelligence services were desperate to 'do something about the Kachin connection'. Denied Chinese support when Beijing started to improve its relations with the Burmese military junta, the KIA was compelled to look to Burma's other big neighbour, India. A senior R&AW official who set up India's links with the KIA says they were given at least two large consignments of weapons between 1990 and 1992 and promised more. The estimates of Indian weapons supplied to the KIA vary between 700 and 900 assault rifles, light machine guns, carbines, grenades and assorted ammunition. For its part, the KIA agreed to deny support, bases, weapons or training to the North East Indian rebel groups. Indeed, for two years, a full team of R&AW agents, equipped with communication equipment, were based in the KIA's 'second brigade' headquarters at Pasao. A Burma-born Indian officer was in charge of this team, which quietly monitored the movement of all North East Indian rebel groups in that strategic corridor.[16]

Apart from denying Kachin support to the North East Indian rebels, the R&AW managed to use their influence with the KIA to deny the NSCN and the ULFA the membership of the Burmese rebel coalition National Democratic Front (NDF) and the Democratic Alliance of Burma (DAB). Both the NSCN and the ULFA were seeking the membership of the NDF and the DAB because that would help them develop a vast fall-back zone in Burma. The KIA leaders regularly visited Delhi and were hosted by two successive R&AW chiefs. When the R&AW discovered that Brangsein had authorized a KIA mission to Pakistan to meet Afghan rebels in order to procure Stinger missiles, the relationship suffered its first strain. The KIA team met Gulbuddin Hekmatyer and tried to negotiate the purchase of the Stinger missiles, but the deal had to be called off when the Indians found out and hauled up Brangsein.

The KIA made another mistake. The Indians insisted on total secrecy of weapons transfer because they were keen to help the KIA but not willing to be seen doing it. The R&AW had asked the KIA to refrain from attacking the two Burmese army camps close to the Indian border near the Pangshau Pass, so that the supply route to the KIA's major base areas could be maintained. Disregarding the R&AW's advice, KIA military wing chief Malizup Zau Mai launched a blistering assault on the two camps, forcing many Burmese soldiers to flee to India and seek shelter at the Indian military base of Vijaynagar. Burmese intelligence soon found out that the KIA had been receiving weapons from India and wasted no time to block the supply routes.[17]

After 1988, Burma received Chinese military hardware worth close to $2 billion that qualitatively augmented the offensive capability of the Tatmadaw. The KIA could just about hold out with Indian assistance but it lost huge areas during the Tatmadaw's winter offensive of 1992–93. In February 1994, it declared a ceasefire with the Tatmadaw, as many of Burma's rebel armies had already done. But though the R&AW–KIA relations failed to grow after the ceasefire, the KIA kept its promise of not allowing any North East Indian rebel group to be based in areas it controls. Nor has it supplied weapons or trained North East Indian rebels ever since.

After 1997, India discontinued all forms of support to the Burmese rebel armies it had helped during 1988–95. The KIA was allowed to retain a 'liaison post' in Delhi, but the National Unity Party of Arakans (NUPA) and Chin National Front (CNF) were hounded out by Indian intelligence.[18] India improved its relationship with the Burmese military junta and one of the key elements of this emerging relationship is the agreement to operate against trans-border rebel groups on a mutual basis. So India denied her territory to be used by the KIA, the CNF or the NUPA, and the Burmese started attacking the NSCN rebel bases in its territory. With its improved military capability, the Tatmadaw has been in control of much of its long border with India.

The only hiccup in this emerging relationship was the capture of 192 Manipuri rebels and the seizure of 1,600 units of weaponry by the Tatmadaw during operations around Tamu in November 2001. India did not take kindly to the Burmese refusal to hand over the rebels, among them some of the top guns of the Manipuri insurgency, like UNLF chairman Rajkumar Meghen alias Sanayaima. Diplomatic sources suggest that the Burmese junta was annoyed by Western media reports sourced to Indian intelligence according to which Rangoon had given shelter to two Pakistani nuclear scientists who were close to the Taliban and were wanted by the Americans. The last thing the junta would want is an American aircraft carrier off its coast poised for punitive action. But despite the occasional hiccups, the Indian and the Burmese armies regularly exchange notes and try coordinating trans-border counter-insurgency operations against the rebel groups. The bonhomie has not helped India much. The Manipuri rebel groups and the ULFA have not been attacked by the Tatmadaw so far.

Only the NSCN's Khaplang group has faced Burmese attacks because its vision of independent Nagaland includes 'eastern Nagaland' which is Burmese territory.

BHUTAN: ALL CLEAR

Given Bhutan's economic and strategic dependence on India, one would have least expected her enemies to find shelter in the land of the Druk Yul. Indian intelligence and its military establishment were slow to react when the ULFA and the NDFB started moving into the southern foothills of Bhutan in 1992–93. For the guerilla captains from Assam, Bhutan was a much more attractive base than far-off Bangladesh. Bangladesh's border with Assam is largely riverine, dominated by a Bengali population that's less than friendly towards the ULFA or the NDFB. Bhutan's terrain, on the other hand, is perfect for guerilla camps—hilly and thick with vegetation. The kingdom is also close to the Bodo and the Assamese heartland, the Manas River and the forests straddling the hilly frontier.

'Operation Rhino', launched by the Indian army in 1992, unsettled the ULFA and sent it scurrying for cover. The first ULFA bases in Bhutan were on the border—Guabari, Ngalam and Kalikhola. But by the end of the decade, the ULFA had set up at least 17 camps in the four southern districts of the kingdom. An Assamese security analyst, with impeccable sources in the state's intelligence and access to interrogation reports of ULFA leaders, has listed the bases used by the ULFA at the peak of its presence in Bhutan.[19] The camps are located at Mithundra, Gobarkunda, Panbang, Diyajima, Pemaghetsal Complex (Khar, Shumar, Nakar), Chaibari, Marthong, Gerowa, Sukhni (Marungphu), where the ULFA General Headquarters are located, Melange, Marsala (Dinghshi Ri), where the ULFA Council Headquarters are located, Dalim-Koipani (Orang), Neoli Debarli, Chemari, Phukatong, Wangphu and Kalikhola. The NDFB also has at least 10 camps in the area.

In the last decade, the bases in Bhutan have provided the ULFA and the NDFB with a very useful operational area. Because the border runs close to districts where the two groups enjoyed some popular support, the bases were used for strike-and-withdraw operations. The camps in Bhutan gave these two groups enormous operational flexibility and were key to their survival as functional groups. When the KLO moved in as well to set up three to four bases around the ULFA's camp of Kalikhola, the Bhutan base area began to resemble the one in Burma during the mid 1980s.

Bhutan, unlike Bangladesh, made no secret of the North East Indian rebel presence in the kingdom. The royal government, however, first tried persuasion with the rebel leaders to leave Bhutan rather than opt for a protracted military operation. In 2003, the ULFA and NDFB shifted some bases from Bhutan. The Assam police and the army organized 'strike groups' of surrendered rebels who had attacked ULFA hideouts in southern Bhutan. It was already becoming increasingly difficult for the ULFA and the NDFB to hold out in Bhutan, when Bhutan's small army unleashed 'Operation All Clear' on the morning of 15 December 2003—a comprehensive one-month long offensive against the bases of the ULFA, NDFB and KLO on a wide are from Daifam in the east to Samste in the west. Indian army chief General N.C. Vij later admitted that at least 650 rebels were neutralized—killed or captured.[20] Among them were some of the top guns of Assam insurgency like the ULFA quartet of Robin Neog, Bening Rava, Robin Handique and Asantha Bag Phukan. One Indian division commander posted in the region later said the 'Bhutanese really delivered the way we wanted them to'.[21]

'All Clear' is now India's best inspiration for moving away from the 'insurgent crossfire' model to one of trans-regional cooperation with neighbours to control trans-border insurgencies in the North East. Indian diplomats and leaders are pressurizing Burma and Bangladesh to do a Bhutan on the anti-Indian rebel armies based in their territory, promising to end aid and support to rebel groups and criminal elements considered inimical to their security by Burma and Bangladesh, without much success so far. But India has stopped help to rebel groups in Burma and Bangladesh in the hope that they would reciprocate. If they don't, India always has the option to resume the 'insurgent crossfire' in the eastern slice of South Asia—as it did up until the end of 1990s. The ethnic groups in CHT of Bangladesh or in the Kachin-Chin Hills and Arakan province of Burma are still as restive as ever and resentful of federal control—like those in India's North East. That's a perfect setting for 'insurgent crossfire'—mutual sponsorship of guerrilla warfare against each other as a favourite low-cost offensive action that's been the name of the game in South Asian statecraft since the colonial withdrawal from the subcontinent. In the west, Pakistan alleges that India is interfering in Balochistan by arming and training Balochi youths in Afghanistan . By agreeing to 'look into information that Pakistan has on threats in Balochistan and other areas' in a formal joint communiqué issued after the meeting of the Indian and Pakistani prime ministers in Egypt in July 2009, India has fuelled speculation of having started a covert tit-for-tat to punish Pakistan for its involvement in Kashmir and in supporting other jihadi groups against India. That already indicates to a pos-sible revival of the insurgent crossfire in the west—if India's patience is taxed by inaction or duplicity by its neighbours in the east, the insurgent crossfire could be back in the east and the North Eastern slice of the subcontinent.

NOTES

1. For a detailed study on these proxy wars, see Subir Bhaumik, 1996.
2. S.P. Sinha, 1998.
3. I was introduced to Colonel Medhi by a common friend, I.H. Malik, at Oxford University. In December 1989, Colonel Medhi gave me a detailed interview on his SSG experiences and also presented me his monograph, called the *Medhi Papers*, which looks at the causes of failure of Operation Gibraltar in Kashmir in 1965.
4. Subir Dutta, a decorated IB official now re-employed with the IB, was in charge of its Moreh outpost when Damkoshiak walked in with his entire group of China-returned guerrillas, surprising the army and the local police.
5. The R&AW's eastern regional chief, P.N. Banerjee, argued that if India did not seize the opportunity provided by the Bengali insurrection in East Pakistan, Delhi would in the long run find it difficult to retain the North East in view of the Sino-Pak axis of support to the myriad rebel groups there. I have notes from a retired official who attended Mr Banerjee's briefings in 1971. For details, see Bhaumik, *Insurgent Crossfire*.
6. The R&AW's former additional secretary B.B. Nandi, former Bangkok and Dhaka station chief of the organization, in an interview with the writer. He is no more.
7. A commemorative volume of the 45th Indian armoured regiment, published in 1983, admitted that its units had fought in Garibpur, deep inside East Pakistan, on 20 November 1971. They demanded battle honour for that successful action rather than for the one in Darsana, which they fought later in the war.
8. Retired R&AW official Gopal Chakma, in an interview with the writer, said a joint secretary of his organization arrived within a week of the coup and asked him to set up contact with the Parbattya Chattogram Jana Sanghati Samity (PCJSS) and its military wing, the Shanti Bahini. Within another week, three PCJSS leaders, including its present chief Santu Larma, were on their way to Delhi, accompanied by that joint secretary.
9. Sudattapriya Chakma alias Dipayan alias Major Roxio commanded Sector Four of the Shanti Bahini until the split within the PCJSS and the fratricidal feud that erupted in 1982. The R&AW decided to disarm the Priti Kumar faction of the PCJSS-Shanti Bahini and Major Roxio was asked to give up his weapons by the R&AW station chief in Agartala, Parimal Kumar Ghosh. During his subsequent days in India, Roxio kept in close touch with me until he returned to Bangladesh in 1998 after the PCJSS signed an accord with Dhaka. Roxio's second-in-command, Suman, settled down in Tripura, completed his degree and joined the Tripura Revenue Service as *tehsildar*.
10. Priti Kumar Chakma, Shanti Bahini leader who in 1977 was in charge of the foreign liaison unit of the PCJSS deployed in Agartala to liase with the R&AW on a regular basis.
11. Parimal Kumar Ghosh served in the BSF intelligence and developed close relations with Zia-ur-Rehman during the 1971 war, when he operated under the pseudonym Captain Ali. He later joined the R&AW and served the organization with distinction in India and abroad, before returning to the BSF as commandant of its Intelligence Training School. For much of the period that India backed the

Shanti Bahini, Ghosh (under the pseudonym Major Choudhury) served as the R&AW station chief in Agartala.

12. Tripura police Special Branch's pamphlet *ATTF-NLFT Camps in Bangladesh*, a copy of which was made available to the writer.

13. Morshed Khan, interview in BBC Bengali Service, 2 December 2002.

14. Assam police special branch chief Khagen Sarmah provided details of these twelve ULFA hideouts in Dhaka at a press conference in Guwahati on 24 July 2007.

15. The *Far Eastern Economic Review* (4 April 2002) and *Time* (21 October 2002) reported in detail the presence in Bangladesh of Al-Qaida and Taliban fighters who are believed to have arrived by ship. Bangladesh dismissed these reports as false but Indian and Western intelligence officials have confirmed them, saying that Osama Bin Laden's number two, Ayman Al Zawahiri, also found shelter in Bangladesh for a while in 2002 after the United States intensified its global search for Al-Qaida elements.

16. The late B.B. Nandi, a former additional secretary of R&AW, set up close links with the KIA during his tenure as R&AW station chief in Bangkok. He developed a personal rapport with KIA chief Maran Brangsein and settled on a quid pro quo: the KIA promised not to help any North East Indian rebel group any more; the R&AW promised weapons and ammunition that the KIA needed to fight the Burmese junta. This relationship was short lived, however, and did not last beyond 1993. The KIA announced a ceasefire with Burmese forces in 1994 and has not resumed fighting the Tatmadaw.

17. B.B. Nandi, interview with the writer, 25 May 2003.

18. The NUPA, who had helped India block the arms route from the black markets of South East Asia through the Arakans, was mercilessly duped by Indian military intelligence. The NUPA was offered two islands in the Andamans, but when its members arrived there by sea in February 1998, six of their leaders were shot dead and the rest imprisoned at Port Blair. The CNF bases in Mizoram were regularly attacked and neutralized by the Assam Rifles. For details on the NUPA's relations with Indian intelligence, see Subir Bhaumik, 2001. Now the whole story has been documented by India's top human rights lawyer Nandita Haksar 2009.

19. Jaideep Saikia. 'Revolutionaries or Warlords: ULFA's Organisational Profile. 'Faultlines'

20. Provin Kumar, 2004.

21. Major General Gaganjit Singh, former Goe, 20th Indian mountain division based at Rangiya on Assam-Bhutan border, interview with the author, 3 February 2004.

6   Guns, Drugs and Contraband

Remote frontier locations, difficult hill and jungle terrain, weak and corrupt local administration and trans-national kinship networks encourage not only insurgents but also big-time criminal syndicates. With its pre-British tradition of opium farming and consumption, its proximity to Burma's infamous Golden Triangle, its remoteness from the Indian heartland (which renders goods from China, Burma and Bangladesh cheaper than those produced in Mumbai or Chennai), and with a thriving demand for weapons created by the unending 'little wars', the North East has become a happy hunting ground for smugglers, arms merchants and drug lords operating within the region and across its borders in the immediate neighbourhood. If ethnicity and religion, land and language, population movements and insurgencies have contributed to the crisis in India's North East, the proliferation of arms, drugs and the contraband economy have pushed it towards what Sanjib Baruah describes as 'durable disorder'. In fact, if the flow of drugs and arms into the North East is not checked, the region may permanently slide into a 'durable disorder' situation one usually associates with Colombia or Afghanistan.

Two major wars engulfed the 'North East' at its peak. During the Second World War, the 'North East' became a major Allied base, first for supplying China through air and road (after the Stillwell Road was commissioned), then for stopping the Japanese offensive into India with Subhas Bose' Azad Hind Fauj in tow. Some of the fiercest battles of the Second World War were fought along the Kohima–Imphal front line. Local tribes like the Nagas and the Kukis were drawn into the fighting as porters, scouts and irregular partisans. As the Japanese and the Allies pulled out of the area towards the end of the war and the fighting spilled into Burma, their armies left behind thousands of weapons in the dense jungles of the frontier region. These were the weapons with which the Naga separatists first fought the Indian security forces.

In 1971, the Bangladesh Liberation War led to a major proliferation of small arms in the region. More than 90,000 Pakistani troops surrendered and many of their weapons found their way into the Bangladeshi countryside and towns, later spilling over into the thriving black market of India's border states, specially in the North East. It is anybody's guess how many weapons recovered from the Pakistani troops were listed by the Indians and by the Bengali guerrillas as seizures and how many just vanished. As a resident of a border town like Agartala during the Bangladesh Liberation War, I have personal knowledge of local gangsters buying Pakistani weapons from corrupt Indian military personnel or from the Mukti Fauj guerrillas. Sheikh Mujib's call to the Mukti Fauj to surrender all their weapons after the war ended evoked a grudging and a very partial response. Many of the North East's second flush of guerrilla movements (the post-1971 groups) initially armed themselves with these weapons.

The continuing civil war in Burma and the policy of insurgency patronage adopted by China, Pakistan, India and Bangladesh have also added to the availability of weapons in the region. After every large-scale surrender of rebel armies, the weapons black market in the region has swelled with fresh weapons. Unsettled conditions in South East Asia have also added to the availability of cheap, easy-to-use light arms. The Vietnam War and the post-1975 conflicts in Indo-China led to a steady flow of modern weapons into the black markets of Thailand and Burma. The National Socialist Council of Nagaland (NSCN), the Manipuri insurgents and the United Liberation Front of Assam (ULFA), and even other smaller North Eastern insurgent groups bought much of their weapons from these South East Asian black markets.

In the mid 1960s, the quality of Naga rebels' small arms inventory was better than the Indian army's. The Pakistanis supplied them with US-made weapons. Later they received Chinese weapons, as did the Mizo insurgents. Estimates made by Indian military intelligence suggest that the Naga Army and the Mizo National Front (MNF) together received no less than 3,000–4,000 assault rifles, automatic carbines, light machine guns, rocket launchers and an assortment of other weapons. Over time, more than 80 per cent of those weapons were either recovered or seized by the Indian security forces; or lost in action in India and Burma; or were deposited with the authorities during en masse surrenders beginning late 1960s. Some of the Naga Army's weapons were retained by those Naga fighters who stayed behind with the NSCN, while some of the MNF's weapons found their way into the black markets of North East.

Some former rebels, however, claim that the Indian estimates of Pakistani and Chinese weapons received by the Naga Army are exaggerated because they are based on the assumption that every guerrilla who went to Pakistan or China came back with at least one weapon. After collating their estimates, it would seem more probable that the Naga Army and the MNF returned with just over 2,000 pieces of small arms. Naga rebel commander Mowu Angami, a veteran of many marches to East Pakistan and later to China, told me before his death in August 2003: 'Only half our boys were fully armed, the rest were carrying supplies of ammunition given with the rifles and the automatics, they were covering a lot of ground over very difficult terrain, so there was no way they could all carry one or two weapons each.'[1] Former MNF leader Bualhranga agrees, but he says that since the marching distance of the MNF groups going to the Chittagong Hill Tracts was much less than the route taken by the Naga Army, the former brought back more weapons from East Pakistan. Similarly, the Nagas brought back more weapons from China because they marched over lesser distances than the Mizos.[2]

While the Naga Army and the MNF depended on 'official' supplies from the Chinese and the Pakistani military (before 1971), the guerrilla organizations that came into existence later had to depend on purchases from the black markets of Burma, Thailand and China. In the last two decades, the NSCN, the ULFA and the National Democratic Front of Bodoland (NDFB) as well as the Tripuri and Manipuri rebel groups have primarily built up their arsenals through (a) purchases from friendly Burmese rebel groups, like the Kachin Independence Army; (b) from Thai black markets;

(c) lately from Yunnan-based Chinese mafia groups, like the Black-house; (d) occasional supplies by the Pakistani ISI shipped to Bangladesh and (e) theft and pilferage from Indian security forces.

In the last two years, the United Wa State Army (UWSA) has set up a large weapons manufacturing facility on franchise from some Chinese ordnance factories. The UWSA is not only the prime source of memphatamine drugs in the region—they are now the single largest source of clandestine weapons supply. The separatists of northeast India, the Islamic radicals of Bangladesh, even the Maoists of Nepal and India have all been receiving their latest supply of Chinese weapons from the UWSA—either directly or through agents.

While the purchases from the Kachins were more in the nature of starter supplies in the 1980s, the procurement from Thai black markets has been substantial. Estimates prepared after collating intelligence data verified with rebel sources indicate that while the supplies from the Kachins would account for barely 200–250 pieces of small arms, the procurement by all post-1980 rebel groups from Thailand has amounted to about 10,000 pieces of assault rifles, carbines, pistols and revolvers, grenade-firing rifles and an assortment of other weapons. In 1999–2003, procurement from the Blackhouse and Ah Hua networks of Yunnan have also accounted for no fewer than 4,000 pieces of small arms, although more than 1,600 of these weapons were seized by Burmese troops during raids on Manipuri rebel bases around Tamu in November 2001. While the arrested Manipuri guerrillas were released, it is not yet clear whether weapons seized from them were also handed back.[3]

The weapons from the Kachins were carried back by the guerrillas over the land border, while those from the Chinese mafia were picked up in Burma and Bhutan.[4] Those purchased in Thailand were brought by sea to Bangladesh, then smuggled back into northeast India by groups of guerrillas marching back. One such large guerrilla column carrying back the weapons brought from Thailand was intercepted by the 57th Mountain Division of the Indian army in April–May 1995. The subsequent 'Operation Golden Bird' was successful in blocking and scattering the column—38 rebels were killed, 118 captured and more than 100 weapons were seized with large quantities of ammunition. Wyakaung beach located south of Bangladesh's coastal town of Cox's Bazaar was the favourite landing spot for these weapons, but at least six other points in the Cox's Bazaar district were used.

The guerrillas of the NSCN, the Manipuri groups, the ULFA and the NDFB would then pick these up and carry them back through one of three routes: (a) the Chittagong Hill Tracts–south Mizoram–east Manipur route, skirting the border with Burma; (b) the Chittagong Hill Tracts–Tripura–west Mizoram–west Manipur route and (c) the Chittagong–Sylhet–Meghalaya–Assam route. In the last several years, the Sylhet–Meghalaya route has been used more frequently by the rebels. The Directorate General of Forces Intelligence (DGFI) has helped the North East Indian rebel groups to safely land these weapons and only on a few occasions have weapons meant for these rebel groups been intercepted by the Bangladesh police, who were misled into believing that the weapons were intended for criminals in that country.

With Bangladesh emerging as the gateway to northeast India for the weapons brought in from Thailand, the rebels in Tripura were the best located to carry them back. Both the National Liberation Front of Tripura (NLFT) and the All-Tripura Tiger Force (ATTF) have secured weapons from the NSCN. The NDFB and the ULFA helped them cache the weapons at their bases in the Chittagong Hill Tracts before they were carried to the respective base areas in the North East. The NSCN, after it started talks with the Indian government, had also 'loaned out' up to 200 rifles and other weapons to the NLFT and the NDFB. The ULFA has followed this practice to some extent, primarily in order to fraternize with other groups like the ATTF, thus protecting weapons-induction routes and securing other tactical advantages.

Earlier in the decade, the Bangladesh police seized truckloads of ammunition and explosives from the ATTF. A former chief of the Bangladesh army, Lieutenant-General Mustafizur Rehman, has alleged that the ammunition seized from the ATTF at Kahalu *upa-zilla* in Bogura was manufactured at the Bangladesh Ordnance Factory.[5] This suggests that the rebels are now receiving ammunition, if not the weapons, from Bangladesh government agencies. Rebel groups have much greater trouble maintaining a steady supply of ammunition—they only need more weapons if they have huge recruitment. Steady ammunition supply is crucial for maintaining the action-profile of the rebel groups against security forces or for defence during counter-insurgency offensives by government forces—and it is a priority for all rebel commanders to locate sources of ammunition supply closer to home.

The seizures in some of the North Eastern states will help indicate the extent of small arms flow into northeast India. Between 1995 and 2000, 1,074 weapons were seized from various rebel groups in Assam. Nearly half of these, 578, were pistols and revolvers, but there were 128 AK-series rifles and 91 other carbines. Of these 1,074 weapons seized or recovered, 723 were picked up from the ULFA. More than 30 kilos of high-grade explosives like RDX were recovered from them during this period.[6] Almost 70 per cent of these weapons were seized or recovered in 1997–99, the peak of counter-insurgency operations in Assam. In Manipur, where the Meitei guerrilla groups have started to regroup, unite and expand their operations after the setbacks in the last decade, the police and army have seized or recovered 269 pieces of small arms during 2000–02. Again, 9-mm pistols accounted for the bulk of seizures—33 in all—closely followed by AK-series rifles.[7] In some states, including Tripura and Assam, there has been very little recovery of weapons from guerrillas who surrendered.

Since 1980, North East Indian rebel groups built up their arsenals largely through their own resources and patronage from foreign countries has been limited to occasional supplies and sanctuary. Therefore, rebel groups have had to resort to large-scale extortion and abductions to raise funds. Weapons acquired in South East Asia or on the Sino-Burmese border cost anything between $1,500 and $1,700 for an AK-series rifle and around $2,000 for a light machine gun, plus an additional 20 per cent for shipping and other costs. The requirement for funds is thus enormous. Since the Nagas and the Mizo insurgents in the 1950–60s got most of their weapons from Pakistan and China and the Manipuri People's Liberation Army (PLA) and the Tribal National Volunteers (TNV) built up much of their arsenal through theft and looting, they did not require the kind of funds that the post-1980 groups have needed.

The ULFA has shown the way on how funds can be raised on a large scale, namely, by systematic 'taxation' of business and industry. The NSCN and the Manipuri groups widened their 'taxation' base, while the Tripura groups turned kidnapping into a business activity whose gross turnover would beat some of the state's regular industries, such as tea and rubber. Some reports received by Indian intelligence suggest that the Pakistani ISI occasionally provided funding to the NSCN, the MNF and then the ULFA, essentially to finance purchase of weapons and explosives. Chinese intelligence set up the initial contacts between the Thai arms cartels and the NSCN, whereas the ULFA gained access to the same cartels through the Liberation Tigers of Tamil Eelam (LTTE).

Unsettled conditions in the region have also boosted the local market for small arms. The revolvers, pistols, AK-series rifles are all available in the various arms bazaars in the North East or nearby in Burma and Bangladesh. Political parties purchase weapons to arm their supporters for survival against insurgents or for use against rivals; so do the crime syndicates that have grown in the region. Dimapur, Agartala, Moreh and Champhai have emerged as entry points for small arms. The NSCN used these markets to build up the Naga Lim Guards, a militia group that fought the Kukis during the bloody fratricidal strife in the 1990s. The Kuki militias also used the Moreh–Tamu route to bring in weapons to build up their arsenal after the dwindling of initial supplies provided by Indian military intelligence, which was trying to turn the Kukis against the NSCN. The Chin rebels of Burma, who treat the Kukis as their ethnic kinsmen, also provided the Kuki militias with weapons.

Newly established Bengali militant groups, like the United Bengal Liberation Force, also used the border markets to arm themselves. While the bigger rebel groups have managed to smuggle in large quantities of weapons from Thailand, the smaller groups have paid a premium to secure the weapons from the black markets that thrive in Bangladesh and Burma. Cox's Bazaar and some coastal towns around Chittagong have thriving arms markets that do not enjoy the visibility of Darra Adam Khel on the Pakistan–Afghanistan border, but nevertheless thrive on regional requirements. Tamu in Burma is what Cox's Bazaar is in Bangladesh. In recent months, large numbers of Chinese assault rifles and automatics have found their way to Tamu to be picked up by the rebels. It is not yet clear whether the Chinese government patronizes mafia syndicates such as Ah Hua and Blackhouse, or whether, like all public-sector industries desperate to make profits in post-Mao China, Chinese ordnance factories (for example, Norinco) do not care whom they sell their wares to, as long as they bring profits.

It is however hard to believe that Norinco and other Chinese ordnance establishments can sell weapons on a large scale to non-state actors without at least tacit approval of the Chinese government. It is still harder to believe that these weapons would easily pass through military-ruled Burma, unhindered and unchecked, to the rebel groups based in the jungles of Sagaing enroute northeast India. There is growing evidence of connivance between Chinese intelligence and the ordnance establishments, as well as evidence of paybacks to Burmese military commanders who allow the weapons to pass through Burmese territory from Yunnan to northeast India. The ULFA has based a mission in Myitkina in Burma's Kachin state to oversee the weapons transfer from Yunnan to its units based in northern Sagaing. Surrendered ULFA (SULFA) rebels have confessed that the group purchased much more weapons than it needed—much of what it purchased through its 'mission' in Myitkina was sold at a premium to Indian and Nepal Maoists, so that the ULFA could pay off its own purchases—like frying fish in its own oil.

That perhaps explains the huge consignment of weapons that the ULFA was bringing in through the Bangladesh port city of Chittagong on the night of 1–2 April 2004 when it was seized by the Bangladesh police. The seized weapons included 690 7.62 mm T-56-I sub-machine guns (SMGs); 600 7.62 mm T-56-2 SMGs; 150 40 mm T-69 rocket launchers; 840 40 mm rockets; 400 9 mm semi-automatic spot rifles; 100 'Tommy Guns'; 150 rocket launchers; 2,000 launching grenades; 25,020 hand grenades; 6,392 magazines of SMG and other arms; 7,00,000 rounds of SMG cartridges; 7,39,680 rounds of 7.62 mm calibre and 4,00,000 cartridges of other weapons. Most of the arms and ammunition were reportedly of Korean, Italian, Chinese and American make. The case was not properly pursued by the Bangladesh Nationalist Party (BNP)–Jamait e Islami coalition government because several of their top functionaries were involved.

But the newly installed Awami League government has reopened the case after it came to power with a massive electoral mandate. The kingpin of the case (and now a key evidence), Bangladeshi arms dealer Hafiz ur Rehman, has been arrested. Rehman has confessed in the court of the Chittagong Metropolitan Magistrate Mohammed

Osman Ghani on 2 March 2009 that ULFA military wing chief Paresh Barua (under the pseudonym of Asif Zaman) had checked into Hotel Golden Inn on Chittagong's Station Road (room number 305) and was actually supervizing the unloading of the weapons at Chittagong's Urea Fertiliser Limited (CUFL) jetty when the police arrived and seized the weapons. Barua was accompanied by NSCN leader Anthony Shimray, Rehman said in his judicial confessional statement (recorded in court under section 164 of Bangladesh Penal Code). This account totally matches the details in a report filed by Anthony Davies in the Janes Intelligence Review (1 August 2004)—so it can be said that much about this sensational weapons seizure was already known in Bangladesh. Hafizur Rehman says that he was introduced to Paresh Barua in 2001 by former Jatiyo Party leader (now absconding) Gholam Faruq Ovi in the house of Bangladesh's film director Ajmal Huda Mithu. Mithu's house is located in Dhanmondi residential area of Dhaka. Rehman confessed that Barua has paid him Rs 50 lakhs (5 million) Bangladesh taka for paying off trawlers, trucks, cranes and dock labour. A copy of Hafizur Rehman's confession is now available with this author.

The Bangladesh CID has now issued look-out notices for Paresh Barua and says it will also question former Industry Minister (and Jamait e Islami leader) Motiur Rehman Nizami, former junior Home Minister Lutfor Zaman Babbar (of BNP) and BNP lawmaker from Chittagong Salahuddin Qader Choudhury (popularly known as SAQA). Choudhury's Continental Shipping was allegedly involved in bringing in the huge weapons consignment using its own ships. Nizami will be questioned because the CFL jetty cannot be used by anyone without clearance from the Industry Department—and Babbar will be questioned because the Home Department provides security clearance for all landings at CFL jetty.

This author learned from highly-placed government sources in Delhi that a top Awami League politician had informed Indian intelligence well in advance about the exact time of the arrival of this huge consignment, when he had come to Ajmer for a religious visit. The politician has been leading the dock labour unions in Chittagong for a while—and these unions had been alerted about the large requirement of labour on the night of 1 April to unload the huge consignment. Special bonuses had been promised to the labour if they cleared the consignment in good time. Indian intelligence conducted a successful disinformation campaign to foil the induction of the consignment. It alerted the Bangladesh police through its own sources in Chittagong, telling them that these were weapons meant for the Awami League, whose General Secretary Abdul Jalil had threatened to bring down the BNP–Jamait government by 30 April. When the police arrived in strength, mysterious phone calls promptly alerted the press.

But while the Chittagong arms haul, the biggest seizure of illegal weapons in South Asia, was successfully foiled, many similar consignments have reached the ULFA through Bangladesh. The ULFA would have brought it—either by sea from Hong Kong, as Jane Intelligence Review's Anthony Davies claims, or by the land route from Upper Burma to the port of Sittwe in the Arakans and then on to Chittagong, as claimed by Assam's security analyst Jaideep Saikia—not merely for arming its own cadres. The recruitment into ULFA has actually dwindled since 2003, so there's much truth in Indian intelligence claims that the ULFA has traded a large part of its weapons import, selling it off to Indian and Nepal Maoists or other buyers in the Indian mainland. While such large-scale weapons proliferation in India serves the objectives of ULFA's external sponsors, the profits from the trade helps ULFA fund its separatist campaign in Assam. Both ways, it serves to fuel separatist violence—arms its own fighters and procure funds from the illicit weapons trade to keep the group going despite reverses in the region.

THE BURMESE DRUG TRAIL

Apart from arms, increasing flow of drugs, such as heroin and methamphetamines, is a major cause of worry for the North East. The region sits at the western end of Burma's infamous Golden Triangle, one of the two largest narcotics producing regions in the world. Though Afghanistan's poppy output has again surpassed that of Burma after the Taliban—who had banned drugs and enforced it ruthlessly—were forced out of power by a US-led military campaign, there is no evidence that would suggest the poppy output of Burma has fallen. It is only that the Afghans have grown more. Burma has attracted more attention in recent years for other reasons—the intensified campaign for democracy during the 2007 Saffron Revolution or the miseries following the 2008 Cyclone Nargis. But Burma's drug output has got less and less attention after the world's attention has shifted away to Iraq and the volatile situation in the Middle East.

The International Narcotics Control Bureau (INCB), in its 2003 global report, has said that more than 70 per cent of the methamphetamines sold worldwide come from the Golden Triangle.[8] The INCB report ranks Burma as second to Afghanistan in opium production. It says international pressure compelled Burma's military rulers to undertake some anti-drug measures that led to a 40 per cent fall in Burma's opium production from its peak of around 2,500 tonnes in 1996. Indian and Western narcotics control officials fear that Burma's military rulers, who maintain close relations with most drug cartels that do not directly challenge the regime, might have 'just started taking it easy' on the drugs front.[9] By all indications, Burma's heroin output, which in the past has shown the ability to increase sharply (for example, from 54 tonnes in the 1970s to 166 tonnes in 1985–95),[10] could now rise again.

What is more worrying about the Golden Triangle is the eight-fold rise in the production of methamphetamines (sold on the street as Speed or Yaba) from an estimated 100 million tablets in 1993 to 800 million tablets in 2002.[11] Amphetamines are cheap and their consumption among the youth is rising throughout the world because they are seen as performance-enhancing drugs. This is a source of concern for India as much as for the West—or even China—because the consumption of amphetamines is rising quickly. Their low cost means that local consumption in the North East would be much higher than that of heroin. In fact, the Burmese military junta not only encourages the sale of drugs in Burma (where it aims to distract the youth from agitations and politics), but it also allows friendly drug cartels to sell their wares openly in towns and villages on the frontier with India and China. A recent report from Burma News International came up with a classic case:

> The unregulated and open sale of drugs has been reported in a village near Bhamo Township, where a large number of local youths are said to be getting addicted to the malaise. Reports said that black opium (Khat Pong), heroin and amphetamines (Yaba) were freely being sold at a village, seven miles away from Bhamo township. The authorities are said to be keeping silent on the matter despite knowing about the drug trafficking

in the region. The drug peddlers and traffickers are let off after simple warnings by the local forces.[12]

Two recent developments in the Golden Triangle do not bode well for the North East's social stability and security. First, traditional drug lords like Khun Sa have been eclipsed by ethnic rebel armies like the UWSA in the Triangle. The Was are former head hunters who formed the bulk of the fighting force of the Burmese Communist Party's (BCP) military wing until they revolted against their Burman commissars in the late 1980s. The once powerful BCP just withered away and its Wa officers took to drugs. Today, the UWSA monopolizes the amphetamine output to the extent that a recent *Time* magazine cover article described the Was as the 'Speed Tribe'. Second, the Wa monopoly over amphetamines has forced traditional drug lords like the late Khun Sa and his successors to reinforce their control over the heroin output. Khun Sa has tried to establish monopoly on the heroin export routes from the Golden Triangle to Laos and Thailand. Three years ago, he imposed a hefty 60 per cent 'profit tax' on smaller cartels, forcing at least three of them to relocate their drug refineries to the borders with India's North East and China's Yunnan province. These three cartels—headed by Zhang Zhi Ming (a former BCP officer), Lo-Hsin Nian and the Wei brothers—have between 14 and 18 refineries in western Burma, mostly in the Sagaing Division and the Chin Hills, but some now as far down as the Arakans.[13]

These cartels are using almost 30 different routes to traffic their drugs into the North East on their way to Western markets. Some of these routes have been identified by India's Narcotics Control Bureau (NCB), but NCB officials admit that the traffickers regularly switch routes to escape their monitoring. The identified routes are as follows:

(a) Behiang–Singhat–Churachandpur–Imphal; (b) Behiang–Singhat–Tipaimukh–Silchar (Assam) and then onward to Bangladesh; (c) Mandalay–Tahang–Imphal; (d) Tamu–Moreh–Imphal; (e) Homalin–Ukhrul–Jessami–Kohima; (f) Mandalay–Tahang–Tiddim–Aizawl–Silchar; (g) Homalin–Khamjong–Shangshak Khullen–Ukhrul–Imphal; (h) Myitkina–Maingkwan–Pangsau Pass–Nampong–Jairangpur–Digboi; (i) Putao–Pasighat–Tezpur–Guwahati;

(j) Tamanthi–Noklak–Kohima–Dimapur; (k) New Somtal–Sugnu–Churachandpur–Imphal–Kohima–Dimapur; (l) Kheinan–Behiang–Churachandpur–Imphal–Kohima–Dimapur; (m) Tahan–Tiddim–Melbuk–Champhai–Aizawl–Silchar; (n) Tahan–Tiddim–Hnahlan–Aizawl–Silchar; (o) Tohan–Vaphai–Khawlailung–Serchip–Aizawl; (p) Tahan–Falam–Ngarchhip–Khawlailung–Serchip–Aizawl; (q) Falam–Dawn–Thingsai–Hnahthial–Lunglei–Demagiri–Chittagong Hill Tracts–Chittagong; (r) Falam–Lungbun–Saitha–Chittagong Hill Tracts–Chittagong; (s) Churachandpur–Ngopa–Aizawl–Phuldungsei–Jampui Hills–Agartala–Chittagong.[14]

While the routes through Manipur and Mizoram have been used for nearly two decades or more, the ones through Nagaland, Arunachal Pradesh and Tripura have just come into use. This has much to do with the location of the drug refineries in Burma. The first of these refineries came up in the Chin state, so the traffickers used Manipur and Mizoram to peddle their drugs. Now, with refineries coming up in Homalin and Putao and in the Arakans, the cartels have to use routes through Nagaland, Arunachal Pradesh and Tripura. The new weapons smuggling routes out of Burma also follow many of these routes because border couriers carry both guns and drugs to maximize profits.

China is already squaring up to face the threat. It has executed more than 20 drug traffickers, seized nearly 70 kilograms of heroin and nearly two million amphetamine tablets during the last three years. Up to 67,500 drug traffickers have been arrested and $25 million and 4.5 million Chinese yuan seized from them. Most of the seizures and arrests were made in Yunnan.[15] China has also joined the six nations' initiative in the Greater Mekong region to fight the drug menace. In January 2002, the six countries—Thailand, Burma, Laos, Cambodia, Vietnam and China—set up a 'Joint Special Task Unit 2002' to coordinate the fight against drug trafficking.

Strangely, despite Delhi's publicized 'Look East' foreign policy, India has not joined the six nations in the fight against drugs. India's narcotics control officials play down the threat from the Golden Triangle, despite clear indications that Burmese drug mafias are increasingly using the North East to send their cargo into Bangladesh, India and Nepal on the way to the global markets. In January 2002, police and customs officials in Mizoram alone seized nearly three kilograms of Burmese heroin and more than 10,000 amphetamine tablets. In neighbouring Manipur, frequent seizures of heroin and amphetamines have been reported. Seizures of 1 to 1.5 kilograms of heroin have been reported from Assam and Tripura. Confessions by the arrested traffickers reveal that the drugs were on their way to Bangladesh, where lax anti-narcotics laws have encouraged Indian and Burmese drug dealers to use that country to ship their cargo to the West and the Far East. But the seizures may just be the tip of the iceberg.

This spurt in drug trafficking through the North East poses a serious threat to the region and the rest of the country for three reasons:

1. Trafficking through the North East has led to a rise in local consumption. In the last two decades, the North Eastern states have witnessed a sharp rise in the number of drug addicts, now estimated by the Indian Council of Medical Research at 1,10,000. Many addicts use intravenous injections and risk becoming HIV-positive. The number of HIV-positive cases in the North East has risen to 12,000 over the last two decades. Manipur and Mizoram have been the worst affected: more than 1,650 people, mostly youths, have died of drug-related maladies. Drug addiction could spread slowly to all the states of the North East and affect the social fabric of the region. The kind of enthusiasm that NGOs in the North East have displayed in enforcing prohibition of liquor has been absent when it comes to fighting drugs—and for understandable reasons. The Burmese cartels that deal in heroin and Speed are much more financially powerful than the Indian domestic liquor lobby. Not only do the Burmese drug lords ensure insurgent protection in the North East (with the exception of the Manipuri rebels, who have attacked both liquor merchants and drug-dealers) but they also manage to influence the levers of power and influence in government and the NGOs.

2. In the past, we have often seen the involvement of serving military and paramilitary personnel in drug trafficking. The trend

seems to be on the rise. This could undermine discipline and morale in Indian armed forces and further weaken the policing of frontiers and checking the drug trade. Besides the armed forces, the drug mafias are undermining the political establishment and even the judiciary. In August 1988, an Indian military major, Balbir Singh Sangha, was arrested with 2.2 kilograms of 'Double Globe' heroin at Dimapur but got away without much ado. My investigations revealed that he had the backing of senior officers, including his division commander. In recent years, many army and paramilitary officials have been caught trying to smuggle out heroin and other narcotics. For every culprit who is caught, there are several others who carry on the trade. Judges and government officials, monks and priests, and surely military and paramilitary personnel have all been found working for the drug mafia. Anti-narcotics officials complain that most drug couriers arrested by them are promptly let off in courts and that police tamper with evidence to ease sentences.

3. Ethnic rebel armies in the North East are beginning to be affected by the 'Burma syndrome'. Like their cousins in Burma, they are beginning to protect the drug mafias. Some Manipuri rebel groups, like the UNLF and the PLA, continue to resist the drug traffickers, meting out exemplary punishment to them. Other groups, however, are turning to taxing drug mafias to raise funds. They are also encouraging tribal farmers to plant poppy, acting as agents of the Burmese drug lords. For example, heroin was seized from a peace-time camp of the NSCN near Dimapur in May 2003. The NSCN, which once abhorred the drug trade and threatened smugglers with dire consequences, has been accused of trying to take control of the drug trade through Moreh. Some analysts say the desire to control the lucrative drug contraband route lies at the heart of the feud between the Naga and the Kuki militias in Manipur.[16]

Unless the new opium plantations are promptly destroyed and gainful agricultural alternatives are provided to tribal peasants, the India–Burma border will soon be dotted with poppy fields. A nexus of rebels, drug lords and local officials is emerging that could further undermine the effective presence of the state and its institutions in the North East. Otherwise India's new 'Look East' policy—an attempt to develop an economic stake for the North East in the country's growing trade with South East Asia—will be defeated by the 'Look West' thrust of the Burmese drug lords who want to tap the booming South Asian market and the drug routes through Bangladesh, Nepal and India as an alternative to the Thailand–Laos route.

A Smuggler's Paradise

It is not merely guns and drugs that are smuggled across the frontiers of India's North East, though these imports are the cause of much concern. Not much contraband comes and goes across the borders with Bhutan and China, but smuggling is rampant on the borders with Bangladesh and Burma. The National Council of Applied Economic Research (NCAER) has estimated that the unofficial trade between India and Bangladesh is worth Rs 1,165 crore. It says only 4 per cent of this happens through the North East, the rest passing through West Bengal. The unofficial trade through Assam and Tripura is estimated at Rs 43 crore annually.[17] The estimate is outdated in view of the sharp rise in Indo-Bangladesh trade in the last decade. Some Bangladeshi studies indicate that at present the unofficial trade figure could be as high as that for official trade. Going by the estimates of Revenue Intelligence, smuggling through Assam, Meghalaya and Tripura accounts for not less than Rs 450 crore at current prices. In Tripura, the unofficial trade is estimated at 50 times the official border trade. According to these estimates, smuggling on the India–Bangladesh border is estimated at around Rs 1,500 crore.[18]

These estimates are arrived at by rough calculations of the local market demand for those products which are regularly smuggled into Bangladesh or Burma, the wholesale purchase of those products by dealers in the North East from heartland Indian states (which can be gleaned from sales tax figures secured from the 'tax gates' on inter-state borders) and seizures made by agencies like customs or the Border Security Force (BSF). The Indian Institute of Foreign Trade (IIFT) has estimated that unofficial trade between India and

Burma—all occurring through the North East—is estimated at Rs 2,200 crore at current prices. According to this study, the Moreh route through Manipur accounts for trade worth Rs 1,600 crore annually, the Champhai route through Mizoram accounts for Rs 500 crore annually and the Longwa route through Arunachal Pradesh accounts for Rs 100 crore annually.[19] The unofficial trade on the India–Bangladesh border is a large portion of the overall trade between the two countries; it is more than 40 times higher than the official trade on the India–Burma frontier. But the accumulation of black money in states on the India–Burma border would be much more than in states on the India–Bangladesh border, because the illegitimate income there is legalized because the states of the India–Burma border are 'tribal states' where most residents enjoy income-tax waivers under law.

The growing contraband traffic on the borders of India's north eastern states has four serious implications for the region: (a) since income from smuggling is illegal, it leads to huge black money generation that is not invested in the region, certainly not in productive manufacturing, and is mostly siphoned off by the smugglers elsewhere in the country or abroad; (b) the political and social influence of the 'smuggler's lobby' grows until it begins to criminalize local society and politics, undermine established social values and administrative structures and subvert traditional leadership with destabilizing consequences; (c) smugglers are utilized by both insurgents and foreign intelligence and (d) powerful vested interests work against legalization of border trade and better relations with neighbouring countries, thus denying residents of a fair share of prosperity that growth in legitimate trade would ensure.

Like the separatist insurgents, whose funds are invested mostly outside the region, the smugglers are inclined to siphon off their profits and deposit their funds where they are less likely to be identified. Thus, the regional economy does not benefit from the unofficial trade with neighbouring countries and the government loses out on huge potential revenue. Instances in which a smuggler invested in an employment-generating industrial production in the North East are rare. In Tripura, a survey conducted by revenue intelligence on the assets of twenty leading smuggling dons in 1998–99 indicated that their assets would amount to not less than Rs 500 crore. Only three had invested in brick fields, committing a small percentage of the assets. Most had invested heavily in real estate in Calcutta and other cities in India or in trade, which generates very little local employment.

The leading drug barons of Manipur have made hardly any local investments and most of their funds have been siphoned off to South East Asia. The insurgent–smuggler nexus grows because one supports the other: insurgents use smugglers to facilitate supplies or for shadowy monetary transactions, while smugglers need protection and unsettled trans-border conditions for their trade to flourish. Only when the insurgents start taxing the smugglers too heavily does the relationship begin to suffer. Such instances are rare. In Assam, smugglers who deal in rhino horn were initially punished by the ULFA because destruction of the wildlife was seen as depleting the 'national resources of Assam'. Even such acts, albeit for populist considerations, have become rare in the region.

While tea estate owners and managers, government officials, rich industrialists and traders have been abducted or killed by the insurgents when they refused to pay the rebels, there is hardly any instance of a leading smuggling don getting killed or abducted by the rebels in any of the northeast Indian states. The protection money is quickly settled and those smugglers who directly serve as procurement agents of the insurgent groups are even exempted from the 'tax'. In the North East, illegal activities like smuggling, illegal logging and destruction of forests and wildlife have thrived on the close rapport between the insurgent and the smuggler until an insurgent has tried to replace the smugglers by trying to take over the trade all by himself. The huge black money generation also means a colossal loss to the exchequer, and the lack of local revenue mobilization and a resource base for the state governments have forced them to depend on central assistance.

A 1998 study on the coal trade from Meghalaya to Bangladesh came to three conclusions: (a) official data relating to the quantity of trade is underestimated; (b) based on calculations of average daily vehicle movement and the volume of coal transported, there was an unofficial trade of at least 1,32,092 tonnes of coal in 1997–98, which was three times larger than the official trade through the border check posts and (c) revenue loss amounted to at least Rs 15.1 crore.[20]

My own investigation in 1993 revealed that food grains carried by railways to Tripura and Mizoram through Assam were reporting up to 25 per cent 'transit loss' at Silchar, where the Food Corporation of India (FCI) has large storage facilities. Enquiries revealed a large number of 'accidents' on grain-carrying trains between Silchar and the north Tripura town of Dharmanagar, while in reality the grains were being diverted to the border and smuggled into Bangladesh. A federal minister from Silchar was found to be the chief patron of this racket and the smugglers, whose fronts ranged from transport companies to hotels, were financing his electoral campaigns.[21] Several politicians in Tripura enjoy the direct patronage of smugglers. A sports club financed by the smugglers and a politician who patronizes them is called 'Bloodmouth' and another is called 'Nine Bullets'. Former Manipur minister Ngurdinglien was named in a report by the Drug Enforcement Agency (DEA) of the United States and his murder was linked to rivalries between two drug mafias seeking monopoly over a lucrative heroin route through his home district, Churachandpur.

This pernicious nexus of insurgents, smugglers and politicians is not unique to the North East. Similar trends exist in other border trades elsewhere in India. In the North East, however, the size of the legitimate economy is much smaller than in other states and the size of the black economy is far more preponderant. In some ways, smuggling enjoys local popular sanction because it facilitates easier availability of essential commodities that are difficult to obtain from the heartland and would be more expensive if imported legally. Garments, bricks and cement from Bangladesh are 30–40 per cent cheaper in Tripura than their Indian-made competitors. Even the former Marxist chief minister of the state, Nripen Chakrabarty, defended 'my poor people's right to cheap clothes from Bangladesh, which your Tatas and Birlas cannot provide'.[22]

For many border villagers, the frontier makes little economic sense. Sending two bags of rice or a headload of sugar into Bangladesh or receiving salt from Burma are not perceived as illegitimate acts. At the peak of the railroad disruptions during the Assam agitation, Nagaland Chief Minister Vizol threatened 'to turn to Burma for everything'.[23] It would be wrong, however, to look at smuggling purely as a problem of law and order that can be tackled by border guards and check posts because the phenomenon is linked to the realities of demand and supply mechanisms in the economy of the border regions. In a study conducted by the Bangladesh Institute of Development Studies (BIDS), economists have observed that 'the asymmetry and the resultant price differentials between the two countries for a vast number of items which are constantly creating opportunities for arbitraging, the incentive structure for smuggling remains very strong, side by side with the increasing flow of legally traded goods'.[24]

Another study by Muinul Islam lists some of the causes for the sharp rise in smuggling on the India–Bangladesh border. It says that due to bureaucratic red tape, high tariff barriers and procedural wrangles involved in the legal trade regime between the two countries, the landing cost of goods smuggled to either side of the border remains lower than legal imports. It blames both the Indian policy of restricting market access to Bangladeshi goods and the Bangladeshi policy of denying legal import of items like cattle (which is regularly carried into Bangladesh during festival seasons) for the rise in smuggling.[25]

Both the BIDS and the Islam studies indicate that (a) Bangladesh's under-developed economy ensures that all surplus is attracted to the trading sector and flows into illegal trade because of higher profits, lesser time and cost overruns during transactions and movement; (b) a 'dependency syndrome' that supports imports of any new item produced elsewhere is at work in Bangladesh; (c) the Wage-Earners scheme in Bangladesh has created a parallel market for foreign exchange that supports large-scale illegal imports; (d) Bangladesh's import liberalization policy since 1986–87 has paved the way for higher market penetration of Indian goods; (e) the wide margin between the landed cost of legally imported items and their domestic retail price in Bangladesh allows importers to promote large-scale corruption that helps them conceal illegal imports within the legal trade through practices such as under-invoicing, mis-classification, wrong-grading, fake declaration, under-assessment and under-weighing and (f) easy institutional credit for import of plant and machinery is used for capital flight through under-invoicing.

Islam rightly argues that while Bangladesh's legal imports from India are 10 times higher than its legal exports, the volume of illegal exports from Bangladesh is increasing compared to illegal imports. This, he claims, is evident from the 'robust showing' of the Bangladesh taka in the border *hundi* (unofficial) markets, though this has no impact on the depreciation of the taka's official value and the dwindling of Bangladesh's foreign exchange reserves. Another Bangladeshi study indicates that the large-scale smuggling on the India–Bangladesh border has 'practically created a free trade regime in the border regions'.[26] This would justify the creation of a sound border trade regime with India's neighbours so that border populations in both countries can benefit from legitimate trading and governments earn more revenue.

Both Bangladesh and Burma as well the states of the North East sit on a huge accumulation of black money. Burma's cash-strapped military junta announced a tax amnesty scheme in 1998–99, under which it was possible to legalize black money by paying a 20 per cent profit tax on the amounts declared. The scheme helped Burma collect $860 million in tax revenues. As the money entered the legal economic system, it led to a real estate boom that soon spread to service sectors, including the hospitality industry. Details of the amounts collected from northeast India by the India's Voluntary Disclosure of Income Scheme are not officially available because the government is committed to keeping the disclosures secret, but sources in Revenue Intelligence indicate it could be more than Rs 700 crores. While ways must be found to bring this money into the productive system of the region, it is also incumbent on the government to curb smug-gling by deterrent measures as well as by sound economic policies that will render it dangerous and unprofitable.

NOTES

1. Naga rebel commanders like Mowu Angami and Thinoselie provided the author with detailed information about the marches to East Pakistan and China—the events during the marches, the kind of training the rebels underwent, the kind of weapons they received and the routes they took to bring them back. Thinoselie even shared his extensive photo collections with me.
2. Bualhranga, a former MNF senator, has also shared rare insights on the marches. It appears that the average Naga or Mizo guerrilla carried on his person almost three times as much ammunition as an Indian soldier would carry on patrol. Since both Naga and Mizo fighters were marching over long distances, they needed to carry sufficient ammunition for the encounters they were expected to have with Indian and Burmese troops.

3. For details of these arrests and seizures, see various *BBC Online* reports during 2001–02 (see http://news.bbc.co.uk/2/hi/south_asia/1658651.stm).
4. After SULFA commander Luit Deuri told the Assam police and the army that he had personally received two consignments of weapons from the Blackhouse mafia in Bhutan in 1995–96. At that time, he was the 'Bhutan base area' commander or G2 of the ULFA. The ULFA also received some weapons and large quantities of Research Developed Explosive (RDX) from the ISI, which were brought into Bangladesh and handed over to the ULFA.
5. Quoted in the Bengali daily *Prothom-Alo*, 6 July 2003.
6. Assam police records (details cannot be provided for reasons of official secrecy).
7. Manipur police records (details cannot be provided for reasons of official secrecy).
8. INCB 2003 annual report, cited in Larry Jagan's 'Southeast Asia Remains Drug Hotspot', *BBC Online*, 26 February 2003.
9. Commissioner of Customs (North East), Donald Ingti, in an interview with the writer. Mr Ingti has been one of the most successful drug policemen in the region.
10. Bertil Lintner, March 2002.
11. *'Burma Prospect' – Focus on Burma Issues*, published at Bangkok by Peaceway, February 2002. Available online at www.burmaissues.org.
12. Burma News International (apex body of six regional Burmese newsgroup), 1 August 2003.
13. Revealed by a senior American Drug Enforcement Agency (DEA) official who requested anonymity, during interviews with the writer in February 2003. He served as DEA representative in both India and Thailand and has intimate knowledge of the movement of drugs from the Golden Triangle through these two countries.
14. Quoted in Phanjaobam Tarapot, 1997.
15. Chinese Vice Minister of Public Security Bai Jingfu, quoted in *Burma Focus*, February 2002.
16. Binalakshmi Nephram, 2002.
17. Sudhakar K. Chaudhuri, 1995.
18. Revenue Intelligence Assessment on Smuggling in North Eastern Region, 2002.
19. Export Potential Survey of the North Eastern Region, IIFT, Delhi, 1997.
20. Rajesh Dutta, 2000.
21. 'Food Scam in Assam, Union Minister Backs Culprits', *Business Standard*, 13 July 1993.
22. Nripen Chakrabarty, interview with the writer, 13 September 1987.
23. Vizol Angami, quoted in *Nagaland Times*, 17 February 1980.
24. A. Gafur, M. Islam and N. Faiz, 1990–91.
25. Muinul Islam, 2001.
26. A. Rahman and A. Razzaque, 1998.

**Elections, Pressure Groups
and Civil Society**

When the Constituent Assembly debated the future arrangement for India's North East, it ran into a crossfire of contrasting standpoints. Always a powerful influence, Mahatma Gandhi was against 'unnatural unions' and he promised to stand between the Nagas and the Indian bullets if Delhi attempted a merger by force. The Mahatma did not live long enough to fulfil his promise, but the tribespeople of the North East, particularly the Nagas, found in his pronouncements a moral benchmark against which all subsequent actions of the Indian state would be judged. Then there was B.R. Ambedkar, the champion of India's vast Dalit underclass, whose analogy equating the North Eastern tribespeople with Native Americans (Red Indians) was ill-conceived but whose support for extensive autonomy to the hill regions was well in order. His argument that the tribespeople of the North East should not be asked for anything more than a token allegiance to the constitution created huge expectations among them. And Bengal leader Sarat Chandra Bose (elder brother of Netaji Subhas Chandra Bose) spoke of a future India as 'an union of mutually supporting socialist republics', raising much expectations about a truly federal post-colonial India.

On the other end of the spectrum was the broad thrust of nationalist thinking, which sought to overturn the colonial policy of insulating the hills from the influences of the plains in an attempt to bring the tribespeople into the 'Indian mainstream'. The integrationists were opposed to special administrative arrangements in the hills. The Assam Congress politicians were against any autonomy for the hill regions and many advocated the end of the Inner Line system. Committed to the Congress ideals of Indian nationalism and having just about saved their own state from being merged with East Pakistan, these Assamese leaders were determined to convert Assam into a 'nation province, ignoring the historical specificity of societal development in colonial Assam',[1] a province that would at once be the 'homeland of all Assamese' and the living land of a vast majority of linguistic, religious and tribal communities, where the ethnic Assamese would dictate the socio-political agenda and steadily assimilate the non-Assamese. Only the Muslim immigrants of Bengali origin were willing to sacrifice their linguistic distinctiveness if their physical and economic security was assured. Neither the Bengali Hindus nor the tribespeople were prepared to accept the Assamese assimilationist agenda.

Jawaharlal Nehru was profoundly influenced by Verrier Elwin, a Cambridge anthropologist, whose advocacy for 'an administration without outside influences and impositions' for the tribal areas had made him the high priest of the country's tribal policy.[2] He favoured drawing the tribespeople into the Indian mainstream but insisted on protecting their culture and traditions, their land and distinctive institutions. In fact, during the initial years, Nehru was in some doubt about whether Indian democracy, which had evolved out of the 'limited elections' under British rule in the rest of the country, would suit the hills of the North East or whether traditional leadership patterns were better suited for the region.

Back in the hills of northeast India, the tribal society was equally divided on the issues at stake. The emerging middle class wanted ballot-box democracy and modern administration; the chiefs wanted the British policy of promoting traditional power structures to continue. But both the chiefs and the emerging tribal middle class had some reservations about their areas being incorporated into India. The notion of self-determination, cleverly promoted by the British in the North East, further complicated the scenario. Though the idea of independent homelands was 'partly romantic and partly political', independent India had to deal with them. There were also the princely states of Tripura and Manipur, which Sardar Patel was keen to merge into India in keeping with his overall strategy of 'dealing firmly' with the native states.

The merger of Manipur and Tripura with India was achieved under somewhat controversial circumstances and a degree of haste and secrecy shrouded their absorption. An armed rebellion swept through the hills of Tripura as the communists played on the tribal's sense of loss to create an atmosphere conducive to revolution. In Manipur, the first expression of separatism came from a communist leader, Hijam Irabot Singh, but there was no armed rebellion like Tripura. Irabot Singh did not find much support and his attempt to link up with the Burmese communists did not work. Singh went to Burma and died on his way back to Manipur. After the communists gave up the 'Ranadive path of armed struggle' and participated in the 1952 parliamentary elections, all seemed quiet in the North East, except in the Naga Hills, where the storm was brewing as the Naga National Council (NNC) insisted on independence. Soon, it became the first real challenge to India's nation-building project.

When Prime Minister Atal Behari Vajpayee, during his meeting with National Socialist Council of Nagaland (NSCN) leaders in early 2003, accepted the 'unique history of the Nagas', he was perhaps recognizing a historical fact that they were the only people in northeast India to have resisted incorporation into the New Republic. The other tribespeople in the North East accepted the Indian constitution and the autonomy provisions enshrined in it without much protest. Those who perceive the North East as a landlocked island of perpetual trouble and mayhem since independence—the 'durable disorder' proponents—must understand that every ethnic group in the North East, except the Nagas, gave India and polyethnic Assam a chance after 1947. It is India's failure to resolve key issues like governance and state reorganization, power-sharing and ethnic balance, economic development and state-building, that has led to alienation, and ultimately rebellions, in the North East.

Five issues have dominated the political discourse in post-colonial northeast India. They have shaped the nature of political mobilization and socialization in the region and influenced the political culture that has emerged there. They are: (a) the basis and pattern of state reorganization—whether a new state should be organized on a purely ethnic principle or on a power-sharing equation by major ethnic groups or remain broadly polyethnic; (b) the emerging dynamics of electoral arithmetic—whether national parties and coalitions could strike alliances with regional groups on the basis of a minimum common programme; (c) the federal issue—what should be the powers and interests of states and the provincial elites governing them; (d) lately, the civil society issue—how much of a space will there be for human rights organizations, youth groups, those with a gender-specific or an environmentalist agenda and (e) the militarization of the region leading to the emergence of a security state that imposed limits on the operation of democracy. These issues have influenced the political dynamics of post-colonial northeast India.

Assam's failure to accommodate the aspirations of the tribespeople was caused by the 'nation province' mindset of its leadership and elite. As the tribals began to agitate for autonomy or independence, the reorganization of the North East became inevitable. This opened the federal issue, that is, the balance of power between the state and the Centre, the national and provincial power-holding elites. Failure to resolve the federal issue led to violent agitations and insurrections, which in turn led to the emergence of the security state in the North East. Tensions across the borders caused by reciprocal sponsorship of insurgencies by India and hostile neighbours lead to ever greater military deployment in the area. The interference of foreign countries and easy availability of weapons fuelled nativist violence, which, in turn, justified for Delhi a large-scale paramilitary as well as a substantial military deployment in the North East. The shadow of the man in uniform has thus continued to influence the political dynamics of the region not the least due to the regular posting of governors in the region who have long years of servce in the armed forces, the police and the intelligence services.

OF NEXUS AND ACCORDS

India's promotion of electoral democracy in the North East and power-sharing deals with moderates and extremists alike led to the emergence of a strange political dynamic, in which the underground began to co-exist with the 'overground'. The mutual sustenance of the 'illegitimate' and the 'legitimate', on the one hand, undermined the rule of law and weakened the roots of democracy, but on the other, allowed flexibility and co-option that helped the Indian state build its legitimacy in troubled areas like Nagaland and Mizoram. In the days of Gopinath Bordoloi, Bishnuram Medhi and B.P. Chaliha, the dividing line between the legitimate and the illegitimate, the ruler and the rebel in the North East, was more pronounced. The Indian political super-structure existed at the top, dependent on the pro-Delhi politicians whose links with the grassroots were often as tenuous as the subservient bureaucracy that sustained the system through the initial years of challenge.

As the Indian political system in the North East came under severe pressure from a large number of insurrectionary movements and popular agitations, it evolved a political culture of co-option and accommodation built around multi-layered power-sharing, shifting ethnic equations and the 'covert' and 'overt' tactical alliances of recognized political parties and underground insurgent groups. As a result, the region's politics has become a confusing cobweb of ethnic vote banks sustained by overground–underground collaboration, where use of systematic and orchestrated violence to achieve power by a preponderant ethnic group or a political party has become a fait accompli. Practically, no insurgent group or political party in the region has managed to stay out of this dynamic. The underground is now as much a part of the regional political dynamic as the recognized political parties, often sharing the same space for power, resources and popular support. The parties need the insurgents to win elections and undermine political rivals, while the insurgents need the parties for survival and support. So even as they challenged the Indian state, they began to replicate it in their own organizational structures and processes and state values influenced their organizational behaviour.

Tactical compulsions soon graduated into covert alliances, as the rebellions were slowly internalized through the growing nexus of the overground and the underground. In some cases, the proclivity of the insurgent groups to the political parties and to the system they initially chose to challenge and undermine has led many of them to return to the mainstream by giving up the path of armed struggle. In other cases, however, the insurgents pursued selective cooperation with political parties even though they remained beyond the system pending a settlement. A few illustrations are as follows:

1. In 1988, the Bengali-dominated Congress struck a deal with the anti-Bengali Tribal National Volunteers (TNV) guerrillas to oust the ruling Left Front. TNV unleashed a wave of attacks on Bengali settlements, killing 114 Bengalis in a month before the elections. The Congress played on Bengali sentiments, demanding military deployment with special powers. The ruling Left Front took a principled stand, trying to resolve the insurgency by political means, keeping the army out to avoid alienating the tribespeople. Bengalis voted angrily against the Left for its failure to provide them security against rebel depredations. Within three months of the Left's ouster from power, Prime Minister Rajiv Gandhi was hugging TNV supremo Bijoy Hrangkhawl before television cameras, an accord was signed and the TNV surrendered its weapons to emerge as a legitimate political party. And what did Hrangkhawl get for giving up his 'fight for tribals'! The chairmanship of a state-level corporation meant for rehabilitating tribals through rubber plantations.

2. The Left learnt from its mistakes. Between 1988 and 1993, it promoted the All-Tripura Tribal Force (ATTF) and used it to embarrass the Congress–Tripura Upajati Juba Samity (TUJS) government, whose claim of 'finishing insurgency' in Tripura was effectively scuttled. The Left returned to power in 1993. Within a few months, a sizable section of the ATTF surrendered but a section remained behind, changing the 'Tribal' for the 'Tiger'. The Congress alleges that the ATTF continues to serve the Left. The Left blames the Congress and its tribal-ally, the Indigenous Nationalist Party of Tripura (INPT), of using the National Liberation Front of Tripura (NLFT) rebels. That the ATTF mostly kills INPT and Congress politicians and the NLFT kills or kidnaps leftists indicate that both allegations are true. The Congress needs a tribal party because its support base is limited to Bengali areas, while the Left is popular in both communities. This electoral requirement justified the 'covert alliance' of 1988 and the 'overt' alliance of the NLFT-backed INPT and the Congress in 2003 and the 2008 elections. On the other hand, the Left needs to counter-act the firepower of the NLFT in the hills and needs a force like the ATTF, which has viciously fought the NLFT. But as the Left

has gained in confidence after winning the 2003 and the 2008 state elections, it has allowed the state police launch operations against the ATTF to win Bengali support by unleashing an all-out offensive against tribal insurgents.

3. The Bharatiya Janata Party's (BJP) politics in the Indian heartland developed around the aggressive political ideal of 'Hindutva'. The NSCN has always promised a 'Nagaland for Christ'. The BJP has no political base in Christian-dominated Nagaland, while the Congress has stalwarts like former Chief Minister S.C. Jamir. Jamir has supported talks to find solutions for the Naga problem but has been against 'undue pampering' of the NSCN. Though it has been negotiating for a political settlement of the Naga problem, the NSCN has not formally given up its demand for Naga independence. In the 2003 elections, the NSCN pushed Naga regional parties to cobble together a coalition with the BJP in a grand plan to oust the Congress. Its guerrilla fighters went into the villages, not asking Nagas to stay away from 'Indian elections' as they had done in the past, but asking them to vote for the Democratic Alliance of Nagaland (DAN) and oust the Congress from power. The NSCN said the coalition would be 'in the interest of peace and permanent settlement of the Naga problem', unlike Jamir's Congress, which was 'subverting the negotiations'. The Congress lost the elections, the BJP ended up with five seats in the Nagaland assembly, opening its account in the Christian-dominated state for the first time, and the NSCN got the government it wanted—one that would support the negotiations and perhaps even step down, like Lalthanhawla did in Mizoram in 1986 to pave the way for the Mizoram accord.

4. In Arunachal Pradesh, the Congress came to power in 1999 by engineering large-scale defections from the local party, Arunachal Congress. It used the breakaway Khaplang faction of the NSCN to cajole the 11 legislators of Tirap and Changlang, the two districts bordering Burma where the Khaplang group was particularly active. Three years later, the Arunachal Congress struck back, engineering similar defections. Its leader, Gegong Apang, used the NSCN's Issac-Muivah faction to oust the Khaplang group from the two

districts and take control of the Tirap–Changlang group of legislators. The BJP backed Apang because he is seen as a long-term political ally. Apang has been against conversions to Christianity and he promotes the animistic 'Donyi Polo' faith and was the first to push an anti-conversion bill in the predominantly Christian hill region. Apang obliged the NSCN by withdrawing the draconian anti-crime ordinance Arunachal Pradesh Control of Organized Crime Act (APCOCA) and by stopping the 'Operation Hurricane' the Congress government had started against it. Pro-NSCN ministers, earlier jailed by his predecessor, were rewarded with cabinet portfolios. Apang wants to regain power in Arunachal Pradesh, the NSCN leaders Muivah and Issac Swu want a 'soft chief minister' in the states neighbouring Nagaland to push its Greater Nagaland agenda and to neutralize the last major base for its factional rival, Khaplang. The BJP wants no trouble with the NSCN and a foothold in Arunachal Pradesh by riding piggyback on Gegong Apang's party. That Sonia Gandhi, an Italian Catholic, leads the Congress comes as a propaganda bonus for 'Donyi Polo' Apang and 'Hindutva' BJP even as 'Nagaland for Christ' NSCN prefers a silence of convenience and helps both.

5. The Asom Gana Parishad (AGP) used the United Liberation Front of Assam (ULFA) as its military arm during its first tenure of power in Assam. The ULFA went about physically annihilating the Congress, the 'collaborators of Delhi'. The Congress pushed for president's rule and sent the army into Assam. The ULFA hit back at the Congress when the party returned to power in 1991 and tried to regain the popular support it had lost during the farcical polls in 1983. The AGP, as a constituent of the left-of-centre United Front, won the elections in 1996 by getting ULFA support on an explicit pre-poll promise to 'review the question of Assam's sovereignty'. But once in power, it seized off its past mistakes and made sure not to fall foul of the Centre. Chief Minister Prafulla Kumar Mahanta backed the Unified Command proposals of Assam's governor S.K. Sinha and the retired army general promptly obliged by denying prosecution sanction to try the chief minister in the Letter of Credit (LOC) scam worth millions. The ULFA, upset with the Unified Command structure, started

attacking the AGP leaders. Several assassination attempts were made against Mahanta and his ministers and the number two in the state cabinet, Nagen Sarma, was blown to pieces by a bomb that exploded under his car. Mahanta struck back and his police unleashed a campaign of secret killings against the ULFA leaders and their relatives by using surrendered militants (called SULFA [Surrendered ULFA] in Assam), far in excess to what the Congress had ever done. The ULFA backed the Congress in the 2001 and did not oppose its bid to recapture power in the 2006 elections. The AGP deserted the Left and struck a deal with the BJP. But it failed to counter the ULFA's strategy of select terror and lost two successive elections. The Congress promptly started pushing for negotiations with the ULFA. Since the 1990s, the ULFA, though now a much weakened rebel force, has managed to ensure that the party it has backed in each election has won.

Whenever in power in Delhi, the Congress has been striking deals with the rebel groups. To bring off a mass surrender or pull off a settlement in an election year was seen as auspicious for electoral prospects. When in power, the BJP followed similar tactics. Besides negotiating with the NSCN, it used MNF's chief minister Zoramthanga to open dialogues with several other rebel groups in the region—with the NLFT in Tripura, the Achik National Volunteer Council (ANVC) and the Hynniewtrep National Liberation Council (HNLC) in Meghalaya, the National Democratic Front of Bodoland (NDFB) in Assam and the Kuki National Front in Manipur. Zoramthanga had reasons to oblige the BJP, or else it starts using the Rastriya Swayamsevak Sangh (RSS) to up the ante in the Bru areas of western Mizoram, where the rebel-turned-chief minister faces trouble from a smaller tribe that complains of Mizo high-handedness.

Now it was the turn of the Congress—the master of accords, fair and foul, useful and ineffective—to cry wolf. Jamir in Nagaland, Lapang in Meghalaya, Mithi in Arunachal Pradesh, Ibobi Singh in Manipur—these former or serving Congress chief ministers started to complain about the 'unholy nexus' between rebel groups and the BJP government in Delhi. Party chief Sonia Gandhi felt that the toppling of Congress governments in Nagaland and Arunachal Pradesh through election and defection in 2003 was a prelude to a determined BJP–NSCN move to bring down Congress governments elsewhere in the region. Gegong Apang joined the BJP with more than 40 legislators, gifting the Hindu nationalists with their first-ever state government in northeast India. The BJP wanted to have as many states under its belt in a year when national parliamentary elections were coming up, the NSCN wanted friendly governments in states neighbouring Nagaland to pursue its 'Greater Naga state' project. It no longer insists on Naga sovereignty but has made it clear that there can be no solution to the Naga problem without integration of Nagas in other states of northeast India with those in Nagaland. Unless they get 'something more' than the 16-point agreement of 1960 that bestowed statehood on Nagaland, the NSCN will have little to justify the miseries Nagas have suffered during the long years of the insurgent movement.

As the interests of national and regional parties and of the underground in the North East converge, the 'unholy' overground–underground nexus is destined to grow. There could be more accords to add to the more than a dozen already signed in the region so far, some almost as farcical as the Shillong Accord or the one in Tripura in 1988, others are more substantive, like the 1960 agreement with the Naga Peoples Convention or the 1986 accord with the MNF. The Shillong Accord was a one-page document that merely reiterated the 'desire of the two sides to pave the way for a final settlement'. The accord in Tripura, except for two clauses containing small concessions, was marked by a reiteration to implement all existing central development schemes in the state.

If Assam bore the brunt of territorial loss during the first major political reorganization of northeast India, Manipur stands the danger of virtual eclipse if the second phase of reorganization follows a possible settlement with the NSCN. The violence in the Imphal Valley against the extension of the Naga ceasefire underscores the Meitei's fear of political decimation. That they targeted the symbols of political office rather than the Nagas during the violent anti-ceasefire protests of 2001 is significant. After the summary boycott of the 1952 parliament polls in the Naga Hills and the Assamese boycott of the 1983 state elections, the Indian political system faces its biggest challenge in Manipur. Any attempt to redraw Manipur's political boundaries will not only lead to a bloodbath but will also completely alienate the Meiteis from the Indian political system and bolster the splintered but increasingly stronger Meitei underground. The agitation against the ceasefire was followed by the emergence of united rebel front, the Manipur Peoples Liberation Front, which has now teamed up with the ULFA and the ATTF. Their subsequent efforts to coordinate the anti-Delhi violence were quite successful. The North East's second major political reorganization, if it ever comes through, will doubtlessly lead to much greater ethnic polarization and violence. It will pit ethnic groups with a recent history of insurgent violence against each other.

The politics of accords in the North East, centring around power-sharing and co-option, have been crucial to India's counter-insurgency strategy in the region—former Lieutenant-General D.B. Sheketkar actually describes this as India's success in 'building legitimacy' in the region. The accords have given the rebels access to power and funds within the Indian system, and their people have got autonomy and distinct political identity. The MNF settled for full statehood for Mizoram, the Assam students settled for limited disenfranchisement of foreigners, the TNV in Tripura settled for reservation of a few more seats in the state legislature for tribals after a decade of violence in which more than 1,500 lives were lost. The NNC settled for an accord to pave the way for a final settlement. Very often, it was not the piece of paper carrying their signature that was important. It was the secret deals involving power-sharing that really mattered.

Laldenga's insistence on taking over as chief minister in an interim administration after the elected chief minister had stepped down delayed the settlement in Mizoram by at least five years as Chief Minister Thengpunga Sailo would not oblige. Lalthanhawla's 'sacrifice for peace' became his strongest electoral card but it also emphasized the element of desperation in Laldenga's quest for a place in the Indian power structure. Zoramthanga has tried to play the mediator for Delhi with many other rebel groups in neighbouring states to secure his position in Mizoram. In the process, however, he came to be seen as Vajpayee's 'hatchet-man' in the North East.

The rebels in northeast India have rarely raised key issues like land, environment, preservation of traditional institutions, culture, development and governance when they negotiated with the Indian state. Delhi is happy they did not. India's post-colonial power structure is comfortable with those who seek power-sharing rather than resource-sharing. In neighbouring Burma, the junta is willing to allow rebels a ceasefire to make quick money by trading in teak, jade and gems but would not discuss autonomy. Pakistan refused autonomy to its eastern wing and that led to the revolt that broke up the country. India is willing to allow both 'money-making opportunities' and a 'share of political power' to the rebels in the North East as part of its strategy of co-option. The Congress had a problem—it had to reckon with its own regional *subahdar*s, like Hiteswar Saikia and S.C. Jamir, who saw peace-making as a threat to their positions. The BJP, with no real political base in the North East, did not face such a problem. From the new crop of rebel leaders negotiating with the federal government, it has the chance to pick and choose trusted political sub-contractors for the future.

ELECTIONS

Except the Naga Hills, no part of the North East opposed Indian electoral democracy after independence. The national parties were not strong in the hill regions because the British had practically forbidden their entry, but they had a strong base in the plains of Assam, Tripura and Manipur. The Congress emerged as the strongest party in Assam and Manipur, closely challenged by the socialist parties. In Tripura, the communists won both the parliament seats in the state in 1952 and 1962, sharing one with the Congress in 1957. Only in 1967 did the communists lose both the parliament seats in Tripura, as the Congress benefited from the growing Bengali migrant vote. As the Congress also took control of the state assembly, the communists changed their strategy and started increasing their influence among the Bengalis.

In Assam, the Congress won 11 of the 12 parliament seats in 1952. In 1957 and 1962, it won nine seats. In 1967, it won 10 of the 14 parliament seats and riding the 'Indira wave' in 1972, it won 13 seats. The Praja Socialist Party (PSP) continued to win two parliament seats until 1967 and the CPI won a seat in 1967. In Manipur, the Congress and the PSP won a seat each in 1952 and the CPI and the Congress shared the two seats in 1967. In 1957, the Congress won both the parliament seats. In 1962, it won a seat and lost the Outer Manipur seat (reserved for Scheduled Tribes) to a socialist Naga candidate contesting as an independent. In 1972, the Congress regained both the seats in Manipur but lost both the seats in Tripura.

In the first 25 years of the republic, the national parties dominated the parliament elections in Assam, Tripura and Manipur. The Congress was challenged by the socialist and communist parties in varying degrees in these states, but managed to win most of the seats in Assam and Manipur. In the state assembly elections, independents supported by regional groups fared better. In 1952, in a house of 108 members, independents won 26 seats and polled 32.2 per cent of the votes. The Congress won 76 seats. In 1957 state assembly elections, independents won 25 seats and 26.8 per cent of the popular vote as against 71 seats won by the Congress. In 1962, the number of victorious independent candidates came down to 20 seats, but when the strength of the Assam assembly was raised to 126 in 1967, the independents came back strongly to win 35 seats. Most of these independent candidates were backed by regional groups active in the hill regions of Assam and not in the plains, where the Congress dominated. Thus, the politics of Assam's valley region was largely dominated by the Congress and the socialist and communist parties in sharp contrast to the politics of its hill regions, which later broke away from Assam. In the hills, the movements for greater autonomy, a separate state or other local concerns were effectively articulated by the local parties and other organizations close to them, who kept the Congress and other national parties at bay.

Nagaland became a full fledged state in 1963 but it took the Congress nearly two decades to come to power. Elsewhere in the hill regions of northeast India also, regional parties held sway for the first 30 years of the republic. Elsewhere in the country, the Congress was largely unchallenged until 1967, but that was not the case in the hills of the North East. The All Party Hill Leaders Conference (APHLC) in Meghalaya, the Mizo Union in Mizoram, the Naga Nationalist Organization (NNO) in Nagaland, all articulated local causes and grew in popularity. The APHLC was at the forefront of the hill state campaign in the Khasi-Jaintia and Garo hills that later became

Meghalaya. The NNO was formed by Naga moderates who broke away from the Naga National Council (NNC) and advocated a peaceful settlement with India. They became an associate organization of the Congress and their leaders cooperated with the Centre to make substance to statehood in Nagaland. When they came to be seen as close to the Congress, they were challenged by the separatist United Democratic Front. The strength of the Naga separatist movement and the limited space left for a pro-Delhi party in state politics forced the NNO to finally join with the Congress.

The Mizo Union was the party of the emerging middle class that opposed the United Mizo National Organization (UMNO), a political platform of the chiefs who opposed democratization. The Mizo Union controlled the district council in the Mizo Hills and ran the first state government in the Union Territory of Mizoram until the space it occupied was taken over by another regional party, the Mizoram People's Conference. It had good relations with the Congress at the Centre but grew apprehensive when the Congress formed a state unit in Mizoram. In only one hill state, Arunachal Pradesh, did the national parties gain a foothold quickly. The fact that Arunachal Pradesh was unaffected by separatism and insurgency or by a powerful regional movement like the hill state agitation in Meghalaya helped the national parties. The Janata Party swept the first elections in the state in 1978 but the Congress quickly reversed the position in the next election, having won over Gegong Apang. Personalities and clan loyalties, ethnic equations and religious positions have always proved to be more important than political ideology in most North Eastern states.

The Congress held power at the Centre continuously until 1977. In the North East, it controlled the state government of Assam (the largest state in its undivided form and still the most populous in the region) and Tripura until 1978. Even after the party's national debacle in the 1977 parliament elections, the Congress continued to remain the single largest party in Manipur, though it could only form governments with support from a number of local parties or independents. But it had to wait until the early 1980s to come to power in Nagaland and Mizoram. It took control of Arunachal Pradesh immediately after losing the first state elections. Gegong Apang, who deserted the Janata Party to join the Congress, gave the party a long tenure of power in the frontier state until the mid 1990s, when he fell out with the party's national leadership and formed his own regional party, the Arunachal Congress. Then he dissolved the Arunachal Congress and joined the BJP, giving the Hindu nationalists the first state government in the North East. In what may be an apt example of the 'personality factor' in the region's politics, Gegong Apang has been chief minister of his state while representing three different national parties—the Janata, the Congress and the BJP—and also a regional party (Arunachal Congress) set up by him.

In Assam, the Congress lost out to the 'Janata wave' mainly due to endemic factionalism within the party in the late 1970s as its ef-ficacy was undermined by the powerful anti-migrant agitation led by the All Assam Students Union (AASU). It came back to power in 1983 through a violent election that was fiercely opposed by the regional groups supporting the anti-foreigner agitation. Prime Minister Rajiv Gandhi signed an accord with the pro-agitation groups who formed the AGP party that swept the 1985 mid-term elections after the Congress government under Chief Minister Hiteswar Saikia had been forced to step down by Rajiv Gandhi. The Congress returned to power in 1991, the AGP came back to power in 1996 only to lose to the Congress five years later. A two-party model emerged in Assam for a while but the BJP has gained substantial political influence in both the Brahmaputra Valley and the Barak Valley during the last eight years. The AGP has a political support base among the ethnic Assamese but it needs either the Left to pull to its side the Bengali-origin Muslims and tea-garden workers or draw on the BJP's vote banks among the Bengali Hindus to create a winning combination against the Congress, which relies on its traditional 'Ali-Coolie' vote banks amongst the Muslims and tea-garden workers.

But the Congress now faces a new challenge in a minority party, Assam United Democratic Front (AUDF) which is led by Maulana Badruddin Ajmal and is blessed by Shahi Imam of Delhi's Jama Masjid as part of a fresh experiment by Indian Muslim leaders to try out a stand-alone Muslim party that could be replicated elsewhere in India. Indian Muslims—or at least many of them—resent being used as vote banks by national parties and are keen to try out a pre-Partition Muslim League kind of party that would give them larger political clout in the Indian system, though not to promote secession. The AUDF sliced into the Congress' Muslim vote banks in Assam, winning 10 seats in the 2006 elections. The Congress was forced to turn to the Bodo Peoples Progressive Front (BPPF) to form a coalition government. The BPPF is largely made up of former Bodo insurgents, its chief Hangrama Mohilary has been one of the region's dreaded bombers, but the Congress finds him an acceptable ally because it has little influence in the Bodo-areas of western and central Assam.

In undivided Assam, regional political parties were initially restricted to the hill regions that broke away. The Congress had led the nationalist movement against the British in the plains, where it continued to control power until the powerful anti-foreigner agitation weakened the political base of all national parties and gave a boost to the forces of Assamese regionalism. In Tripura, however, the regional forces have been restricted to the tribal areas of the state. The communists and the Congress remain the major contenders for state power, but the Congress does not have a base in the tribal areas and has been compelled to align with the TUJS and the INPT. The communists retain some support in the tribal areas, but it is well below the levels of support it enjoyed in the hills of Tripura during the 1950s and 1960s. Its support base has sharply increased among the Bengali migrants at the expense of the Congress, which has to play soft on the tribal issue to maintain its alliance with the TUJS, and now with the INPT.

The Congress, however, is back in power in Manipur. Despite endemic factionalism, it ran the state government in the 1980s and for much of the 1990s. While Chief Minister Rishang Keishing provided the Congress some stability through the 1980s despite a number of powerful insurgent movements, the party lost its way under weak leaders like R.K. Joychandra Singh. It came back to power under the leadership of W. Nipamacha Singh but, like Gegong Apang in Arunachal Pradesh, Nipamacha fell off with the party's national leadership and formed the Manipur State Congress. Manipur has had several phases of legislative instability. During 1967–75, it saw five successive governments in eight years. In the 1996–2002 period, it experienced four governments. After a period of president's rule, the Congress, under the leadership of Chief Minister Ibobi Singh, emerged as the single largest party in the Manipur assembly during the 2002 and the 2007 elections. It formed the government with the support of the communists and two regional parties. So far, the Congress government has survived but the state's BJP chief Rajkumar

Dorendra Singh (who first joined the Congress by defecting from the Manipur Peoples Party and later deserted the Congress to join the BJP) has been trying to line up regional parties to bring down the Congress government. On the other hand, Congress Chief Minister Ibobi Singh has been accused of using insurgent groups to keep the regional parties under pressure.

Like Manipur, Meghalaya is another state where legislative instability has been endemic and almost continuous. The state is now under president's rule after a coalition government of regional parties was brought down by defection of five legislators. Though the coalition survived the trial of strength on the floor of the House by the Speaker's casting vote, Meghalaya governor R.K. Mooshahary, a former chief of the Border Security Force (BSF), recommended central rule. Ruling coalitions, like the ousted Meghalaya Progressive Alliance (MPA), have gone to the extent of agreeing to rotate chief ministers to ensure their survival in the state. Meghalaya is one state where no single party has attained a clear majority in an election or has been able to hold on to the majority won in the election.

It has been a long tale of coalition politics, one sustained wholly by considerations of power-sharing. Such power-sharing arrangements can assume ethnic dimensions. In 2008, the Congress emerged as the single largest party in the state assembly elections but the Nationalist Congress Party led by former Congress Speaker in Lok Sabha, Purno Agitok Sangma, thwarted the Congress efforts to form a coalition, by teaming up with other regional parties. Then he agreed to allow a Khasi tribal politician Donkuper Roy to be the state's chief minister for two and a half years on the understanding that Roy steps down and allows Sangma, a Garo tribal, to become chief minister for the remaining two and half years. This is when political power-sharing has become coterminus with ethnic power-sharing. Sangma's ambition, however, remained unfulfilled as central rule was imposed on Meghalaya in March 2009.

Only the states of Tripura and Assam have had less of the *Aya Ram, Gaya Ram* phenomenon (rampant and regular defections) and hence more legislative stability. Tripura's travails lasted for just over a year during the 1977–78 phase. Since then, the Left Front has ruled Tripura continuously but for a five-year period in 1988–93, when the Congress–TUJS alliance came to power. The culture of defections and changing political loyalties has been largely absent in Tripura, particularly among the ruling Left, which produced some role-model politicians like Nripen Chakrabarty, Dasarath Deb and Biren Dutta. The Congress witnessed some turbulence in the mid 1970s in the post-Emergency soul-searching within the party and many dissident party leaders left to join the Janata and the Congress for Democracy. Most of them returned to the party fold, and have not left it since. The smaller tribal parties have been subjected to splinterization and regrouping. The TUJS split thrice before it was compelled to join forces with the Indigenous People's Front of Tripura (IPFT) (renamed Indigenous Nationalist Party of Tripura [INPT]) under pressure from the NLFT rebels. Both the INPT and the NLFT have now split. Tribe loyalties, personality clashes and religious tensions between tribal leaders (traditional Hindus and converts to Christianity) account for the instability in Tripura's tribal politics.

Assam's legislative instability peaked during the early years of the anti-foreigner agitation but it stabilized after 1985 into a pattern where voters have not usually given a party more than one term in power. Thus, the AGP came to power in 1985, the Congress ousted it in 1991, the AGP returned to power in 1996 and lost again to the Congress in the 2001 state assembly elections. The Congress returned to power in the 2006 state elections, but only with support from the Bodo party. In the years after independence, the Congress built a solid vote bank among the immigrant Muslims, the tea-estate labourers, the Hindu refugees from East Pakistan and the tribals through a 'catch-all strategy', even as it maintained a strong presence among the Assamese caste-Hindus by supporting movements like the one against the Barauni refinery. It lost its support among the Assamese after the state's break-up in 1972. Later, it lost the support of the Bengali Hindus and Muslims after the 1985 accord, but while the Bengali Hindus gravitated towards the BJP, the Muslims returned to the Congress fold largely because they have no alternatives. Many of them may be going over to the Assam United Democratic Front (AUDF) now, undermining the Congress' traditional support base in Assam. The tribals in Assam have started supporting community-specific organizations to promote demands for autonomy. The AGP found a strong support base among the Assamese caste-Hindus as it emerged from the anti-foreigner agitation. It has found a natural ally in the BJP because both parties want stronger measures to prevent illegal migration from neighbouring countries. The BJP is slowly eating into the AGP's Assamese base, however, as many Assamese caste-Hindus feel that only a national party like the BJP can deliver on the infiltration problem.

Arunachal Pradesh experienced unusual stability, almost stagnation, during the long years of Congress rule until Apang's rupture with the party's national leadership. Since then, instability has grown but the state's politics is still determined by Apang's position: now in power, now out of it and again back in it. After losing Apang, the Congress made a brief comeback, with Mukut Mithi leading the charge to topple Apang's Arunachal Congress government in 1999. Mithi's Congress government has now fallen into a similar legislative coup, with Apang engineering a huge split in the Congress, running away with 40 of the 56 legislators of the party. Mizoram has also been largely stable, except during the split in the MNF in 1987 that brought down the government of one-time rebel chief Laldenga and returned the Congress to power. All the major parties in the state—the Mizo Union, the People's Conference, the Congress and now the MNF—have enjoyed power for full five-year terms.

The legislative instability in northeast India has been caused by a combination of the following factors: (a) a political culture based on parochial loyalties, personalities and ethnic affiliations and not on ideology or long-term vision; (b) the small size of the assemblies, mostly comprising 40 or 60 members (only Assam has an 126-member assembly), which makes it possible to topple a ruling party or coalition by engineering the defection of a small group of legislators; (c) the designs of parties or coalitions in power at the Centre, as a result of which the office of the governor and the services of the central intelligence services are frequently misused to put in power a government of the Delhi's choice or bring down if it does not like; (d) the emergence of powerful vested interests (business–contractor lobbies, insurgent–NGO and military–bureaucrat combines) who seek to bring down a government that refuses to oblige; (e) endemic corruption, as a result of which legislators change loyalties when promised ministerial berths or chairmanship of state-owned corporations and (f) growing political competition. When these factors combine in a state, systemic instability is sure to follow.

Legislative instability in the North East is responsible for (a) the poor quality of governance reflected in the lack of success in conceiving and implementing development programmes, particularly in infrastructure; (b) the unusually large size of ministries and the wasteful expenditure in providing the ministers with bureaucratic and security support (in most states of the North East, up to 80 per cent of the legislators supporting ruling parties and coalitions find a place in the state council of ministers); (c) the high level of corruption because legislators want to accumulate resources to sustain their political careers in the event of losing power; (d) the uncertainty in administration, particularly during the ups and downs of coalition politics, when a single party fails to get majority and horse-trading starts and (e) the lack of political vision and the poor quality of leadership.

These problems, however, are not unique to the North East. Legislative instability is as much a phenomenon in Uttar Pradesh as in Meghalaya. Personality factors are as much a feature of Tamil Nadu's politics as Arunachal Pradesh's. The narrowing effects of ethnic politics in northeast India finds a ready parallel in the parochial caste equations of the cow-belt, and although these local dynamics are different, the political limitations they impose are quite similar. Ethnic or religious violence in the North East has been as profound and as brutal as in Gujarat and its impact on elections as profound. In the 50 years of the republic, India's ballot-box democracy has produced a leveler effect that cuts across the regions. The political landscape in the country's remote North East has been as much affected by the elections as any other part of the country. I have met many Nagas, Mizos and Manipuris who fiercely oppose Indian influences and even support secession but nevertheless vote in all elections. In some states like Tripura, the turnout has been as high as 90 per cent. And insurgents no longer ask people to boycott elections—rather they pressurize them to vote for the party of their choice. Notwithstanding a feeling of helplessness to change the system that is often corrupt, the ethnicities of the North East have taken to elections with greater enthusiasm than to India's other passion—cricket.

Pressure Groups and Civil Society

Across the North East, student and youth groups have emerged as powerful pressure groups in local politics. During the British rule, groups like the Asomiya Deka Dal picked on local issues and articulated concerns that bigger national parties were not willing to take up. After independence, these groups multiplied not only in Assam but elsewhere in the region. Every single state in northeast India now has powerful statewide student unions. More than taking up campus or educational issues, which they also do, these unions have led agitations on key political issues and set the agenda for local politics. They have been at the forefront of movements to resist demographic changes that threaten many states in the region. These student unions have remained largely independent of direct political affiliations, preserving their distinct organizational identity, unlike the student affiliates of the national political parties. They have been the training ground for political aspirants and a catchment area for recruitment by political parties. In the process of political socialization and mobilization, these student unions have played a major role.

The All Assam Students Union (AASU) has been the strongest of them. It led several agitations for Assam's economic development before it started the 'mother of all agitations' during 1979–85 on the issue of illegal migration from neighbouring countries. During this anti-foreigner agitation, the AASU held centre stage with so much authority that Assam's established political parties were rendered almost irrelevant. The federal government was forced to negotiate with the AASU and other regional groups supporting the agitation for the detection and deportation of the illegal migrants. For four years, until the bloody elections in 1983, there was no organization in Assam that could remotely challenge the AASU's authority. The installation of the Congress government in the 1983 elections did lead to repression but Prime Minister Rajiv Gandhi was quick to realize that there could be no peace in Assam unless the issues raised by the AASU were addressed and a settlement arrived at with the students. After the AASU signed the agreement with the Indian government in 1985, most of their top leaders, like the organization's president, Prafulla Mahanta, and the general secretary, Bhrigu Kumar Phukan, left to form a regional political party, the AGP.

The AASU, however, retained its distinctive organizational identity and did not end up as a student affiliate of the AGP. Now much weaker than before, its image considerably affected by the corruption and incompetence of its former leaders who made it big in state politics, the AASU nevertheless has remained consistent on the illegal migration issue. The national political scene has changed, however.

In the 1980s, the federal government was unwilling to accept that the illegal migration problem was serious. There was a tendency to see the problem as a fallout from the Partition. In the 1990s, the federal government led by the Hindutva forces went a step ahead of groups like the AASU to acknowledge the problem. They have hijacked the 'infiltration card' of the AASU though they interpret migration in religious terms, which is not acceptable to the AASU.

Other ethnic groups have emulated the Assamese insofar as they all have student unions that are equally dominant in local politics. Like the AASU's role in the anti-foreigner agitation, the All Bodo Students Union (ABSU) played a leading role in the Bodo agitation for a separate state. Both the movements were marked by violence. The Bodos finally settled for an autonomy arrangement in 1993 and it was the ABSU that signed the agreement with Delhi along with the Bodo Peoples Action Committee. The agreement was not implemented, largely due to the obstructive attitude of the Assam government, which was unwilling to concede autonomy to the Bodos over the entire area earmarked for it. A decade later, a new autonomy deal has now been signed with the insurgent Bodoland Liberation Tigers Force (BLTF). The deal for setting up an autonomous council was endorsed by the ABSU. The subsequent tensions between the insurgents and the student leaders notwithstanding, the ABSU remains a key player in Bodo politics.

The All Assam Minority Students Union (AAMSU) played a role in resisting the AASU movement. It was temporarily overshadowed by the minority political party, the United Minorities Front (UMF), which emerged as a potent force in the aftermath of the 1985 Assam accord. The rise of the AUDF has somewhat undermined the faction-ridden AAMSU but it is still around and takes extreme positions on minority protection issues.

The All Manipur Students Union (AMSU), the Naga Students Federation, the Khasi Students Union (KSU) of Meghalaya, the Mizo Zirlai Pawl (MZP) and now the Young Mizo Association (YMA) of Mizoram and the Tribal Students Federation (TSF) of Tripura have all been at the forefront of the movement to expel illegal migrants. On this issue, they enjoy a degree of popular support from their communities. These organizations have also been vocal on issues like development and environment, language and better economic deals for use of local resources by the federal authorities. For some, these student-youth groups are the 'saviours' of the community and defenders of its vital interests, but for others they represent the 'fountainhead of parochialism' and 'extra-constitutional forces' in the politics of northeast India. They nevertheless continue to enjoy much influence in almost every state of the region.

The AMSU has led the movement for the recognition of the Manipuri language and for its inclusion in the Eighth Schedule of the Indian constitution. In 2001, it was at the forefront of the agitation to scrap the extension to Manipur of the Naga ceasefire, which was seen as a prelude to parceling off Naga-inhabited areas of the state to the neighbouring state of Nagaland. The TSF has consistently articulated the demand for expulsion of Bengali migrants who entered the state after 1949, when the erstwhile kingdom merged with the Indian Union. The All Arunachal Pradesh Students Union (AAPSU) led the agitation to expel the Chakmas and the Hajongs who came from East Pakistan and were settled in what was then the North-East Frontier Agency (NEFA). The KSU has stridently opposed uranium mining in the Domiosiat-Wakkhaji region in the West Khasi Hills because it fears large-scale radiation hazards for the local villagers, similar to those witnessed alongside India's main uranium mines at Jadugoda in Jharkhand state. The Naga Students Federation (NSF) successfully agitated to stop oil exploration in Nagaland until the state agreed to pay royalties and provide local employment. The YMA has led the pogrom against the Brus and the Chin migrants in Mizoram.

The student and youth groups have thrived on the margins of the Indian political system, in the buffer space between political parties and the insurgent groups. The national political parties were seen by many as not appropriately reflecting the concerns of the ethnic communities while the insurgents were seen as 'going too far', so the student and youth groups emerged effective options to take up local concerns with some aggression but pragmatic enough to negotiate deals with the authorities at the right opportunity. These groups have provided future leaders and activists to both the national and regional political parties. Many of the future insurgent leaders also started off in the student movement. For example, many top ULFA leaders started off with the AASU during the heady days of the anti-foreigner agitation. Government repression convinced them that the politics of mass mobilization would not take the Assamese anywhere and that armed struggle was the only answer. A number of TSF leaders, like Mantu Koloi in Tripura, ended up in guerrilla organizations like the NLFT. But most student leaders ended up in overground political parties, regional or national, and entered the legislatures.

It is not just the student-youth groups, however, that have exerted influence in the politics of the North East. Some traditional institutions like the Naga Hoho remain as powerful as the political parties and enjoy considerable social acceptance. In recent years, human rights organizations, gender-specific groups and social platforms have become part of the emerging civil society architecture in the conflict-torn region. The Indian military-security establishment has viewed these groups as 'an extension of the insurgencies' and has often sought to 'expose their close links' with the separatist organizations. But government and intelligence agencies have often used the services of these civil society pioneers to open dialogues with the underground leadership. The social consensus in support of peace that these civil society groups have been able to generate has proved useful to the federal political-bureaucratic establishment. The military has claimed that these groups acted as 'force multipliers' for the underground in combat, but they have often ended up as 'force multipliers' in the cause of peace and settlement. For instance, the church has long been accused of supporting insurgencies in the North East, but it is the church that took the first decisive initiatives for peace in Nagaland and Mizoram. The peace-making roles of Reverend Longri Ao in Nagaland and Reverend Zairema in Mizoram have not only been appreciated in their states but also in the corridors of power in Delhi.

The human rights arena has been the new war theatre in the battle for the hearts and minds of the people. The military has been compelled to introduce human rights in its training curriculum. The human rights groups in the North East have often been accused of double standards because while they have been critical of the military, they are seen as soft in pulling up the insurgent groups when the latter perpetrate mass killings or select assassinations. Thus, although the impartiality and credibility of the North East's human rights movement have been challenged by the military-security establishment, the human rights debate has come to dominate the civil society discourse in the region.

The Naga Peoples Movement for Human Rights (NPMHR) made an impact on Naga society when it set out to expose the excesses of the security forces. Its first effective campaign to highlight the military's excesses followed an ambush by the NSCN guerrillas at Namthilok in which more than twenty Sikh soldiers of the Indian army were killed in early 1982. Five years later, the NPMHR undertook the biggest mobilization of witnesses in the history of India's human rights movement when it gathered more than 600 witnesses to back up allegations of extra-judicial killings and extensive torture perpetrated by Indian security forces in Naga areas of Manipur after the NSCN had looted away more than 100 weapons in a raid on an Assam Rifles camp at Oinam. The NPMHR had managed to secure the services of one of the best human rights lawyers in the country, Nandita Haksar. Some of the early activists of the NPMHR rose in the Asian indigenous peoples' movement. For example, Luithui Luingam, one of the NPMHR's founders, even headed the Asian Indigenous Peoples Pact at one time.

The Meira Paibis in Manipur have aggressively promoted the strongest gender platform in northeast India, one that fights against alcoholism, drugs and other social evils but also serves as a great mass mobilizer to prevent the possible break-up of Manipur. They have played the lead role in the movement against the draconian Armed Forces Special Powers Act (AFSPA) and some of its elderly members even stripped naked in front of the Assam Rifles headquarters in Imphal, with placards saying: 'Indian army, come and rape us.' The AMSU, the All Manipur United Clubs Organization (AMUCO) and the Meira Paibis form a formidable triumvirate in Meitei society that will fight its last battle against a possible break-up of the state if Delhi decides to dissect Manipur and hand over Naga-inhabited territories to appease the NSCN. They demonstrated their strength and social support during the agitation against the AFSPA after the brutal killing of a Manipuri girl Thangjam Manorama in July 2004.

The Naga Mothers Association has also played an important role in enforcing prohibition and in fighting against drugs in Naga society. Its pioneering role in trekking to the NSCN bases in Burma to kick-start the peace process in Nagaland is well documented. The NSF, the NPMHR and the Naga Mothers Association form an effective civil society triumvirate that has helped carry forward the peace talks between the NSCN and mobilized the support for peace in Naga society. That yearning for peace has compelled both the NSCN and the Indian government to keep the dialogue going despite its very slow progress. In the years since the NSCN started its negotiations with the Indian government, the democratic space has widened in Naga society. The pen and the microphone have somewhat, if not fully, replaced the gun as instruments of political discourse and there is greater freedom of debates in Naga society on crucial issues than was the case during the long years of conflict.

The Naga people have also made it clear that they will not tolerate blatant warlordism any more. Several incidents in which NSCN guerrillas were lynched were reported from the towns of Nagaland in recent years. At Mokukchung, hundreds of Nagas lynched two guerrillas of the NSCN's Khaplang faction after they killed a student in broad daylight. One guerrilla of the NSCN's Issac–Muivah faction was beaten to death at Tuensang by a mob complaining of guerrilla excesses. Militarism has taken a toll on Naga civil society for years. But now for the first time in almost five decades, the Nagas are experiencing uninterrupted peace for a long time as a result of the Delhi-NSCN ceasefire. Having already expressed themselves against Indian militarism through the human rights forums, these civil society groups are beginning to take on Naga militarism with some firmness.

In the 1970s, Brigadier Sailo's civil liberties movement in Mizoram brought about change in the ground situation. A brutalized society suddenly found a new voice, one of reason and sense. A generation that has grown up hearing talk of 'regrouped villages', 'cordon and search' and 'preventive detention' were suddenly going over the Universal Declaration of Human Rights and the provisions of the Indian constitution that provide for fundamental rights. The Civil Liberties and Human Rights Organization (CLAHRO) in Manipur and the Manab Adhikar Sangram Samity (MASS) in Assam have established the human rights and the civil society agenda in their own states on a firm institutional footing, despite the enormous harassment and repression they continue to face.

Like the student organizations that formed the North East Students Organizations (NESO) to coordinate their activities through a common agenda from a united platform, the human rights groups in the North East have developed a regional network to articulate their concerns. The biggest challenge for the region's fledgling human rights movement is to carry the campaign against the AFSPA and the Disturbed Areas Act to a successful finale. The Indian government was forced to set up a committee with a retired Supreme Court judge to examine the AFSPA but then, under possible pressure of the military, decided not to implement the committee's recommendation to scrap the Act. But even tough Indian policemen, like Assam Police Chief G.M. Srivastava, have advocated withdrawing the AFSPA, at least for a while.[3]

As the frail Meitei woman Irom Sharmila's unending fast for scrapping of the AFSPA nears a decade, more and more people are coming out in her support not only in Manipur but elsewhere in the region—and even in mainland India. As the yearning for peace grows and the civil society shapes up all across the North East, the insurgent groups and the government will have to heed the spirit of the times and work to end the region's endemic conflicts. After 60 years of strife, there is a growing realization in the North East that peace is more difficult to achieve than war.

NOTES

1. Gurudas Das, 2002.
2. Verrier Elwin, 1959. Also see, *Verrier Elwin* 1964.
3. G.M. Srivastava advocated withdrawl of AFSPA, at least temporarily, in a seminar organized by the Centre for Peace and Development Studies in Guwahati on 17 March 2009.

8   The Crisis of Development

Many have blamed the rebellions in India's North East on the region's economic backwardness and lack of development. It has been argued that the North East is an endowed region, gifted with many natural resources, but the endowments have not translated into economic growth and development. That widened the gap between expectation and achievement among its predominantly Mongoloid ethnicities and the alienation of the fringe from the core has intensified. Instead of investing in the region's infrastructure and allowing market forces to do the rest, the country's federal government pumped huge quantam of funds to sustain the region's economy. Only recently has it dawned on Delhi that such huge fund flows have led to little development of infrastructure. The Vision 2020 document for North East, prepared by the Department of Development of North Eastern Region (DONER) and the North East Council, admits:

At independence North Eastern Region was among the most prosperous regions of India. Sixty years on, the Region as a whole, and the States that comprise it, are lagging far behind the rest of the country in most important parameters of growth. The purpose of this Vision document is to return the North Eastern Region to the position of national economic eminence it held till a few decades ago; to so fashion the development process that growth springs from and spreads out to the grassroots; and to ensure that the Region plays the arrow-head role it must play in the vanguard of the country's Look East Policy.[1]

In a free-market economy which India is evolving into, the influence of globalization and liberalization will be profound. In such a situation, the North East will miss the bus unless it has adequate infrastructure to attract investments. The Vision 2020 document noted that if the country's economy is growing at 9 per cent per annum (as it was before the global economic slump), the North East's economy will have to grow at the rate of 13.5 per cent to catch up with the national standards of living. Fund flows from Delhi will perhaps continue to help the region in its catch-up game, but only if results are discernible over a reasonable time frame. Or else the North East will remain a basket case, an unsustainable dole-economy. The Vision 2020 identified three 'critical non-economic requirements' that will condition the region's economic performance:

1. law and order, especially internal security;
2. good governance, including governance at the grassroots through institutions of local self-government, and
3. diplomatic initiatives with the neighbourhood of the North East to secure what the Minister of External Affairs has described as the 'new paradigm' where 'foreign policy initiatives blend seamlessly with our national economic development requirements'.

So far, the North Eastern states have received a very high rate of per capita central assistance, several times more than poor heartland states like Bihar, because they have been treated as 'special category' states by the Indian government. But that's not really produced the desired results in development. The National Development Council earmarks 30 per cent of the total plan allocations for these states as central assistance for state plans. These 'special category' states receive 90 per cent of the plan assistance as a grant and 10 per cent as a loan, while other Indian states receive only 30 per cent as grant and 70 per cent as loan. The support to these states from the central devolution (Planning and Finance Commissions) accounts for over 80 per cent of the per capita revenue receipts in this region. Tables 8.1 and 8.2 illustrate the importance of fund flows from the Centre for North Eastern states.

Thus, the contention that India has neglected the development needs of the North East is far from true, if one were to base such an

TABLE 8.1
Ratio of Gross Transfers from the Centre to Aggregate Disbursement
of the North Eastern States

(%)

State	1985–90 (avg.)	1990–95 (avg.)	1995–96 (R.E.)	1996–97	1997–98 (R.E.)	1998–99 (R.E.)
Arunachal Pradesh	79.7	86.4	85.8	87.6	86.5	86.9
Assam	72.5	65.0	68.2	75.3	68.5	62.8
Manipur	86.6	81.0	78.1	75.8	76.1	73.1
Meghalaya	86.3	77.4	78.1	80.7	75.1	72.4
Mizoram	95.2	84.4	84.8	79.6	85.9	84.6
Nagaland	82.9	75.7	72.6	76.2	77.6	76.9
Tripura	83.2	83.1	88.5	83.8	80.6	78.2
India	45.3	40.1	41.6	40.4	41.2	40.4

Source: Gulshan Sachdeva, *Economy of the Northeast*, 2000.

assertion on the volume of fund transfers to the region. As Table 8.2 reveals, gross fund transfers into the North East during the 1990s totalled to more than Rs 60,000 crore and net transfers (after accounting for interest payments and loan repayments) amounted to more than Rs 50,000 crore. Not surprisingly, the region's basic socio-economic indices also compare favourably to the national average. At Rs 5,070 per annum, the region's per capita income is above the national average of Rs 4,485. The proportion of the population below the poverty line (33 per cent) is also less than the national figure (39 per cent). Even access to electricity—at 44 per cent of all households—is just above the national average of 43 per cent; access to health centres/hospitals within five kilometres stands at 47 per cent, as against a national average of 41.2 per cent. In terms of roads, industrial development and other indices of infrastructure development, however, the region lags far behind the rest of the country.

Much of the considerable funds from the Centre have not been used to develop infrastructure that could, in turn, draw investments and create jobs. Very few new industries have come up since the British departed. Traditional industries like tea and oil are in great difficulty, victims of high production costs, poor yields, falling markets and extortion by insurgent forces. Railroad expansion in the region has been notoriously slow—some states like Mizoram and Manipur have almost no railways at all. And Tripura's capital

TABLE 8.2

Devolution and Transfer of Resources from the Centre to the North East, 1990–91 to 1998–99

(Rs in crore)

State	Gross devolution and transfer total	Annual average	Net devolution and transfer total	Annual average	Net state domestic product at current prices, average of six years 1990–91 to 1995–96	Ratio of annual net transfer to NSDP (p.c.)
Arunachal Pradesh	5,489.18	609.91	5,274.47	586.05	750.83	78.05
Assam	25,160.62	2,795.62	18,865.51	2,096.17	12,462.83	16.82
Manipur	5,583.20	620.36	5,216.18	579.58	1,070.50	54.14
Meghalaya	4,994.40	554.93	4,613.97	512.66	1,101.83	46.53
Mizoram	4,837.87	537.41	4,511.35	501.26	520.16	96.37
Nagaland	6,607.16	734.13	5,781.43	642.38	950.83	67.56
Tripura	7,266.94	807.43	6,784.24	753.80	1,355.67	55.60

Source: Gulshan Sachdeva, Northeast Council, 2002.

Agartala has only recently been connected by rail. Inland water transport systems that could have boosted intra-regional cargo and passenger movement and also shipping to and from the heartland via Bangladesh failed to develop because of lack of federal and provincial initiative. The Vision 2020 document recommends huge outlays for road building and extension of railways all over the region.

The region's distance from the heartland should have justified prioritized development of telecommunications and speedy development of broadband Internet services. With its high literacy rates and relatively better exposure to English education due to the efforts of Christian missionaries, the North East would have been ideally poised to take advantage of the information technology boom. But the chief ministers of the North Eastern states would go to Delhi to lobby for more funds for the state plan rather than fight for better infrastructure that could promote growth and attract investment. The funds they managed to secure from Delhi were wasted to promote employment in government. The result: a bloated bureaucracy and a huge government workforce whose inefficiency and corruption makes it a liability rather than an asset for the states.

This is not to underestimate the inherent limitations from which the region suffers. With the exception of Assam and Arunachal Pradesh, the other North Eastern states are small in size. Except Assam, none has a large population. The local market for any product made in the region is therefore quite limited. Except for Assam, the manufacturing industries in the rest of the region never took off. The smallest state in the region is Tripura (10,486 square kilometre) and the lowest in population, according to the 2001 census, is Mizoram (8,91,058 inhabitants). The density of population varies from 13 (Arunachal) to 340 (Assam) inhabitants per square kilometre, and the cultivable arable land in the largely hilly region is rather sparse. The largest state in the region is Arunachal Pradesh but only 4 per cent of its total area of 83,743 square kilometre is cultivable. Population is largely dispersed, residing mainly in the hills. This makes development of infrastructure—roads, telecommunication, water supply and electricity, health facilities—very expensive, consuming, at times, double the expenditure incurred for similar purposes in the mainland states. The fact that much of the material for construction has to be shipped from the mainland states over great distances compounds the problem.

The Partition burdened the region with the need for new infrastructure as the pre-1947 links through eastern Bengal were suddenly severed. The distance from the Indian mainland has added to the economic disadvantage, in terms of higher transportation costs of raw material from sources of supply and of finished goods produced in the region to potential markets. Lack of a sufficiently large regional market and the consequent lack of economies of scale have worked against setting up of new industries even as the old ones have languished. Some have argued that Assam's economy would have taken off if India had set up a big refinery in the state and not in Barauni immediately after independence and had followed it up by a gas cracker plant to use the more than Rs 3,000 crore worth of associated gas available.[2]

Downstream industries could have taken off on a large scale but that did not happen. It has not helped Assam when it got what it wanted after years of agitation. Now, Assam's crude output has fallen, raising fears that the large Numaligarh Refinery may be under-utilized or would have to get crude from outside the region or through foreign imports. Reliance Industries wasted more than a decade after it signed the Memorandum of Understanding (MOU) with the Assam government (and got most of the concessions it wanted) before deciding to back out of the proposed gas cracker plant in Upper Assam. Such delays have led to unacceptable time and cost overruns. It may now be necessary to explore whether the proposed gas cracker project continues to remain viable or not. Since new industries failed to take off in Assam, the rest of the North East was denied the spillover effect. Consequently, all the North East Indian states remain at the very bottom of the process of industrialization in India, despite possessing rich resources.

Resources by themselves do not result in a buoyant economy. The North East has a proven exploitable reserve of 864 million tonnes of coal, a recoverable reserve of 421 million tonnes of hydrocarbons (267 million tonnes of crude oil and 154 million tonnes of gas in oil equivalent) and a hydroelectric power potential of nearly 60,000 MW. Assam and Arunachal Pradesh are endowed with rich oil-bearing shale formations that could yield 15 billion tonnes of recoverable oil. Though commercially expensive to exploit now, these deposits could become a real asset when oil reserves elsewhere in the country begin to dry up and the rising global oil prices make imports prohibitive. Despite such energy endowments, the region suffers from acute power shortages. Huge queues for gas cylinders can be seen in all major towns and cities. Guwahati, the largest town in the North East, suffers from a perpetual water crisis, despite being located on the banks of one of the nation's mightiest rivers. Car hire rates in the region are higher than anywhere else in the country even though Assam's five refineries produce substantial quantities of petroleum products.

Poignant examples of development failures abound all across the region. In Upper Assam's Rohmaria area, villagers are so upset with the government's failure to tackle river erosion that they have stopped Oil India Limited (OIL) from commercial exploitation of the rich oil deposits in the area. Thirty eight villages have been swallowed away by the merciless Brahmaputra in the past two decades but the Assam government is unmoved, though the state's present Water Resources Minister Prithvi Majhi is elected from the assembly consituency under which Rohmaria falls. The villagers have nothing against OIL but they have stopped their oil production in 1999 only to force the government to do something about erosion. But the 'economic blockade' of the OIL facilities for 10 years now has not given the villagers of Rohmaria the desired result. But the OIL, which, like other oil companies under some pressure to produce more oil in Assam, is lost. There was a time when Assam did not have enough refineries to process the crude it produced. Now it has refineries with an installed capacity of 7 million tonnes but its annual crude output is hovering around 5 million tonnes for several years.

In India's liberalizing and increasingly globalizing economy, where opportunities are growing, the North East is at an obvious disadvantage caused by physical distance from the mainland. During the five decades of socialist planning, India's federal government stuck to its freight equalization policy that denied its eastern and North Eastern states any locational advantage. The political leadership of the North East did not fight against such policies and even West Bengal only rarely raised a feeble voice. West Bengal and Assam, whose economies are closely linked and can only grow together, worked at cross-purposes, carried away by the lure of easy employment in the public sector. Only if Indian manufacturing companies focus on trans-border markets in neighbouring countries like China, Burma or

Bangladesh will the North East emerge as a production and trading hub. For that to happen, the regional environment in South Asia would have to change and that would largely depend on the success of India's economic diplomacy in the region. A major breakthrough has already been achieved with Bangladesh; where the new Awami League-led coalition government has agreed to allow India the use of the Chittagong port for accessing its North Eastern region and also designated Ashuganj (very near Tripura's capital Agartala) as a new port of call under Article 23 of the Inland Water Transit and Trade Agreement. This will mean huge transport cost savings for goods taken to the North East (by sea to Chittagong and then by river to Ashuganj and by rail to Agartala) and will bring down expenditure for executing all major projects in the region.

The political reorganization of the region was designed to pacify ethnic unrest. The criteria of economic and financial viability were not applied to the new states and those like Nagaland, which were created to take the sting out of the secessionist movements, were given the obvious commitment that Delhi would largely underwrite the cost of governance. At least four North Eastern states (Nagaland, Assam, Manipur and Tripura) have been suffering the consequences of severe insurgency, which diverts both financial resources and attention from development to security issues.

In Assam, for instance, the expenditure on police and on maintenance of law and order has gone up from Rs 99 crore in 1986–87 to Rs 724.99 crore in 2001–02. The police force has increased to around 75,000. This is mainly due to insurgency and worsening law and order. Since 1990–91, the Assam state government has claimed nearly Rs 1,100 crores as re-imbursement from the Centre on security-related expenditure. The Centre has cleared only about Rs 350 crore. It has been alleged that there was discrimination in this respect because in Punjab the entire amount of loan taken for security-related expenditures was written off by the Centre.

Indeed, if one were to blame insurgency in those states on lack of development, far too simplistic an explanation, one would see the working of the vicious cycle unwittingly created: lack of development leading to insurgency and then insurgency leading to lack of development. Some states, like Assam, Arunachal Pradesh, Tripura and Manipur, have to bear the brunt of annual floods and landslides. Floods in the Brahmaputra and Barak Valleys of Assam cause serious erosion, loss of life and livestock and heavy damage to infrastructure and property retarding agricultural productivity on account of risk avoidance and sandcasting, disrupting communications and education and posing health hazards ... The flood damage to crops, cattle, houses and utilities in Assam alone between 1953 and 1995 is estimated at Rs 4400 crores with a peak of Rs 664 crores in a single bad year.[3]

The assessed flood-prone area in Assam alone is estimated at 3.15 million hectares or 92.6 per cent of the cultivated land. In 1992–93, almost half of this land (1.63 million hectares) did not have any flood-management structures. Even the limited flood-management structures that do exist are poorly maintained. The master plan prepared by the Brahmaputra Board involves Rs 1,848 crore at 1995 prices for short-term measures and Rs 50,000 crore for long-term measures up to 2050. In the meantime the state governments continue with fire-fighting operations and provide flood and natural calamity relief causing a heavy drain on their otherwise meagre resources. The floods have created so much uncertainty that there has been very little investment aimed at commercializing agriculture and fisheries.

The region imports more than Rs 700 crore worth of foodstuffs and fish from other parts of the country every year. The Assam government has sunk thousands of deep tube wells in the past six years and this is beginning to have a positive impact on the state's agriculture. Most states in the region, however, do not pay enough importance to modernizing agriculture, though it remains the mainstay of the region's economy. Tripura, for instance, spent only 4 per cent of its budget on promotion of agriculture, though the potential for commercializing it is evident with the success of rubber and a host of other plantation crops in the state. The Vision 2020 documents stresses that the real boost to North East's can come only by 'some kind of a green revolution'.

The North Eastern states have a tremendous potential in tourism that has not been exploited at all. Tourism generates a much higher level of employment for every penny invested. The North East has ethnic diversity, climatic variations, game parks like Kaziranga and Manas, lakes like Umiam and Loktak, the sub-Himalayan landscape of Arunachal Pradesh and a massive river like the Brahmaputra. There is huge scope for ethnic tourism, game tourism, nostalgia tourism (which can be promoted in Britain among descendants of those who served in the tea gardens of the North East), winter sports and adventure tourism and even golf tourism (in Shillong). Most state capitals and major cities of the North East are barely one to two hours flying time from Calcutta and barely another two hours from Bangkok. Despite an Air India flight that now connects Guwahati to Bangkok (three hours flying time), Assam and the North East have failed to draw even a small percentage of the tourists who come to Thailand. The North East has been identified as a tourist destination but again lacks the infrastructure and the marketing drive to attract tourists. A sporadic elephant festival or a rhino festival will not help. Insurgency in the North East will not deter tourism because Africa's civil wars have not deterred tourists from going there. When states like Haryana have developed very profitable roadside tourism by setting up motels on the road to Delhi over a largely barren rocky red soil country, it defies logic why the North East, so richly endowed with flora and fauna, landscape and ethnic diversity cannot develop a viable tourism industry.

The governments should spend on developing tourism infrastructure, the private sector should provide the enterprise. The Assam Tourism's Calcutta office has shown some drive in recent months by some aggressive marketing to take advantage of the turmoil in Darjeeling. A huge percentage of Bengali tourists, who account for the biggest chunk of the domestic tourists in India, have been drawn to Assam by skilful projection of Assam's past linkages with Bengal, its attractive sites like the Kaziranga wildlife park and the Kamakshya temple and also by projecting the three-in-one advantage (a visit to Assam can easily take the tourist to the neighbouring states of Meghalaya and Arunachal Pradesh). Even tea companies, whose profit margins are shrinking, can explore the option of diversifying into tourism. With West Bengal and Sikkim, the North East can form a very profitable tourist circuit. When locals make money from tourists, the animosity towards outsiders will decline. As a result of the SARS scare in South East Asia and the Maoist rebellion in Nepal and the serial bombings all over the Indian mainland (Hyderabad, Bangalore, Jaipur, Bombay, Ahmedabad, Delhi, Lucknow and Varanasi have all been hit by the serial bombings in the last three years) the Bengal–North East axis has the opportunity to become a viable alternative for domestic and foreign tourists—specially after the decline in intensity of the separatist movements in the North East.

Since most North Eastern states have very little industry and a small population, much of it belonging to Scheduled Tribes who do not pay income tax, their tax base, except in Assam, is narrow and limited. The largest contributor to the net state domestic product is the tertiary sector, which is comprised mostly of services dominated by public administration. Except in the case of Assam and to some extent in the plains of Manipur and Tripura, income from those sources are beyond the purview of the tax net. Except Assam, which levies an agricultural income tax, agricultural income in the rest of the region is not taxed. Unfortunately, barring Assam, the manufacturing sector is very small. The secondary sector is mostly made up of construction work, mainly roads and government buildings, and financed by the federal organizations.

The lack of industrial growth in the region has compounded the problem. Assam's tea industry is in the doldrums, its production costs rising and auction prices falling over the years and exports to other countries increasingly challenged by cheaper teas from Sri Lanka, Kenya and China. Assam's oil industry is affected by falling crude output that is not even enough for the existing refineries in the state. Bringing in imported crude through Haldia to sustain the Assam refineries will again go against the logic of setting them up. The plywood industries have been affected by the Supreme Court's order against commercial tree-felling. While the traditional industries are languishing, new-age industries like information technology have not come to the region. All this has contributed to a narrow tax base. The federal Income Tax department, however, expects tax revenues to go up because they expect considerable spin-offs from the nearly Rs 35,000 crores that is likely to be invested to boost the region's infrastructure.

It is obvious that huge fund transfers from the Centre, though sustained for more than five decades, have not led to a corresponding level of acceleration in the region's development. The per capita net state domestic product (NSDP) of all the North Eastern states, except Arunachal Pradesh, Nagaland and Mizoram, is lower than the national average, while the per capita central assistance is higher than the national average for all states except Assam (see Table 8.3). The per capita central assistance has come down for most of the North Eastern states and during the Tenth Plan period they are under considerable pressure to generate their own revenues or face economic collapse.

TABLE 8.3
**Net State Domestic Product (NSDP) and Per Capita Central Assistance
for North Eastern States**

(in rupees)

State	Per capita NSDP	Per capital central assistance	
Arunachal Pradesh	10,205	14,936 (2001–02)	15,213 (1999–00)
Assam	6,288	838 (2001–02)	1,190 (1999–00)
Manipur	6,914	4,476 (2001–02)	4,134 (1999–00)
Meghalaya	7,862	3,960 (2000–01)	3,282 (1999–00)
Mizoram	9,750	9,518 (2000–01)	9,654 (1999–00)
Nagaland	9,758	4,692 (2000–01)	5,288 (1999–00)
Tripura	5,083	3,183 (2000–01)	3,950 (1999–00)
All other states (average)	9,725	1,619 (2000–01)	1,712 (1999–00)

Source: Gulshan Sachdeva, 2000.

Commenting on the problem, the leading economist of the region, Jayant Madhab Goswami says:

The North Eastern States have not done well; their per capita Net State Domestic Products [NSDP] are lower than the all India average. Indeed, Assam, the biggest economy in the region, has only 61 per cent of the all India average; and, 41 and 21 per cent of those of Maharashtra and Delhi respectively. While India's Gross Domestic Product [GDP] has been growing at an average of over 6 per cent in real terms, the economies of North Eastern states were growing at a much lesser rate during 1992–99. In a few states high growth was noticeable in some years. This was mostly due to higher construction [mainly roads] activities financed by the Central Government in certain years.[4]

FINANCES IN THE DOLDRUMS

The North Eastern states are now heavily dependent on the Centre to bail them out of the doldrums created by rampant fiscal profligacy. Assam and Manipur were on the verge of bankruptcy and the two state governments are unable to pay salaries to their employees on time. They were getting increasingly dependent on overdrafts from the Reserve Bank to wriggle out of tight situations. The other states are slightly better off, but since they also spend much of their resources on salaries, pensions and to service interest payments, they could face similar problems as Assam and Manipur. Growth of their revenue is not commensurate with their rising expenditure. These states are borrowing heavily to meet revenue expenditure and to service debt. But in spite of such huge borrowings, government employees in many states often go without salaries for months together. Wasteful expenditure on populist schemes—all justified by the need to win hearts and minds in a counter-insurgency situation–add to the woes of public finance in the North East. The gross fiscal deficits of all the North Eastern states are rising, as indicated in Table 8.4.

TABLE 8.4
Gross Fiscal Deficits of North Eastern States and Some Selected Mainland States, 1998–99 to 2000–01

(Rs crore)

State	1998–99	1999–00	2000–01
Arunachal Pradesh	55.4 [4.3]	59.3 [3.7]	224.7
Assam	338.2 [1.6]	1,605.8 [6.4]	1,923.5 [7.1]
Manipur	106.2 [4.6]	655.8 [25.7]	234.4 [8.3]
Meghalaya	147.3 [5.8]	209.1 [7.4]	280.1 [8.7]
Mizoram	132.3 [11.6]	179.1 [13.2]	197.6
Nagaland	243.2 [11.1]	249.0	358.8
Tripura	118.4 [3.4]	290.3 [7.6]	427.3 [10.2]
Haryana	2,240.4 [5.9]	2,132.5 [5.1]	2,405.9
Kerala	3,012.2 [5.9]	4,536.6 [7.7]	4,363.7
Orissa	3,420.4 [11.5]	3,746.1 [10.4]	3,005.4
West Bengal	7,109.1 [6.7]	11,666.4 [9.5]	11,220.9 [7.8]

Source: Centre for Monitoring of Indian Economy (CMIE): Public Finance 2002 and Eco-nomic Survey 2001.
Note: Figures within brackets indicate percentage of NSDP.

The problem with the North Eastern states is that their own revenue resources form a very small portion of the NSDP (see Table 8.5).

TABLE 8.5
State Revenue Sources as a Percentage of Net State Domestic Product, 1999–2000

Assam	6.6	Haryana	11.5
Manipur	3.2	Himachal	9.3
Meghalaya	6.6	Kerala	8.9
Nagaland*	3.6	Orissa	7.4
Tripura	4.7	West Bengal	8.9

Source: Data from CMIE: Public Finance 2002 and Economic Survey, 2001.
Note: *Nagaland figure for 1998–99.

It is evident that there is still some scope to raise revenue within the states. The same point can be looked at from a different angle. The revenue-raising efforts of the North Eastern states as a proportion of per capita NSDP are shown in Table 8.6, which again drives home the point that the North Eastern states are under-taxed.

TABLE 8.6
Per Capita State Revenue as a Percentage of Per Capita Net State Domestic Product, 1999–2000

Assam	6.5	Haryana	10.7
Manipur	3.0	Himachal	18.4
Meghalaya	6.9	Kerala	9.8
Nagaland	3.6	Orissa	7.2
Tripura	5.4	West Bengal	4.6

Source: Compiled from CII: Public Finance 2002 and Economic Surveys. Population figures are of 2001 provisional census. State revenue includes tax and non-tax sources.

Though the financial resources of the northeast Indian states are limited, there are some taxes that they can raise effectively. Sales tax and state excise yield a lot of revenue to the states. Taxes on professions, agricultural income tax, tax on property and capital transactions, land revenue, stamps and registration fees, taxes on commodities and services, central sales tax, taxes on vehicles, taxes on goods and passengers and entertainment also contribute substantially to the state's exchequer. While sales tax contributes between 50 and 70 per cent of the revenue of most states, strangely it contributes very little to the state revenues in Arunachal Pradesh, Mizoram and Meghalaya. In Arunachal Pradesh, only 10 per cent of the state's own tax revenue of Rs 4.09 crore in 1991–92 was contributed by sales tax. When the state's own tax revenue grew to Rs 25.64 crore in 1996–97, the sales tax accounted for only 2 per cent of revenue. State excise, however, contributed between 50 and 70 per cent of the state's own tax revenue. On the other hand, the state excise contribution in Assam, Manipur and Nagaland remains small. Three reasons explain the low sales tax collections: (a) the states want to provide goods—the cost of which is already high due to high transport costs—at the lowest possible rate; (b) the states are not willing to give outside businessmen sales tax numbers that could form the basis for future residency claims and (c) some states, like Mizoram, practice prohibition.

Non-tax revenues in the North Eastern states consist essentially of interest receipts, receipts from lotteries, revenues from economic and general services. In the case of Assam and to a lesser extent Arunachal, Nagaland and Tripura, royalties from production of oil and natural gas form a part of non-tax revenue as well. These states do not make much effort to recoup the cost for providing economic services like irrigation, power, transportation and water supply. If the state governments do not hesitate to charge full or close to full cost for providing these services, their revenue situation would improve to some extent.

Oil royalty paid by Oil and Natural Gas Corporation (ONGC) and OIL seems to be the only major source linked with production and since the rate of the royalty has been increasing since the Assam agitation, income from oil and gas royalties is rising. But the Nagaland government has been sitting on its oil reserves in Champang, not allowing oil companies to drill and produce after the NSCN chased the ONGC away in the mid 1990s. By adopting prohibition, Nagaland and Mizoram deprived themselves of a huge source of excise revenue. The rebels have imposed prohibition in Manipur, again depriving the state of critical excise revenue. The Supreme Court's ban on commercial tree-felling in forest areas has also affected the revenue of most of the North Eastern states.

The receipts of the North Eastern states are accrued primarily from central assistance, coming in the form of grants, shared taxes and loans. While all states together received Rs 64,142 crore in 1994–95, this increased to Rs 1,56,305 crore in 2000–01, within six years. This assistance formed 38.6 per cent of total receipts of the states in 1994–95 and 43 per cent in 2000–01. Clearly, dependence on the Centre has increased for all the states. Central assistance forms between 65 and 92 per cent of total revenue in the North Eastern states (see Table 8.7). Arunachal Pradesh's and Mizoram's own revenue receipts are not more than 10 per cent of total revenue. Per capita devolution from the Centre to the states is also quite high.

Among the North Eastern states, Assam's liquidity problem seems to be worst, as Table 8.8 suggests. While the total expenditure grew at an annual average rate of 12.9 per cent during the five-year span from 1995 to 2000, total receipts grew at the rate of only 5.4 per cent. Though the figures do not suggest it, Manipur's situation became very serious during the last three years. While introducing the

TABLE 8.7

**Total Central Assistance (Grants, Shared Taxes, Loans and Advances)
as a Percentage of States' Total Receipts, 1999–2000**

Assam	65	Haryana	32
Manipur	67	Himachal	32
Meghalaya	66	Kerala	26
Nagaland	81	Orissa	49
Tripura	76	West Bengal	47

Source: Data from CMIE: Public Finance 2002.

TABLE 8.8

**Annual Average Growth Rates of Total Receipts and Total Expenditure
from 1995–96 to 1999–2000**

States	Total receipts annual growth rate	Total expenditure annual growth rate
Assam	5.4	12.9
Manipur	22.1	22.9
Meghalaya	15.6	15.8
Nagaland	14.2	10.8
Tripura	16.5	15.0
Haryana	4.5	4.7
Kerala	15.3	16.8
Orissa	15.3	15.4
West Bengal	17.8	20.0
All States	13.4	32.1

Source: Data from CMIE: Public Finance 2002.

2002–03 budget, the finance minister of Manipur had to admit that 'the state's financial health at this juncture is extremely precarious. The mismatch between our resources and expenditure is too glaring and it is depressing to see that it is also widening at too fast a pace'. The Assam finance minister similarly said that 'the fiscal scenario was extremely grim when this government assumed charge, with the State Government in a quagmire of debts, deficits and overdrafts'.

While Assam and Manipur are facing severe financial crises, other North Eastern states are slightly better off. Their fiscal management is better. Out of 26 states studied in 1999–2000, 19 had revenue deficits. Of the seven states that enjoyed a revenue surplus, five were from the North East. Even these five states, however, now are slipping into a difficult fiscal situation, largely because they have failed to contain expenditure on salaries, pensions and debt services. Assam spent 78 per cent of its total expenditure on salaries, pensions, interest payments and repayment of loans in 2000–01. Tripura and Manipur spent 62 per cent and 67 per cent, respectively, in 2002–03. Salaries do not include travelling allowances, other perks and establishment expenses. If these are included, the percentage goes up substantially. Table 8.9 shows interest payment and loan repayment as a percentage of total expenditure in 1999–2000 as compared to 1994–95.

TABLE 8.9
Interest Payment and Loan Repayment as a Percentage of Total Expenditure

States	*1999–2000*	*1994–95*		*1999–2000*	*1994–95*
Assam	22.5	22.7	Haryana	18.9	8.4
Manipur	10.4	10.6	Himachal	18.6	14.4
Meghalaya	11.1	9.5	Kerala	18.0	16.4
Nagaland	17.4	12.0	Orissa	16.0	19.8
Tripura	12.8	11.8	West Bengal	17.6	17.9

Source: Data from CMIE: Public Finance 2002.

Assam and some other states are borrowing more and more from the market to meet revenue deficits. As a result, debt service charges have increased as a proportion of total expenditure. Except for unusual circumstances, debt is incurred to create income-earning assets through which debt can be redeemed. The central government plan loans are also for creating assets. Assam and some other states, because of the pressure created by revenue deficits, are simply using the loans for meeting revenue deficits. For the special category states, the Planning Commission agreed that 20 per cent of plan financing can be utilized for meeting revenue deficits.

In the case of Assam, the annual expenditure on salaries, wages, other allowances and pensions constituted 126 per cent of the state's own revenue receipt in 1990–91; it increased to 243 per cent in 2001–02. The average annual salary of a government employee in Assam increased from Rs 22,281 to Rs 96,003, an increase of over four times between 1990–91 and 2001–02. Assam's Committee on Fiscal Reform (COFR) remarked:

> During interactions with departmental officers COFR gathered the impression that in most departments there were excess staff. Although

not individually identified, such surplus employees can be taken out of the salary at any time without any detriment to Government of Assam's performance. To be precise, a one per cent downsizing of State's bureaucracy would on a rough estimate result in a saving of Rs 44.13 crore annually.[5]

The Assam Development Report of the Planning Commission (2002) made a very strong point that 'the bloated government has also led to a fiscal crisis. The government has a monthly overdraft of Rs 200 crores ... Downsizing government is a most pressing imperative if Assam is to develop faster'. Says economist Jayant Madhab Goswami: 'The story of Assam is not unique; in fact it is the same story all over the North East.'[6]

All the North Eastern states have failed to create the right kind of atmosphere to attract investment in the private sector. Most have announced 'new' industrial policies during the last few years but unsteady law and order, physical distances from markets and lack of infrastructure and better investment opportunities elsewhere in the country have failed to enthuse domestic or foreign investors. It has been left to the state governments to create employment. The number of government servants as a percentage of the state's population is much higher than the national average, which stands at one employee for every 113 inhabitants. The ratios in the North East are as follows: 1:17 in Nagaland, 1:20 in Mizoram, 1:29 in Tripura, 1:31 in Manipur, 1:37 in Arunachal Pradesh and 1:105 in Assam. As all the governments are overstaffed, their salary and pension budget keeps mounting. Some of the North Eastern states have now entered into MOU with the Union Finance Ministry for immediate help on fiscal reforms. Assam, Manipur and Nagaland have already entered into MOUs on medium-term fiscal reform; the other states may follow.

The North Eastern states must enforce immediate tax reform with selective enhancement of rates across the board, apply ruthless expenditure control, disinvest in loss-making public sector undertakings, radically improve governance and make it accountable. The rates of sales tax, land revenue, state excise, motor vehicles tax, passenger and goods tax, electricity duty and other utility charges must be enhanced across the region. The Sixth Schedule areas and the hill states do not impose income tax on people who belong to Scheduled Tribes. It is high time that taxation in this country is rationalized and everybody falling in the taxable brackets should be taxed. There is no reason why the rich and wealthy in the hill areas of the North East should not pay income tax. The rate of the profession tax should also be increased. A high-level commission made this recommendation:

> The performance of the North East states in mobilizing additional resources for development has been poor. Clearly for accelerated development of the region, it is imperative that the state governments in the region rein in non-plan expenditure and substantially step up additional resource mobilization ... All North Eastern states or those segments of tribal population hitherto exempt from income tax should voluntarily accept the principle of taxation in accordance with the ability to pay subject to the proviso that the net proceeds or additionality be credited to a special development fund for the concerned state/district council for a stipulated period say, 15 years. The rates of tax would be marginally lower than the all India rates in all the states for an initial period.[7]

Unless the non-plan expenditures of all the North Eastern states are heavily controlled and the wasteful ones curtailed, unless the size of state cabinets is kept at a minimum, the development process will continue to suffer. The huge fund transfers from Delhi will lead to little if no development. The expenditure on salaries, pensions and on-interest servicing will continue to eat up 85 to 90 per cent of ex-penditure, as is the case now. For all cash-strapped states, it is time to undertake some unpopular measures on the lines of the ones sug-gested by the COFR for the state of Assam, namely, '(a) curb on fresh employment and reduction of government employees at the rate of 2 per cent per year over the next five years; (b) freezing of dearness allowances and dearness relief for at least three years; (c) curb on travel and control of expenditure on vehicles; and (d) reduction on aid to autonomous bodies at the annual rate of 10 per cent during the next five years and thereafter stabilizing at 50 per cent of all current level and urging them to be self-reliant. All these can be reviewed after three years if the finances improve.'[8]

Throughout the North East, state governments are heavily burdened with loss-making public sector industries that are proving to be a drag on their budgets. In Assam alone, out of the 49 public sector undertakings (PSUs), 30 now have negative net worth.

Again, while the total capitalization in the 49 PSUs is about Rs 4,500 crore, their total accumulated loss is Rs 4,060 crore. Dues to financial institutions amount to Rs 1,500 crore. In one instance, the Assam government had to release Rs 104 crore in 2000–01 and Rs 64 crore in 2001–02 to enable the Assam State Electricity Board to clear its dues to North Eastern Electric Power Corporation (NEEPCO), otherwise electricity supply would have been stopped to the entire state. The majority of the 54,500 employees in these PSUs are idle. Many are not receiving their salaries for months or even years. The number of such PSUs in other states is much smaller because of the general lack of industrialization in those states but each has many useless, loss-making units like the Nagaland Paper Mill and the Tripura Jute Mill, which must either be sold off or liquidated to avoid the huge losses that have made them financially non-viable. The other option is to turn the relative better-off units into joint ventures by giving at least 51 per cent equity to the private sector. This will ensure that these industries are run by professional managers rather than useless politicians or bureaucrats who are not commercially oriented and look at these units as personal pastures for distributing favours or siphoning off funds for personal use.

For better governance, the North Eastern states must ensure devolution of powers at the panchayat or village council level, rationalize and reduce government departments and introduce e-governance to achieve higher productivity and transparency. The financial crisis calls for help from the central government in terms of additional devolution or ad hoc grants or a moratorium on servicing central loans. On the other hand, states and their citizenry have to bear the additional burden. The central government has to bear the burden of creating infrastructure while the states have to earmark a higher level of expenditure to achieve accelerated development. The current level of economic growth will not help solve the high unemployment problem faced by these states, nor bring them closer to the more advanced states of India.

On the contrary, the gap between the advanced states and the North Eastern states is likely to widen. Globalization and new economic policies (1991–92) have not helped them. The North Eastern states must realize that they must govern themselves better and make a success of their development projects rather than use them as milking cows; the central government also has to play a vital role in helping them achieve higher and equitable growth. To begin with, the credit–deposit ratio in the North East must improve, as the present levels are far from satisfactory (see Table 8.10). The state governments have to take some responsibility for the recoveries, otherwise banks, in a new competitive environment, will be reluctant to extend credit.

TABLE 8.10
Credit–Deposit Ratio in the North Eastern States, March 1999

State	Credit–deposit ratio (p.c.)
Arunachal Pradesh	19.25
Assam	32.61
Manipur	47.60
Meghalaya	19.11
Mizoram	23.40
Nagaland	21.25
Tripura	35.00

Source: NEC 2000.

The North Eastern states are now under heavy pressure to improve revenue collection during the 10th Plan. Table 8.11 shows that the targets are indeed stiff.

TABLE 8.11
Stipulated Percentage Rise in the North Eastern States' Own Tax Revenues

(%)

State	States' own tax revenue	Share in central tax revenue
Arunachal Pradesh	129.1	(–) 32.0
Assam	52.4	28.2
Manipur	86.5	(–) 13.5
Meghalaya	61.4	(–) 9.1
Mizoram	252.8	(–) 33.4
Nagaland	40.1	(–) 55.5
Tripura	30.5	(–) 18.0

Source: *The Statesman*, 5 August 2002.
Note: The rise is during the 10th Plan as against the 9th Plan.

This will not be an easy task, unless leakages in revenue collection and wasteful expenditure are curbed with a heavy hand and the region's endemic corruption is controlled firmly. Every state in the region has its own share of scams—in state lotteries, health and public works, irrigation, police, and almost in every government department—resulting in loss of thousands of crores to the state exchequer. One single swindle, related to the Nagaland state lottery and involving at least three ministers in successive governments, is said to have led to loss of more than Rs 5,000 crore to the state's exchequer. The Letter of Credit (LOC) system has also led to scams in many of the North Eastern states as development funds have been siphoned off through fraudulent LOCs against works that were never performed. Flood protection embankments that existed on paper were often not found on the ground. In recent months, the Indian government has alleged that a large percentage of the development funds pumped into the North East have regularly found their way to rebel coffers through a nexus involving local politicians, bureaucrats, contractors and insurgents.

The Rebel Economy

The Indian Home Ministry has drawn up a blacklist of more than 800 non-governmental organizations (NGOs) in the North East that are said to be receiving government funds to carry out development projects. 323 of these blacklisted NGOs are in Meghalaya alone. Of the Rs 5 billion in development funds that the state received in 2002–03, Rs 1.5 billion were routed through these NGOs. There are a total of 8,000 NGOs in Meghalaya, serving a small population of barely 2.5 million people. Many ministers and bureaucrats have set up NGOs in the name of their close relatives to siphon off vital development funds. An Indian minister in charge of the North Eastern states, C.P. Thakur, alleged that up to 20 per cent of the funds pumped into the region were reaching insurgents' coffers.[9]

Whereas state governments in the North East fail to raise enough tax, the separatist rebel groups are accused of 'taxing' the people far too much. Rebel groups have enforced their own 'Land Revenue and Trading Act', 'Household Tax' and at least 17 different kinds of taxes. The rebels tax those who deal in forest produce and bamboos, they tax shops and businesses, they impose taxes on houses, farms and transport plying through the highways. No economic activity in the North East escapes the 'taxation' net of the rebels. Generally, the rebel groups have adopted two techniques for fund-raising: (a) taxing households and families systematically on the basis of their incomes and endowments and (b) asking for huge one-time lump sum payments. Many rebel groups have started off by demanding huge lump-sum amounts running into millions of rupees from business houses and companies and then settled down to a pattern of regular monthly or annual pay-offs. Some rebel groups, like the ones in Tripura, have mostly negotiated ransoms after abductions, rather than to abduct someone for not paying up.

The tea industry throughout the North East has been the worst hit. As many as eight rebel groups have been raising huge amounts from the tea estates in Assam and Tripura. The tea estates in these states have been subjected to 'taxation' by rebels from neighbouring states like Nagaland. Once the government realized it was important to deny the rebel groups their main source of financing, the tea companies came under a scanner. Senior executives of Tata Tea were booked for providing funds to the ULFA. Some tea companies even indicated the payments made to the rebel groups in their annual balance sheets.

It is not only tea, however, that is 'taxed' by the rebels. All other industries and trades are subjected to 'taxes' by the rebel groups. The NSCN, though now committed to a ceasefire agreement with the Indian government, has used the last 12 years of peace to improve its 'tax collections' in Nagaland, Manipur, Arunachal Pradesh and Assam. On the national highway that connects Nagaland and Manipur to the rest of the country, the NSCN has set up road blocks that extort money from the trucks travelling into the two states. Since Manipur, with hardly any railways, is totally dependent on this highway for its survival, the NSCN and Naga organizations close to it have turned the screws on by resorting to blockades whenever they want to score a political point. This extortion on the highway has been ruthless and systematic. The NSCN leader Thuingaleng Muivah has justified this by saying that his group needs 'revenue to run our government'.

The ULFA, the NDFB, the NLFT, the ATTF and the MPLF have all intensified their tax-collection drives. During the 2002 Manipur elections, the Meitei rebel groups forced all candidates to pay lakhs of rupees to be able to contest the elections. The rebels, who have boycotted 'stage-managed Indian elections' in the past, did not call for a boycott—they 'taxed' the candidates. Nearly Rs 30 million was raised and much of it was spent on the Burmese military officials for securing the release of 192 guerrillas and leaders who had been arrested in Tamu in November 2001. By the end of March 2002, all the UNLF and the PLA leaders and guerrillas arrested in Burma had been released. In the rundown to that election, every political party, including the one that had originated from agitation against the Naga ceasefire, had to pay the UNLF and the PLA. Not a single politician who contested that election escaped extortion.

The NSCN, the ULFA, the NLFT and the ATTF have all secured funds from political parties for their backing during the elections. While these groups stick to their secessionist rhetoric, they do not flinch from opportunities for fund raising even if it means covert support for parties contesting Indian elections. Even smaller groups like the ANVC or the HNLC in Meghalaya have streamlined their fund collections. The ANVC taxes the border trade with Bangladesh, kidnapping coal traders and customs officials only to release them for ransom. One researcher has revealed how the ULFA raised funds by subverting the public distribution system in Assam.[10] The bulk of the essential commodities meant for the poorer sections of the population found their way to the black market through dealers who had close links with the ULFA, generating up to Rs 600 million a month, much of which found its way into the ULFA's coffers. Now the ULFA, from its bases in Bangladesh and Burma, is heavily into the illicit regional arms trade, buying cheap Chinese made weapons from front groups like the Was and then selling them at a premium to other North Eastern rebel groups, Maoists in India and Nepal (until the Nepal Maoists gave up their armed movement and entered electoral politics) and a wide array of Islamist groups in Bangladesh and India.

An intelligence assessment, believed to be a very conservative estimate by some, estimated that 14 rebel groups have raised Rs 750–800 crore since 1980, when the NSCN was formed.[11] The stronger groups, like the NSCN and the ULFA, have formal annual budgets. One of the recent ULFA annual budgets, reproduced in Table 8.12, gives an idea of how the rebel formations spend.

A close look at this budget indicates that the ULFA spends more on teeth than on tail. Much of the funds are spent on arms purchases,

TABLE 8.12
United Liberation Front of Assam (ULFA) Budget, 2001–2002

Sl No.	Expenditure	Amount (Rs)
1.	Expenditure in council HQs	2,35,25,000
2.	Expenditure in general HQs	1,00,90,000
3.	Expenditure in travel	1,90,00,000
4.	Expenditure in battalion HQs	1,00,28,000
5.	Expenditure on arms purchases	7,00,30,000
6.	Expenditure on foreign missions	2,50,04,000
7.	Expenditure on special operations	2,05,00,000
8.	Expenditure on rations items	4,11,00,000
9.	Expenditure on district committees	1,05,07,000
10.	Expenditure on *anchalik* units	15,75,000
11.	Expenditure on social welfare	1,08,07,000
12.	Expenditure on medical services	2,06,07,000
13.	Expenditure on dresses and uniforms	90,75,000
14.	Expenditure on publicity campaigns	2,25,20,000
15.	Expenditure on women's battalion	1,50,00,000
16.	Emergency expenditure	1,75,10,000
17.	Expenditure on Raising Day celebrations	15,00,000

Source: Jaideep Saikia, former security advisor, Government of Assam.
Note: Presented at the ULFA General HQs (Sukhni Basti, Bhutan) on 18 March 2001.

special operations and 'foreign missions'. While the weapons add to the group's firepower, the 'foreign missions' maintain crucial links to arms dealers and assets for propaganda and liaison with other rebel groups as well as foreign agencies supporting them. Other rebel groups also spend more on armaments and operations than on non-combat overheads. So, in some ways, the governments in the North East can learn a quick lesson from the way the rebels spend their money.

Some top rebel leaders have invested a lot of money elsewhere in the world in personal accounts, stocks and companies. A home ministry report on North East militants says that several militant leaders, including ULFA's commander-in-chief, Paresh Baruah, and the NSCN-IM's general secretary, Thuingaleng Muivah, have invested in stocks of multinational companies. The secret report, obtained by this correspondent, claims that Muivah bought 12,450 shares worth $1,25,000 (equivalent to Rs 70 lakhs) listed to an Irish multinational company, well known for the production of consumer goods. Interestingly, Muviah's name figures in the list of the company's board of directors. Dhaka-based Paresh Baruah is the head of a company called Karimuddin Export Pvt Ltd, which has 325 employees. In Bangkok, Muivah's nephew Paul and his Thai wife, Walaila K. Luengdong, own a toy manufacturing company. The Manipur UNLF chief, R.K. Meghen, also has huge investments in blue chip companies in Thailand, Hong Kong and Singapore.

Indian intelligence is said to have unearthed this 'corporate face' of rebel operations when it tried to track down Isaac Swu in Ireland. Isaac is said to have flown from Amsterdam to Dublin to attend a board meeting of the Irish multinational. Muivah at that time was in a Bangkok jail, and hence he is believed to have sent Swu as his nominee to the board meeting. The report says that the NSCN-IM prepared a 'balance sheet' showing an expenditure of Rs 20 crore, but it is actually worth $50 million as its chief has invested in real estate, shares, hotels and proprietorship of several companies. The NSCN-IM is said to make over Rs 150 crore per annum through extortion and other means, while the main source of money is from taxation of truck drivers: each truck passing through Kohima has to pay Rs 500 as protection money to the NSCN-IM. Extortion money from Assam is being pumped into export and other trading businesses via Dhaka, where Baruah has several permanent safe houses. The ULFA is said to have even invested in Bangladesh's Transcom company that publishes the top English and Bengali dailies of Dhaka, *Daily Star* and *Prothom Alo*.[12]

Recently, there was a spate of reports in the Indian media about Paresh Barua trying to relocate a lot of his assets to South Africa and Portugal. Barua does not deny handling 'a lot of money' but his personal lifestyle is surely not corporate. Muivah and Issac also lead austere lifestyles. Much of the funds raised are spent on routine expenses such as cadre salaries, arms purchases and operational expenses, but huge funds are also invested in companies and stocks so that the rebel groups do not have to worry about funds in future to keep the organization going. On the other hand, some rebel leaders, like the NLFT top brass, lead a profligate life, replete with wine and women. Leaders of the NLFT and the ATTF have set up transport companies in Bangladesh and run regular luxury bus services in Chittagong and the hill tracts. Many rebel leaders, according to the Home Ministry report, have huge investments in shipping companies in Bangladesh. The companies make profits and ship weapons for the rebels. The deposits at one account in a foreign bank travel from account to account through teller arrangements and other modern e-commerce devices. Once money reaches a foreign account through the hawala channels, it is transferred to several accounts through e-commerce channels.[13]

Herein lies the misfortune of the North East. Corrupt politicians siphon funds and buy property elsewhere in India and abroad to conceal their ill-gotten wealth; even rebel leaders invest elsewhere in the world. If the region's corrupt political leaders, bureaucrats and rebel leaders invested their money in profit-making ventures in the North East, they would have done some service to the region, whose sentiments they exploit for achieving political objectives and personal opulence. It is time for the leaders of the region to realize that their states will no longer receive the kind of federal largesse they have been used to, not least because they have failed to utilize the entire quantum of federal development funds that have come their way. Since it is now mandatory for all union ministries to set aside 10 per cent of their budget for the North Eastern states, the region has benefited from a higher fund flow in recent years. Due to poor infrastructure, lack of innovative schemes and inefficient governance, the state governments could not utilize all the funds they received.

Not so long ago, Indian rural development minister M. Venkaiah Naidu disclosed that the North Eastern states failed to utilize Rs 324 crore out of the Rs 976 crore provided to them in the 2000–01 fiscal year. This was partly due to the lack of viable development schemes but mainly because the states could not meet their share of the contribution. The states have to provide 25 per cent for centrally funded projects while Delhi meets the remaining 75 per cent of the expenditure. Mr Naidu said that Assam alone lost Rs 600 crore of central funds for rural development between 1996 and 2000 because it failed to provide its share of contributions.[14] The North Eastern states are now demanding that they be asked to provide only 10 per cent matching contribution.

In India's emerging free-market economy, however, such preferential treatment may not continue for long. Loss-making ventures and unproductive workforce are both on their way out. No state will be able to afford them because the federal government will not be in a position to fund them. It is time to tighten belts and work out projects that will make profits and employ efficient people. Across the borders lie opportunities that the North Eastern states must learn to exploit. Business opportunities in Bangladesh or Burma must be grabbed by the North Eastern states without waste of time. Economic linkages with distant Delhi, based on one-way dependence, will not help anymore. Business linkages, based on mutual profit, with neighbouring countries will benefit the states of northeast India. The mindset in the region—Delhi will fund us because it has an interest to keep us in the Union—will have to change.

NOTES

1. Northeast Vision 2020 document, finalized by the DONER and the Northeast Council at its Agartala meeting on 12–13 May 2008.
2. B.G. Verghese, 1996.
3. Atul Sharma, 2002.
4. Jayant Madhab Goswami, 2002.
5. Report of the COFR appointed by the Assam Government, 2001. The state government is yet to act on the recommendations.
6. Goswami, *op.cit.*
7. Shukla Commission Report (Transforming the North East), 1997.
8. COFR report.
9. Subir Bhaumik's report titled 'India Blacklists 800 NGOs' published in *BBC Online*, 18 June 2003.
10. Ajai Sahni, 2001.
11. Directorate of Military Intelligence's special note on 'Financial Status of Insurgent Groups in Northeast India', June 2002.
12. Sunita Paul, 2008.
13. Ministry of Home Affairs, special report on 'Investments in Foreign Countries by Militant leaders from Northeast India', April 2001. Some details of the ULFA's investments in Bangladesh are also available in the Home Ministry document 'Bleeding Assam'. Sources in the ministry say these details were secured from Bangladesh intelligence, who obtained details about the ULFA's investments from arrested General Secretary Anup Chetia.
14. Venkaiah Naidu, in an interview to NDTV, 3 August 2008.

9   The Road Ahead

What explains the crisis in India's North East? Why and how has India's nation-building project gone wrong in the far frontier region? Sixty years into its post-colonial journey, India needs to figure out why the North East has remained a troubled periphery and whether it is possible to change it into a vital bridgehead with South East Asia and southwestern China, so that both the region and the nation gain meaningfully. The geographical distance from the mainland has translated into a psychological distance that can both be bridged now. The physical distance can be reduced by development of transport infrastructure and modern technology, the psychological distance can be bridged by changes in attitudes, policies and a vision of a shared and prosperous future. While Delhi's policy on the North East is undergoing some change, much more remains to be done.

A vision document that projects the North East as the 'arrowhead' of the country's 'Look East' policy, as part of a shared transnational economic space with South East Asia and southwest China is a perfect, though delayed, acknowledgement of the reality that the North East is where India looks less and less India and more and more like the highlands of South East Asia. But a statement of vision is only the beginning of a new policy. To make that vision translate into reality, a huge change is needed in the way the national and regional bureaucracy and the political parties function. India has to resolve the festering ethnic conflicts and the separatist movements not by use of force or Kautilyan techniques but by key structural changes in its polity that would accommodate these battling ethnicities in a future India that's truly federal.

The 'special federal relationship' that the National Socialist Council of Nagaland (NSCN) and the Indian government has worked out—but that has been kept such a closely guarded secret—could well provide the kick-start of the structural change of Indian polity. Though surrounded by states that looks headed for failure—especially Pakistan—India can look back at its six decade of post-colonial journey with some confidence. It does not need a mighty Centre anymore, in spite of the challenges posed by trans-regional terror. It does not need to turn India into a security state. It may still be not feasible to expect India evolving into Sarat Bose's ultimate vision of a 'collection of republics' but India cannot be a powerful body with just a strong head and chest—it needs strong limbs, which is why it needs strong states. India should emulate the European Union and grow into a strong and vibrant federation by consensus us. It can well avoid the mainstreaming, assimilationist usges of a Chinese Middle Kingdom or go for the leveler effect of an American 'melting pot'. Because the European model of shared civilization base is the closest to the Indian reality. That will help India resolve its festering separatist conflicts in the North East and elsewhere and help it evolve into a major power.

But these conflicts cannot be merely resolved through piecemeal deals that will create homelands that are largely illusory, especially if the North East has to be turned into a political space that supports the vision of a trans-national economic space the Vision 2020 documents is talking about.

Sanjib Baruah aptly summed up the problem of the region:

A large number of 'tribal' people entitled to protective discrimination under the Indian Constitution live in those (North Eastern) states. The rights of 'non-tribals' to land ownership and exchange, business and trade licenses and access to elected office are restricted. A number of these tribal enclaves now are full-fledged states. One of the unintended effects of this regime of protective discrimination is that the notion of exclusive homelands for ethnically defined groups has become normalized in the region. In a context of massive social transformation that attracts significant numbers of people to the region, this has generated an extremely divisive politics of insiders and outsiders.[1]

Identity, Governance, Development

The crisis of India's North East has largely centred round the questions of identity, governance and development. The *crisis of identity* has been evident at *four* levels: (a) tribes have so far failed to evolve as nationalities either by themselves or as part of a larger generic identity so even when a 'Naga' or a 'Mizo' organization fights for a homeland, tribes and clans seek to assert their identity within the movement and weaken the generic identities; (b) the larger generic identities like the Nagas and the Mizos or even a larger nationality like the Assamese have failed to rise beyond its primordial boundaries and envisage a polyethnic regional identity for the North East; (c) the ethnic groups in the North East continue to be confused about their identity in India—some realize secession is not a viable option, much as cultural assimilation with the dominant pattern of the mainland is not possible or desirable, but there is a clear lack of consensus on how to institutionalize the relationship between the locality, province and the nation in the North East and (d) the ethnic groups are very hostile to settlers from outside the region or the immediate neighbourhood, even those who settled or were settled in the area more than a 100 years ago.

The attitude of the power-holders in Delhi does not make the problem any easier. Nation-states evolve, they cannot be built or constructed, like high-rise buildings. The federal centre of the nation-state can play the facilitator and the developer, even a bit of a shepherd, but it can play the builder at its own peril. The self-proclaimed patriot in saffron or khadi in Delhi, however, fails to realize that the multiplicity of identity is a fact of life in post-colonial India, as it was throughout India's long history. The history of trans-regional empires in India—Hindu, Muslim and British—does not add up to more than eight to 900 years. The rest of India's long history of a few 1000 years is the history of independent provinces—from the *Solasamahajanapad* (16 great provinces) before the rise of the Magadhan empire to the scores of kingdoms that were subjugated by the British, much of India's history has centred round the provinces. It changed after the British but the viceroys of London allowed many powerful kingdoms (called Native States) to survive and rule their subjects. So the tunnel vision of the 'Hindu, Hindi, Hindustan' can only unsettle what has so far been a far-from-happy federation.

An Assamese or a Khasi, a Naga or a Mizo—or for that matter, a Bengali or Punjabi or a Tamil—can *also* be an Indian without any apparent contradiction. An ethnic identity can easily survive under the over-arching Indian civilizational identity. A J.M. Lyngdoh or a Bhupen Hazarika, a Sachin Devvarman or a Somdev Devvarman may be the pride of his community, the crowning jewel of his tribe, but he can be as much of a role model for the rest of the country as anyone else. Identities as constructs operate in multiple layers in a vast subcontinental country like India—and they can easily co-exist if tolerance of diversity is institutionalized in the political and administrative culture of the nation-state.

A recent debate on the pages of the Calcutta *Statesman* resurrected the question of whether there could be a 'North Eastern identity'. Assamese film-maker Bhabendra Nath Saikia was upset when all film-makers from the region were grouped under the 'North East' category while others were categorized according to the languages in which the films were made. 'We often use the term South India but does it mean that we club together Kerala and Tamil Nadu or Adoor Gopalakrishnan and Mani Ratnam?' asked Bhabendra Nath Saikia. Here's a strong cultural counter-point to Rangan Dutta's desire to see a North Eastern identity emerge loud and clear. Some give the 'North East' identity a chance but many, like Sanjib Barua, believe the 'North Eastern' identity has not worked. Joining the debate on the North Eastern identity, he said in a recent *Statesman* article:

> The use of the term northeast India goes back to the radical redrawing of the region's map and the creation of the North East Council. In retrospect, these were little more than a hurried and short-sighted exercise in political engineering ... the mistrust of democracy on the part of the new dispensation was evident right from the beginning. Initially, the NEC did not even include the elected chief ministers of the states. It was made up of Governors... from today's vantage point, the project of political engineering that produced the category northeast India must be pronounced a failure. The cosmopolitan Indian's blind faith in the magic of economic development will not produce new identities in the region.[2]

The North East can actually do without a flurry of new identities. Identities can never emerge as watertight compartments in the North East. The over-arching presence of a Naga National Council (NNC) or an NSCN has not meant an end to student unions and churches based on separate tribes in Nagaland. A Meitei in Manipur is happy with his proud racial identity, but in Tripura he wants to be recognized as a Scheduled Tribe in order to secure better access to opportunities. It is true that the 'North Eastern' identity is a top-down flow from the country's power centre—this is how Delhi wants to make sense of the region as a directional category. It is true that governments cannot dictate the formation of identities, but it is also true that evolving identities are not absolutes and can change with circumstances. The nation-state and a distinct geo-political region like the North East impose fresh challenges for identity management for people who are still wedded to the distinct boundary of the tribe and the clan. But if people from different tribes speak English or Hindi with an Assamese fellow-traveller up to Bongaigaon and then start speaking in Assamese as the train enters West Bengal and Bihar to emphasize a commonality that is not reinforced by ethnicity, language or religion, can we write off a case for a 'North Eastern' identity, at least in reaction to other parts of heartland India? No easy answers, but much to ponder about.

The *crisis of governance* has manifested itself on *four* levels: (a) lack of ethnic tolerance and the failure to manage plurality that led to the break-up of bigger states like Assam; (b) lack of ideological moorings, administrative competence and political loyalties that has led to inefficiency and instability in the regional political system and translated into a lack of capacity for handling core governance issues effectively; (c) the emergence of an unholy nexus between the politician, the insurgent and the contractor-businessman that has subverted the vitality of the region's politics and its economy and (d) lack of a regional vision and failure to take advantage of opportunities in countries across the borders.

The *crisis of development* has happened due for *four* reasons: (a) a near-total dependence on the Centre for funds and even for ideas on programmes for development; (b) unacceptable levels of spending on non-productive government employment and lack of invest-ment in development of infrastructure that can sustain growth and generate higher volumes of employment in the long run; (c) siphoning off of funds through corruption and mismanagement, causing huge 'leakages' and (d) failure to develop trade and business links within the region and with neighbouring countries.

Economy and Governance rather than ethnicity should be the basis for future policy in the North East. Trade routes, access to ports in Bangladesh and Burma, the alignment of the proposed Trans-Asian highway—considerations such as these should dictate the agenda for policy. Any proposed territorial reorganization should be put on hold because creation of more non-viable states or redrawing the boundaries of the existing ones will create more problems than it will solve.

The burden of ethnicity is a legacy that the North East will have to live with. The fluid process of nationality formation in the region is further complicated by federal policies that accepted ethnicity as the basis for creating new states. It is time to examine seriously whether ethnicity should continue to be the basis for political and territorial reorganization in the region. Perhaps states created merely on the basis of ethnicity now need a higher degree of administrative and economic integration around a regional body like the North East Council to create a 'grow-together' environment crucial for the region's future prosperity and development. The 'magic of economic development' should not be seen as a solution to all the problems of the region, but since the conflict of battling ethnicities has much to do with control over scarce resources or lucrative resources (for example, the Naga–Kuki feud to control the drug contraband route out of Moreh), the need for economic development and for the emergence of a consensus on key resource-sharing issues cannot be wished away.

Crucial to the region's future is Assam, once the region's largest and still its most populous and most ethnically diverse state. More and more ethnic groups want to break away from Assam, even as the religious schism in the state's two valleys, Barak and Brahmaputra, begins to widen. If Assam is balkanized by further splits, the North East will be left without its strongest pivot for economic growth and political stability. Two alternative scenarios can unfold in the North East if the movements for separate homelands gain momentum in Assam in the backdrop of an attempt to create a 'Greater Naga' state by integrating the Naga-inhabited territories of Manipur, Assam and Arunachal Pradesh with the present state of Nagaland:

Scenario One

Assam breaks up further, two new tribal states are carved out of it, one for the Bodos and one for the Karbis and Dimasas, and a patch in western Assam inhabited by the Koch-Rajbongshi tribals is handed over to a new Kamtapur state largely carved out of West Bengal. And if a 'Greater Nagaland' is created, Assam and Manipur are badly truncated. If this happens, Nagaland may emerge as the new political powerhouse in the region. But greater competition amongst Naga tribes for power and resources within a Greater Naga state may undermine its emerging clout. As Assam becomes smaller through fragmentation, political and economic competition may exacerbate the religious divide in both the Brahmaputra and the Barak valleys, obscuring ethnic and linguistic divisions, but setting the stage for a much more dangerous form of conflict in the backdrop of growing Islamic radicalism in neighbouring Bangladesh.

If this happens, the tribals in Tripura may take advanatage of a Bengali Hindu–Muslim divide in Tripura and push for a separate state carved out of the present autonomous district council area. In that case, the present state of Tripura will survive as a small elong-ated north–south stretch of plains hugging the eastern borders of Bangladesh and barely connected to the rest of India through Assam. A partition will compel the Bengali-dominated western plains of Tripura to join the Barak Valley either in a truncated Assam or as part of a separate Bengali state in the Barak Valley. Meghalaya may not escape the split-up wave and the Garos may end up getting a separate state. The Bharatiya Janata Party (BJP), which has a limited presence in the region, may seek to augment its influence and political clout by unexpected alliances that marginalize the Congress-ruled states of Assam and Manipur and the Left-ruled state of Tripura. The BJP has created new states elsewhere in India—they can upset the *status quo* in the North East to gain allies and influence in the region if they come back to power in Delhi.

Scenario Two

A more of a *status quo*, in which Delhi refuses to go ahead with any further territorial reorganization in the North East. More autonomous councils may be created in Assam to pacify the tribals while a religious divide across the two valleys may intensify and benefit the BJP. If the BJP senses it can achieve power in Assam by using the growing religiosity of politics in the Brahmaputra and Barak valleys, it may stay away from breaking up Assam any further. In that case, it may also desist from creating a 'Greater Nagaland'. This will exacerbate the NSCN's dwindling credibility and weaken it in Nagaland. At the same time, a tenuous peace will hold in Manipur. The *status quo* will also hold in Tripura and Meghalaya, but Mizoram may have to create more autonomous structures to pacify smaller tribes like the Brus.

If Assam breaks up and the NSCN manages to secure a 'Greater Nagaland' by aggressive negotiations with Delhi, the fulcrum of power in the region will shift further east and the stage will be set for more unrest within the region. If the Naga 'national worker' replaces the *Asomiya Dangoriya* (gentry) as Delhi's next political sub-contractor in the region, the transition to a new power balance may not be an easy one. Assam has endured diversity in its politics and society since before British rule. Its political and social leadership emerged from the Ahom empire, which governed the largest area in the east of the subcontinent prior to British rule. Though Assam's post-colonial leadership failed to manage plurality and transition effectively, the new generation of its leaders are beginning to learn from the humbling experience of the great break-up of 1972.

This holds true with both its overground and underground leaders. A young Assam minister, Pradyut Bordoloi, told a recent seminar in unambiguous language: 'Assam is a plural state and those in government here have to address themselves to the concerns of all communities.'[3] One can discern that India's obsession with creating a monolingual state like West Bengal is finally over, not the least because even a much more homogenous state like West Bengal is beginning to experience divisive forces on its fringes, like in Darjeeling. And though the ULFA's stated objective of 'an independent and a federal Assam' may never be achieved, it reveals a vision that has transcended the limiting boundary of ethnicity, language and religion and sets a political model for the very plural region.

By contrast, the Naga leadership is still fractious and unable to get over the pull of the tribe and the clan, much as the leadership in Bihar or Uttar Pradesh cannot get over the caste identity. Smaller separatist groups in the North East had followed the NSCN as a role model for decades in their fight against India, but Muivah's world of enemies and friends, of 'reactionary traitors' and 'revolutionary patriots', is a set-top box that defies flexible and pragmatic political programming. Bravery and dynamism, capacity to survive and fearlessness in combat are the Naga's forte, tolerance of dissent and management of diversity is not. The NSCN sees itself as a sun in a sky with no place for anybody else. Even a reconciliation commission consisting of some of Nagaland's respected civil society leaders is dismissed as undesirable by the NSCN because it cannot accept the emergence of any other credible platform in Naga society. Its former comrades in the region's underground no longer trust the NSCN—it is seen as the odd one that 'broke the pack to jump on to India's bandwagon when there was no need for such a move'.[4]

NEW STATES OR *STATUS QUO*

The territorial integrity of Assam, Manipur and Tripura is crucial to the future stability of the North East. These are, and have been, multi-racial, multi-lingual and multi-religious states and if the region has to make a beginning in effective management of plurality and change, these three states have to stay the way they are. Pacifying the aspirations of the Nagas or other tribes cannot be done at the cost of breaking up any of these three states. If such a break-up does happen, it is the end of the road for plural societies in the North East. The Nagas must be offered a just political deal that allows their kinsmen in Ukhrul and Senapati, Tamenlong and Chandel, Tirap and Changlang to maintain close development and cultural links with Nagaland within an inter-state Naga council operating dir-ectly under the North East Council, through which special develop-ment funds can be channelled into these hitherto neglected districts.

Instead of district councils, the Naga areas of Manipur and Arunachal Pradesh can be reconstituted into two territorial councils as part of the inter-state Naga Council and a special development budget can come to them from the Centre. Nevertheless, these areas should remain in Manipur and Arunachal Pradesh. A compact Naga vote in Manipur can translate into a sizeable Naga legislative presence in the Manipur assembly that can give Manipur a Naga chief minister again, like Rishang Keishing in the past. The Tirap–Changlang lobby has decisively emerged as the king-maker in Arunachal Pradesh.

Any attempt to parcel off these Naga areas to Nagaland will reduce Manipur to less than half its present size and have disastrous consequences for the state and the region. To settle the Naga insurgency, Delhi will have to bargain for a bloody urban insurgency that can spread well beyond the Imphal Valley. The Nagas are capable of dominating the politics of two states besides Nagaland in a decisive way if they maintain the *status quo* and play their cards well. Manipulations for a 'Greater Nagaland', however, will only isolate the Nagas in the North East. From a role model of consistency in struggle and sacrifice, the NSCN will be reduced to an eyesore, a predator eyeing everyone else's territory. And the Nagas of Ukhrul, Senapati, Tirap and Changlang have much more to gain in power-political equations if they stay with Manipur and Arunachal. In a 'Greater Nagaland', they will only make up the fringes.

'Greater Nagaland' raises questions similar to those raised by 'Greater Bengal'. For the sake of hypothesis, how much say will a Bengali from Tripura have in a 'Greater Bengal' that may consist of 140 parliament members, 70 per cent from present Bangladesh and perhaps 25 per cent from West Bengal? Will he prefer to forego political and economic control of a state just to be able to live in a political unit that is woven round his ethnic and linguistic identity? At the peak of his clout, former Union Minister Santosh Mohan Dev was referred to as 'a Sylheti cat amongst Bengali pigeons' in the headline of a front page report in the *Statesman*. Emotionally, a Bengali is likely to be swayed by the idyllic appeal of a 'united Bengal' as much as a Naga is by the concept of a 'Greater Nagaland'. But as prudence gets the better of emotions, a Naga in Manipur or Arunachal Pradesh may realize he is better off with autonomy in Manipur or Arunachal Pradesh, much as a Bengali from Tripura and Assam has very little to gain from a 'Greater Bengal'.

Furthermore, how is it that 'Eastern Nagaland' suddenly dropped out of the NSCN agenda and became 'Burma's Naga areas'? Why must Nagaland be treated as incomplete without the Nagas of Manipur or Arunachal Pradesh if the Hemi and the Khieumengan can be left behind to languish in Burma? Is it because the trans-border base area in Burma is no longer needed now that the NSCN is in a peace-making mood? The Burmese Nagas have had the worst of both worlds so far—they missed out on any development whatsoever in Burma and they faced military offensives for harbouring the NSCN. Do they deserve nothing for their sacrifices? The Nagas deserve the 'special federal relationship with India' but such an arrangement should not be limited to them. If it works for the Nagas, all other ethnicities and nationalities in North East should be allowed to enjoy it. Other separatist groups in the region, still fighting the Indian state, should walk out of the jungles and consider dropping their sovereignty agendas and join the negotiations, alongside the NSCN if not with it, and all of them should work together to give the whole of North East a 'special federal relationship' that may tackle its crisis of identity within India. If the Nagas are dropping their sovereignty agenda after 50 years of fighting, the rest of North East's battling ethnicities should learn from the Naga experience rather than go through the whole of it themselves.

And though Muivah, a veteran of the long marches to China, has good reason to push his people in Manipur to join Nagaland, former Chief Minister S.C. Jamir has a point when he claims that 'Greater Nagaland' should be taken up on the agenda only if it is conclusively established that all Nagas living in other states indeed wish to join Nagaland. According to Jamir, that urge has not been in evidence in spite of an option given to the Nagas outside Nagaland under provisions of the 1960 agreement.[5] It is again a situation in which a Santosh Mohan Dev or a Manik Sarkar, when pitted against a Pranab Mukherjee or a Priya Ranjan Das Munshi, or against a Biman Bose or a Buddhadev Bhattacharya, begins to realize his political future lies in his own land and he can count more on an Assamese or a Tripuri tribal politician than his co-linguists in the same party.

In Assam, smaller tribes and nationalities will demand autonomy and powers for local self-government. The Assamese will do well to concede them, but no further break-up of Assam is either acceptable or desirable. No further change in Assam's demography and no more illegal migration into Assam are desirable either. If the state disintegrates further, the case for a multi-racial, multi-lingual political entity in the North East will be lost forever. Assamese separatism, manifest in the ULFA, is weakening because the Assamese power-holder group continues to have a strong stake in a united India. It resents the potential break-up of Assam and the marginalization of the once-huge province but it needs India to protect its valleys from large-scale illegal migration from neighbouring Bangladesh. To avoid any further break-up of Assam, the Assamese leadership will have to work on a comprehensive structure of autonomy for the tribespeople to satisfy their homeland demands. One of the important processes of the Assamese nationality formation was the slow but steady assimilation of the smaller tribes and nationalities—a process that was ruptured by the excesses of the Assam agitation and the ethnic nature of Assam's politics thereafter. That process can be restored only if the smaller tribes and nationalities are led to believe that they have a stake in Assam. From the Assamese—and the North East perspective—it is crucial to restore the *Asomiya* nationality formation process. One can only accept the withering away of the region's pivot nationality at its own peril.

CONFLICT RESOLUTION AND ETHNIC RECONCILIATION

Any process of conflict resolution in Assam cannot focus, as is so often done by political and administrative decision-makers, only on opening a dialogue with a particular insurgent group like the ULFA. Any strategy for conflict resolution in Assam would have to focus on: (a) the aspirations of the smaller nationalities and tribes who have stopped identifying themselves with the *Asomiya* 'mainstream'; (b) the aspirations and security concerns of the minorities and (c) the aspirations of the *Asomiya* power-holder groups.

It will not be easy to harmonize these aspirations, but an attempt will have to be made on the basis of give-and-take so that the framework for an overall solution can be worked out. Some measures are inescapable if Assam has to chart out an effective roadmap for conflict resolution:

1. Work out a constitutionally and politically viable structure of extensive autonomy that will decentralize governance, provide the smaller tribes and nationalities local self-rule and resources to sustain it, and create for them a strong stake in the present state of Assam. One needs the political will to implement such a structure of autonomy to avoid future homeland demands that can rip apart the state.

2. Try to revive civil society in conflict zones, revive the traditional leadership and strengthen its position by making concessions to them. Isolation is what rebel groups are always apprehensive about and one good way to create among them an urge to give up armed struggle is to leave them with no choice outside established civil society. Security operations are essential to contain insurgencies but they should not undermine civil society structures because when that happens, the rebels create alternative social platforms that undermine the state.

3. Propose negotiations with rebel groups not for the sake of it. Negotiations should be started only when the government is clear about the bottom line and the kind of concessions it can make. The process of negotiation must be transparent; otherwise violent situations are likely to recur, as happened after the extension of the Naga ceasefire to Manipur.

4. The process of negotiation should be handled by a liaison committee headed by a senior politician and assisted by representatives from the Home Ministry, Law Ministry, IB and R&AW, the state governments concerned and civil society leaders in the region. Great care should be taken to finalize the composition of the liaison committee and negotiations should not be unduly drawn out. Wearing down and splitting a rebel group makes tactical sense, but is a poor long-term strategy of conflict resolution. A detailed exercise about possible constitutional amendments should be initiated by the Centre, with close support from the state government and the Law Ministry, to pave the way for meaningful autonomy in the region. The political will to create a multi-ethnic ethos of power sharing and governance should be amply demonstrated.

Tripura can take the lead in charting out a unique strategy of ethnic reconciliation by decommissioning the Dumbur hydroelectric project that ousted thousands of indigenous tribesmen from their ancestral lands. The heartburn over steady land loss among Tripura's indigenous tribal population was exacerbated by the submergence of a huge swathe of arable lands in the Raima-Sarma Valley as a result of the Gumti hydroelectric project in south Tripura. This project not only disturbed the fragile ecology of the area, but also left a permanent sense of loss in the tribal psyche. A 30-metre-high gravity dam was constructed across the river Gumti about 3.5 km upstream of Tirthamukh in south Tripura district with an installed capacity of 10 MW. The dam submerged a valley area of 46.34 sq. km once it was commissioned in 1976. This was one of the most fertile valleys in an otherwise hilly state, where arable flatlands suitable for wet rice agriculture amount to a mere 28 per cent of the total land area.[6] Official records suggest that 2,558 tribal families were ousted from the Gumti project area but this number includes only those families who could produce land deeds and were officially owners of the land they occupied. Unofficial estimates varied between 8,000 and 10,000 families, or about 50,000–60,000 tribespeople were displaced by the project.

In the tribal societies of the North East, ownership of land is rarely personal and the system of recording land deeds against individual names is a recent phenomenon. Before the dam, the hills around the present project area were sparsely populated and the area was almost wholly under dense forest cover. After the hydroelectric project was commissioned, almost half of the tribal families displaced by the dam moved into the hills in the river's upper catchment area. The roads built to move construction material opened up the rich forests of the area to illegal loggers. The surplus-producing tribal peasantry lost their rich flatlands and were forced to revert back to slash-and-burn *jhum* cultivation that caused irreparable damage to the ecology of the upper catchment of the Gumti. The Gumti hydroelectric project must be decommissioned for four reasons:

1. It is now producing only 7 MW of electricity even in the peak monsoon season when the reservoir is full. The state government says it has been able to restore the project's output to the original installed capacity of 10 MW. It also says that while the running cost of the project is around Rs 3 crore per annum, it supplies nearly Rs 21 crore per year through the sale of electricity. Officials in the Tripura power department describe the project as 'very profitable'. Experts, however, claim that siltation levels will continue to increase and unless the reservoir can be dredged, there will be no rise in output. The power output from this project will progressively diminish, making it a white elephant.

2. With its rich natural gas reserves and major gas thermal power projects in the pipeline (including one with the capacity to generate 500 MW against the state's current peak demand of 125 MW), it is a waste of funds for Tripura to invest in the Gumti hydroelectric project. An ideal power strategy for Tripura would be to produce around 500–600 MW of electricity, feed half of that into the North Eastern grid, use 150–200 MW within the state keeping in mind the rising demand, and sell the balance of 100 MW to Bangladesh for a short duration until Bangladesh is able to meet its own demand. India has promised, in a September 2009 agreement with Bangladesh, to supply 100Mw of electricity to the power-starved country and Tripura, because of its proximity to Dhaka, Sylhet, Chittagong and Comilla, is the best place to do this from.

3. Since more than 45 sq. km can be reclaimed from under water if the Gumti hydroelectric project is decommissioned, a huge fertile tract of flatland would be opened up for farming and resettlement of the landless tribal peasantry of the state. Approximately 30,000 tribal families, perhaps the whole of the state's landless tribal population, can be gainfully resettled in this fertile tract. Before the dam, the fertility of the Raima-Sarma valley was a talking point in the state. After so many years under water, this tract is likely to be very fertile. Tripura is a food deficit state and turning this area into a modern agrarian zone will solve the state's food problem. The problem of tribal land alienation, believed to be the root cause of tribal insurrections in the state, can thus be addressed at the same time. Conflict resolution requires symbolic gestures as well as substance and decommissioning the dam could provide both. Indeed, never before has a large development project been dismantled to preserve the interests of an indigenous people.

4. If almost the entire tribal landless population of the state can be gainfully resettled in the Gumti project area, it will free the hilly forest regions from human pressure. Since most of these landless tribals practise *jhum* or slash-and-burn agriculture, which is dangerous for the ecology of the hills and the forests, it is essential to resettle this entire population. Unlike the plains, the hills cannot take the high pressure of human settlement. From an ecological viewpoint, therefore,

the resettlement of the landless tribals of Tripura in the re-claimed Gumti project area will be welcome. The state's forest cover, now receding, will improve; degraded forests may be turned into gainful plantations through large-scale private investments.

This decommissioning proposal should be implemented before ethnic polarization between Bengali settlers and indigenous tribes-people reaches unmanageable proportions. The state is still ruled by the Left Front, a left-of-centre coalition that enjoys support among both Bengalis and tribespeople. Tribal parties and militant groups will support the dam's decommissioning while Bengali extremist groups are not yet powerful enough to resist it. A political dialogue can be initiated to create the proper climate for decommissioning and the creation of an alternative economy. Even the security agencies may benefit from this settlement—a happily settled tribal popula-tion, easily monitored, is less troublesome than if it is spread out over a vast hill region with a poor economy that creates empty stom-achs and angry minds.

Arunachal Pradesh should be developed as the powerhouse of the region. With several power projects on the anvil, this sparsely popu-lated state is well on its way to becoming one of the nation's major sources of hydroelectric power. India needs energy desperately to plug its widening power gap but it will have to implement these huge hydel power projects only after appropriate environmental audit. It is true far less people will be displaced by these projects in sparsely populated Arunachal Pradesh than anywhere else in this crowded country, but the state has several major bio-diversity hotspots and game sanctuaries that cannot be sacrificed for power alone. India will also have to modernize its hydel power management so that lower riparian communities in Assam are not subjected to 'created floods' caused by sudden release of monsoon-time surplus water to save the dams from structural pressure. And Indian engineering has to ensure that the huge dams in Subansiri and elsewhere in Arunachal Pradesh can withstand a 1950 Assam earthquake and not collapse to start a deluge in the lower riparian region. The North East is a seismic hotspot, the faults in the Assam–Arakan geosyncline experience up to 200 micro tremors each year. Many geo-scientists like Assamese seismologist M.M. Saikia feel another big earthquake is due anytime now in the North East. So, Delhi's plans to turn Arunachal Pradesh into a power-house (to meet the country's huge power needs as it grows into a tiger economy competing with China) must be carefully implemented after accommodating the region's environmental and displacement concerns, so that the interests of the locality, province and the nation are all in a win-win order. That's easier said than done but there cannot be any short-cut on this.

The state government of Arunachal Pradesh also needs to open up a few select plains districts of the state bordering Assam to food-processing companies so that they can accommodate integrated captive farms and factories producing niche products. The tribes in the uplands should be encouraged and trained to cultivate medicinal plants and select crops that provide substantial cash returns (for example, asparagus).

A comprehensive land use policy should be formulated and implemented for the entire region. If tribal farmers do not graduate beyond subsistence farming and are forced to live from hand to mouth, they will turn to poppy cultivation. Cultivation of rice and major cereals should be left to the plains of Assam, Tripura and Manipur. The hills should be planted with highly paying niche vegetables, medicinal plants and fruits. Top companies producing herbal medicines should be encouraged to sign deals with autonomous councils who should take it on themselves on how to get the tribals into high-return farming. The councils should also develop marketing divisions to tap high-volume customers or for doing value-added marketing. If the autonomous councils fail to work out area-specific land use strategies and deliver some critical agricultural extension services, they will lose the rationale for existence. And if farmers in North East don't earn from land, they will turn over their remote farms to Burmese druglords and grow poppy.

The northeastern states should concentrate on agriculture, fisheries and dairy farming. This is to promote self-sufficiency in food and develop niche crops for exports. It would not only save millions of rupees now wasted every year to bring food products from outside the region but would also rejuvenate the rural economy and provide a springboard for food-processing industries and limited exports. This would reduce pressure on the tertiary sector to provide employment. 'Back to land and roots' might be a useful slogan for a generation of tribesmen. So far, the land has not given many returns but it can if new farming techniques and an intelligent crop strategy is adopted.

The next priority should be developing tourism in close coordination with West Bengal. Tourism has much higher employment and income-generating potential than sunrise industries like information technology. The North East has huge tourism potential. Since West Bengal is the gateway to the region, tourist packages should be developed in close coordination with West Bengal, which has also not exploited its potential for tourism. Bengalis are also a dominant segment of the domestic tourist market. If properly tapped, the Bengali traveller can prop up tourism in the North East, after the troubles in Darjeeling and the serial explosions in the rest of the country. Special initiatives to attract foreign tourists could be made jointly by West Bengal and the North Eastern states. Calcutta, the Sundarbans and Darjeeling can be marketed along with Kaziranga (a rhino sanctuary), Shillong, Cherrapunji and Manipur as a fortnight getaway for the adventure-seeking foreign tourist. If tourists bring in income, the region's dislike of outsiders will also begin to dilute.

The third priority should be to develop key industries targeting the regional market and the neighbouring countries and a smaller number of niche products for the global markets. In a globalizing market economy, five-year plans are out and entrepreneurs must make the most of sudden opportunities. For example, the Kerala government jumped into the market to sell its bottled coconut water in the aftermath of the Coke-Pepsi pesticide controversy, but the Tripura government failed to take advantage and increase sales of its high-quality pineapple and orange juices. Former Mizoram Chief Minister Zoramthanga has talked much about the quality of passion fruit in his state and Mizofed passion fruit products are high quality. But his plan to get an Australian company to start a processing plant has not worked so far. The Mizoram government may also do well to try and get a major Indian or foreign company to produce Ginger Ale in the state to utilize the quality ginger available and market this as a health drink with a fixed purchase quota for the defence services. The smaller states of the North East need only a few successful industrial projects to set the ball rolling, even as agriculture and tourism will provide the base for a leap in per capita income.

Last but not the least, the North East will have to be developed more as a trading than as a manufacturing hub. For that, Indian diplomacy has to succeed in eastern South Asia so that trade with

Bangladesh, Burma and China may grow. Trade with China is growing at some speed but it has yet to benefit the border regions of the two countries. It is in the interests of both Beijing and Delhi that their border regions figure more prominently in the bilateral trade. If India, China and Russia can emerge as one solid trading block and the frontier regions of these countries manage to benefit from the process, the integration of their frontier tribes and smaller races with the heartlands will become easier. For trade to grow, however, peace and stability are a must in frontier regions like the northeast. Delhi has to undertake some urgent measures in the North East to turn the troubled region into one of growth and peace:

1. Rampant migration from other Indian states into the region should be discouraged. There must be a strict national labour policy for protecting the interest of indigenous populations. Only if higher skills are not locally available should people from other states be allowed to work in the North East. This surely contradicts the provisions of the Indian constitution and any executive order designed to protect the interests of local labour is likely to be challenged in the courts. Nevertheless, such measures would be a sure way of avoiding conflict.

2. Illegal migration into the region from Bangladesh, Nepal and Burma must also be stopped. Since resources are scarce and the region's agrarian economy cannot take any further load of population, any major inflow of migrants is bound to create ethnic or religious backlash or both. For example, the Mizos, who once considered themselves ethnic cousins of the Chins from Burma, now resent fresh Chin migration into Mizoram.

3. Protection of land of indigenous peoples is a must because land alienation is one of the major sources of ethnic conflict in northeast India. If tribals lose land on a large scale, insurgency will follow and lead to large-scale displacement.

4. Extensive autonomy for tribal regions must be provided before the tribes start agitating, not after they have already taken the road to militancy.

5. Having recommended autonomy for indigenous people and protection for their land and share of scarce resources, it is

important to work out a multi-ethnic ethos of governance. No province in India can be totally homogenous in ethnic or religious terms and minorities are bound to remain. Even if the minorities happen to be illegal migrants who had entered the region at some stage, their present generation cannot be faulted for the decision of their ancestors. Empowerment of indigenous populations should go hand in hand with a tough policy against insurgents who resort to ethnic cleansing and violent militancy. There is no reason such groups should be legitimized or unnecessarily placated because such actions encourage other rebel groups to surface.

6. Once displacement has taken place, it is important to provide security to the affected population and organize their return to ancestral villages as soon as possible. Delay may turn the camps into recruiting grounds for militant groups.

7. Security operations should be further humanized and draconian acts like the Armed Forces Special Powers Act should be scrapped. Greater emphasis should be on strengthening intelligence so that only genuine insurgents are targeted and no police or military unit should be allowed to go ahead with Manipur or Assam-type secret killings in which relatives of insurgents, innocent civilians, are targeted.

8. Saturation deployment of security forces should be avoided, force levels should be decided after meticulous calculations of actual requirement because efficient and coordinated handling of forces under Unified Commands reduces the need for too many men in uniform on ground and that can ease tensions even in the worst of insurgency theatres.

Into the first decade of the new millennium, India's North East stands at the edge of a new reality. Return of peace and imaginative planning can ensure a turnaround for the economy. Restoration of pre-Partition links with neighbouring countries can work wonders for trade and business. Resolution of the conflicts that have festered can set the stage for the creation of better transport and communication infrastructure. Multiplicity of identity is acceptable as long as it does not become a source of continuing conflict that saps the vitality of an otherwise vibrant region. Identity-management and development of a political culture of tolerance are needed in the North East.

Ethnic identity is highly contextual. Donald Horowitz points out that 'in what was the eastern region of Nigeria, an Ibo may, for example, be an Owerri Ibo or an Onitsha Ibo, but in Lagos, he may simply be an Ibo and in London, he is a Nigerian'.[7] Much like an Angami in Nagaland will become a Naga in Delhi and an Indian in London. Even rebel leaders who fought India's state-centric nationalism for several decades, like Muivah, now travel on Indian passports. Horowitz details many situations where battling ethnicities realized the futility of perpetuating the conflict and decided to manage it. northeast India is one region that desperately needs an agenda of ethnic reconciliation that can be implemented both from the top and at the grassroots because if the ethnic conflicts intensify—and there are indications that this could happen in states like Manipur, Tripura and Assam—the drug lords will step in to take advantage of the disturbed conditions, forcing the region to remain a troubled periphery with no light at the end of the tunnel.

LOOK EAST VAGARIES

The essential logic of a 'Look East' foreign policy—and the way the North East is seen as fitting into it—is not difficult to see. India's efforts to use the North East as bridgehead to link up with the tiger economies of South East Asia and China is in keeping with the emerging dynamics of Asia's geo-politics and geo-economics. But if that becomes a justification for Delhi's growing bonhomie with the xenophobic Burmese military junta at the expense of India's natural allies in the pro-democracy movement, it would adversely affect both India and its North East. Burma will never attain its pre-independence economic pre-eminence unless it can get rid of the military junta and become a democracy. The military junta is in China's interest—Burma will remain a Chinese backyard so long as the generals run the country and its resources will be freely available for Chinese exploitation. But only if Burma becomes a democracy can it attract huge Western and Asian investments that will help its economy grow like neighbouring Thailand. And if Burma remains a basket case, India's 'Look East' will bump into the Great Wall called Myanmar (as Burma is now called) and go no further. All the grandiose transport links through Burma will remain ineffective.

At the moment, India is only playing a catch-up game with China in Burma. So it is placating the military junta. This will not help. The generals have not obliged India by attacking the North Eastern rebels in its territory; they are sending the Arakan gas to China through a pipeline now under construction; they are doing nothing to stop the flow of deadly drugs to India. India also enjoys an adverse trade balance with Burma. In the last decade or so that India has tried to play footsie with the Burmese generals, Delhi has achieved very little. So as the Pagoda Nation heads for its first elections in two decades, India should join the West in decisively supporting the pro-democracy movement and National League for Democracy headed by Nobel Laureate Aung Sang Suu Kyi.

India not only has to overcome the democracy deficit in its North Eastern region. It has to play a decisive role in overcoming the democracy deficit in the immediate neighbourhood. Bangladesh has voted the Awami League back to power with a decisive and sweeping mandate. But as the February 25 Bangladesh Rifles mutiny shows, the Awami League regime is always in danger of being subverted by Islamic fundamentalists who enjoy access to huge petrodollar funding from the Middle East. Much as it is important for India to have the secular-democratic Awami League-led alliance in power to sort out the North East's problems of trans-border insurgency and for restoration of the region's pre-Partition transport links, it is equally important to have a democratic regime in Burma to address India's security concerns emanating from the insurgencies, from the growing illegal trade of drugs and weapons and to counteract China's growing influence in the Pagoda Nation. Supporting the cause of democracy in the neighbourhood is not wasteful luxury for India—it is a sound investment in securing its own position in the North East.

Basic structural changes in the polity to accommodate the aspirations of the battling ethnicities of the North East will nicely fit in with efforts to turn the region into a trans-national economic space linking India with the economies of South East Asia—but this will work only if the neighbourhood is freed from the pernicious influences of military rule or fundamentalist control. So a democratic Burma and a secular-democratic Bangladesh is essential for a trouble-free North East.

For early four decades, people in India's North East have lived in the shadow of the gun. The literature of the region reflects this unfortunate reality. Indira Goswami's *The Journey*, Arupa Patangia Kalita's powerful novel *Felanee* and short stories like 'Someday, Sometime Numoli', Manoj Goswami's *Samiran Barva is Coming*, Sebastian Zumvu's story 'Son of the Soil', Temsula Ao's 'These Hills Called Home: Stories from a War Zone', Binabati Thiyam Ongvi's story, 'He's Still Alive', Dhrubajyoti Vrora's trilogy on the insurgency, Rita Choudhury's novel Ai Samay, Sai Samay (These times, Those Times), to name a few, have dealt with these themes in much detail. Aruni Kashyap's first novel, *The House with a Thousand Novels* explores why so many young people in the region have taken up arms to fight the Indian State. This is something that Delhi needs to seriously ponder about before it works out a coherent policy for the North East.

NOTES

1. Sanjib Baruah, 2002.
2. Sanjib Baruah, 2003b.
3. Pradyut Bordoloi, inaugural address at *Conflict Resolution in Assam*, a seminar organized by the Institute of Conflict Management, November 2002.
4. Paresh Barua, interview with the writer, broadcast on BBC Bengali Service, 20 July 2003.
5. S.C. Jamir, quoted in the *Times of India*, 24 July 2003.
6. Malabika Dasgupta, 7 October.
7. Donald Horowitz, 1991.

Bibliography

Aditya, R.N. 1970. *Corridors of Memory*. Calcutta: KLM Firma.

Agrawal, M.M. 1996. *Ethinicity, Culture and Nationalism in Northeast India*. Delhi: Indus Publishing.

Aggarwal, S. Kailash (ed.) 1999. *Dynamics of Identity and Inter-group Relations in North-East India*. Shimla: Indian Institute of Advanced Studies.

Alam, K. 1983. *The Development Experience in Assam*. Guwahati: Dutta Barua & Co.

Alemchiba, M. 1970. *A Brief Historical Account of Nagaland*. Kohima: Naga Institute of Culture.

Allen, B.C. 1905. *Gazetteer of Naga Hills and Manipur*. Delhi: Mittal Publications (Republished).

Ao, Lanunungsang A. 2002. *From Phizo to Muivah: The Naga National Question in North-East India*. New Delhi: Mittal Publications.

Arbuthnott, J.C. 1907. *Note from Camp Mauplong to Fort William*, 26 September. Quoted in Suhas Chatterji. 1985. *Mizoram under British Rule*. Delhi: Mittal Publications.

Barbora, Sanjay. 2008. 'Under the Invisibility Cloak—Reimagining the "Northeast", *Biblio*, 13(5&6), May–June. Also available online http://www.biblio—india. org/archives/08/MJ08.asp?mp=Mj08

Barpujari, H.K. 1980. *Assam in the Days of the Company (1826–42)*. Guwahati: Spectrum.

———. 1981. *Problems of the Hill Tribes: Northeast Frontier (1873–1962)*. Guwahati: Spectrum.

———. 1998. *North-east India: Problems, Policies and Prospects* (Guwahati: Spectrum Publishers, 1998).

Baruah, Sanjib. 1999. *India against Itself: Politics of Nationality in Assam*. Philadelphia: University of Pennsylvania Press.

———. 2002. *Economic and Political Weekly*, 12 July.

———. 2003a. 'Citizens and Denizens: Ethnicity, Homelands and the Crisis of Displacement in Northeast,' *Journal of Refugee Studies*, 16: 44–66.

Baruah, Sanjib. 2003b. 'Government Cannot Dictate Identity', *The Statesman*, 11 October.

————. 2003c. 'Look East but via Northeast', *Indian Express*, New Delhi, 12 December.

————. 2004. *Durable Disorder: Understanding the Politics of Northeast India.* Delhi: Oxford University Press.

————. (ed.) 2009. *Beyond Counter-Insurgency: Breaking the Impasse in Northeast India.* Delhi: Oxford University Press.

Bhaumik, Subir. 1994. *Nagas, India and the North-east.* London: Minority Rights Group.

————. 1996. *Insurgent Crossfire: Northeast India.* Delhi: Lancers.

————. 1998. 'Northeast India: The Evolution of a Post Colonial Region', in Partha Chatterjee (ed.), *Wages of Freedom: Fifty Years of the Indian Nation state.* Delhi: Oxford University Press.

————. 2001a. 'Treachery: How an Indian Officer Betrayed Burmese Rebels', a four-part series in *Times of India*, 11–15 April.

————. 2001b. *The Accord That Never Was: Analysis of the 1975 Shillong Accord.* South Asia Peace Audit Series. Kathmandu: South Asia Forum for Human Rights.

————. 2003. 'Bangladesh: The Second Front of Islamic Terror', in O.P. Mishra and Sucheta Ghosh 'Terrorism and Low Intensity (eds) *Conflict in South Asian Region.* Delhi: Manak Publishers.

————. 2005. 'Ethnicity, Ideology and Religion: Separatist Movements in India's Northeast', in Satu. P. Limaye, Robert Wirshing and Mohan Malik (eds), *Religious Radicalism and Security in South Asia.* Honolulu, Hawaii: Asia Pacific Center for Security Studies.

————. 2006. 'Guns, Drugs and Rebels—India's Burma Policy', *Seminar*, Delhi.

Bhattacharjee, Pravas Ranjan. 1993. *Economic Transition in Tripura.* New Delhi: Vikas Publishing House.

Bhattacharya, Anadi. 1987. *Tripura o Tripuri: A Collection of Essays.* Udaipur.

Bhattacharya, Harihar. 1999. *Communism in Tripura.* Delhi: Ajanta.

Bhattacharyya, Hiranya Kumar. 2001, *The Silent Invasion: Assam Versus Infiltration.* Guwahati: Spectrum Publications.

Bhattacharjee, J.B. (ed.) 1982. *Social Tension in Northeast India.* Calcutta: Research India Publications.

Bhattacharjee, S.R. 1989. *Tribal Insurgency in Tripura: A Study in the Exploration of Causes.* Delhi: Inter-India Publications.

Bhuyan, B.C. 1989. *Political Development of the North East.* New Delhi: Omsons Publications.

Bordoloi, B.N. 1972. *District Handbook: United Mikir and North Cachar Hills.* Shillong: Tribal Research Institute.

————. 1984. *The Dimasa Kacharis of Assam.* Guwahati: Tribal Research Institute.

————. 1991. *Tribes of Assam Part-III.* Guwahati: Assam Institute of Research for Tribals and Scheduled Castes.

Bordoloi, B.N., Thakur, G.C. Sharmah, Saikia, M.C. 1987. *Tribes of Assam Part-I.* Guwahati: Assam Tribal Research Institute.

Bordoloi, B.N., Thakur, G.C. Sharmah. 1988. *Tribes of Assam Part-II*. Guwahati: Assam Tribal Research Institute.

Brajamani, S. 2003. *Economic Growth in Manipur: An Empirical Analysis*. Manipur: S. Romesh Singh.

Bhuyan, Arun Chandan and De, Sibopada. (ed.), 1999a. *Political History of Assam Vol. III 1940–47*. Guwahati: Publication Board Assam.

———. 1999b. *Political History of Assam Vol. II 1920–1939*. Guwahati: Publication Board Assam.

———. 1999c. *Political History of Assam Vol. I 1926–1919*. Guwahati: Publication Board Assam.

Bose, Ashish, Tiplut Nongbri and Nikhilesh Kumar. 1990. *Tribal Demography and Development in Northeast India*. Delhi: B.R. Publishing Corporation.

Buzzi, Camilla and Ashild Kolas 2008. 'Northeast India and Myanmar: Looking East towards a Dead-End?' presented at Borders and Beyond: The Northeast in India's Security and Foreign Policy, Department of Political Science, Cotton College, Guwahati, Assam, India, 21 February.

Chakrabarty, Saroj. 1984. *The Upheaval Years in Northeast India*. Calcutta: Saraswati Press.

Chatterjee, Suhas. 1985. *Mizoram under the British Rule*. Delhi: Mittal Publishers.

Chaube, S.K. 1973. *Hill Politics in Northeast India*. Delhi: Orient Longman.

Chaudhuri, Sudhakar. K. 1995. 'Cross-Border Trade between India and Bangladesh', Working Paper No. 58, NCAER, New Delhi.

Conboy, Kenneth and M.S. Kohli. 2002. *Spies in the Himalayas: Secret Missions and Perilous Climbs*. Delhi: Harper Collins-*India Today* joint venture publishing.

Coupland, Reginald. 1944. *British Obligation: The Future of India*. London: Wiley.

Das, Amiya Kumar. 1982. *Assam's Agony*. Delhi: Lancers.

Datta, P.S. 1990. *Ethnic Movements in Poly Cultural Assam*. Delhi: Har-Anand Publications.

Das, Gurudas. 2002. 'Probable Options: Cementing the Faultlines in Assam', *Faultlines* 11 (April).

Das, Gurudas and R.K. Purkayastha. (ed.) 2000. *Border Trade: North-East India and Neighbouring Countries*. Delhi: Akansha Publishing House.

Das, Samir Kumar. 1997. *Regionalism in Power*. Delhi: Omsons Publications.

Das, Ratna. 1997. *Art & Architecture of Tripura*. Agartala: Tribal Research Institute, Government of Tripura.

Das, M.N. and Manpong, C.M. 1993. *District Administration in Arunachal Pradesh*. Delhi: Omsons Publications.

Dasgupta, Malabika. 1989. 'The Gumti Hydel Project of Tripura', *Economic and Political Weekly,* 7 October.

Datta, P.S. 1991. *Northeast: A Study of Mobility and Political Behaviour*. Guwahati, New Delhi: Omsons Publications.

———. 1993. *Autonomy Movements in Assam*. New Delhi: Omsons Publications.

———. (ed.) 1995. *North East and the Indian State: Paradoxes of a Periphery*. Delhi: Vikas Publishing House.

Dhar, Maloy Krishna. 2005. *Open Secrets: India's Intelligence Unveiled*. New Delhi: Manas Publications.

Deka, Kanak Sen. 1991. *Youths in Turmoil: Assam*. Calcutta: Gurupada Chaudhury.

Deka, Kanak Sen. 1993. *Assam's Crisis: Myth and Reality*. New Delhi: Mittal Publications.

Dev, S.C. 1987. *Nagaland: The Untold Story*. Calcutta: Pearl Publishers.

Directorate of Military Intelligence. 2002. Special note on 'Financial Status of Insurgent Groups in Northeast India', June.

Dutta, Rajesh. 2000. 'Coal Export from Meghalaya to Bangladesh', in Gurudas Das and R.K. Purakayastha (eds), *Border Trade: North-East India and Neighbouring Countries*. Delhi: Akansha Publishing.

Elwin, Verrier. 1959. *A Philosophy for NEFA, North-East Frontier Agency*. Shillong: Government of Assam Press.

———. 1964. The Tribal World of Verrier Elwin. Bombay: Oxford University Press.

Egreteau, Renaud. 2003. *Wooing the Generals: India's New Burma Policy*. Delhi: Authorspress, Centre de Sciences Humaines.

Gafur, A.M. Islam and N. Faiz. 1990–91. *Illegal International in Bangladesh: Impact on Domestic Economy* (Phase 1 & 2) Dhaka: Bangladesh Institute of Development Studies.

Ganguly, J.B. 1987. 'The Problem of Tribal Landlessness in Tripura', in B.B. Datta and M.N. Karna (eds), *Land Relations in Northeast India*. Delhi: People's Publishing House.

Gohain, Hiren. August 1973. 'Origins of the Assamese Middle Class', *Social Scientist*.

Goswami, Dilip. 1974. 'Elites and Economic Development', *The Northeast Research Bulletin*, Vol. V, Dibrugarh University, Dibrugarh (Assam).

Goswami, Jayant Madhab. 2002. 'Commentary on the Fiscal Situation in Northeastern States', *Dialogue*, July–September. Available online at www.asthabharati.org.

Guha, Amalendu. 1977. 'Planter's Raj to Swaraj Freedom Struggle and Electoral Politics in Assam (1826–1947)'. Delhi: Indian Council of Historical Research.

———. 1980. 'Little Nationalism Turned Chauvinist: Assam's Anti Foreigner Upsurge (1979–80)', *Economic and Political Weekly*, Special Number (October), Bombay.

Gopalkrishnan. R. 1995. *Insurgent Northeastern Region of India*. Delhi: Vikas.

Gundevia, Y.D. 1975. *War and Peace in Nagaland*. Dehradun: Palit and Palit.

Haksar, Nandita. 1996. 'Movement of Self Assertion in the Northeast', in Madhushree Dutta, Flavia Agnes and Neera Adarkar (eds), *The Nation, The State and Indian Identity*. Calcutta: Stree.

Haksar, Nandita. (forthcoming). *The Rogue Agent: How India's Military Intelligence Betrayed the Burmese Resistance*. Delhi: Penguin.

Haokip, T.T. 2002. 'Ethnic Conflicts and Internal Displacement in Manipur', in C.J. Thomas (ed.), *Dimensions of Displaced People in Northeast India*. Delhi: Regency Publications.

Hazarika, Atul (ed.) 1957. *Asom Sahitya Sabhar Bhasanvali*, Vol. 2 Sibsagar. Guwahati: Asom Sahitya Sabha Prakashani.

Horam, M. 1988. *Naga Insurgency: The Last Thirty Years*. Delhi: Cosmo Publications.

Horowitz, Donald. 1991. 'Ethnic Conflict Management for Policy-Makers', in Joseph V. Montville (ed.), *Conflict and Peace Making in Multi-Ethnic Societies*. New York: Lexington.

Hussain, Monirul. 2000. 'Post-Colonial State, Identity Movements and Internal Displacement in Northeast India', presented at the International Conference on Forced Migration in South Asian Region, organized by the Centre for Refugee Studies, Jadavpur University, 20–22 April.

Hussain, Monirul (ed.). 2005. *Coming out of Violence: Essays on Ethnicity, Conflict Resolution and Peace Process in Northeast India*. Delhi: Regency Publications.

Islam, Muinul. 2001. 'Trade and Economic Cooperation between Bangladesh and the Bordering Indian States: A Victim of Policy-Induced Distortions', paper submitted at the Bangladesh Institute of International and Strategic Studies, Dhaka, 21–23 August.

Jafa, V.S. 1999. 'Administrative Policies and Ethnic Disintegration: Engineering Conflicts in India's North East', *Faultlines*, 2 August.

Kar, Bodhisatva. 2009. 'When was the Postcolonial? A History of Policing Impossible Lines', in Sanjib Baruah (ed.) *Beyond Counter-Insurgency: Breaking the Impasse in Northeast India*. Delhi: Oxford University Press.

Karlekar, Hiranmoy. 2005. *Bangladesh: The Next Afghanistan*. Delhi: Sage Publications.

Kumar, Pravin. 2004. 'External Linkages and Internal Security: Assessing Bhutan's Operation All Clear', *Strategic Analysis*, Delhi, 28(3), July–September.

Lianzela. 2002. 'Internally Displaced Persons in Mizoram', in Thomas (ed.), *Dimensions of Displaced People in Northeast India*. Delhi: Regency Publications.

Lintner, Bertil. 1990. *Land of Jade: Journey through Insurgent Burma*. Bangkok: White Lotus & Kiscadale, Edinburgh (Scotland).

———. 1999. *Burma in Revolt: Opium and Insurgency since 1948*. Bangkok: Silkworm Books.

———. 2002a. 'Beware of Bangladesh: Cocoon of Terror', *Far Eastern Economic Review*, 4 April, 13: 14–17.

———. 2002b. 'Ethnic Movements in Burma: From Insurgency to Terrorism', paper delivered at the Seminar on Terrorism and Low-Intensity Conflicts in South Asia, held at Jadavpur University, March.

Lokendrajit, Soyam. 1988. 'Identity and Crisis of Identity: A Case Study of Manipur' in *Manipur: Past and Present* (ed.) N. Sanajaoba. Delhi: Mittal Publications.

Mackenzie, Alexander. 1884. *Memorandum on the Northeastern Frontier of Bengal*. Calcutta: Government of India Press.

Mackenzie, Alexander. 2001. (republished). *The North East Frontier of India*. Delhi: Mittal Publications.

Marwah, Ved. 1995. *Uncivil Wars: Pathology of Terrorism in India*. Delhi: Harper Collins Publishers India.

Mills, J.P. 1982. *The Rengma Nagas*. Nagaland: Directorate of Art and Culture, Government of Nagaland.

———. 2003. *The Ao Nagas*. Nagaland: Directorate of Art and Culture.

Mishra, Omprakash; P.V. Unnikrishnan and Maxmillian Martin. 2000. 'India' in Global IDP Survey Project and Norwegian Refugee Council, *Internally Displaced People: A Global Survey*. London: Earthscan.

Misra, Tillotama. 1980. 'Assam: A Colonial Hinterland,' *Economic and Political Weekly*, 9 August, Bombay.

Misra, Udayon. 2000. *The Periphery Strikes Back: Challenges to the Nation state in Assam and Nagaland*. Shimla: Indian Institute of Advanced Study.

McCoy, Alfred. 1972. *The Politics of Heroin in Southeast Asia*. New York: Harper and Row.

Muivah, Thuingaleng. 2003. 'Nagas Set Terms for Peace', *BBC Online*, South Asia page, posted on 22 July 2003.

Namo, Dalle. 1987. *The Prisoner From Nagaland*. Kohima: United Publisher.

Nag, Sajal. 1990. *Roots of Ethnic Conflict: Nationalities Question in Northeast India*. Delhi: Manohar.

———. 1998. *India and North-East India: Mind, Politics and the Process of Integration 1946–1950*. New Delhi: Regency Publications.

———. 2002. *Contesting Marginality: Ethnicity, Insurgency and Subnationalism in North-East India*. Delhi: Manohar Publishers.

Northeast Council. 2000. *Annual Report*.

Nayyar, V.K. 1991. *Threat from Within: India's Internal Security Environment*. Delhi: Lancer.

Nephram, Binalakshmi. 2001. *South Asia's Fractured Frontier: Armed Conflict, Narcotics and Small Arms Proliferation in India's North East*. Delhi: Mittal Publications.

Nibedon, Nirmal. 1978. *Nagaland: The Night of the Guerillas*. Delhi: Lancer.

———. 1980. *Mizoram: The Dagger's Brigade*. Delhi: Lancer.

———. 1981. *Northeast India: The Ethnic Explosion*. Delhi: Lancer.

Nuh, V.K. 1986. *Nagaland Church and Politics*. Nagaland: V. Nuh & Bro.

———. 2001. *Struggle for Identity in North-east India: A Theological response*. Guwahati: Spectrum Publications.

Pakem, B. 1990. *Nationality, Ethnicity and Cultural Identity in Northeast India*. Delhi: Omsons.

——— (ed). 1997. *Insurgency in Northeast India*. Delhi: Omsons.

Pandey, Nischal. 2008. *India's Northeastern Region: Insurgency, Economic Development and Linkages with South-east Asia*. Delhi: Manohar Publishers.

Paul, Sunita. 2008. 'When the Media turns Evil', *Global Politician* website, 8 June.

Pillai, S.K. 1999. 'Anatomy of an Insurgency: Ethnicity and Identity in Nagaland', *Faultlines*, 3 November. Available online http://www.satp.org/satporgtp/publication/faultlines/volume3/Fault3-GenPillai.htm.

Phadnis, Urmila. 1989. *Ethnicity and Nation Building in South Asia*. Delhi: Sage Publications.

Prabhakara, M.S. 1987. 'Land: The Source of All Trouble', *The Hindu* (Chennai), 15 July.

Rahman, A. and A. Razzaque. 1998. *Informal Border Trade between Bangladesh and India: An Empirical Study in Selected Areas*. Dhaka: Bangladesh Institute of Development Studies.

Rajagopalan, Rajesh. 2008. *Fight Like a Guerilla: The Indian Army and Counter-Insurgency*. Delhi: Routledge Taylor & Francis Group.

Raman, B. 2002. *Intelligence: Past, Present and Future*. Delhi: Lancer.

Rammohan, E.N. 2007. *Insurgent frontiers: Essays from the Troubled Northeast*. Delhi: India Research Press.

Reid, Robert. 1983 [1944]. *History of the Frontier Areas Bordering on Assam: From 1883–1941*. Delhi: Eastern Publishing House. Printed first by Assam Government Press.

Roy Burman, B.K. 1995. *Indigenous and Tribal Peoples and the UN and International Agencies*. Rajiv Gandhi Institute for Contemporary Studies, Paper. No 27.

Rustomji, Nari. 1983. *Imperilled Frontiers: India's Northeastern Borderlands*. Delhi: Oxford University Press.

Sachdeva, Gulshan. 2000. *Economy of the North-east: Policy, Present Conditions, and Future Possibilities*. Delhi: Konark.

Sahni, Ajai. 2001. 'The Terrorist Economy in India's Northeast', *Faultlines* 8 (April). Available online at http://www.satp.org/satporgtp/publication/faultlines/volume8/Article5.htm.

Saigal Omesh, Tripura. 1978. Concept Publishing Company, Delhi.

Saikia, Jaideep. 2001. 'Swadhin Asom or Brihot Bangla' (Independent Assam or Greater Bengal) in *Contours*. Assam: Sagittarius.

———. 2001. 'Revolutionaries or Warlords: ULFA's Organisational Profile. 'Faultlines', Available online at http://satp.org/satporgtp/publication/faultlines/volume9/Article4.htm.

———. 2004. *Terror Sans Frontiers: Islamist Militancy in Northeast India*. Delhi: Vision Books.

———. (ed.) 2006. *Bangladesh: Treading the Taliban Trail*. Delhi: Vision Books.

———. (ed.) 2007. *Frontier in Flames: Northeast in Turmoil*. Penguin.

———. (ed.) 2009. *Terrorism: Patterns of Internationalisation*. Delhi: Sage Publications.

Sarin, V.I.K. 1982. *India's North-East in Flames*. Delhi: Vikash Publishing House.

Sharma, Atul. 2002. 'Why Assam Continues to Decelerate', *Dialogue*, July–September. Available online at www.asthabharati.org. Last accessed on 3 August, 2009.

Sinha, A.C. (ed.) 1994. *Youth Movements in North-East India: Structural Imperatives and Aspects of Change*. Delhi: Indus Publishing Company.

Sinha, S.P. 1998. 'Insurgency in Northeast India: The External Dimension', *Journal of the United Services Institution*, Vol. 3(July–September): 14–19.

Singh, K.S. (ed.) 1996. *People of Tripura*. Vol. XLI. Calcutta: Seagull Books.

———. 1993. *People of India: Sikkim* Vol. XXXIX Calcutta: Seagull Books.

———. 1994a. *People of India: Meghalaya*. Vol. XXXII. Calcutta: Seagull Books.

———. 1994b. *People of India: Nagaland* Vol. XXXIV Calcutta: Seagull Books.

———. 1995a. *People of India: Mizoram* Vol. XXXIII Calcutta: Seagull Books.

———. 1995b. *People of India: Arunachal Pradesh* Vol. XIV. Calcutta: Seagull Books.

———. 2003. *People of India: Assam* Volume XV Part Two. Calcutta: Seagull Books.

Singh, Rajkumar Manisana. 2000. *A Short Constitutional History of Manipur 1891–1971*. Imphal: Smt Usha Devi.

Singh, Bhupinder. 2002. *Autonomy Movements and Federal India*. Delhi and Jaipur: Rawar Publications.

Singh, Prakash. 2001. *Kohima to Kashmir: On the Terrorist Trail*. Delhi: Rupa & Co.

Singh, B.P. 1987. *The Problem of Change: A Study of North east India*. Delhi: Oxford University Press.

Singh, L.P. 1994. National Policy for the Northeast, Unpublished Paper, Delhi, *Seminar*. Thomas, C.J. (edited), *Dimensions of Displaced People in Northeast India*. Delhi: Regency Publications.

Syiemlieh, R. David. 2000. *Survey of Research in History on North-East India 1970–1990*. Delhi: Regency Publication.

Tarapot, Phanjoubam. 1997. *Drug Abuse and Illicit Trafficking in North Eastern India*. Delhi: Vikash Publishing House.

Tribal Research Institute. 1974. *The Problem of Transfer and Alienation of Tribal Land in Assam*. Guwahati: Tribal Research Institute.

Thomas, C. Joshua. 2002. *Dimensions of Displaced People in North-East India*. Delhi: Regency Publications.

Thomas, C. Joshua, Das Gurudas. 2002. *Dimensions of Development in Nagaland*. Delhi: Regency Publications.

Thomas, C. Joshua; Gopalakrishnan, R., Singh, R.K. 2001. *Constraints in Development of Manipur*. Delhi: Regency Publications.

Tyson, Geoffrey. 1992. *Forgotten Frontier*. Guwahati: Spectrum Publications.

Verghese, B.G. 2001. *Reorienting India: The New Geo-Politics of Asia*. New Delhi: Konark Publishers.

———. 2004. *India's Northeast Resurgent: Ethnicity, Insurgency, Governance, Development*. Delhi: Konark Publishers.

Weiner, Myron. 1978. *Sons of the Soil: Migration and Ethnic Conflict in India*. Delhi: Oxford University Press.

Zairema, Reverend. 1978. *God's Miracle in Mizoram*. Aizawl: Synod Press & Bookworm.

Zehol, Lucy. 1998. *Ethnicity in Manipur: Experience, Issues and Perspectives*. Delhi: Regency Publications.

Index

About the Author

Subir Bhaumik is the East India Correspondent of the BBC World Service for the last 15 years. He has reported on North East India and the countries around it for three decades since his previous assignments with Press Trust of India, *Ananda Bazar Patrika* and Reuters News Agency. As a journalist he has broken some of the biggest stories in North East India, Bangladesh, Myanmar and the Himalayan countries of Nepal and Bhutan.

He was Queen Elizabeth House Fellow in Oxford University (1989–90), during which he completed has first book *Insurgent Crossfire* (published by Lancers in 1996). He has been a Fellow at Frankfurt University and done projects with prestigious institutions like the East-West Center, Washington. He has presented nearly 40 papers in seminars at home and abroad and written more than 25 articles for volumes edited by leading scholars (some published by SAGE India) like Partha Chatterjee, Ranabir Sammadar, Robert Wirshing, Sanjib Baruah, Samir Das and Jaideep Saikia. He is also a popular TV anchor, a corporate risk analyst and a media trainer. He is the Working President of the Guwahati-based North East Policy Alternatives and a Founder-member of the independent think tank, the Calcutta Research Group.